Praise for *The Second Civil War*

"Timely and compelling . . . In describing the history of partisanship in this country Mr. Brownstein writes with both an authoritative understanding of the political dynamics in Washington and a plain spoken common sense." —Michiko Kakutani, *The New York Times*

"Brownstein presents both a biting critique of current political practices and an investigation into their origins."
—Art Winslow, *Los Angeles Times*

"Provocative." —Alan Brinkley, *The New York Times Book Review*

"Brownstein knows what he's talking about."
—Jonathan Yardley, *The Washington Post*

"Brownstein eloquently laments the consequences of ['hyperpartisanship'] . . . and offers some fascinating remedies."
—Mort Kondracke, *Roll Call*

"An engaging and insightful analysis of an important subject that should be read by all who care about the nation's political health."
—Claude R. Marx, *The Washington Times*

"[*The Second Civil War*] lays out a complex history with lucid precision, painting a damning portrait of contemporary politics that's sure to provoke and captivate readers."
—*Publishers Weekly* (starred review)

"Astute examination of a stymied system." —*Kirkus Reviews*

PENGUIN BOOKS

THE SECOND CIVIL WAR

Ronald Brownstein, formerly the chief political correspondent and columnist for the *Los Angeles Times*, is political director of Atlantic Media Co., publishers of *The Atlantic Monthly*, *National Journal*, and The Hotline. A frequent political commentator on both network and cable television, he was named a finalist for the Pulitzer Prize for his coverage of the 1996 and 2004 presidential elections.

THE SECOND CIVIL WAR

HOW EXTREME PARTISANSHIP HAS
PARALYZED WASHINGTON AND
POLARIZED AMERICA

Ronald Brownstein

PENGUIN BOOKS

PENGUIN BOOKS

Published by the Penguin Group

Penguin Group (USA) Inc., 375 Hudson Street, New York, New York 10014, U.S.A.
Penguin Group (Canada), 90 Eglinton Avenue East, Suite 700, Toronto,
Ontario, Canada M4P 2Y3 (a division of Pearson Penguin Canada Inc.)
Penguin Books Ltd, 80 Strand, London WC2R 0RL, England
Penguin Ireland, 25 St Stephen's Green, Dublin 2, Ireland (a division of Penguin Books Ltd)
Penguin Group (Australia), 250 Camberwell Road, Camberwell,
Victoria 3124, Australia (a division of Pearson Australia Group Pty Ltd)
Penguin Books India Pvt Ltd, 11 Community Centre, Panchsheel Park, New Delhi – 110 017, India
Penguin Group (NZ), 67 Apollo Drive, Rosedale, North Shore 0632,
New Zealand (a division of Pearson New Zealand Ltd)
Penguin Books (South Africa) (Pty) Ltd, 24 Sturdee Avenue,
Rosebank, Johannesburg 2196, South Africa

Penguin Books Ltd, Registered Offices:
80 Strand, London WC2R 0RL, England

First published in the United States of America by The Penguin Press,
a member of Penguin Group (USA) Inc. 2007
Published in Penguin Books 2008

1 3 5 7 9 10 8 6 4 2

Copyright © Ronald Brownstein, 2007
All rights reserved

THE LIBRARY OF CONGRESS HAS CATALOGED THE HARDCOVER EDITION AS FOLLOWS:
Brownstein, Ronald.
The second civil war : how extreme partisanship has paralyzed Washington
and polarized America/by Ronald Brownstein.
p. cm.
Includes bibliographical references and index.
ISBN 978-1-59420-139-4 (hc.)
ISBN 978-0-14-311432-1 (pbk.)
1. Political parties—United States.   2. Political culture—United States.
3. Opposition (Political science)—United States.   4. Divided government—United States.
5. United States—Politics and government—2001–   I. Title.
JK2261.B84 2007
973.931—dc22
2007014696

Printed in the United States of America
DESIGNED BY NICOLE LAROCHE

For Eileen, my beautiful reward,
and for Taylor and Danny, my boys of summer

Contents

THE SECOND
CIVIL WAR

PREFACE

A DAY IN JUNE

After two terms as America's first president, George Washington used his farewell address to preach the benefits of unity and warn his young nation about the dangers of "permanent alliances" with foreign powers. Dwight Eisenhower, in his farewell address after his two terms in the White House, urged Americans to restrain the unaccountable power of the "military-industrial complex."

When Republican Representative Tom DeLay of Texas retired under fire in June 2006 after nearly twenty-two years in Congress, he chose to warn against a different threat: too much cooperation between the Democratic and Republican parties.

This might not have seemed a pressing danger to many in the Capitol or anyone around the country watching the evolution of American political life over the past several decades. On most issues, the two parties now spend most days at each other's throats. On both sides, the number of legislators who seek to build alliances across party lines, or even dissent from their own party on key votes, is much smaller than a generation ago. Reversing the famous dictum of Carl von Clausewitz, in contemporary Washington politics often seems the extension of war by other means.

DeLay could claim some credit for that condition. A former pest exter-minator and Texas state legislator from Sugar Land, Texas, outside of Houston, he was first elected during Ronald Reagan's landslide victory in 1984. Intently religious and devoutly conservative, DeLay always recoiled from the conciliatory, deal-making style that House Republican leaders, led by Bob Michel of Illinois, applied to their relationship with the Demo-cratic House majority in the 1970s and 1980s. But DeLay was also a skilled practitioner of practical politics, accomplished at building the alliances with other members that provide the foundation for advancement in the House. In 1989, DeLay placed a bad bet when he managed the losing cam-paign of moderate Ed Madigan against Newt Gingrich, the leader of young House conservatives, for the position of minority whip. But DeLay rebuilt enough support to defeat a moderate as secretary of the Republican conference in 1992. And when Republicans gained control of the House and Senate in 1994, DeLay won the whip job himself. (In the process, he defeated the preferred candidate of Gingrich, who had advanced to speaker when Republicans gained control.) When Gingrich stepped down as speaker after the disappointing Republican losses in the 1998 election, and his successor Bob Livingston also resigned amid a personal scandal, DeLay demonstrated his rising power by engineering the election of Illinois Republican Denny Hastert. Four years later, when fellow Texan Dick Armey stepped down as House majority leader, the number two position in the House leadership, DeLay replaced him without opposi-tion. Hastert was never the DeLay puppet some believed, but there was no question that DeLay exerted at least as much influence as the speaker over the direction of the Republican majority in the House.

DeLay operated with a broad vision and a precise attention to detail. He worked relentlessly to tighten the links between the Republican major-ity and the business community by providing the latter greater access and ability to influence legislation, but he also pressured them to tilt their po-litical contributions more toward the GOP, and to hire more Republicans as lobbyists. Inside the House, his principal priority was to maximize Republican unity and minimize opportunities for Democratic influence. DeLay's overriding goal was to advance the most conservative agenda possible in a manner that framed the differences between the parties as sharply as possible. He did not fear passing legislation on razor-thin party-line votes; indeed, it often appeared that he preferred bills that pushed to the right so far that they attracted only the bare minimum of votes required to pass. Anything less meant the legislation conceded too much to those resisting the conservative agenda, not only Democrats but moderate Republicans. He was like a meat cutter who prided in his ability to slice closer to the bone than anyone else.

DeLay succeeded to a remarkable extent in imposing his vision. Even though House Republicans operated with a narrow margin of majority throughout DeLay's years in the leadership, they moved their agenda through the institution much more smoothly than Democrats had with larger margins in the years before the GOP takeover. DeLay was so central to those efforts, he earned the nickname "the Hammer" for his ability to nail down winning coalitions.

In June 2006, though, DeLay seemed to be leaving the House one step ahead of an angry mob. Over the years his hardball tactics had prompted several rebukes from the House Ethics Committee. In the months before his resignation, several of his former aides pleaded guilty to various offenses in an ongoing investigation centered on Republican lobbyist Jack Abramoff, who had earned millions of dollars in fees from Indian gambling interests, and had shared the wealth in the form of contributions and overseas trips directed primarily toward Republican legislators. Questions continued to swirl around DeLay's own relationship with Abramoff, who pleaded guilty himself to a series of charges and announced his intention to cooperate with prosecutors five months before DeLay's speech. More pressingly, a prosecutor in Texas had indicted DeLay, accusing him of laundering corporate money through the Republican National Committee to help elect a Republican majority in the Texas state legislature in 2002. (DeLay intended the new majority to redraw the state's congressional districts in a way that allowed Republicans to win more seats, which is exactly what the legislature did the next year.) The combination of the Texas indictment and the Abramoff investigation led restive House Republicans to demand that DeLay step down as majority leader. When he was stripped of that perch, DeLay decided to walk away from the House altogether, and he resigned his seat.

So DeLay was bloodied when he stepped to the House floor to deliver a farewell speech late on the afternoon of Thursday, June 8, 2006. But he was definitely unbowed. DeLay began his speech with a few conventional observations about finding inspiration in the great monuments to Washington, Jefferson, and Lincoln on the Washington Mall. Then he turned in a characteristically defiant direction:

> In preparing for today, I found that it is customary in speeches such as these to reminisce about the good old days of political harmony, and across-the-aisle camaraderie, and to lament the bitter, divisive partisan rancor that supposedly now weakens our democracy.
>
> Well, I cannot do that because partisanship, Mr. Speaker, properly understood, is not a symptom of democracy's weakness but of its health and its strength, especially from the perspective of a political conservative.
>
> Liberalism, after all, whatever you may think of its merits, is a political philosophy and a proud one with a great tradition in this country, with a voracious appetite for growth.
>
> In any place, or any time, on any issue, what does liberalism ever seek, Mr. Speaker? More. More government, more taxation, more control over people's lives and decisions and wallets. If conservatives do not stand up to liberalism, no one will. And for a long time around here, almost no one did.
>
> Indeed, the common lament over the recent rise in political partisanship is often nothing more than a veiled complaint instead about the recent rise of political conservatism.

The problem with Washington, DeLay continued, was not politicians who compromised too little but those who compromised too much. "Now, politics demands compromise," he acknowledged. But

> we must never forget that compromise and bipartisanship are means, not ends, and are properly employed only in the service of higher principles.

It is not the principled partisan, however obnoxious he may seem to his opponents, who degrades our public debate, but the preening, self-styled statesman who elevates compromise to a first principle.

For the true statesmen, Mr. Speaker, are not defined by what they compromise, but by what they do not.

DeLay was nothing if not forthright. He had built his career on advancing an agenda that sharply separated Republicans from Democrats, often through means that proved as divisive as his goals. At the end of the road, he saw no reason to apologize. If the reluctance to compromise was the true measure of statesmanship, future generations would be dismantling statues of Daniel Webster and Henry Clay and erecting them to Tom DeLay.

ABOUT THREE HOURS after DeLay finished his speech, several hundred people gathered in a ballroom at the Riviera Hotel in Las Vegas. The people in the room agreed with virtually none of DeLay's views. Most of them considered him an unethical zealot. Yet almost universally they shared his prescription for political success. Just as DeLay wanted Republicans to stand up more firmly against Democrats, the men and women who gathered at the Riviera wanted Democrats to fight more fiercely against Republicans.

The occasion that brought them to Las Vegas was the first convention for readers of the popular liberal Web site Daily Kos. Markos Moulitsas Zuniga, a former Army officer, had founded the site four years earlier while working as a project manager for a company that designed Web sites. Thousands of people checked in every day to read his latest offerings and the postings from the other "Kossacks," who congregated on the site to trade political news, share outrage over the latest maneuvers from Bush and congressional Republicans, and demand that Democrats resist the Republican agenda with more fervor and commitment.

In every way the conference measured the widening influence inside the Democratic Party not only of the Kos community in particular but more generally the activists organizing on the Internet through dozens of liberal Web sites, especially the giant liberal online group MoveOn.org. The YearlyKos convention attracted not only readers of the site from around the country, but the cream of the national political press corps, officials from a wide assortment of liberal groups, and an impressive array of Democratic leaders, including the party chairman, Howard Dean, and the Democratic leader in the Senate, Harry Reid. Four Democrats at the time considering a 2008 presidential race all made the long trip to Las Vegas. On the convention's last morning, the assembled Kossacks received validation of another sort when Moulitsas appeared on *Meet the Press*, the most watched of the Sunday interview shows.

Even with all the big names milling through the halls, the conference, organized by volunteers, had an agreeably ramshackle feel. The hotel looked like it hadn't replaced its carpets since the Rat Pack roamed Las Vegas. The ceilings were low, the light dim. At the conference itself, most people wore jeans and T-shirts. In a crowded conference room, liberal authors lined up to sign books, and organizers for causes (a group dedicated to organizing "the Christian left," a campaign to raise the minimum wage) tried to recruit volunteers. One man arrived in a pickup truck covered on almost every available inch with bumper stickers deriding Bush. "When fascism comes to America," insisted the most pointed of them, "it will be wrapped in a flag and carrying a cross." In the hallway before the opening session, one man wore a T-shirt emblazoned with a picture of Bush and the words "I'm not with stupid."

All of this represented a physical manifestation of the fervent opinions that filled the Daily Kos Web site every day. But in other ways the crowd that gathered for three days of speeches, panels, and intermittent comedy routines did not fit many of the expected stereotypes about Democratic Internet activists. They were not especially young (there was more gray hair than ponytails), they seemed to come as much from conservative small towns (Elgin, Texas, or Fremont, Michigan) as the cosmopolitan centers of big city liberalism, and they were not all die-hard liberals (though most clearly were). The unifying thread was their passionate partisanship. Each one that I spoke with over three days saw politics through much the same lens as Tom DeLay: as a clash between political coalitions with views of the world so incompatible that compromise was almost always misguided. The names that provoked the loudest catcalls from the YearlyKos audience were not Bush or any of his Republican allies, but Democrats the crowd thought cooperated too much with the GOP. The declarations that drew the loudest applause were calls for Democrats to fight Bush more fiercely. "We don't want Neville Chamberlain Democrats," one speaker insisted. "We want Muhammad Ali Democrats."

DeLay saw greater partisan conflict as a means of advancing conservative goals. The Kossacks saw more conflict as essential to resisting conservative goals and reviving a left-of-center agenda. Each vision derived energy from the other. The more Republicans pursued the uncompromising ideological agenda DeLay promoted, the more they strengthened the voices in the Democratic Party that opposed any cooperation with the GOP. The more Democratic activists pressured their party to pursue a scorched-earth opposition to the GOP, the more they strengthened the conservatives like DeLay who proclaimed it pointless to seek agreements with Democrats. DeLay and the Democratic Internet activists who gathered in Las Vegas could not have been more dissimilar in almost every possible respect. But each sought to reconfigure their political party to the same specifications—as a warrior party that would commit to opposing the other side with every conceivable means at its disposal. In that they were hardly alone. Among the most ardent activists in both parties, the only cause that attracted bipartisan support in the first years of the twenty-first century was the extermination of bipartisan cooperation. That reciprocal passion has produced a political environment marked by unstinting conflict between the parties and the virtual collapse of meaningful collaboration between them. What this unrelenting polarization of political life means for the parties, the electoral system, and the country is the subject of this book.

★

CHAPTER 1

AMERICA DIVIDED

A merica is the richest and most powerful country in the world. It may be the richest and most powerful country in the history of the world.

But it cannot agree on a plan to reduce its dependence on foreign oil.

Nor can it balance its federal budget.

It can't provide health insurance for the nearly one in six Americans without it, either.

It can't agree on a plan to improve security at its borders and provide a humane way to deal with the estimated twelve million illegal immigrants working in its fields and factories and restaurants.

It can't align the promises it has made to seniors through Social Security and Medicare with the tax burdens that future generations realistically can bear.

It can't agree on the steps to rebuild economic security for middle-class Americans in the age of global economic competition. It can't formulate a strategy for reducing the emissions of the gases that contribute to global warming and potentially disruptive changes in the climate.

It cannot agree on an approach to fight the threat of Islamic terrorism, at home and abroad, in a way that unites the country with shared purpose.

None of these problems are new. All have been discussed for years in the media. All are the subject of constant debate in Washington. In most cases the options for dealing with them are limited and familiar.

Why, then, has America failed to make more progress against these challenges?

The answer, above all, is that the day-to-day functioning of American politics now inhibits the constructive compromises between the parties required to confront these problems. The political system has evolved to a point where the vast majority of elected officials in each party feel comfortable only advancing ideas acceptable to their core supporters—their "base," in the jargon of modern campaigns. But progress against these problems, and almost all other challenges facing America, requires comprehensive solutions that marry ideas favored by one party and opposed by the other. It's implausible, for instance, to imagine that we can address the long-term challenge of Social Security and Medicare without both reducing benefits and increasing taxes. Or that we can regain control of our borders without significantly toughening enforcement and creating a legal framework for the millions of illegal immigrants already in the United States. Or that we can reduce our dependence on foreign oil without reducing consumption and increasing domestic production. Yet in each of those cases, and all the others listed above, most elected officials in one of the two major parties will not accept half of that solution. The result is to prevent us from using all of the tools available to attack our problems. One side proposes to control the deficit solely through spending cuts; the other side almost entirely through tax increases. One party proposes to produce more energy, the other to conserve more energy. In fact, to make meaningful progress against any of these problems, the answer is almost always that we will need to do both. Yet because each party seeks to impose its will on the other—and recoils from actions that might challenge its core supporters—it cannot propose comprehensive solutions. We are left with either-or alternatives—increase production or reduce consumption, cut benefits or raise taxes—when the challenges demand that we apply solutions built on the principle of both-and.

This book examines how we have reached this dangerous impasse. It rests on an unambiguous conclusion: The central obstacle to more effective action against our most pressing problems is an unrelenting polarization of American politics that has divided Washington and the country into hostile, even irreconcilable camps. Competition and even contention between rival parties has been part of American political life since its founding. That partisan rivalry most often has been a source of energy, innovation, and inspiration. But today the parties are losing the capacity to recognize their shared interest in placing boundaries on their competition—and in transcending it when the national interest demands. On some occasions—notably efforts to balance the federal budget and reform the welfare system under Bill Clinton, and an initiative to rethink federal education policy in George W. Bush's first year—they have collaborated on reasonable compromises. But for most of the past two decades the two sides have collided with such persistent and unwavering disagreement on everything from taxes to Social Security to social and foreign policy that it sometimes seems they are organizing not only against each other, but against the idea of compromise itself.

Against this backdrop of perpetual conflict, America is living through a transformation of its political life. For most of our history American political parties have functioned as loose coalitions that lightly tether diverse ideological views. Because the parties were so diverse, they have usually operated as a force that synthesized the diverse interests in American society. As the great political historian Richard Hofstadter once wrote, "In our politics, each major party has become a compound, a hodgepodge, of various and conflicting interests; and the imperatives of party struggle, the quest for victory and for offices, have forced the parties to undertake the business of conciliation and compromise among such interests."

That definition is obsolete. From Congress and the White House through the grassroots, the parties today are becoming less diverse, more ideologically homogeneous, and less inclined to pursue reasonable agreements. American government, as we'll see in the chapters ahead, usually has worked best when it is open to a broad array of views and perspectives, and seeks to harmonize a diverse range of interests. Today the dynamics of the political competition are narrowing the perspectives of each party in a manner that pushes them toward operating as the champion of one group of Americans against another—with dangerous results for all Americans. Reconfigured by the large forces we will explore in this book, our politics today encourages confrontation over compromise. The political system now rewards ideology over pragmatism. It is designed to sharpen disagreements rather than construct consensus. It is built on exposing and inflaming the differences that separate Americans rather than the shared priorities and values that unite them. It produces too much animosity and too few solutions.

Political leaders on both sides now feel a relentless pressure for party discipline and intellectual conformity more common in parliamentary systems than through most of American history. Any politician who attempts to build alliances across party lines is more likely to provoke suspicion and criticism than praise. "People want you to choose sides so badly in modern politics, there is no ability to cross [party lines]," said Senator Lindsey Graham, a conservative but iconoclastic Republican from South Carolina. "You are one team versus the other and never shall the twain meet. If it's a Democratic idea, I have to be against it because it came from a Democrat. And vice versa."

Richard A. Gephardt of Missouri, the former Democratic leader in the House of Representatives, used almost the exact same terms to describe the changes he experienced during the twenty-eight years he served in the House before retiring after 2004. "There is no dialogue [between the parties]," he said. "You are either in the blue team or the red team, and you never wander off. It's like the British Parliament. And I never thought about it that much when I came, but it was very different then. It wasn't a parliamentary system, and people wandered off their side and voted in committee or on the floor with the other side. There was this understanding that we were there to solve problems."

The wars between the two parties that take place every day in Washington may seem to most Americans a form of distant posturing, like border clashes between two countries they could not find on the map. But this polarization of political life imposes a tangible cost on every American family—a failure to confront all of the problems listed above with sensible solutions that could improve life for average Americans. Less tangibly but as importantly, extreme partisanship has produced a toxic environment that empowers the most adversarial and shrill voices in each party and disenfranchises the millions of Americans more attracted to pragmatic compromise than to ideological crusades. The reflexive, even ritualized, combat of modern politics leaves fewer and fewer attractive choices for all Americans who don't want to be conscripted into a battle between feuding ideologues or forced to link arms with Michael Moore or Ann Coulter.

KEN MEHLMAN, the campaign manager for Bush in 2004 and chairman of the Republican National Committee during part of his second term, does not exaggerate when he says America is now living through an era of "hyperpartisanship."

The defining characteristics of this age of hyperpartisanship are greater unity within the parties and more intense conflicts between them. On almost every major issue, the distance between the two parties has widened, even as dissent within the parties has diminished. Interest groups in each party are escalating their efforts to enforce ideological discipline on elected officials. Each party has demonstrated greater willingness to employ confrontational tactics that earlier generations considered excessive.

This new political order, as we'll see, has some of its roots in the strategies liberals pursued in the first decades after World War II to promote more disciplined and ideologically unified parties. But over roughly the past fifteen years, the Republican Party has contributed more than the Democrats to the rising cycle of polarization in American politics. That's partly because the GOP has controlled a larger share of political power during that time; Democrats have not had as much opportunity to implement a philosophy of government. But it's mostly because conservatives, eager to reverse decades of liberal policies, have embraced both ends and means that accept high levels of division as the price for ambitious change. Since the GOP takeover of Congress in 1994, and especially since Bush's election in 2000, the Republican Party has grown into a centrally directed, ideologically coherent institution that demands loyalty, isolates and punishes dissent, and mobilizes every conceivable resource allied with it against the other side.

Bush and his advisers greatly accelerated this process by rejecting the assumption that controlling the center of the electorate is the key to success in American politics. Instead, he has tolerated, and at times even seemed to welcome, division as the price of mobilizing his core supporters behind an aggressive agenda that splits the country and the Congress. Under Bush, the GOP has set the pace in adopting confrontational legislative tactics, tethering Congress to the White House, discouraging internal disagreement, constructing an electoral strategy that relies more on exciting its base than courting swing voters, and advancing an agenda, often on razor-thin party-line votes, that aims to meet the preferences of its supporters with as little concession as possible to those outside of its coalition.

The ferocity of this challenge rattled the foundations of the Democratic Party. During the Bush years Democratic leaders faced rising demands from their own base to abandon Bill Clinton's centrist model of governing and reconfigure the party into a mirror image of the highly partisan warrior party that the president and his political "architect," Karl Rove, had designed for the GOP. In fact, Democrats are unlikely ever to match (or even pursue) the level of centralized control and ideological conformity achieved by Republicans because they rely, as we'll see, on a much more diverse electoral coalition. But Democrats are moving fitfully in the same direction, as more party activists push their party to emulate the Republican model. The Democrats have not been the principal engine of polarization, but they have not been immune to its effects either.

On some fronts, the change in the political environment can be measured quantitatively. On major votes, nearly all Republicans and Democrats on Capitol Hill now line up against each other with regimented precision, like nineteenth-century armies that marched shoulder to shoulder onto the battlefield. For the past half century *Congressional Quarterly*, a nonpartisan political magazine in Washington, has tracked the extent to which House and Senate members vote with a majority of their party on contested votes. Both Republicans and Democrats are standing with their own party against the other on about 90 percent of the votes, a level of lockstep uniformity unimaginable only a generation or two ago. Rather than seeking to bridge their differences, the vast majority of legislators in

PARTISAN UNITY IN CONGRESS

Years (President)	House Republicans (%)	House Democrats (%)	Senate Republicans (%)	Senate Democrats (%)
1957–60 (Eisenhower)	69.7	70.0	67.3	66.3
1961–68 (JFK/LBJ)	70.6	67.8	64.4	61.7
1969–76 (Nixon/Ford)	65.6	62.9	61.4	62.6
1977–80 (Carter)	71.0	67.2	64.0	65.3
1981–88 (Reagan)	72.6	76.3	75.5	73.5
1989–92 (G. H. W. Bush)	75.5	80.5	78.3	78.8
1993–2000 (Clinton)	86.8	82.0	86.4	85.4
2001–2004 (G. W. Bush)	90.0	85.5	89.0	85.0

Source: Congressional Quarterly Weekly Reports, *January 1, 2007.*

each party now reflexively vote against any initiative that originates with the other. The table above tracks the level of party unity in congressional votes under every president since Dwight Eisenhower's second term. In both chambers, and in both parties, the trend toward a parliamentary level of loyalty is unmistakable.*

The same trend toward division is evident in the way Americans look at the president. Polls over the past half century show it has become increasingly difficult for presidents to win approval from voters across party lines. Dwight Eisenhower, Lyndon Johnson, even Richard Nixon all attracted significant support from voters who identified with the opposite party. But since then the gap has steadily increased between the way Americans in the president's party assess his job performance and the reviews he receives from Americans in the other party. Under Bush, this difference has widened to unprecedented, almost unimaginable, heights: Bush has excited his own party and infuriated the other as much as any

---

* Using a different set of measures, the political scientists Nolan McCarthy, Keith T. Poole, and Howard Rosenthal have calculated that House and Senate members are voting with their parties today at the highest levels since the 1890s.

PRESIDENTIAL APPROVAL BY PARTY

Year	President	Democratic Party (%)	Republican Party (%)	Gap (%)
1956	Eisenhower	54.1	92.8	38.7
1964	Johnson	84.1	61.6	22.5
1972	Nixon	39.0	83.4	44.4
1976	Ford	36.3	69.2	32.9
1980	Carter	53.5	22.5	31.0
1984	Reagan	28.8	88.4	59.6
1992	G. H. W. Bush	15.7	70.5	54.8
1996	Clinton	82.8	22.1	60.7
2004	G. W. Bush	15.2	90.5	75.3

Source: Calculations from Gallup surveys; data by party provided in 2006 by Professor Gary Jacobson, University of California (San Diego).

president in modern times. The above table tracks the average approval rating each president since Eisenhower has received from voters in the two parties in Gallup Organization surveys during the year they were seeking reelection—the moment at which Americans are rendering their most important judgments on their performance.

As we'll see in Chapter 6, the trends in election results over the past several decades add to the portrait of a political system increasingly divided between stable, divergent, and antagonistic camps. Ideologically, culturally, and geographically, the electoral coalitions of the two major parties have dispersed to the point where they now represent almost mirror images of each other. As this re-sorting has proceeded, each party has established powerful regional strongholds in which it dominates the presidential vote as well as House and Senate races. Each party, in other words, is consolidating its control over a formidable sphere of influence that provides it a stable foundation of support. The flip side is that each party is losing the ability to speak for the entire nation as it loses the capacity to effectively compete in large sections of the country.

THERE ARE TWO dangers in examining today's conflicts between the parties and their allied coalitions. One is to ignore the similarities to the past. The second is to ignore the differences.

Many commentators who downplay the significance of today's partisan wars correctly note that there was never a golden age in American political life when statesmen entirely transcended party to advance the national interest. Politics has always been a rough game; as early as 1797, Thomas Jefferson complained that the factional disputes in the new republic were so heated, "Men who have been intimate all their lives, cross the streets to avoid meeting, and turn their heads another way, lest they should be obliged to touch their hats."

But the level of conflict between the political parties today, the intensity of their disagreements, and the difficulty they face in reaching reasonable compromises is not typical either. American politics is evolving toward greater partisanship and ideological rigidity than it experienced through most of the twentieth century, though in many respects it is moving along a track that is taking it back to the future.

This book will argue for a new way of understanding the cycles of conflict and cooperation between the parties. It will show that relations between the two parties have moved through four distinct phases over the history of modern American politics, a period that traces back roughly over the past 110 years.

The first phase, which stretched from 1896 through 1938, saw the parties pursue highly partisan strategies for governing in a period of sharp party conflict. This era, which will be explored in Chapter 2, was the period in modern American political life most like our own, and in many ways the political system today is re-creating the advantages and disadvantages of that time.

The second (the subject of Chapter 3) saw an erosion of partisan discipline that forced presidents from Franklin D. Roosevelt through John F. Kennedy into the longest sustained period of bipartisan negotiation in American history. This is the period that most closely approaches an ideal of cooperation across party lines. Although the political system in those years was flawed in many respects, its best aspects contain important lessons for us today.

The third period, ranging from the mid-1960s through the mid-1990s, was a period of transition, in which the forces that had sustained that bipartisan system waned and the pressures for more partisan confrontation intensified. (These will be explored in Chapters 4, 5, and 6.)

The final phase, the culmination of those pressures, is our own period of hyperpartisanship, an era that may be said to have fully arrived when the Republican-controlled House of Representatives voted on a virtually party-line vote to impeach Bill Clinton in December 1998. (Chapters 6 through 10, from different angles, will all explore this period.)

The resurgence of partisanship over the past several decades confounded the expectations of political scientists in the middle to late twentieth century. Most analysts predicted that the parties might be eclipsed by television (which provides politicians a more direct relationship with voters), the ability of candidates to raise large sums of money on their own, or the rise of independent voters.

Instead we have moved into an era when partisanship at every level, from the voters to elected officials, is the most powerful force in political life. "The two political parties are really strong in a way they haven't been in years," Mehlman correctly notes. "Not strong that as the chairman of the Republican Party I'm a big dog; that's not what it is. Strong in the sense that . . . joining a political party means something. Political parties are no longer divided along lines that are arbitrary: religion, race, what your economic status is. They are now divided along [the lines of] what your ideology is, which is much more durable. We live in an era of very strong parties."

These strong parties, as noted above, are reminiscent in many ways of the dynamic parties that anchored the age of intense partisanship around the beginning of the twentieth century. But the competition between the parties today is unique in one critical respect: In the early years of the twentieth century, the country was deeply divided but not closely divided. It was deeply divided, because a large gulf separated the priorities of most Republicans and most Democrats throughout that era. But it was not closely divided, because Republicans and Democrats each assembled dominant coalitions that constituted a clear majority of the country during the

years when they held power. Conversely, in the period of greater bipartisan negotiation, between the late 1930s and the mid-1960s, the country
was closely but not deeply divided. It was closely divided because the tendency of dozens of conservative Democrats, and a smaller number of moderate Republicans, to routinely cross party lines left neither side with a
reliable majority in Congress throughout this era. But it was not deeply
divided, because the very instability of the system encouraged presidents
from each party to pursue mostly centrist agendas.

Today America is deeply and closely divided. The ideological differences between the parties are as great as at any time in the past century.
But the country is split almost exactly in half between the two sides. Deeply
and closely divided is an unprecedented and explosive combination. Voters
for the losing side always feel unrepresented when the other party wins
unified control over government. But for most of our history those voters
could look to heretics in the majority coalition (liberal Republicans or conservative Democrats) who championed an approximation of their views.
And in most cases—under William McKinley and Theodore Roosevelt,
or Franklin Roosevelt and Lyndon Johnson—the disaffected faced the reality that the other side, at that moment, represented a preponderant majority of the country. Neither was true while Republicans controlled the
White House and Congress through most of Bush's presidency. Nearly 49
percent of the country voted against Bush in 2004, but few Republican
leaders, inside his administration or in Congress, held views close to almost
any of those voters. The size of the losing electoral coalition was much
greater than in most previous periods of unified government, but their
influence inside the governing coalition was smaller. For most of his presidency this dynamic allowed Bush to govern in a manner that satisfied his
base while excluding perhaps a greater share of the electorate than at any
previous point in American history. The operation of that system, and its
consequences for Bush, the two parties, and the country, will be explored
more in Chapters 7 and 8.

THE POLARIZATION OF American politics is an enormously complex,
interactive phenomenon. Its roots trace into factors far beyond the workings

of the political system itself, into changes in social life, cultural attitudes, and America's place in the world. The tendency toward polarization has been fueled, on the one hand, by the rise of feminism and the gay rights movement, and on the other by the increasing popularity of fundamentalist and evangelical churches. It draws strength from the questions about America's international role opened by the end of the cold war. And it has been influenced by changes in residential patterns that appear to have increased the tendency of Americans to settle among neighbors who share their political views.

This book, though, will focus on the changes within the political system that have carried America into the age of hyperpartisanship: the changing nature of the party coalitions; the role of organized constituency groups in shaping the political debate; the shifts in the way the media interacts with political life; the changes in the rules and practices of Congress; and the strategies pursued by presidents and other political leaders. All of these changes are diminishing our capacity to resolve conflicts. Indeed, as we'll see in the chapters ahead, almost every major force in American political life now operates as an integrated machine to push the parties apart and to sharpen the disagreements in American life.

The consequences of hyperpartisanship are not all negative. The new alignment offers voters clear, stark choices. As recently as 1980 less than half of Americans told pollsters they saw important differences between the Republican and Democratic parties. Today, three fourths of Americans say they see important differences. With the choices so vividly clarified, more Americans are participating in the political system. Over 122 million people voted in 2004, nearly 17 million more than just four years earlier. The number of people who volunteered and contributed money to campaigns has soared too. One study found that the number of small donors to the presidential campaign increased at least threefold, and perhaps even fourfold, from 2000 to 2004. Many of those small donors made their contributions through the Internet, which has demonstrated an extraordinary ability to connect ordinary citizens to politics. The liberal group MoveOn.org is the best example: It has over 3 million members who not only direct torrents of cash toward favored candidates and stacks of e-mails to Capitol Hill, but get up from their computers to participate in everything from candlelight vigils on the Iraq War to bake sales. The political blogs are often intemperate, but they have created vibrant communities that discuss and debate political issues with remarkable verve and intensity. They daily disprove the easy assumption that Americans are fundamentally apathetic about the choices their leaders make in their name.

The rise in political conflict is a measure of vitality in another respect, too. As we will see in Chapters 3 and 4, American politics is more polarized in part because it is more diverse and open. Far more interests than half a century ago have a voice in shaping the national agenda. That has required the political system to deal with difficult issues, from civil rights for minorities to protection of the environment, it largely submerged during the era of the greatest bipartisan cooperation around World War II. Many of these issues inherently provoke strong emotions and conflict. That is unavoidable and in some ways admirable. Political peace bought at the price of ignoring problems is usually temporary and almost always counterproductive: It produces mounting frustration and growing alienation, the way the bipartisan refusal to confront the South over segregation did through the early 1960s. The conflict that comes from including a greater variety of voices in decisions is to be welcomed, not feared.

It's also a mistake to blame the ideologues in both parties for this system, or at least to blame them too much. There have always been true believers in American politics. Sometimes they function as a negative force, as they did, say, in the Joe McCarthy era. Today they inhibit progress when they lean too heavily on the parties to reject compromise. But ardent believers also play a valuable role in the political system by challenging the status quo. What Hofstadter wrote about utopian parties applies to the true believers of left and right today—they can be useful by bringing "neglected grievances to the surface." John Kennedy considered the civil rights activists a nuisance; when the freedom riders mounted their brave campaign to integrate interstate travel on hazardous trips through the South, Kennedy once told his top civil rights aide to have them "call it off." But they persisted, at great personal risk, and forced him to move more quickly than he wanted to obtain desegregation of interstate buses. Few interest groups can claim such a moral high ground today. But they also serve by pressuring the parties to confront problems they might otherwise ignore. The agitation of environmentalists has made it more difficult for politicians to ignore global warming; conservative groups pressure Washington to acknowledge the long-term difficulty of funding the current promises under Medicare and Social Security. Without ideologues, the system can mistake drift for consensus.

Likewise, it is a mistake to blame the rise in political combat primarily on political consultants. Political consultants are a force for conflict in campaigns because as a group they love negative advertisements. But they are not a consistent force against compromise in government. Some of them preach the gospel of "feeding the base" to win elections; that has been the central focus, for instance, of Bush's political team. Others, in both parties, still worry about alienating moderates and independents in the many states that don't lean decisively to either party. Most, in the end, can argue it round or argue it flat: They run polarizing campaigns for politicians who prefer to polarize and centrist campaigns for candidates who want to conciliate. If anything, most political consultants prefer to keep every possible vote in play: that inclines many of them against the most ideological approaches.

Yet it is impossible to deny that in a period of polarization, politicians, consultants, and activists can find it in their short-term interest to accelerate the spiral of division. Surrendering to polarization often appears an easier, and safer, political course than confronting it. Bush made polarization work for him in both the 2002 and 2004 elections by generating an enormous turnout of the Republican base. Congressional Democrats maximized their influence during Bush's second term by uniting solidly against his agenda, especially his plan to restructure Social Security. Reaching out across party lines takes a very long arm when the two sides begin almost every debate so far apart. In particular, the ambition and edge of Bush's agenda—his determination, as he often expressed it to aides, not to play "small ball"—pointed him in directions on many issues so far from the preferences of most Democrats that it sometimes seemed it might be easier to find common ground between the interests of the cow and the slaughterhouse.

In this environment, politicians who appeal for compromise often appear weak, naive, or worse, enablers of the other side. Yet it is a dangerously self-fulfilling prophecy for politicians to view themselves as soldiers in an army whose only legitimate goal is to destroy the other. The more elected officials accept that logic the more they harden the divisions that inspire the argument in the first place. Ultimately, breaking the cycle of polarization will require elected officials—almost certainly beginning with a future president—to take a leap of faith that a constituency for reasonable compromise still exists in America.

Nothing is certain in politics, but there's considerable evidence that such a gamble would pay off. As we'll explore in Chapter 6, one critical reason American politics has grown so polarized is the consistency of ideological belief in each party—the solidifying dominance of conservative views among voters and officeholders in the Republican Party, and to a lesser extent, the ascent of liberals in the Democratic coalition. But the *intensity* of belief among average voters isn't the principal problem. The weight of evidence suggests American politics isn't so polarized because large numbers of Americans have suddenly grown deeply, ardently ideological in their view of the world. The number of deeply committed ideologues in America, though difficult to measure precisely, probably isn't much larger today than at earlier points in our history, which is to say minuscule. In the biennial political surveys conducted by the University of Michigan, the percentage of adults who call themselves very liberal over the past three decades has soared from 1 percent to . . . 2 percent. The share that calls itself very conservative has exploded from just 1 percent to 3 percent. In that survey, after the 2004 election, half the voters in both red and blue states placed themselves in the three most centrist categories.

None of this suggests an electorate suddenly dominated by crusaders. If anything, it suggests an electorate that might be more receptive than commonly believed to a problem-solving, pragmatic politics that tempered the hostilities between the parties. Given the political choices they are now presented, Americans align in sharply defined, and increasingly antagonistic, camps. But that doesn't mean many Americans might not accept, or even prefer, less adversarial choices. In the spring of 2006, a group of veteran political operatives from both parties launched an Internet-based effort to draft a centrist third-party candidate for 2008. (We'll look at that possibility more closely in Chapter 10.) As part of their planning, they

funded a poll that measured American attitudes toward the political system. The survey found enormous disenchantment over the unstinting
conflict between the parties. Three fourths of those polled agreed, "The
bickering between Republicans and Democrats in Washington is getting
in the way of solving the nation's problems." An even greater number—82
percent—agreed that "America has become so polarized between Democrats and Republicans that Washington can't seem to make progress
solving the nation's problems."

Such findings support the verdict of Stanley B. Greenberg, a veteran
Democratic pollster who advised the presidential campaigns of Bill
Clinton, Al Gore, and John Kerry, when he concludes: "The country
doesn't like this politics. It doesn't like to be sorted; it doesn't like to be
forced into an agenda that follows these lines. There are still lots of voters
who don't fit into these pigeonholes." Matthew Dowd, the senior strategist and chief pollster for Bush's presidential campaigns in both 2000 and
2004, expresses the same conclusion in even more emphatic terms. "I think
there is a big opportunity for movement," he said. "I think an election
could come along that all of a sudden is not a close election if somebody or
some party speaks to the mixed . . . group while still maintaining part of
their party. . . . Because I think people in this country want something that
brings them together, not something that separates them. I think people
want that sense of community, they want that sense of connection."

It would be naive to understate the difficulties of building an electoral
coalition centered on constructive compromise. Here the key is to watch
what people do, not what they say. Americans may say they dislike partisan bickering, but more of them are aligning more reliably with one party
or the other. When centrist solutions to problems such as immigration,
the budget, or welfare are offered in polls they almost always attract broad
support. But when they are presented in the real world, against a backdrop
of praise from the leaders of one party and condemnation from leaders of
the other, support often fractures along the familiar party lines. Building
consensus in this environment is a formidable challenge.

But the best evidence is that it's not an insurmountable one. Constructing broad agreements is more difficult today than in the first decades after
World War II because more interests must be accommodated. But, as

we'll see, even amid the rising partisan tensions of the past four decades, the two parties have come together for important agreements on the environment (under Richard Nixon), tax reform and the stabilization of Social Security (under Ronald Reagan), the federal budget (under George H. W. Bush and Bill Clinton), and welfare reform (under Clinton again).

American politics isn't breaking down because the country's disagreements are inherently more difficult to bridge today than they were while those men sat in the White House. It is breaking down because too few political leaders resist the rising pressures inside the parties for ideological and partisan conformity that make it more difficult to bridge our disagreements. Ideological voices are louder than perhaps ever before in all aspects of American politics, from Congress to the media, but that isn't because deeply ideological voters now dominate the American electorate. At its core, the problem isn't too many ideologues but too few conciliators willing to challenge the ideologues, and partisan warriors on each side demanding a polarized politics. The first step toward lowering the temperature in American politics is a political leadership that would rather douse fires than start them.

Today, though, the impulse to harmonize divergent interests has almost vanished from the capital. Rather than promoting consensus, Washington manufactures disagreement. In both parties, many politicians see it in their interests to widen, not narrow, the underlying divisions in society. Americans today are sincerely divided over the role of government in the economy, foreign policy (especially the Iraq War), and perhaps most intractably, cultural and social issues. But no one would say Americans are divided as violently and passionately as they were over civil rights and the Vietnam War in the 1960s, or the rise of the corporate economy in the 1890s, much less slavery in the 1850s. In each of those periods, the differences between Americans were so profound that they were expressed not just with words, but with fists, and clubs, and ultimately guns. (Think Kent State, the Homestead Steel strike, and John Brown, not to mention the Civil War.) Clearly the *country* has been more polarized than it is today. What's unusual now is that the *political system* is more polarized than the country. Rather than reducing the level of conflict, Washington increases it. That tendency, not the breadth of the underlying divisions itself, is the defining characteristic of our era and the principal cause of our impasse on so many problems.

The road to this point has been paved by the long list of factors that we will explore in the chapters that follow. It has been manifest in hundreds, even thousands, of discrete decisions, yet the overall direction has been unwavering. The center in American politics is eroding. Confrontation is rising. The parties are separating. And the conflict between them is widening.

With so many centrifugal forces at work, this era of hyperpartisanship won't unwind easily or quickly. No one any time soon will confuse American politics with the era of good feeling that virtually eradicated partisan competition early in the nineteenth century. The forces encouraging polarization are now deeply entrenched, and they are unlikely to be entirely neutralized: Many of the most antagonistic features of American politics over the past fifteen years are likely to endure indefinitely. But that doesn't mean the country has to be as sharply and relentlessly divided as it is today. The parties have cooperated before to reach commonsense solutions that advance the national interest and could do so again. An exploration of how the parties have cooperated, or failed to, over the past century, shows the opportunities that are still available—and the risks of failing to seize them.

CHAPTER 2

THE AGE OF
PARTISAN ARMIES

The presidential election of 1896 was the first that contemporary Americans would recognize as a distant ancestor of the modern campaign for the White House. In its style, the contest between Republican William McKinley and Democrat William Jennings Bryan gestured toward a fading past but mostly welcomed an approaching future. McKinley, the stately and serene Ohio governor, respected the nineteenth-century tradition that disdained personal campaigning for the White House; he famously remained at home on his front porch in Canton, receiving carefully selected delegations of supporters. But around him, Republicans organized an extensive, expensive public relations campaign that functioned as an overture for the multimedia onslaughts of the twentieth century. Under the direction of Cleveland industrialist Marcus (Mark) Hanna, the shrewd strategist behind McKinley's rise, Republicans dispatched an army of promotional speakers, distributed over 120 million pieces of literature, and even hired two cameramen to produce a rudimentary campaign film of McKinley chatting (where else?) on his porch. Bryan, the thundering Nebraska populist who opposed McKinley as the Democratic nominee, shattered tradition even more emphatically: He mounted a tireless three-month cross-country railroad tour that saw him speak to as many as 5 million people on 250 scheduled stops and untold more unscheduled appearances.

The 1896 election anticipated the politics that would follow not only in its form, but in its content. It began an argument between Republicans and Democrats over the role of government that has continued ever since. From the time of Thomas Jefferson and Andrew Jackson, Democrats had been a small-government party that sought to limit Washington's role in the economy. To nineteenth-century Democrats, support for limited government was a form of populism. The rich and well-connected, they reasoned, would use government as a tool to exploit the farmer and ordinary workingman through special favors. But Bryan and his supporters began the process of separating Democrats from that tradition, which had grown anachronistic as railroads, trusts, and great financial institutions accumulated massive economic and political power in the decades after the Civil War. In policy, and even more in rhetoric, Bryan pointed Democrats toward their modern philosophy of an activist government that would attempt to protect ordinary people ("the struggling masses," as he called them) by regulating and taming the power of business ("the idle holders of idle capital"); he opened doors that Woodrow Wilson and Franklin D. Roosevelt later would storm through.

Bryan's movement away from the Democrats' Jeffersonian heritage established a bright-line distinction—the clearest contrast in any presidential race in decades—with McKinley. The affable McKinley crystallized the Republican vision of government as a partner with business in the monumental project of industrializing America. Republicans consecrated the alliance primarily through support for a high tariff that protected American manufacturers against competition from foreign imports (while also functioning as a tax on American consumers who paid inflated prices). The underlying issue Bryan and McKinley debated—can Washington best promote prosperity and opportunity by challenging the free market or by deferring to it?—has remained at the heart of American politics ever since.

For our purposes, the collision between McKinley and Bryan had a third major consequence: it opened the era in American political life most like our own. The election of 1896 ended a period of extended political disorder. By the mid-1870s, the political allegiances forged in the Civil War—with Republicans as the dominant party of Union and Democrats as the discredited sympathizers of rebellion—were eroding in most of the country. But the parties had not established any new basis for firm attachments to voters. Neither developed bold or coherent responses to the forces upending American life—industrialization, immigration, the shift of population to the cities, and the growing economic power of corporations and the trusts. Both remained trapped in a minimalist view of Washington's responsibilities to those struggling against these currents—farmers, workers, the new arrivals from Europe crowding into urban tenements.

Unable to meet emerging needs, neither party could establish a lasting advantage. In Washington instability ruled. In the four elections from 1880 through 1892 no president won a majority of the popular vote. Nor did any win a second consecutive term. For only four of the twenty years from 1876 through 1896 did one party achieve unified control over the White House and the House and Senate. Congressional majorities were frequently narrow and always fragile. Inside Congress, leadership was weak and party discipline rare. Major issues, such as currency reform or the tariff, often split both parties. Surveying the scene with disdain, a young political scientist named Woodrow Wilson complained in 1885, "No one exercises the special trust of acknowledged leadership."

Through the early 1890s, the ground remained unstable as the electorate careened through temperamental swings in allegiance. Finally, in the confrontation between McKinley and Bryan, the differences between the parties sharpened and the balance of power between them hardened. The collision of these two visions in 1896 produced a clear victory for McKinley and the forces of industrializing America. For the next sixteen years, and again from 1920 through 1932, Republicans would control the White House by sweeping the Northeast, the Midwest, the West Coast, the Great Plains, and in the best years, the Mountain West as well. Promising, and mostly delivering, prosperity, they welded together a dominant coalition of the wealthy, small business owners, and much of the urban laboring class. For most of this era, the Republicans were the party of broader reach, with a much wider geographic appeal than the Democrats and a much more encompassing mission: In these years, as political scientist

Everett Carll Ladd, Jr., aptly noted, the GOP "was the party of industrial nation-building." Except under Wilson and Franklin Roosevelt, Democrats were reduced to pockets of regional discontent in the South (where Republicans remained disqualified by their stain as the "party of Northern aggression" in the Civil War), some big cities (where new immigrants were herded to the polls by resourceful political machines like Tammany Hall in New York), and, to a more limited extent, the Plains and Mountain West states drawn to Bryan.

The election of 1896 imposed order on the previous generation's political instability. And that new order inaugurated a forty-year period in which American politics was defined by intense conflict between remarkably unified partisan coalitions that remained stable until moments of sudden wrenching change. From the election of McKinley in 1896 through the reelection of Franklin D. Roosevelt in 1936, one party or the other held unified control of the White House and both chambers of Congress for all but six years. With power partitioned so cleanly, the parties felt little incentive for bipartisan cooperation—and pursued almost none of it. It was an unsentimental age, when both parties exercised the authority they held without much concern about the priorities of any interest outside of their electoral coalition. John J. Ingalls, a Republican senator from Kansas, had predicted the age's ethos in 1890 when he declared, "Government is force. Politics is a battle for supremacy. Parties are the armies." This was the age of partisan armies.

In this era, Republicans dominated Washington for two long periods, from 1896 through 1912, under the presidencies of McKinley, Theodore Roosevelt, and William Howard Taft; and again from 1920 through 1932, during the administrations of Warren Harding, Calvin Coolidge, and Herbert Hoover. Democrats held the initiative during Woodrow Wilson's presidency, from 1913 through 1920, and the first years of Franklin D. Roosevelt's New Deal, from 1932 through 1938.

These presidencies diverged in their styles, their goals, and their success at achieving those goals. But they shared common characteristics that defined the age of partisan armies. One was a grant of preponderant power from the electorate. Voters not only provided the parties' unified control over Congress and the White House, but usually afforded them overwhelming control. From 1896 through 1910, Republicans averaged a fifty-eight-seat advantage over Democrats in the House and a twenty-four-seat advantage in the Senate; from 1921 through 1930, the GOP held, on average, seventy-nine more seats than the Democrats in the House and thirteen more in the Senate. That meant Democrats lacked the strength to force concessions, or even much consideration, from Republicans through almost all of those years. During these periods, Democrats were so weak that in contemporary accounts, they appear as a whisper, an afterthought, an irrelevance; almost all the debates that mattered in those years occurred solely within the Republican Party. Republicans were a more competitive minority under Wilson (after his first two years). But against Franklin Roosevelt, the Republicans were as depleted as Democrats had been in the earlier periods of Republican control: After the 1936 election, Republican strength in the House and Senate fell to the lowest point it would reach in the twentieth century. With few exceptions, this was an age of commanding majorities.

Second, the parties represented clearly delineated constituencies. Except during Theodore Roosevelt's presidency, Republicans in Congress and the White House during this period identified with business as thoroughly as they ever did before or have since: "Never before, here or anywhere else, has a government been so completely fused with business," the *Wall Street Journal* declared during the 1920s. Republicans also drew reliable support from Midwestern farmers, and when times were good, from industrial workers attracted by "the full dinner pail," as McKinley called it. But, amid all these voices, the GOP left no doubt about its highest priority. With only intermittent exceptions, Republicans in this era pursued the policies favored by the Eastern financial and corporate elite: hard money, high tariffs, and limited federal regulation. In turn, business provided the ruling Republicans not only a formidable foundation of electoral and financial support but a mission—building a strong, industrial, national economy—broad enough to attract others to the party's banner.

The Democratic coalition was always more diverse and conflicted. At the party's lowest points during the period, the Democratic coalition was defined mostly in negative terms: It comprised only the pieces (Catholics, Southerners, and sometimes Western farmers) that felt unwelcome in a

Republican Party centered on Protestantism, the industrial economy, and the burgeoning states of the Northeast and Midwest. In a real sense, the Democrats during long stretches of this period existed only in the margins the GOP left unfilled. But in the moments when Democrats achieved the clearest definition—first under Wilson and later Franklin Roosevelt—the party established a positive identity as the voice of all the groups looking to government to tame the rising corporate economic order: the reforming middle class, struggling farmers, and increasingly over time, organized labor. At those points the lines between the parties were sharply drawn.

The contrasts in the parties' constituencies, and the decisiveness of their victories, encouraged a third defining characteristic of this age: a philosophy of party government. This period was shaped above all by the determination of its leaders to advance their agendas in ways that maximized unity within their own party and minimized the influence of the other. Both Republican and Democratic presidents governed by maneuvering for consensus within their own coalition rather than building alliances with likeminded legislators from the opposition party (with FDR, during his first years, the conspicuous exception). The ruling party almost always preferred to overwhelm its opposition rather than persuade or even divide it. Presidents and congressional leaders prioritized party discipline, often punishing dissenters by withholding campaign funds and patronage or blocking their preferred committee assignments; the imperious Republican House speaker Joseph G. Cannon removed three reform-minded committee chairmen in one sudden strike just before Congress convened in 1910. Presidents displayed little tolerance for mavericks and crusaders. To a supporter who wrote Taft asking why he didn't do more to support reformers challenging Cannon's autocratic rule in the House, Taft replied: "I ask you how a man of sense . . . can expect me to do otherwise than support the regular organization in the House. . . . I must rely upon the party and party discipline to pass the measures that I am recommending." Taft, Wilson, and Franklin Roosevelt all participated in purges of dissident members—each with limited success at best. And the vast majority of rank-and-file members, especially in the Republican Party, absorbed the ethos of the times. "[T]he unity of the party on all questions is of paramount importance," one Republican senator declared early in the period. Around the same time, Republican senator Thomas C. Platt of New York wrote to one of the GOP's preeminent Senate leaders, "What you say goes. Kindly keep me posted as to what you do, so that I may not go astray."

Even these powerful centralizing tendencies did not completely extinguish disagreement within the parties. Democratic differences extended beyond the divisions between progressives drawn toward activist government and "Jeffersonians" or "Bourbons" who clung to the party's ancestral small-government ideology. During the march to Prohibition after World War I, rural "drys," from the South and West, feuded with Northern "wets" defending the right of their immigrant constituents to unwind with a stein of beer after a long day at the docks or in the forge; the shameful subjugation of Southern blacks increasingly split the party at the Mason-Dixon Line. But all of these disagreements afflicted Democrats most when Republicans controlled government. Out of power, Democrats amply justified the acid judgment of Taft, who declared in 1904, "The great difficulty about the Democratic party is that it is not a party at all, in the proper sense of that term. It is a conglomeration of irreconcilable elements that have no solidarity so far as carrying through any policy affirmatively is concerned." Yet when Democrats held power in this period, under Wilson and through Franklin Roosevelt's first term, they suppressed their differences long enough to pass most of those presidents' agendas. In this age of powerful partisanship, ideological divisions did not prevent Democrats from exercising power when voters provided them the opportunity.

The same was true of Republicans. Throughout these decades the GOP consistently divided between the business-oriented conservatives who dominated the party and a minority of insurgent progressives who pressed for political reform and more federal oversight of industry. The progressives were a powerful force in the first period of Republican control, especially after the dynamic Robert M. La Follette of Wisconsin brought his hurricane personality and ambition into the Senate in 1906. By the time Republicans regained power after Wilson's two terms, the GOP balance of power had tilted decisively to the conservatives. Still, Republican Progressives like La Follette and George Norris of Nebraska continued to battle with the conservative Republican presidents of the 1920s; even Herbert

Hoover faced conflicts between old guard and progressive Republicans, who pressed for a more aggressive response to the Depression.

Yet the dissidents never threatened the ruling Republican vision. During each period of Republican control, GOP progressives achieved relatively few victories. Sharing the partisan assumptions of the time, the Republican progressives almost always tried to work within the GOP rather than to build coalitions across party lines. When they did try to ally with Democrats—on railroad reform under Theodore Roosevelt and to lower tariffs under Taft—they failed miserably. In a polarized political system, the progressives in each party were logical allies in the search for compromises between business and its critics, but the progressives never found a way to consistently work together.

Instead, party discipline shaped the era. Political scientists who track the history of roll-call voting have found that in both the House and the Senate, Republicans and Democrats voted with their own party, and against the opposition party, more consistently in the years just before and after 1900 than they would at any other point in the twentieth century. During most congressional sessions in those years, legislators from both parties, in both chambers, voted with their side on contested issues as much as 90 percent of the time or more—a staggering testament to the elevation of party that shaped the era. Only amid the polarized politics of the early twenty-first century is the level of party discipline in Congress returning to such heights again.

The era of partisan armies foreshadowed many of the virtues and defects of politics in our own time. The sharp lines of division between the parties, and the suppression of differences within them, produced stable and efficient governing coalitions. During their first period of control, the Republicans followed a remarkably consistent governing strategy for fully sixteen years. Though Theodore Roosevelt pressed against the consensus, and the party held unity toward the end only by dodging issues like the tariff and currency reform, the GOP dominated this era with a business-friendly agenda that evolved only modestly from McKinley through Taft, and accelerated the nation's historic industrialization and urbanization. In the 1920s Republicans again unified behind a similar course of lowering taxes, raising tariffs, and restraining federal regulation. The two periods of

Democratic ascendance during this era produced torrents of landmark leg-islation that built much of Washington's modern regulatory and social welfare state, from the Federal Reserve Board to Social Security. In office, each party produced a clear and unambiguous record that provided voters a clear choice.

But the system had two great weaknesses. The first proved more a problem for Republicans. Because the two parties drew support from such distinct economic and geographic pools, and so rigidly enforced discipline on their members, the political system in this era encouraged insularity. It was a system that provided few, and often no, political concessions to any interest not allied with the party in power. Shrewd in promoting the cre-ation of a powerful industrialized America, the Republican leaders were shortsighted in too often equating that mission with support for the most powerful industrialists themselves. During both its periods of preemi-nence, the GOP paid little attention to voices outside of its business-centered coalition. In their first period of control, Republicans offered little to labor, slighted middle-class reformers uneasy about the rise of cor-porate power, and slowly alienated farmers squeezed by the high-tariff, tight-money policies demanded by the party's Eastern industrial base. In the second period, the GOP pursued much the same course. Each time the Republican leadership, focused almost exclusively on the needs of its core supporters, made too little effort to balance those needs against other interests in society. In both periods of Republican control, the party's con-gressional leadership isolated and marginalized the progressive dissidents, who raised alarms about the growing discontent. Determined to stifle dis-sent inside the party, they failed to recognize the strength of the popular sentiment it embodied. As a result, the GOP allowed grievances to build that destroyed its hold on power, first in 1912, then again in 1932.

Democrats could not be quite so insular. Typically, their coalition always contained more diverse and contradictory elements: Northern lib-erals and Southern racists, ardent progressives and corporate lawyers. That required them to juggle more complex demands than the Republicans; Wilson and Roosevelt, for instance, could never dismiss the leaders of business as thoroughly as McKinley or Coolidge could dismiss the *critics* of business. Yet Democrats were not immune to the narrowing tendencies that weakened the Republicans in this era: When Franklin Roosevelt turned sharply to the left after his first few years, he accelerated a backlash on the right that effectively cut his presidency in half.

The experience of the era's other Democratic president, Woodrow Wilson, demonstrated the second central weakness of this deeply polarized political system. Because Wilson chose to govern on a purely partisan basis, he lacked the goodwill he needed to recruit Republicans into common cause when he came upon a problem too large to be solved by one party alone: leading America into a new international role after World War I. Later, Herbert Hoover would face a similar equation when confronted with the Depression. Both of those presidents, their parties, and ultimately the nation would pay heavy prices for their inability to draw on all of America's talents at moments of great challenge.

PARTISANSHIP IN PRACTICE

Before the age of partisan armies ended, the president would emerge as the undisputed focal point of American politics. But the first important steps toward establishing central command over the parties were taken on Capitol Hill.

Even as the electorate sorted into a more stable alignment in the 1890s, a small group of political innovators in Congress moved to establish the party discipline that had lapsed in the first decades after the Civil War. The first milestone came in 1890 when the corpulent, cold-eyed Republican speaker Thomas B. Reed of Maine rewrote House rules to eliminate the minority party's ability to block bills. The minority's most powerful weapon in the nineteenth-century House had been its ability to prevent action by refusing to answer present during roll calls; that denied the majority the quorum required for action. On Wednesday, January 29, 1890, without warning even his allies, Reed instructed the clerk to record as present and not voting all the Democrats who refused to answer when the speaker sought to bring up a contested election from West Virginia. Democrats erupted in outrage, but Reed made the change stick: No longer could the minority stalemate the majority through the House equivalent of a Senate filibuster.

"Reed's rules," later adopted as well by Democrats when they took control, moved the House into a new era by unequivocally establishing the majority party's control over the institution. When Reed's Republican friend and rival, Joseph G. Cannon of Illinois, was elected speaker in 1903, he built on his predecessor's breakthrough with changes that maximized his leverage over not only the minority party but his own members. A profane, cigar-chewing, tobacco-spitting staunch conservative from rural Illinois, "Uncle" Joe Cannon seized authority over committee appointments; decided which bills reached the House floor through his chairmanship of the House Rules Committee; and maintained control over which legislators would be recognized to speak or offer motions on the floor. No speaker ever controlled the House more completely.

No single individual emerged with quite so much authority in the Senate. But the upper chamber witnessed an equally powerful shift to centralized control. Under the reliable Republican majorities that began in 1898, Senate power flowed toward what became known as the "Four." First among equals in the Four were Nelson W. Aldrich of Rhode Island and William B. Allison of Iowa; they were supported by Orville H. Platt of Connecticut and John C. Spooner of Wisconsin. Albert J. Beveridge, the perceptive and ambitious Republican senator from Indiana, once described the group (in a description paraphrased by two historians) as "a marvelous combination composed of Aldrich as manager, Allison as conciliator and adjustor, Spooner as floor leader and debater, and Platt as designer and builder." The Four's power rested on their positions on key committees (all four sat on the Finance Committee; Platt chaired the Judiciary Committee and Allison the Appropriations Committee); their influence over committee assignments (which fell under the control of Allison, as chairman of the committee that decided the appointments); and their power, largely through Aldrich, over campaign funds from the GOP's business supporters.

The Four were not monolithic; the stocky, bearded Allison, who faced more progressive dissent at home, was more conciliatory than the imperious Aldrich, a self-made millionaire who corruptly compounded his millions through investments with wealthy men who benefited from his decisions in the Senate. Aldrich preferred to work behind the scenes;

Spooner, a former railroad lobbyist, was a gifted debater. Nor could the Four always impose their will: Initially they resisted the rush toward war against Spain in 1898, only to surrender to the tide. Yet on key issues, the Four almost always came together to steer the Senate as forcefully as Cannon did the House. Meeting in Platt's modest Washington apartment, or during summers at Aldrich's opulent Rhode Island mansion, the Four "promoted their friends and isolated their enemies" to unify Senate Republicans behind an agenda that promised prosperity through unstinting government support for business.

McKinley mostly deferred to the leadership of the Four. Theodore Roosevelt, who succeeded to the presidency after McKinley's assassination in 1901, was more dynamic and less tractable. "[W]e will have to both pull the load and apply the brakes," Cannon wrote to one ally after Roosevelt won his own full term with a resounding victory in 1904. Yet the institutional strength of the GOP congressional leadership discouraged Roosevelt from openly breaking with them, though his instincts sometimes tempted him. Aldrich and his allies reflexively resisted any federal action that impinged on the freedom and prerogatives of business. Roosevelt's view was more subtle. He feared the widening conflict between classes, and between labor and business. He wanted his party to be seen as more than the voice of one faction. In 1904 he declared, "It would be a dreadful calamity if we saw this country divided into two parties, one containing the bulk of the property owners and conservative people, the other containing the bulk of the wage-workers and the less prosperous people generally." Roosevelt considered modest reform the antidote to revolution; he believed, one sympathetic historian wrote, "His primary task lay in making his party bend and adapt to change and discontent."

But Roosevelt was unwilling to separate decisively from an unbending Republican mainstream that resisted almost all his efforts to broaden the party's agenda and appeal. "I'm just a president," Roosevelt said of Aldrich, "and he has seen a lot of presidents." Roosevelt did try to soothe social tensions, and he reached out to constituencies beyond the GOP's business and rural Midwestern base, with conservation initiatives, regulation of food and drugs, and modestly toughened oversight of the powerful railroads loathed by Western farmers. But his desire for party harmony, and his own cautious instincts, discouraged him from pursuing other initiatives with potentially broad appeal, like lowering tariffs or systematically challenging the trusts. Roosevelt never felt entirely comfortable with the dissidents in his own party. And despite his regular conflicts with Republican conservatives he made only fleeting attempts to build alliances with progressive Democrats sympathetic to his agenda; the one time he made a sincere effort, on railroad reform, Senate Democrats could not provide the votes he needed, and Roosevelt was compelled to accept a compromise forged by the GOP Senate leadership. Once Roosevelt left the White House, he formulated (as we'll see in Chapter 10) a brilliant conception of the presidency that challenged the binary partisanship of his era. But as president he governed in a manner that mostly upheld it. When it came to his agenda for reforming Washington and reshaping the Republican Party, Roosevelt inverted his famous maxim on foreign affairs: He spoke loudly, but carried only a small stick.

Under Taft, who succeeded Roosevelt in 1908, Republican unity finally disintegrated. On Capitol Hill, more members rebelled against the heavy yoke of Cannon and the Four. In 1910, progressive Republicans joined with Democrats to strip Cannon of his seat on the Rules Committee and to create the discharge petition, which allowed dissident House members to bring legislation directly to the floor for a vote by obtaining enough signatures from their colleagues. In the upper chamber there was no comparable moment of revolt. But the power of the Senate Republican leaders attenuated from age and illness: Platt died in 1905 and Allison in 1908; Spooner, harassed by progressive insurgents in Wisconsin, resigned in 1907; Aldrich, ailing and feeling his power ebb, did not seek reelection in 1910.

With the leaders' iron grip on Capitol Hill loosening, long suppressed tensions between old guard conservatives and the Republican progressives exploded around the hapless Taft. During his presidency the two sides feuded over tariff reform, railroad regulation, the currency, conservation, and almost everything else of consequence. Taft, lacking Roosevelt's dexterity and elemental will, alienated the progressives by tilting step-by-step toward the old guard; in 1910, he even supported unsuccessful efforts from Aldrich and Cannon to purge dissident House and Senate members in party primaries.

Large Democratic gains in the congressional election of 1910 should have signaled to Taft and the GOP congressional command that their refusal to advance a meaningful economic reform agenda was alienating not only the interests outside of their coalition, but even elements ordinarily inside it—small businesses and Midwest farmers frustrated by currency and tariff policies that favored the industrial East. In his final two years Taft made some gestures toward reform, but he had allied too closely with the congressional conservatives to press them toward effective action to lower tariffs or stabilize the monetary system. Taft's deference toward the old guard provided the spark, or perhaps the excuse, to ignite Theodore Roosevelt's mercurial ambition. The former president challenged his protégé for the Republican nomination in 1912, and when that failed, bolted the party to run against Taft as a "Bull Moose" independent. The epic three-way contest that followed with Democrat Woodrow Wilson (and actually, a fourth candidate, socialist Eugene Debs, who carried 6 percent of the vote) dramatized the cost of a governing strategy that heard so few voices. Taft finished a weak third in the popular vote, trailing not only Wilson but also Roosevelt. After capturing thirty states in 1908, Taft won just Utah and Vermont in 1912. Large Republican losses in the Senate and House of Representatives capped his repudiation. The Republican ascendancy, which had ended the post–Civil War political disorder and inaugurated an era of regimented, martial partisanship, was over.

Yet the underlying governing strategy of the Republican command— unify the party, reward your friends, isolate your opponents—didn't change when Democrats moved into control of the House, the Senate, and the White House after 1912. Wilson and the new Democratic leadership did not share the ends of McKinley and Aldrich and Cannon, but they largely sought to emulate their means.

As a political scientist, president of Princeton University, and then governor of New Jersey, Woodrow Wilson had long been an unstinting advocate of assertive executive power and party-centered government. As president, Wilson placed those beliefs into action. Operating with a comfortable Democratic majority (especially in the House), Wilson chose to govern by unifying his party rather than by reaching out to Republican progressives close to his views. "Like a British Prime Minister," one historian wrote, "Wilson viewed his own party as an alliance of men of the same ideological persuasion, with himself as head of a party government."

That impulse was in one sense understandable. Democrats were eager to exercise power again after Republicans had controlled the White House for the sixteen years before Wilson's election. And exercise power they did, in a concentrated and creative burst of lawmaking that demonstrated—as did Franklin Roosevelt, Lyndon Johnson, and to some extent George W. Bush after them—how a unified partisan majority could impose dramatic change. With the help of able Senate Democratic leader John Kern of Indiana, Wilson bridged the differences in his party much more effectively than Roosevelt had in his. In his first four years Wilson and the Democratic Congress passed a succession of landmark progressive bills. They created the Federal Reserve Board and the Federal Trade Commission, and banned child labor. They lowered tariff rates and raised income taxes on the affluent.

These were undeniable achievements. But they came at a high cost. Wilson failed to expand his coalition significantly, either in Congress or the country. Wilson had few personal relationships with politicians in the other party. Nor did either side gain any experience in negotiating their differences to an acceptable solution. As John Milton Cooper, Jr., one of the most insightful historians of the period, put it, "Nearly every leading Republican cordially despised Wilson, while the president regarded most of them with anger and contempt."

Even the Republican Progressives who had battled with the conservative old guard under Roosevelt sided with the GOP mainstream against Wilson on most issues. Wilson did not use his patronage powers to court progressive Republicans, and the administration and congressional Democrats excluded them almost completely from the drafting of Wilson's landmark legislation. (Tellingly, progressive Republicans supported Wilson most on the one first-term priority when Democrats involved them in the formulation of the plan: the legislation establishing the Federal Trade Commission.) Even the *New Republic*, a new liberal magazine sympathetic to Wilson, recognized that his unwillingness to reach beyond his party was driving Republican progressives back into alliance with the old guard conservatives they had battled under Roosevelt and Taft.

Wilson's "scrupulous loyalty to his own party and his determination to govern by means of a party machine and the use of partisan discipline," the magazine lamented, "has resulted in the recrudescence of merely partisan Republicanism."

The chasm between Wilson and the Republicans captured a principal political risk of the age—one that has recurred in our own time. Because the parties exercised power on such a partisan basis, with so few concessions to the other side, each virtually guaranteed that much of the country would feel deeply disenfranchised no matter which side controlled Washington. It was a system designed to breed resentment among the excluded.

That became apparent when Wilson, after his sterling record of legislative achievement in his first four years, broadened his support only modestly in the 1916 election. Several prominent independents active in Roosevelt's third-party challenge from 1912 endorsed Wilson. And without the presence of a third-party candidate to splinter the vote, Wilson increased his percentage of the popular vote from 42 percent in 1912 to 49 percent in 1916. But Wilson's margin of victory over Republican Charles Evans Hughes, measured as a share of the popular vote, was at the time the smallest ever for a reelected president. Wilson won ten fewer states than he captured four years earlier. In most of the Midwestern states with the strongest reform sentiments—Iowa, Minnesota, Wisconsin—Wilson fell short, partly because he did not receive support from any prominent elected Republican progressive. "The dominant spirit of this campaign," declared one leading Senate Republican reformer, "is reunion among Republicans." In the election, Republicans also gained seats in both the House and Senate, narrowing the Democratic advantage in both chambers. Wilson returned to Washington in 1917 standing on a narrow ledge.

And on that narrow ledge, Wilson was presented with a challenge that did not lend itself to solution through the partisan means both parties had employed for the previous twenty years: the building of a consensus for reshaping America's role in the world. Wilson failed to meet that challenge largely because of the limitations of the intensely partisan governing style he had pursued throughout his presidency. Those limitations undermined him after World War I, when the Senate rejected American participation

in the League of Nations, the centerpiece of his plan for encouraging
international stability and preventing another global conflict.

A PARTISAN FAILURE

Though the broad outlines of the League of Nations story are familiar, it
is worth recounting in some detail, because it demonstrated, in a way still
relevant today, the costs that a purely partisan governing strategy can impose. To take the United States into the league, Wilson needed support
among Republicans as well as Democrats, in the country broadly, and in
the Senate specifically. But he did not possess the skills, the vocabulary, or
even the inclination to court such support. Thin-skinned, resistant to criticism or even ideas that contradicted his own beliefs, Wilson approached
the league with an unwavering conviction in his cause and an inability to
empathize with the arguments or political needs of those who resisted it.
Wilson and George W. Bush differed in most important ways, but the two
men shared a common conception of leadership: the belief that the president's job was to identify the "right" solution to a problem, and then drive
toward it over all obstacles. And just as it would in Iraq and the war on
terror under Bush, that approach unnecessarily polarized the country over
Wilson's league.*

When Wilson asked Congress for a declaration of war in April 1917 he
insisted, "The world must be made safe for democracy." The centerpiece
of his plan for doing so was a league of nations that would commit the
world's leading nations to protecting each other against aggression, by collective military action if necessary. This idea had strong Republican heritage. Roosevelt may have suggested it first in 1910 when he urged "those
great powers honestly bent on peace . . . [to] form a League of Peace."
Five years later Massachusetts senator Henry Cabot Lodge, a close friend
of Roosevelt, also endorsed the idea. Wilson followed in May 1916.

---

* The acerbic and querulous Robert La Follette described Wilson in terms that Bush's critics might have
lifted verbatim ninety years later: Wilson, La Follette maintained, was "cocksure and stubborn while his in-
experience and ignorance of more than the merest smattering on the problems, and his intense political partisan feeling renders him almost impossible."

By then Roosevelt had soured on the idea, and Lodge soon followed. Both came to fear that the league would entangle the United States "in every European quarrel," as Roosevelt once put it. Both concluded that America could safeguard its security more by building its own strength than by participating in collective action. Each found Wilson's vision of the league excessively, even dangerously, idealistic. Many Republicans shared their concerns. Partisan and personal spite may have sharpened the disagreements, but a genuine difference separated the two sides.

But that disagreement hardly seemed unbridgeable. Neither Roosevelt nor Lodge was an isolationist; both had long promoted an active American role in international affairs. Isolationist sentiment was powerful among other Republicans, especially away from the East Coast. But when the Senate began debating the league in 1918, one newspaper survey counted only eight senators as unalterably opposed to American participation under any circumstances. Likewise, when *Literary Digest* surveyed newspaper editors that year, it found that just 12 percent wanted the United States to reject the league entirely. Both in Congress and in public opinion, the raw materials existed for Wilson to fashion a deal.

Yet Wilson consistently failed to mine them. When the United States entered World War I in April 1917, he did not seize the obvious opportunity to encourage national unity and temper partisan hostilities. As Cooper wrote, Wilson "made almost no effort to give the other party a sense of participation or a stake in the conduct of the war." During the 1918 congressional elections, with the guns in Europe nearly stilled, Wilson made another fateful decision. Two weeks before Election Day he urged voters to elect Democratic majorities that would send the world the message that Americans "wish me to continue to be your unembarrassed spokesman in affairs at home and abroad." It was an unusually crass effort to convert patriotic sentiment into partisan advantage, and it backfired, badly: Republicans won a one-seat majority in the Senate and a forty-four-seat majority in the House.

The result provided Lodge an unparalleled position from which to frustrate Wilson's designs: After the victory Republicans named him as both majority leader and chairman of the Senate Foreign Relations Committee. Lodge was a formidable adversary, a Massachusetts patrician who traced his ancestors back to the Puritans, and who had served in the Senate since 1893. Like Wilson, he was one of the few genuine intellectuals to thrive in elected office. Lodge had edited the erudite *North American Review* (where he once published an article from the young Woodrow Wilson), earned one of the first Ph.D.'s in history ever granted by Harvard, and then taught at Harvard before turning to politics in the 1880s. Both he and Wilson were keen students of politics. At the most important moments of their careers, though, each proved a terrible practitioner.

When the war ended in November 1918, Wilson compounded the political miscalculation he began by managing the war itself in such an exclusionary manner: He did not take any senators or any prominent Republicans with him to the peace talks in Paris. Wilson included only one nominal Republican on his delegation: Henry White, a former ambassador to Italy and France. Though friendly with Roosevelt and Lodge, White lacked the stature to shape Republican opinion that national figures such as Elihu Root, Theodore Roosevelt's secretary of state, or William Howard Taft might have brought.

Republicans behaved just as badly as the peace talks began. Both Theodore Roosevelt and Lodge sent letters to British negotiators attempting to undermine Wilson's position while the president was still negotiating the Treaty of Versailles. Lodge moved more publicly to undercut Wilson in early March 1919. On the Senate floor Lodge announced that he had signatures from thirty-seven Republican senators (a list that quickly grew to thirty-nine) opposing the league in the form that Wilson was negotiating it. No one missed the announcement's meaning: If Lodge's votes held firm, he had more than enough to deny Wilson the two-thirds majority he needed for ratification of the peace treaty.

Through 1919, the two sides circled each other, approaching and then retreating. Wilson denounced Lodge's maneuver before he returned to Europe for the next stage of the peace talks, but the president nonetheless negotiated some changes in the treaty that responded to the Senate concerns. Republicans moved somewhat in Wilson's direction too. Largely because of Root's constructive influence, the center of opinion in the GOP moved away from seeking amendments in the treaty itself, which would require Wilson to reopen negotiations with other nations, likely an impossible task. Instead, following a Root suggestion, internationalist Republicans increasingly focused on approving the treaty with reservations, which amounted to unilateral statements of how the United States interpreted its obligations under the treaty. The most important and intractable reservation would limit America's responsibility to commit military force in a crisis under the league's Article X.

A floating group of seven to ten moderate Republicans, who became known as mild reservationists, tried to position themselves through the summer of 1919 as the brokers of a deal to secure approval for the treaty. First they blocked the hard-core opponents by indicating they would vote with Democrats to kill amendments. Then they tried to leverage Democrats into accepting reservations by declaring they could attract as many as twenty Republican votes for approval with such qualifications. Together with forty-five Democrats, that would provide enough votes for ratification. It wasn't clear the group had the stature and reach to attract that much support in the GOP, but Wilson never tried to find out. In August, when the Republican group was maneuvering most energetically, Wilson squelched them by renouncing any compromise. Wilson instead took his case to the country with a grueling nationwide speaking tour in September 1919. His health, already fragile, broke. Four days after his return to Washington, Wilson suffered a stroke that left him an invalid through the remainder of his presidency.

Through the fall of 1919 the legislative battle concluded in an atmosphere of confusion and bitterness. Wilson, still mostly confined to his sickbed, pressured Senate Democrats to reject compromise, and urged them to vote down the treaty if a series of reservations from Lodge (including one that virtually nullified Article X) were attached. Months of division and fractionation culminated in a political failure of historic proportions on November 19, 1919. The Senate considered a resolution to approve the treaty without reservations and a resolution to approve it with Lodge's reservations: Each failed to attract even a majority, much less the two thirds required. Most senators insisted they wanted the United States to participate in the league. That was Wilson's highest priority, too. Yet the two sides could not find a way to achieve it. With stalemate, the majority that claimed to support the treaty produced a result that pleased only the minority that preferred to kill it entirely.

Wilson dug in, adamantly rejecting further compromise. Lodge was equally obdurate. After a futile final cacophony of votes in March 1920, the treaty died in the Senate, and with it, Wilson's hope of an engaged America helping to maintain international order and suppress the rise of tyranny. The Republican presidents who held the White House for the twelve years after Wilson stepped down in 1921 let the treaty languish. Wilson was visionary in understanding that America needed to become the linchpin of any global alliance to maintain international stability. But he failed to recognize that in seeking a shift of that magnitude, demanding party loyalty or bluntly insisting on the rightness of his cause was insufficient. With the league he was asking Americans to abandon an aversion to foreign commitments that had colored the nation's foreign policy since its founding. Change that big needed consensus, which required compromise. Wilson was correct in his conclusions, but misguided in his methods. Rarely has a leader been so farsighted and myopic at the same time.

Wilson had achieved much through an aggressive governing strategy that sought to maximize unity in his party and minimize the influence of the other. Yet his inability to surmount the limitations of that approach doomed the most important initiative of his two terms. With the failure of the league Wilson's presidency ultimately tumbled into the chasm between the parties that he had accepted, and even expanded, during his eight tumultuous years.

TWO MORE MAJORITIES

Wilson didn't fall alone: He took down the Democratic Party with him. In 1920 the pleasant but mediocre Ohio Republican senator Warren Harding won a landslide victory in the presidential race by promising "not heroism, but healing, not nostrums but normalcy." Harding carried in with him overwhelming Republican majorities in the House and Senate.

Thus began another decade of unified, purposeful Republican control of Congress and the White House.

Under Harding and his two successors, Calvin Coolidge and Herbert Hoover, the conservative wing of the GOP restored its dominance over national policy. None of those three presidents showed much inclination to reach out beyond that single faction and its supporters in the business community. The three Republican presidents, and their congressional Republican allies, governed with adamantine consistency and crimped perspective. Hoover, a dynamo as commerce secretary under Harding and Coolidge, was a more subtle and serious thinker than the two predecessors he served. But all three held a narrow view of Washington's responsibilities. Each believed government's principal role was to support business. "The law that builds up the people is the law that builds up industry," declared Coolidge. "The sole function of government," Hoover echoed later, "is to bring about a condition of affairs favorable to the beneficial development of private enterprise." That faith stirred them to raise tariffs on imports, cut taxes on business and the wealthy, limit government spending, retrench federal regulation, discourage the organization of unions, and resist intervention in agricultural markets to boost struggling farmers.

Little in the GOP agenda courted those whose needs conflicted with the dominant business culture: farmers, urban reformers, the few militant outposts in organized labor. Even the relatively strong showing of a third-party progressive challenge in 1924 from La Follette and Montana Democratic senator Burton K. Wheeler (who polled nearly 17 percent of the vote) failed to encourage a broader perspective from the White House or congressional majority. On issue after issue the Republican governing majority of the 1920s reduced politics to a simple equation of supporting their allies, marginalizing their opponents, and limiting the reach of government. It was a closed circle that delivered benefits to the business interests that sustained it financially and intellectually. And so long as those business interests also delivered relative prosperity to most workers, the system enjoyed a clear majority of electoral support—especially against a Democratic Party offering no clear or cohesive alternative.

But the rigidity of this political system, like the rigidity of the Republican coalition that ruled from McKinley through Taft, ultimately destroyed it. When the Depression struck, Herbert Hoover did not respond as passively as he is often accused. Hoover did not oppose government activism as obstinately as Coolidge; an engineer by training, Hoover believed government's principal role was to encourage and support voluntary communal action. His response to the stock market crash and the deepening depression initially focused on such exhortation.

The lingering crisis, like a quickening undertow, tugged Hoover toward a more direct federal role. Eventually he proposed the Reconstruction Finance Corporation, which would make direct loans to banks, railroads, and other business. But Hoover did not travel nearly far enough to address the unprecedented demands that cascaded upon him as unemployment, homelessness, and desperation grew. He pursued half measures in a crisis that demanded bold and large departures. Hoover and his allies in the Republican congressional mainstream clung to old ideological certitudes by raising tariffs through the Smoot-Hawley Act in 1930, which compounded the crisis. Though eventually forced to give some ground, Hoover also resisted Senate progressives, led by the formidable New York Democrat Robert F. Wagner, pressing for more federal spending on public works and relief. And when the indefatigable Senator Norris steered legislation through Congress to create jobs and develop the Tennessee Valley (through the construction of dams that would harness the river and provide electricity for growth), Hoover, like Coolidge a few years earlier, responded with a veto. In each of these ways, Hoover traced the bars that imprisoned him. He was trapped in a political and intellectual system that prized ideological consistency and partisan unity over flexibility, experimentation, and cooperation.

No one anywhere in the American political environment had developed a comprehensive response to the calamity. But Hoover had listened to, and represented, such a narrowly constrained range of interests for so long that he could not fully engage other sources of ideas and energy—the Senate progressives agitating for public works; the economists and intellectuals formulating the first demands for government to stimulate purchasing power through deliberate federal deficits. It was as if his vision had narrowed in a way that blinded him to all but a few pale colors of the spectrum. Like Wilson with the league, Hoover failed to recognize that he faced a challenge so large that he could not respond to it while ignoring concerns outside of his traditional coalition. And like Wilson, Hoover suffered a historic repudiation in 1932, as Franklin D. Roosevelt swept into the White House, carrying commanding Democratic House and Senate majorities with him.

Roosevelt's presidency ended the era of stable, disciplined, and usually polarized partisanship that began with McKinley's election in 1896. On the surface the Roosevelt years seemed more to confirm than challenge that pattern. Through his tenure in the White House, Roosevelt governed with Democratic majorities, often overwhelming Democratic majorities, in the House and Senate. He worked closely with the Democratic leaders in both chambers, mostly the burly Joseph T. Robinson of Arkansas in the Senate and the bullet-headed Sam Rayburn of Texas in the House. He conscientiously sought good relations with the local machines and urban bosses—Ed Kelly in Chicago, Ed Flynn in the Bronx—who exercised so much power in his faction-ridden party. Yet under Roosevelt the foundations of the old partisan approach to governing collapsed—first through his initiative, and then through the initiative of his opponents.

Roosevelt engaged a much broader segment of society in the search for solutions than any of his predecessors in the partisan era. His vision was wider, his approach to governing more elastic and inclusive. Unlike Theodore Roosevelt and Woodrow Wilson, FDR systematically sought alliances with like-minded progressives in the opposition party. In the 1932 campaign FDR welcomed support from Republican progressives who formed the National Progressive League, and limited his attacks to the GOP leadership rather than the Republican Party itself. He named to his initial cabinet two prominent Progressives with roots in the Republican Party—at Agriculture, the mystical Henry A. Wallace (whose father had served as Harding's agriculture secretary), and at Interior, the flinty Harold Ickes (who had stampeded into the Bull Moose party with Theodore Roosevelt in 1912). As his treasury secretary, Roosevelt picked a third, admittedly lapsed, Republican, business executive William H. Woodin.

No other president in the age of partisan armies had been as open-minded as Roosevelt about drawing advice from diverse sources and pursuing initiatives that responded to divergent constituencies. He juggled, balanced, and appropriated ideas from almost all directions. In a speech during the 1932 campaign at Oglethorpe University in Georgia, he provided a prophetic summary of his governing philosophy when he committed himself to a policy of "bold, persistent experimentation." In a presidency of audacious advances and sudden detours that crossed and sometimes collided, that unflagging commitment to forward motion remained the most consistent element. Roosevelt absorbed from other authors, in both parties, many of the initiatives that became signatures of the New Deal. During the transition between his election and his inauguration, Roosevelt took an emotional journey to Muscle Shoals, Alabama, with Norris, where they watched the waters pour through the spillways in the great Wilson Dam built by the federal government during World War I, and cemented their shared commitment to constructing a network of dams that would tame the Tennessee River and revitalize the Tennessee Valley. Around the same time, Roosevelt received Senators Robert M. La Follette, Jr., of Wisconsin and Bronson Cutting of New Mexico, two progressive Republicans who had supported him in 1932, at his home in Warm Springs, Georgia. The two pressed their case for direct federal relief grants to the states; Roosevelt agreed, and included the proposal in his agenda. He even enlisted Hoover's outgoing staff in the Treasury Department to help draft the Emergency Banking Act that stabilized the nation's banks and began the breathless, historic sprint of Roosevelt's first one hundred days. Later that spring, after initial skepticism on both fronts, Roosevelt accepted the arguments from Senate progressives like La Follette, urging significant increases in federal public works spending, and from a bipartisan congressional group that included Michigan Republican senator Arthur Vandenberg promoting federal deposit insurance for banks. Roosevelt initially displayed little more enthusiasm for supporting unions. But he provided some last-minute rhetorical support, and his signature, when Robert Wagner, New York's dogged, meticulous Democratic senator, maneuvered through Congress the National Labor Relations Act of 1935 that enshrined the right of workers to organize.

In this first stage of the New Deal, Roosevelt sought to govern mostly by harmonizing interests. He rejected the ethos of the partisan era that had encouraged each party to view the electorate as immutably divided into fixed camps of friend and foe. His role as president, Roosevelt declared, was "to find among many discordant elements that unity of purpose that is best for the Nation as a whole." Many of his initial proposals drew broad support among congressional Republicans as well as Democrats. Conservative Democrats, skittish about some of the ways Roosevelt was expanding federal power, were reassured (for a time) by his continued call for discipline in spending. Roosevelt studiously avoided partisan rhetoric, even through the 1934 midterm election. (One irritated Democratic congressman later wrote the White House to ask "whether or not the President has . . . ever used the word 'Democrat' since, as the Democratic party's nominee, he took office.") Roosevelt conspicuously praised Republican progressives like La Follette, who had allied with him.

Though many of his initiatives, by strengthening organized labor and stiffening federal regulation, strained his relations with business, Roosevelt initially hoped to engage corporate leaders as well. The centerpiece of his initial economic agenda attempted to institutionalize his vision of a government that would "cement our society . . . into a voluntary brotherhood of freemen, standing together, striving together, for the common good of all." The National Industrial Recovery Act, proposed by Roosevelt and approved by Congress in the first one hundred days, rested on the assumption that government could help balance and reconcile the interests of business, labor, and consumers. The act suspended antitrust laws and empowered the new National Recovery Administration to negotiate compacts under which entire industries would agree to maintain wages and hours for workers in return for permission to raise prices by limiting production. (The act also provided the first protections for union organizing, which were later buttressed by Wagner's bill, in 1935.) The NRA, for all the frenetic enthusiasm of its director, Hugh S. Johnson, ultimately contributed little to recovery. It was too literal an expression of Roosevelt's vision of social harmony. It choked on bureaucracy, the limits of planning to control an economy as vast as America's, and the inevitable tendency of business and labor alike to squeeze every possible advantage from the system. And yet, with the ubiquitous Blue Eagle as its symbol, the NRA also symbolized some of the best instincts of the early New Deal: Roosevelt's desire to bind together a society being pulled apart by unprecedented social and economic strain.

The centrifugal forces of the time were too great to allow Roosevelt to maintain his position as what James MacGregor Burns memorably called "national father . . . bipartisan leader . . . President of all the people." Over the next four years Roosevelt, under pressure from friends and opponents alike, snapped back to a governing philosophy closer to the party-centered, polarizing strategies of his predecessors. Ironically, his shift toward a more partisan and ideological approach sparked a backlash from conservatives that ended the age of partisan control and created a new, diffused, calculus of power in Washington.

The historic sequence of events began when Roosevelt tilted decisively to the left in 1935. Historians still debate his motivation. But Roosevelt faced strong incentives to move toward a more partisan stance. From one side he saw the limits of his efforts to win support among groups to the right of center: increasingly open criticism from the business community and the formation of the confrontational American Liberty League, composed mostly of conservative former Democrats and business leaders. From the other he saw signs of increasing vitality on the left such as the excitement surrounding Senator Huey Long, the whirling populist demagogue from Louisiana, who hinted at a third-party 1936 presidential run on his "share our wealth" platform. Increasing resistance from the conservative-dominated Supreme Court, which struck down the NRA, the Agricultural Adjustment Act, and then even New York's minimum wage law from 1935 through 1936, also hardened his resolve.

Roosevelt never entirely abandoned his earlier posture; as late as 1937 he could still declare "a plague on both your houses" during the historic wave of sit-down strikes that created the modern industrial labor movement. But the tone and strategy of his presidency changed after 1934. In 1935, he passed a historic but unambiguously partisan and liberal agenda that began with a huge appropriation for work relief, continued with Wagner's National Labor Relations Act and a bill to regulate public utility holding companies, and was capped by the creation of Social Security, Roosevelt's crowning legislative achievement. In 1936, he sharply escalated his rhetorical attacks on business and the wealthy, "the royalists of the economic order." And after winning a decisive reelection in 1936, a landslide so emphatic that he carried all but two states and led Democrats to commanding House and Senate majorities that virtually reduced Republicans to a rump group, Roosevelt in 1937 aimed at what appeared to be the last force in American life capable of resisting his agenda: the Supreme Court.

That decision proved a turning point in his presidency. In February 1937, Roosevelt proposed a "court-packing" bill that would allow the president to appoint one new Supreme Court justice (up to six in all) for each sitting justice who did not retire at age seventy. The idea stirred resistance across ideological and partisan lines: a wide array of congressional conservatives, mainstream Democrats, and even many progressives in both parties linked arms to kill it. But while Roosevelt's miscalculation provoked a broad-based backlash, it had its most lasting impact in emboldening conservative opposition to the administration. The court fight broke the dam that had suppressed the internal disagreements in the Democratic coalition.

Though the party held large advantages in the House and Senate, its majorities relied heavily on support from Southern Democratic legislators. And though some of the Southerners were loyal New Dealers (such as Claude Pepper in Florida and Sam Rayburn in Texas), many others had little affinity for Roosevelt's increasingly liberal and activist plans. In the crisis atmosphere of Roosevelt's first years, the Southerners had mostly supported his agenda, though they often exacted a toll by structuring programs in ways that minimized their value to blacks. But the Southerners grew increasingly restive as Roosevelt's agenda collided more directly with the region's low-wage, low-tax, antiunion economic model, and they mobilized against any hint that the federal government would challenge the state-sponsored segregation that defined the Southern social order.

After the court fight, the Southern discomfort burst into the open. Through 1937 and 1938 conservative Southern Democrats joined with congressional Republicans to block FDR's proposals to create a succession of Tennessee Valley–type public authorities across other regions and to centralize more authority in the president by reorganizing the executive branch. After the House passed antilynching legislation, Southern Senate Democrats blocked it with a filibuster in 1938 (while Roosevelt passively sat by). Legislation to prohibit child labor and establish a minimum wage and a forty-hour workweek squeezed through Congress, but only after laborious resistance by Southerners who felt it endangered their region's low-wage economy. "The Roosevelt of 1938," insisted North Carolina's Democratic governor, "does not appear to be related by blood or marriage to the Roosevelt of 1933."

Roosevelt accepted the gauntlet from the Democratic conservatives. Like Taft and Wilson, he sought to reestablish his leadership and clarify his party's ideological course by purging congressional dissidents. The experience was no happier for him than for his predecessors. Through 1938 Roosevelt intervened in a series of Democratic primaries to back New Deal candidates against conservatives. Democrats he supported won Democratic Senate primaries in Kentucky, Alabama, and Florida. Roosevelt's opposition helped oust a conservative New York Democrat who had blocked his initiatives as chairman of the House Rules Committee. But each of the three senators he targeted most directly survived: Walter George in Georgia; the racist "Cotton" Ed Smith in South Carolina; and Millard Tydings in Maryland. (Soon after beating back the challenge, Smith told George that Roosevelt was his own worst enemy. To which George reportedly replied, "Not as long as I am alive.") The results in the 1938 general election compounded Roosevelt's disappointment: Republicans gained seven seats in the Senate and seventy-five in the House. The Republicans had come through the valley of darkness: They were once again a competitive party. Never again would their numbers in Congress fall as far as during Roosevelt's first term.

The failure of the purge, and the Republican resurgence in November 1938, ended Roosevelt's ability to consistently exert his will on Congress. The emerging conservative coalition could not significantly roll back the New Deal, but it could block its expansion: The wages and hours bill Roosevelt signed in 1938 proved the last major New Deal domestic initiative to become law.

This reversal of fortune did more than derail Roosevelt's domestic agenda for his remaining years in the White House. It ended the era that began with McKinley's election and the centralization of power by the Republican congressional leadership in the 1890s. With intermittent exceptions, the period from 1896 through 1937 had been shaped by strong partisan majorities that allowed presidents and like-minded congressional majorities to pass clearly defined agendas while conceding little to their opposition. For the next quarter century, no president would enjoy that luxury. Instead they would be compelled to negotiate endlessly to construct evanescent legislative majorities in a system that shattered party discipline and diffused power between liberal and conservative factions in both parties. Indeed, negotiation—often reluctant, frequently stalemated, but sometimes strikingly productive—among the divergent interests between and within the parties would so characterize the next quarter century in Washington that it could be called the Age of Bargaining.

★

CHAPTER 3

THE AGE OF BARGAINING

In the long summer of 1937, with his legislative agenda in ruins, Franklin Roosevelt's blood pressure seemed to rise every time he looked down Pennsylvania Avenue toward the Capitol. At Cabinet meetings he sniped at Vice President John Nance Garner, who he believed had encouraged the conservative rebellion against his court-packing plan. Roosevelt summoned the Democratic legislative leaders to the White House one evening in early August, and then derisively laughed out loud when they tried to mollify him with a list of obscure bills that Congress had cleared over the previous seven months. Other visitors—a newspaper publisher no longer as ardent for the New Deal, two Southern Democratic senators who fought Roosevelt's priorities, then came looking for federal assistance to cotton farmers in their states—received similar tongue lashings. The "audacious rout of his whole program has left the President angry and embittered," wrote one Washington journalist that summer. "Men close to him say they have never seen him so aroused."

These were new emotions for Franklin Roosevelt in his dealings with Congress. But they would become uncomfortably familiar. In his first term Roosevelt had governed behind an impregnable congressional majority so commanding that even Republicans often felt compelled to join it. After the fall of the court-packing plan and the rise of the alliance between Republicans and conservative Southern Democrats, that majority disintegrated. Across the country Roosevelt remained an immensely popular figure, a symbol of optimism and resolve. But in Congress he was a diminished force. "He could not maneuver as he once had," James MacGregor Burns correctly concluded. "Victory depended on conciliating key congressmen and clearing labyrinthine channels."

That sort of arduous bargaining would become the way of life not only for Roosevelt through the remainder of his presidency, but for each of his next four successors: Harry Truman, Dwight Eisenhower, John F. Kennedy, and Lyndon B. Johnson (at least until his landslide victory in 1964). For the next quarter century—roughly the period from the conservative resurgence in 1937 to the passage of the Civil Rights Act in 1964—almost every important decision in Washington required intense consultation and negotiation between and within the parties. Although Democrats controlled the White House for nineteen of those twenty-seven years, and held both chambers of Congress for all but four of them, they could not impose their agenda as the dominant party had done from McKinley through Franklin Roosevelt's first term. Nor could Republicans consistently advance their ideas. Significant achievements almost always required at least some compromise across party lines. To the extent that this age of bargaining had an ethos, it was supplied by Lyndon Johnson— a towering figure through the period, first as Senate majority leader in the 1950s, and then as president in its final days. "It is the politician's task to pass legislation," Johnson later told his biographer, Doris Kearns Goodwin, "not to sit around saying principled things."

This is the era most likely to be remembered as a golden age of statesmanship and cooperation in Congress—the sharpest contrast to the unrelenting partisanship of our own time. And in some ways the time indeed fit that picture. Political life during these years was slower and less frenetic than today. Everett Dirksen of Illinois, later the Senate Republican leader, took the bus to work when he was first elected in 1951. Sam Rayburn, the Democratic speaker of the House, had time many days for an afternoon walk that took him from the Capitol around the Library of Congress and the Supreme Court, where he liked to inspect a white oak tree at the edge of the grounds that he had planted in 1949. Tradition still carried great weight. This was the heyday of the Senate as "the world's most exclusive club," or the "Citadel," as *New York Times* reporter William S. White labeled it in his classic 1957 book of that name. First-term senators were expected to listen, not speak, until they had served their apprenticeship. Committee chairmen ruled their fiefdoms with enormous independence. Television intruded occasionally but was not yet a consistent factor in the capital's life. Most of Congress's work took place in quiet conversations out of public view, where deals were struck and accommodations hatched.

Politicians had fewer demands on their schedules. They did not spend as much time raising money. Nor were there talk radio or cable television shows recruiting them to fill every spare moment denouncing the other party. Most important, since jet travel was not yet common, they did not travel back to their home states and districts nearly as often as they would later. That left more time for them to loosen their ties and trade tales, often over bourbon or scotch. Rayburn, the taciturn, bald-headed, powerfully built Texas Democrat who led the House as speaker during every year of Democratic control from 1941 through 1961, gathered allies late almost every afternoon into his small hideaway office on the Capitol's ground floor for drinks and gossip; Harry Truman, then the vice president, was at one of those sessions in April 1945 when he learned of Franklin Roosevelt's death. Rayburn's "Board of Education" sessions brought together only Democrats, but the fraternizing extended across party lines. After 1954, when Democrats controlled both the House and Senate, Eisenhower sometimes invited Rayburn and Johnson to his family quarters for unpublicized evenings of drinks and casual conversation. Moderate Republican senator George Aiken of Vermont ate breakfast every day with moderate Democrat Mike Mansfield of Montana. Rayburn and Joseph W. Martin, the leader of House Republicans during the 1940s and 1950s, were so close that when Rayburn was once asked whether he would travel to Massachusetts to campaign against Martin he replied, "Hell, if I lived up there, I'd vote for him."

Washington could still be a very rough place. Hubert Humphrey championed the civil rights cause with a stirring address at the 1948 Democratic convention. When Humphrey arrived in Washington the next year as a

senator from Minnesota, Southern Senate Democrats ostracized him fero-
ciously. Joe McCarthy's rampages through the early 1950s against domestic
Communists, real and imagined, set a bitter tone for all debates over national
security. Beneath the veneer of dignity, comity, and reserve, the Senate was
a minefield for those who resisted the bipartisan conservative alliance that
wielded great power through these years. Their bills would often languish;
when seats opened on the most powerful committees, their applications
would be denied. Howard Shuman, an aide to the liberal Illinois senator
Paul Douglas, who arrived with Humphrey in 1949 and became with him a
leader of those who fought the conservative alliance, would later recall, "If
senators didn't join the coalition that existed at that time among Southerners, Westerners, and trans-Mississippi Republicans, to protect segregation,
to protect oil and gas, to protect public works, to protect cotton and tobacco
and wheat, and to give the water projects to the Western states, if they didn't
join that coalition, they didn't get into the club."

Yet during these years the tone of politics, and the strategies the dominant figures on both sides employed, were less confrontational and partisan, more conciliatory and pragmatic than Washington had typically seen
from McKinley through Roosevelt, or would usually see again after 1964.
Partly that reflected all the social factors—the absence of television, the
greater personal bonds between politicians—that shaped Washington life
from the end of World War II through the early 1960s. A larger contributor was the problem-solving orientation of many of the era's key figures,
from Johnson and Rayburn, to Eisenhower and Kennedy, to Joseph Martin
and Senator Robert Taft among the congressional Republicans. Though
divergent in their philosophical beliefs, all largely shared Johnson's conviction that their principal purpose was to "pass legislation" and produce
progress rather than to deliberately provoke confrontations between the
parties that might shape the next election. "That's vanity . . . not politics,"
Kennedy chided one aide who encouraged him to mount a legislative fight
he knew he could not win.*

---

* Among presidents in this era, Truman was the great exception: In his upset 1948 reelection victory, he used
the "do-nothing" Republican Congress as a foil after it rejected, as he knew it would, the ambitious liberal
domestic agenda he proposed at the Democratic convention. Yet even Truman, as we'll see, built an extraordinarily successful partnership with Republicans on foreign policy.

The men, and they were all men, who rose to the top of this era generally distrusted ideologues and resisted political strategies that encouraged the parties to launch crusades against the other. (Taft was probably most comfortable with those tactics, but Democrats found that even he could be a flexible deal maker at times.) Without stretching the point too far, it's possible that the common experience of combating first fascism and then communism left this political generation understandably suspicious of appeals that mobilized mass audiences behind sweeping ideological systems promising integrated answers to all questions; this was, after all, the era in which sociologist Daniel Bell could write approvingly of "the end of ideology." "The biggest danger to American stability," Lyndon Johnson insisted, "is the politics of principle, which brings out the masses in irrational fights for unlimited goals, for once the masses begin to move, then the whole thing begins to explode. Thus it is for the sake of nothing less than stability that I consider myself a consensus man."

But it was not just by personal inclination that so many of this period's leaders joined Johnson in declaring themselves "consensus" men. Circumstance also forced the choice upon them. Men like Eisenhower, Kennedy, Johnson, and Rayburn did not pursue the assertive, partisan, and polarizing strategies of McKinley, Aldrich, Cannon, and Wilson largely because in this era those strategies could not succeed.

AN INTRICATE PUZZLE

The defining characteristic of the age of bargaining was the diffusion of political power. This was the central political fact of this time—the axis around which all other events in American politics and government revolved. Though Democrats held a partisan majority in Congress for almost all of this period, they did not control an ideological majority: Their control of Congress rested uneasily on the mismatch between ideological and partisan loyalties. The Democratic majority relied upon votes from conservative Southern Senate and House members who consistently allied with Republicans on many domestic issues but still would not leave the Democrats to formally identify with the party of Lincoln and Grant.

Republicans were divided between moderates and conservatives as well. In fact, the divisions were so profound and enduring that political scientists spoke of a four-party system in Congress: liberal and moderate Republicans, mostly from the Northeast and West Coast; old guard conservative Republicans, mostly from the Midwest and rural areas elsewhere; the conservative Democrats concentrated in the South; and the moderate to liberal Democrats from everywhere else.

Each of these four groups coalesced around vivid leaders. The conservative Republican champions included Taft and his fellow Ohio senator, John Bricker, in the early years of the period, and later on Arizona's dynamic Barry Goldwater in the Senate, and Charles Halleck of Indiana in the House; Aiken of Vermont and Arthur H. Vandenberg of Michigan provided early leadership for the Republican moderates, and they were reinforced later by men such as Jacob Javits of New York and Clifford Case of New Jersey. Liberals rallied to senators such as the voluble Humphrey and the intellectual, idealistic Paul Douglas, and to leaders in the House such as Missouri's Richard Bolling, who for decades led the fight to reform congressional rules that entrenched conservative power. Finally, there were the Southern Democrats, men like the stentorian Walter George of Georgia (whom Roosevelt had tried and failed to purge) and the viciously racist James O. Eastland of Mississippi, who stood sentinel at the barricades of segregation behind the leadership of the austere and reserved Richard Brevard Russell, Jr., of Georgia, a figure who maneuvered with such tactical brilliance for his morally tarnished cause that he inspired comparisons even among his opponents to Robert E. Lee.

The size of the four groups shifted somewhat over time as the two parties' fortunes oscillated. But their relative strength was remarkably consistent, as political scientist Mack C. Shelley II found in a detailed study of Congress during this period. By examining voting records, Shelley tracked the size of the four "parties" in Congress throughout the era. Although Democrats controlled the House for all but four years from 1939 through 1964, Shelley found that the largest group in the chamber was almost always the conservative Republicans. Liberal Democrats (including some from the South) usually ranked second. Close behind were the conservative Democrats, mostly from the South but with pockets of support elsewhere. The moderate Republicans were always the smallest of the four groups, but even they sometimes constituted as much as a quarter of House Republicans. The Senate divided along similar lines.

None of these groups alone was large enough to pass legislation. Any accomplishment required significant support from at least two, and sometimes more, of them, especially in the Senate, where a minority could block action with the filibuster. The struggle to assemble such coalitions provided this era its distinctive character. Truman, Eisenhower, and Kennedy, the presidents for most of this period, all identified most with their party's moderate to liberal bloc. But each needed to navigate through all of these groups to advance their ideas.

Throughout this time, no matter which party held the White House or controlled the gavels in Congress, the most consistently influential force in Washington was the alliance of conservative Southern Democrats and conservative congressional Republicans that became known as the "conservative coalition." The coalition was always informal. Its leaders, such as Taft and Russell in the Senate or Halleck and Democrat Howard W. Smith in the House, did not set a common strategy or commit to a joint agenda. Yet after the court-packing fight in 1937, conservatives in both parties and both chambers repeatedly coalesced around common priorities. As Lyndon Johnson memorably put it, Taft and Russell, through the early 1950s, ran the Senate "with a wink and a nod." The alliance revolved around an implicit quid pro quo: The conservative Republicans provided Southern Democrats the votes to block civil rights legislation, and the Southerners provided Republicans the votes to block proposals from liberal Democrats to expand the federal government's involvement in social needs like education or housing (many of which the Southerners feared anyway as possible threats to segregation). Year after year the coalition pushed for lower taxes, less spending on social programs, more money for defense, and restrictions on unions. And during its heyday, from the late 1930s through the early 1960s, it won most of the fights that it entered.

The conservative coalition thwarted most of Truman's domestic agenda. It joined arms with Eisenhower to limit government spending and resist new federal activism. It stymied many of Kennedy's most ambitious domestic proposals and forced him to modify others. The coalition derailed national health care under Truman and shelved Medicare under Kennedy. It muscled through legislation restricting unions in 1947 and 1959. It stood implacably against the dreams of liberals for a more activist and engaged government that would clear slums, construct public housing, and help local governments build new schools and hire more teachers.

Yet the conservative coalition was not a monolithic or invulnerable force. Generally, it was more effective resisting liberal ideas than advancing its own. It suffered more defeats in the last years of the age of bargaining after a Democratic landslide in 1958 infused Congress with a new generation of liberals such as Edmund Muskie of Maine and Eugene McCarthy of Minnesota. The possibility of attracting votes from African Americans in Northern cities gradually tugged Republicans away from their half of the bargain—the commitment to defend segregation. And on other fronts, conservative Republicans and Southern Democrats did not always find common cause. There were subtle but persistent differences between them. The Southern Democrats opposed most social welfare programs as adamantly as the Republicans but were more open to government spending, such as public works, meant to stimulate economic development. Nor did the Southerners share the conservative Republican hostility to international alliances and the strategy of containment in the cold war. Shelley found the conservative coalition in the House united as a cohesive bloc on only about one fourth of the contested votes under Truman and one fifth under Eisenhower and Kennedy. In the Senate, the numbers were similar. In a divided Washington, the conservative coalition was first among equals. But it did not rule consistently.

No one did. Legislators from all four camps found themselves winning and losing votes, often in unstable combinations. In this environment, building successful coalitions for all but the most consensual ideas was like assembling an intricate puzzle. Concessions to any group could alienate another.

In his first term, for instance, Eisenhower reached beyond his Republican base by proposing federal assistance to help states build new schools for the burgeoning baby boom. Northern Democrats, led by Adam Clayton Powell, the flamboyant African American representative from Harlem, responded by proposing an amendment that would bar states operating segregated schools from receiving any of the money. Eisenhower, timid on civil rights but also fearful of losing Southern support for his construction plan, opposed the idea; but enough Republicans joined the Northern Democrats to pass Powell's amendment when the bill reached the House floor in 1956 (two years after the Supreme Court, in *Brown v. Board of Education*, had declared "separate but equal" education unconstitutional).

That coalition, though, dissolved as quickly as it formed. Many of the Republicans who saw political value in voting with Powell against segregation were much less enthusiastic about Eisenhower's underlying proposition of increasing Washington's role in funding education. Those Republicans shifted back into their traditional alliance with the Southern Democrats, who fiercely opposed the bill after the House attached Powell's antisegregation amendment. When the final proposal came to a vote in the House on July 5, 1956, enough Republicans who had earlier backed Powell joined with the Southern conservatives to kill the legislation decisively.

This was not an uncommon occurrence. The four great groups in Washington moved like planets that traveled along distinct orbits: They would briefly align, then drift apart. In such a confusing and complex environment, the White House and the presidents from both parties could count on unwavering support from a smaller share of senators and House members than presidents can today. But fewer legislators were entirely out of reach. The result left the presidents from Roosevelt through Kennedy in a position not unlike European leaders who presided over parliaments with a bewildering array of small parties, as James MacGregor Burns recognized. "The consequence of the four-party system is that American political leaders, in order to govern, must manage multi-party coalitions just as the heads of coalition parliamentary regimes in Europe have traditionally done," he wrote in his 1963 book, *The Deadlock of Democracy*.

POWER DIFFUSED

This system did not eliminate conflict between the parties. But it muted and diffused that conflict. After Truman, who fought with Republicans across a wide range of domestic issues, the presidents who followed through the age of bargaining only rarely squared off in clearly defined confrontations with the opposition party. The disputes within the parties—among Democrats on civil rights, among Republicans on foreign policy—often generated more emotion than the disagreements between them. Presidents preferred to work through their own party, but inevitably grew frustrated at the lack of discipline. In his diary Truman raged about "consarned S.O.B. so-called Democrats." "My greatest troubles come up within the Republican Party," Eisenhower lamented in late 1953. On more than one occasion, presidents in the age of bargaining needed support from the opposition party to protect them from rebellious elements in their own.

On domestic issues Eisenhower usually governed through the conservative coalition of old guard Republicans and Southern Democrats that supported his limited view of government's responsibilities. But on foreign policy Eisenhower relied heavily on mainstream Senate Democrats, whose centrist foreign policy views more closely matched his own, to block conservative Republican initiatives. One case in point was a proposed constitutional amendment from Ohio Republican senator Bricker, an old guard conservative, to limit the president's treaty-making power. The tussle over Bricker's amendment, a ferocious fight at the time almost forgotten now, aligned the parties in a way difficult to imagine today. Although Eisenhower, just before the Senate vote in 1954, declared himself "unalterably opposed" to the amendment, most Senate Republicans still voted for it; Senate Democrats provided Eisenhower the decisive votes to reject the amendment, voting more than 2 to 1 against it.

An even starker example of the era's complex line-crossing politics came during Kennedy's first year. The fight pitted Kennedy and Rayburn directly against the alliance of Republicans and conservative Democratic Southerners that gripped the House. Kennedy aimed at a fortress of the conservatives' power: their hold on the House Rules Committee.

Control of the Rules Committee provided conservatives a commanding weapon in the House. Each year House committees approved a vast torrent of bills and proposals; the Rules Committee was the narrow isthmus through which they all needed to pass to reach the House floor. The committee determined which bills would receive debate on the floor, how long they would be debated, and what amendments could be offered. It had been created as a tool of leadership: Cannon, recall, used his chairmanship of the Rules Committee to cement his hold over the House around the turn of the twentieth century. But since the 1930s the committee had fallen into the hands of the bipartisan conservative coalition, which used it to block liberal proposals or demand they be diluted before allowing them to the floor. In theory, the Rules Committee could be circumvented if a House member collected signatures from a majority of his colleagues on a "discharge petition" to move a bill directly to the floor; in practice, that was such a daunting prospect that only two petitions had succeeded between 1938 and 1960.

Liberal frustration with the committee mounted after 1955, when Virginia Democrat Smith assumed the chairmanship. He was a shrewd and determined conservative who still lived in the home where his mother had lived during the Civil War. First elected to the House in 1930, Smith ruled the committee as a classic midcentury congressional baron, and demonstrated little concern for the congressional leadership or the White House. Trying to shelve civil rights legislation in 1957, he simply disappeared from Washington, leaving the committee unable to meet; later word surfaced from Virginia that he had been busy inspecting a barn that had burned down on his dairy farm. After Kennedy and Johnson were nominated at the Democratic convention in 1960, they stood at the Kennedy family compound in Hyannis Port and asked Congress to return for a special session that would highlight the party's agenda for the fall campaign. Kennedy declared that he and Johnson would devote their "full energies" to passing five bills: federal aid to education; more public housing; an increase in the minimum wage; labor law reform; and Medicare, a program of federal medical coverage for the elderly. The Democratic Congress passed none of them that year. Except for Medicare, which expired from other causes, Smith's Rules Committee played the central role in blocking all of them. Smith was known as "Judge" for a stint on the bench in Virginia during the 1920s, but to liberals he often seemed judge, jury, and executioner.

Seventy-seven at the time of Kennedy's victory in 1960, Smith did not project power. One journalist described him at this time: "Wraithlike and gray—gray, bushy eyebrows, thin gray hair combed back, gray complexion, gray suit, blue-gray necktie." He walked with a slight stoop. But Smith was unbending in his defiance. After the election he pledged his determination to block "radical, wild-eyed spendthrift proposals that will do the country severe damage."

Smith had the leverage to support his threat. As Kennedy took office, Democrats held a solid 8 to 4 majority on the Rules Committee. But only six of those Democrats were loyal to Rayburn and the new president. Smith and his principal Democratic ally, William Colmer of Mississippi, joined with the committee's four Republicans to create an equal conservative bloc. That allowed Smith to block action, because a rule needed a majority of votes to pass.

Kennedy and Rayburn realized that the new president's agenda could be stillborn unless they loosened Smith's grip. The most obvious means to do so would be for the Democrats to remove Smith as chairman because of his disloyalty to the party agenda. But no one apparently was willing to contemplate such a direct challenge to the principle of seniority, the practice, dating back to the nineteenth century, of allowing the longest-serving members to rise to the chairmanships of committees in the House and Senate.

Instead, Rayburn first proposed to temporarily enlarge the Rules Committee by adding two Democrats and one Republican—which would create a one-vote majority for Kennedy. When Smith rejected that idea, Rayburn returned with a more confrontational solution: He said he was considering removing Colmer from the committee (since he had not supported Kennedy in the 1960 election) and replacing him with a loyal Democrat. That idea always might have been a ploy. Two of Rayburn's biographers believe the speaker floated the purge notion so that Southerners would consider enlarging the committee a less threatening option. Indeed, when Southern Democrats threatened to vote with Republicans to name the House Speaker if Rayburn purged Colmer—a maneuver that could have allowed the GOP to control the House—Rayburn quickly abandoned the idea. Rayburn returned to his original proposal of enlarging the committee and scheduled the issue for a vote in January 1961.

To this point the dispute had been fought out solely among the two warring wings of the Democratic Party. But Rayburn needed approval from the full House to enlarge the committee. That brought into the mix the two wings of the congressional GOP. Halleck, the aggressively conservative party leader in the House, leaned hard on his members to oppose the change; a *Time* magazine correspondent saw him literally grab one Republican by his suit jacket to deliver a harangue against "packing" the committee. The pressure from Democratic leaders and the White House (including emissary Lyndon Johnson, now Kennedy's vice president) was just as intense. Kennedy understood the substantive stakes in this procedural skirmish. "We can't lose this one," he told his legislative liaison Lawrence O'Brien. "The ball game is over if we do."

Kennedy did not lose the fight. But he did not win it in the way he anticipated. Kennedy was a new president, Rayburn a beloved Democratic icon. Democrats held a majority of eighty-nine seats in the House. Yet even with a direct appeal from both men, so many Southern Democrats defected on the vote that Democrats could not pass the enlargement plan on their own. The plan succeeded only because the Republican attempts at imposing party discipline also failed. Despite Halleck's pressure, twenty-two liberal Northern Republicans crossed party lines to vote with the moderate and liberal Democrats and a minority of Southern Democrats loyal to Kennedy; those Republicans provided the votes that allowed the enlargement plan to pass by a mere five votes. "We repudiate any suggestion of a coalition with Southern Democrats," the twenty-two dissidents declared. Only the votes of liberal Republicans disillusioned over the longtime conservative alliance protected Kennedy from Southern Democrats who wanted to combine with Republicans against him. Rayburn, who died less than ten months later, called the experience "the worst fight of my life."

Political alignments this tangled produced far-reaching effects. One was to depress partisan polarization in the electorate. The age of bargaining discouraged Americans from viewing political fights and political leaders purely in partisan terms. To a greater extent than before or after, Americans in this period regularly witnessed presidents standing with legislators from the opposition party against members of their own. In our era, the near constant conflict between presidents and members of the opposition party in Congress sends a clear cue to voters from that party to view the president as a threat. But the parties' leaders in Washington did not send that signal nearly as consistently during the age of bargaining. That helps explain why in Gallup Organization polls Eisenhower's approval rating through both of his terms routinely topped 70 percent, with Democrats nearly as enthusiastic as Republicans. Even against the highly political backdrop of a reelection campaign, Eisenhower's approval rating among Democrats never fell below 49 percent in 1956 Gallup polling (and reached as high as 67 percent). Kennedy's approval rating among Republicans did not fall below 50 percent for his first fifteen months in office, and averaged nearly 46 percent through the next year. As Johnson marched to his landslide reelection in 1964, his ratings among Republicans fell below 60 percent only once.

The most common complaint about the politics of this period was that it promoted *too much* consensus. Political scientists complained that the fractures within the parties denied Americans sufficient choice in both governing and elections. In September 1950, after almost four years of work, a sixteen-member commission of the American Political Science Association published a lengthy report that urged the development of what it called "a more responsible two-party system." In "an era when it is no longer safe for the nation to deal piecemeal with issues," it wrote, America needed parties strong enough to pass "coherent programs" when in power, and to provide clear alternatives when in opposition. Without ever saying so directly, the committee clearly yearned for America's parties to behave more like the centrally directed, tightly disciplined parties found in parliamentary systems abroad. Parties infused with greater discipline, the report argued, would offer Americans both more progress and more accountability. As it was, the committee believed, American government offered too little of either. Because Republicans and Democrats were both so divided internally, the party holding power often could not pass the program on which it campaigned. "In a two-party system," the committee wrote, "when both parties are weakened or confused by internal divisions or ineffective organization it is the nation that suffers." And because the ideological differences between the two sides were frequently muddled, voters were too often denied a clear choice at election time. "Alternatives between the parties are defined so badly that it is often difficult to determine what the election has decided even in broadest terms," the committee declared.

Thirteen years later the political scientist James MacGregor Burns raised a similar alarm in his book *The Deadlock of Democracy*. The problem with Washington, he insisted, was a political environment that had promoted too much consensus and prevented either party from implementing a distinctive, sharply defined agenda. Four-party politics, Burns declared, had produced a "dangerous cycle of drift and deadlock in our national affairs." Compelled to govern by "consensus and coalition," Washington was incapable of bold steps at home or abroad. "While the demands on our government pile up at a feverish pace, the system shows no sign of relaxing its grip on the levers of action," he wrote.

Inside the parties, these indictments found the most support from the most ideological voices. Though Republican conservatives won many legislative skirmishes, the age of bargaining increasingly frustrated them. They ached for a GOP strategy that would challenge the New Deal legacy of activist government more directly than Eisenhower's cautious "modern Republicanism" or the legislative deal making of the party's congressional leadership. A few months before the disastrous 1958 midterm election, a *Wall Street Journal* survey of local Republican leaders found many complaining that Eisenhower's centrism had extinguished the animating spark of difference between the two parties. "The difference between the two parties' basic policies has narrowed to a point where [Republican activists] become discouraged or apathetic," lamented one "Midwest party leader," who said the GOP was struggling to recruit volunteers for the campaign season. Republican senator Barry Goldwater of Arizona, who would ignite the modern conservative movement as the GOP presidential nominee in 1964, fanned those embers through the fading Eisenhower years. "It should be evident that a oneness, or 'me-tooism,' in American politics is dangerous to our system," he declared in 1960.

But if the age of bargaining irritated conservatives, it infuriated liberals. Liberals, inverting the conservative indictment, charged that the centrist, business-oriented Democratic congressional leadership, Rayburn in the House, Johnson in the Senate, had enfeebled the party by failing to present a clear alternative to Eisenhower. In the liberal analysis, Johnson and

Rayburn limited the party's electoral appeal by excluding the problems not only of blacks but also of the poor and big cities from the national debate in an emasculating search for party unity with conservative Southerners. From the heights of Franklin Roosevelt, the compliant congressional leadership had brought "the Democratic party to its lowest point in twenty-five years," the chairman of the liberal Americans for Democratic Action insisted halfway through Eisenhower's presidency.

The liberal frustration increased exponentially after Kennedy replaced Eisenhower. The liberals faced a situation difficult to explain or accept. Democrats held the White House for the first time in eight years. They held both chambers of Congress, on paper, by large majorities (with 263 Democrats in the House and 65 in the Senate). And yet they could not move the most ambitious elements of the president's program.

Kennedy's problem was the same problem that had confounded Roosevelt after 1938 and Truman throughout his presidency: In Congress, Kennedy had a partisan but not an ideological majority. It was the enduring Democratic dilemma in the age of bargaining. In each chamber the Democrats' numerical advantage rested on the party's overwhelming strength in the South. Some of those legislators, such as the veteran moderate senators John Sparkman and Lister Hill of Alabama, and the iconoclastic populist representative Wright Patman of Texas, consistently supported the national Democratic agenda. But as the early fight over the Rules Committee demonstrated, most did not.

Seniority solidified the Southern power on both sides of Capitol Hill. The seniority system favored the Southerners because they faced virtually no competition in a Southern political order built around the twin exclusions of African Americans, who were almost all denied the right to vote, and Republicans, who were disqualified by their association with the Civil War. While the shifting tides of national sentiment could sweep legislators from other regions in or out of Congress, toppling them from the ladder of seniority, the Southerners stood safely beyond the waves. Year by year, decade by decade, they climbed toward chairmanships that under the seniority system they could hold for as long as they remained in Congress, which in many cases meant as long as they drew breath.

Through the 1930s and 1940s, Southerners consistently held the chairmanships of about half the committees in both the House and Senate when Democrats controlled the majority; through the 1950s the Southern control grew even more lopsided in both chambers. Even when liberals gained seats their increased strength broke against the stronghold of seniority. In 1958, benefiting from recession and the Eisenhower administration's fading energy, liberal and moderate Democrats made huge gains in the congressional election. The number of Democrats from outside the South surged, rising by forty-eight in the House and by fifteen in the Senate. In both chambers, non-Southerners, almost all of whom stood to the left of center, significantly outnumbered the Southerners in the Democratic caucus. Yet when Congress reconvened in 1959 Southerners held more than three fifths of the chairmanships in the Senate and about two thirds in the House. And those committee chairs, like the Southerners who chaired committees under Roosevelt and Truman, voted with the conservative coalition against the priorities of centrist and liberal Democrats at least as often, and frequently more often, than congressional Republicans.

The tension inherent in this situation boiled over in the Kennedy presidency, when the Democrats most skeptical about his agenda exercised the most power over its fate. In the Senate of 1961, Southerners chaired eleven of the sixteen committees; in the House it was thirteen of twenty-one. These chairs included men deeply estranged from Kennedy's vision. In the House only three of the thirteen Southern committee chairs supported him on at least three quarters of the votes on which he took a position. Four of them supported him less than half the time. Smith, unbowed by his defeat over enlarging his committee, voted with Kennedy on only a little more than one third of the key votes.

In the Senate the story was the same. Just two of the eleven Southern committee chairs (Sparkman and Hill) voted with Kennedy as much as three fourths of the time. Five of the eleven Southern committee chairmen voted with Kennedy less than 40 percent of the time. When the session opened, Joseph Clark, a liberal Democratic senator from Pennsylvania, moved to oust two profoundly conservative committee chairmen because they supported party positions so infrequently. The Democratic caucus refused: Like the House during the fight over the Rules Committee, it would not confront so directly the principle of seniority. And the two chairmen, Harry Byrd of Virginia at Finance, and James Eastland of Judiciary, responded to that vote of confidence by each supporting Kennedy on only about one fourth of the issues on which he took a position.

Provocations like these deepened the liberal dismay over the age of bargaining. It inspired them to begin a crusade whose first significant impact would not be felt until after Kennedy's presidency, and whose full implications would not manifest until Republicans won control of Congress in 1994. The liberals pressed a comprehensive congressional reform agenda with interlocked goals—breaking the power of congressional conservatives and creating more disciplined, ideologically cohesive parties. They saw no contradiction between those aims; indeed, they considered the second goal essential to the first. The left mounted its reform crusade on the conviction that "conservative power [in Congress] rested on unfair institutional protections rather than strong electoral support," wrote congressional historian Julian E. Zelizer, whose study of the effort provides the basis for much of what follows. In fact, though, the left's assumption was flawed. Conservative power in Congress rested on support from substantial elements of the public. It survived even after the congressional rules that benefited conservatives were swept away or retrenched. The result was that the reform drive produced an outcome its architects could not have imagined: more disciplined and ideologically cohesive parties that *increased* the strength of congressional conservatives.

Congressional liberals and their allies in the Democratic coalition, groups such as the AFL-CIO, the National Association for the Advancement of Colored People, and the liberal Americans for Democratic Action, first laid siege in the 1940s to the congressional rules and practices that they believed favored the conservative coalition. The principal motivation for the reform effort was the conservative success in thwarting meaningful civil rights legislation. But liberals also saw the conservative strength as a threat to all other elements of their domestic agenda, from health care to education. They pressed to reconfigure a broad range of rules that they believed unfairly advantaged their opponents. "Conservative and sectional forces have set up roadblocks which are making it nearly impossible to move forward with progressive legislation," Shuman, the hard-nosed leg-islative aide to Paul Douglas, wrote in 1957. "If there is to be even some modest measure of protection for the public welfare, Congressional insti-tutions themselves must be re-examined and revised."

The left's most visible target was the Senate filibuster, which allowed a minority of senators to block action on legislation indefinitely. The filibus-ter provided the last line of defense for Southerners, usually working in alliance with conservative Republicans, against civil rights legislation; they used it to block Wagner's antilynching legislation in 1938, and an effort, four years later, to eliminate the poll tax. Liberals repeatedly sought to lower the threshold for ending a filibuster, from two thirds of the Senate (the level set in 1917) to a simple majority. But throughout this era they never amassed the strength to wrest the weapon away from the South; in 1949 conservatives actually raised the hurdle by requiring votes from two thirds of all senators, not just two thirds of those present, to break a fili-buster. Despite repeated challenges, reformers made no meaningful prog-ress in their efforts to restrict the filibuster until the 1970s, long after Congress had settled the principal disputes over civil rights.

The reformers enjoyed more success in challenging a pillar of conserva-tive strength in the House of Representatives. An unfair tilt toward rural areas in the way congressional districts were constructed inflated the con-servatives' influence in the House. State legislatures, themselves heavily influenced by rural interests, typically drew congressional districts in urban and suburban areas that contained far more voters than districts in rural parts of their states; in Georgia, one urban district contained three times as many people as the smallest rural district. The result was to provide rural areas in many states with more congressional representation than their population would justify. And that, as the liberals recognized, unfairly enlarged conservative strength in the House (as well as in state legisla-tures). Congressional liberals and groups such as the AFL-CIO raged against this imbalance through the 1950s, but, unsurprisingly, could never tempt the dominant conservative coalition into reforms that would dilute its power.

Eventually, though, the Supreme Court destroyed the system. In a series of decisions beginning with the landmark 1962 *Baker v. Carr* ruling, the Court established the principle of "one person one vote," and directed states to draw districts for Congress and state legislatures with roughly equal populations. After congressional efforts to overturn the decisions failed, states undertook a frenzy of redistricting. Predictably the effort diminished the influence of the countryside: by one count, the number of predominantly rural districts plummeted from 214 in 1964 to 130 just eight years later.

The conservative white Democrats who dominated Southern delegations in the House were gradually squeezed between the declining influence of rural voters and the rising presence of Southern African Americans, who moved steadily into the electorate after the passage of the Voting Rights Act in 1965. This was all as the reformers predicted. Yet the principal result of that squeeze would not be the election of more moderates from suburban Southern districts, as the reformers had hoped, but the replacement of rural Democrats with Southern Republicans who typically stood even further to the right. (Later the South would send a growing number of liberal African American Democrats to the House, reducing the traditional right-of-center white Southern Democrats from the other direction.) These changes would narrow the differences within the Democratic Party as truly conservative voices diminished. But they would widen enormously the differences between the parties in Congress, as the loss of conservative and even moderate Southerners moved the Democrats to the left, and the infusion of adamantly conservative Southerners carried the Republican Party further to the right. For those watching carefully, the warning that redistricting reform might produce unanticipated effects came almost immediately in Virginia. In 1966, Representative Howard Smith, the liberals' old antagonist on the Rules Committee, was compelled to run for reelection in a redrawn district that included more suburban voters and African Americans. A young liberal lawyer named George Rawlings, Jr., defeated the aging Smith in the primary—but then lost the seat to a Republican in November. Rawlings's defeat was an early pebble in what would become an avalanche of Republican gains across the South over the next quarter century.

The third front in the liberal reform push was the successful assault on the House Rules Committee that culminated in 1961. The reformers' final priority targeted the seniority system. Seniority, which began informally around the Civil War and hardened after the rule of the Four and Joe Cannon, provided legislators enormous autonomy. It freed them to break from the party consensus without fear that their colleagues could retaliate by stripping them of their positions on committees (as Cannon often did). The inviolability of seniority made an impossibility of serious party discipline. In the age of bargaining, that benefited the Republican moderates who sometimes sided with Truman or Kennedy, but mostly it empowered the conservative Southern Democrats who regularly voted with Republicans. Complaints among liberal Democrats about seniority simmered through the 1950s. "The consequences of this system are disastrous for liberal Senators," Shuman wrote in his 1957 indictment of congressional rules. The discontent moved closer to a boil after the liberal gains of 1958. After being denied a seat on the Finance Committee or the Democratic Policy Committee, Senator Clark of Pennsylvania wrote Lyndon Johnson in 1959, "I don't believe you can indefinitely 'sit on the lid' supporting the chairmen of standing Committees selected by seniority, many of whom are not in sympathy with the principles and platform of the modern Democratic party." Two years later Clark mounted his unsuccessful effort to remove Byrd and Eastland.

That effort's failure surprised no one. When Senator Stephen Douglas, the Illinois Democrat who beat Abraham Lincoln in the epic 1858 Illinois Senate race, opposed a party position on slavery that year, his fellow Senate Democrats summarily stripped him of his chairmanship of the Committee on Territories. Cannon wielded similar cudgels against his enemies in the House. But since the fall of Cannon and the Four, such examples were rare. In 1925, Republicans removed thirteen members from their committee assignments for supporting Robert La Follette's third-party presidential bid the previous year. But the Democrats did not punish any of their thirty Southern legislators who backed Strom Thurmond's "Dixiecrat" presidential challenge to Truman in 1948, despite calls from liberals to strip them of their committee assignments. Nor did Democrats strip seniority from Adam Clayton Powell and Southern Democrats who backed Eisenhower in 1956. And in 1961 Rayburn retreated from the option of removing Colmer from the House Rules Committee.

Clark and his colleagues were ahead of their time. But the issues they raised would prove critical in the transition to today's political system of hyperpartisanship. Not until the 1970s would another generation of congressional liberals overturn the seniority system. Yet, like the rise of "one person one vote," the fall of seniority would not produce the results liberals expected. The abandonment of seniority as the means of selecting committee chairmen would encourage somewhat more party discipline among Democrats from the mid-1970s through the 1990s. But only Republicans, after seizing control of Congress in 1994, would leverage the change to its maximum effect. The liberal effort to marginalize conservatives by undermining seniority would later become a principal tool for Republican leaders like Newt Gingrich and Tom DeLay to advance the most conservative agenda since the 1920s. Indeed, in almost every way, the liberal drive to reform congressional rules would become a monument to the law of unintended consequences.

THE AGE OF BARGAINING: AN ASSESSMENT

Apart from the enlargement of the Rules Committee, the liberal assaults on the institutional structure of conservative power in Congress came too late to benefit John F. Kennedy. The conservative coalition largely held through his presidency. During his "thousand days," Kennedy squeezed some victories through Congress—an increase in the minimum wage, a juvenile delinquency program, the Peace Corps, a trade expansion act, the nuclear test ban treaty in 1963. But the conservative coalition functioned as a very narrow filter on him. Kennedy, whose own interests bent more toward foreign policy anyway, passed none of his most ambitious domestic proposals: health care for the elderly; aid to education; and the legislation he belatedly proposed, under pressure from the growing civil rights movement, to finally end state-sponsored segregation.

Lyndon Johnson, after Kennedy's assassination, would pass that historic civil rights bill in 1964. The Civil Rights Act would prove the last major event of the age of bargaining. A few months later, in the 1964 election, Johnson carried in such commanding Democratic congressional majorities in his landslide victory over Barry Goldwater that he would become the first president since Franklin Roosevelt's first term who did not need to bargain extensively with the opposition party or dissident members of his own to pass his program.

What legacy did the age of bargaining leave? In many ways it was a flawed political system. The extensive negotiation required to build a majority for any policy discouraged dramatic change. The system allowed only for incremental, not revolutionary, reform. It was more congenial for presidents with modest domestic agendas (Eisenhower and to some extent Kennedy) than for those with greater ambitions. Truman, who lacked the subtle touch on domestic issues this system demanded, failed to achieve almost any of his major priorities at home. The era's fractured politics too often encouraged temporizing, delay, and complacency. It discouraged bold, morally clarion leadership. (Eisenhower from the White House and Lyndon Johnson as Senate majority leader, for instance, both shamefully stood aside far too long as Joseph McCarthy rampaged.) It marginalized too many issues, from the needs of the poor to the gathering threats to the environment, which lacked sufficient champions in the mainstream of the two parties. The concentrated burst of classic polemics that appeared from left and right in the early 1960s—from the left, *The Other America, Silent Spring, The Feminine Mystique, The Port Huron Statement,* and from a different angle, Barry Goldwater's *The Conscience of a Conservative* and Milton Friedman's *Capitalism and Freedom*—all testified to the belief that the era's seeming harmony relied on silencing its most impassioned voices. Of course, the greatest shame of the system is that until its final days it safeguarded a regime of brutal state-sponsored segregation that denied the rights of millions of black Americans. For all these reasons, the age of bargaining is not a political system that anyone would seek to resurrect today.

But for all its defects the system possessed one great virtue: It compelled political leaders who held contrasting views and represented differing constituencies to talk and listen to each other. Almost everything important that happened required bargaining between and within the parties. That meant political leaders, on almost any major decision, needed to consider and, as much as possible, harmonize a wide range of opinions. As Robert Caro vividly recounted it in *Master of the Senate*, his monumental biography of Johnson during the 1950s, the passage of the 1957 Civil Rights Act was a challenge that rivaled in its complexity the construction of the pyramids. It required Johnson to juggle impatient liberal Democrats, obdurate Southerners, Westerners with their own parochial priorities, Republicans conflicted between their desires to pass a bill and to embarrass the Democrats, and even contending factions inside the Eisenhower administration. The far more consequential 1964 law required maneuvers nearly as complex, including a sustained siege of Everett Dirksen, the florid Senate Republican leader, by Hubert Humphrey, the leader of the liberal forces behind the bill.

Because the real divisions cut across party lines, the need for bargaining was as urgent when one party held unified control of government as when power was divided between them. Consider the gyrations John F. Kennedy undertook to produce his economic policy at a time when Democrats, recall, held not only the White House, but both chambers of Congress. After running his campaign on the theme of "getting the country moving again," Kennedy looked to invigorate the economy he inherited from Eisenhower. Kennedy's liberal advisers, economists like Walter Heller and John Kenneth Galbraith, prescribed a dose of Keynesian stimulus: government deficits to jump-start growth. But greater deficits faced resistance from Douglas Dillon, the Republican Kennedy had appointed as treasury secretary, as well as deficit-minded Democrats on Capitol Hill, like Harry Byrd, the archconservative from Virginia who chaired the Senate Finance Committee.

Only after more than a year of intense negotiations inside and outside the administration did Kennedy agree to deliberately widen the federal deficit in the hope of stimulating the economy. Once Kennedy crossed that bridge, he immediately faced a second fork. One set of advisers (led by Heller) wanted to provide the stimulus by cutting taxes. Another set (led by Galbraith) wanted to increase public spending. Kennedy's personal preferences inclined toward the latter, but his political sense bent him toward the former. Even after Kennedy settled on a tax cut, he was pressured into a final accommodation: To satisfy Wilbur Mills, the

Democratic deficit hawk who chaired the House Ways and Means Committee, Kennedy agreed to couple his tax cut with further cuts in federal spending. Eventually the package cleared Congress, after Kennedy's assassination.

The point isn't that Kennedy reached a golden mean with his choices: It's that in making the choices he was compelled to consider a wide range of opinion even though his party controlled all levers of government. The space between Heller or Galbraith and Dillon, much less Harry Byrd, was large enough to accommodate the opinion of most, if not a vast majority, of Americans. Balancing the demands of such a divergent party required Kennedy to formulate policies that offered at least some recognition to a broad range of sentiment in the country.

Sometimes the need to harmonize so many viewpoints produced a lowest-common-denominator minimalism. The 1957 Civil Rights Bill, despite its symbolic value as a foundation for future action, largely fit that description. But the pressure to consider so many perspectives also meant that when Washington finally reached an important decision it could cement an enduring national consensus. The Civil Rights Act of 1964 did exactly that in sweeping away segregation. Washington had delayed far too long before reaching that point. But when Congress finally acted, it acted for the nation, with both parties and all regions from outside the South irresistibly affirming the demand for change inside the South.

BARGAINING AT ITS BEST

The finest hour of the age of bargaining, the one that most clearly demonstrated its capacity to forge a lasting national agreement, came early in the period. The occasion was the development of America's post–World War II foreign policy under Harry Truman. In many histories the construction of a bipartisan strategy for resisting the Soviet Union and contesting the cold war seems almost inevitable, more a work of nature than of men and women. And indeed powerful underlying forces pushed the parties toward agreement. The unprecedented national mobilization for World War II had created a culture of cooperation in national security that attenuated but remained potent through the first postwar years. The global havoc of World War II, and the sobering fear of an atomic arms race, enormously weakened the isolationist argument that dominated the 1920s and early 1930s. Fear of the Soviet Union provided a spur even for those who did not concede they had been wrong before World War II.

And yet, reviewing this story, it's striking how much work, how much *bargaining*, it took to bridge the space between the parties. It's worth recounting this experience in some depth because it shows the principal aspect of the age of bargaining that deserves excavation—a systematic effort by farsighted political leaders to broaden support for policy by including both parties in its development.

The path toward a bipartisan consensus for enlarging America's international role after World War II began with a bipartisan consensus against enlarging it before the war. The turn inward that began with the rejection of the League of Nations under Woodrow Wilson still determined American foreign policy through the 1930s. While the world convulsed toward war, an alliance of Democratic and Republican isolationists in Congress hobbled Franklin Roosevelt with restrictive neutrality laws that prevented him from applying economic pressure on Germany, Japan, and Italy or providing meaningful aid to their targets. After Adolf Hitler invaded Poland in 1939 Congress finally loosened the neutrality laws. But even in June 1940, the Senate Foreign Relations Committee blocked Roosevelt from sending modern planes and ships to the Allies.

Pearl Harbor temporarily silenced the isolationists and unified the country. But Roosevelt, with Woodrow Wilson's failure firmly in mind, understood that solidarity during war could crumble with peace. As Roosevelt fought World War II, he remained as dedicated as Wilson a generation earlier to securing a lasting peace by establishing an international organization to resist aggression. But, unlike Wilson, Roosevelt recognized that committing America to a permanent role in the world was a job too big for one party to accomplish alone. Roosevelt reversed Wilson's strategy so completely it is almost as if he used it as the model for what he would not do.

Roosevelt began seeking Republican support for his foreign policy long before America entered the fighting. After the European war erupted in

1939, his first instinct was to appoint both Alf Landon, his Republican opponent in 1936, and Frank Knox, Landon's running mate, to his administration. When Landon balked (fearing that Roosevelt might use him to promote his ambitions for a third term) Roosevelt let the idea simmer for nearly a year. But in June 1940, Roosevelt unveiled a master stroke: He appointed Republican Henry Stimson, the secretary of war for William Howard Taft and secretary of state for Herbert Hoover, as secretary of war, and Knox as secretary of the Navy. Just before the United States entered the war, Roosevelt reached out to Republicans again in an almost unprecedented way: He chose as Supreme Court chief justice Republican Harlan Fiske Stone.

During the war Roosevelt's commitment to bipartisanship, and even consultation with his own party, flagged: Senators in both parties complained that he shared too little information about his diplomacy. But he never entirely forgot that he needed to expand his lines of communication and contain the partisan conflict on foreign affairs. Roosevelt offered Wendell Willkie, his dynamic Republican opponent in 1940, various jobs, and encouraged him in the round-the-world journey that became the basis of his phenomenally successful book *One World* in 1943. During the 1942 congressional election Roosevelt pointedly refused to echo Wilson's call from 1918 for the voters to send him a Democratic Congress; when the Democratic National Committee chairman, rather innocuously, charged that a Republican majority Congress would be a disaster, Roosevelt repudiated him. He moved slowly on the planning for the United Nations to give himself more time to build consensus at home as well as abroad. Roosevelt was initially unenthusiastic about providing Congress much of a role in shaping American participation in the UN, but eventually recognized the need to build acceptance and moved boldly to achieve it: In February 1945, FDR (harvesting an idea first planted by a Republican senator at a 1943 meeting) appointed Democratic senator Tom Connally of Texas and Republican Arthur Vandenberg of Michigan, the chairman and ranking member of the Senate Foreign Relations Committee, to serve on the U.S. delegation to the San Francisco conference organizing the UN. That proved a brilliant maneuver: When Connally and Vandenberg returned to Washington both men "were recognized as the authorities in the Senate" on the UN charter, as one senior

Senate aide later recalled, and helped guide it to a remarkably uneventful approval. Roosevelt had already died when the Senate debated the UN charter in July 1945. But the 89–2 vote to join testified not only to the distance American opinion had traveled since the end of World War I, but to the gulf between the political skills of Wilson and FDR.

Roosevelt's death left Harry Truman, his vice president, to devise America's plan for the postwar world. Initially overwhelmed, Truman moved with growing confidence to place America at the center of an international system designed to rebuild Europe and Asia and contain the threat of communism. As a former senator, Truman exceeded Roosevelt in his determination to invest Republicans in his plan. As much as anything else, it was Truman's success in constructing those domestic alliances that allowed him to forever change America's international role.

The key figure in that historic achievement proved to be Vandenberg, the Michigan Republican. Vandenberg came from solid Republican stock: His grandfather had attended the 1860 Republican convention that nominated Abraham Lincoln. Attracted to politics even as a teenager (he told friends in high school he wanted to be a senator), Vandenberg enlisted in the progressive wing of the GOP behind the banner of Theodore Roosevelt. As a young editor at the *Grand Rapids Herald*, he editorialized for railroad regulation, tough antitrust enforcement, and protection for women and children working in factories. Rejecting the Midwestern Republican isolationism common around him, the young Vandenberg endorsed Theodore Roosevelt's vision of an aggressive, even imperialistic, America confidently imprinting its will upon the world.

In 1928, when a Democratic incumbent died, Michigan's Republican governor appointed Vandenberg to the U.S. Senate. In Washington he tried to find a middle space between the GOP old guard that considered Herbert Hoover too liberal and the Republican progressives who harassed Hoover from the left. After Roosevelt's landslide election in 1932, Vandenberg continued to occupy that ground, voting frequently for New Deal initiatives and pressing Republicans to offer constructive alternatives when they opposed FDR's ideas.

In his early Senate years, under both Hoover and Roosevelt, Vandenberg had retained his commitment to at least modest international engagement.

But Vandenberg tilted sharply right as Roosevelt veered left after 1935. Vandenberg's movement upended even his earlier convictions on foreign policy.

Through the remainder of the 1930s Vandenberg embraced an uncompromising isolationism and fiercely resisted each step of Roosevelt's effort to lead America into the fight against fascism. After Vandenberg helped sink Roosevelt's proposal to loosen the neutrality laws in 1939, FDR was so enraged that, in a private tirade, he included the Michigan senator in a list of Republicans who should have statues erected in their honor in Berlin "with the swastika on them." Even the outbreak of World War II didn't shake Vandenberg from his new course. In 1940, Vandenberg sought the Republican presidential nomination as an isolationist (losing to the internationalist Willkie). To a constituent questioning how Vandenberg could look away as Europe burned, he wrote that year: "since I do not intend to take 'the last step' in this bloody direction [toward war], I also do not propose to take the 'first step' or any other step."

Yet once war came, Vandenberg's beliefs increasingly pinched him, like shoes that no longer fit. As early as 1943 he mused in his diary about the need for "far greater international cooperation" after the shooting stopped. In January 1945, writing the words on his own typewriter (and with suggestions from *New York Times* correspondent James Reston), Vandenberg came full circle. In a dramatic speech on the Senate floor he pronounced isolationism dead and declared: "I do not believe that any nation hereafter can immunize itself by its own exclusive action."

The best explanation for Vandenberg's reversal may be that he realized he needed new means to reach his old goals. In the years before Pearl Harbor he saw isolationism as the mechanism for keeping the United States out of war; after the global destruction of World War II, and the development of atomic weapons, he realized that only engagement and international cooperation could maintain peace. Roosevelt died before he could benefit much from Vandenberg's conversion. But Truman pushed through the opening with skill and determination. The partnership between Vandenberg and Truman became the bookend to the rivalry between Henry Cabot Lodge and Woodrow Wilson; the model, to this day, for how compromise among politicians can build public consensus for difficult choices.

Even after Vandenberg renounced isolationism, Truman and his team easily could have found plenty of reasons to ignore him. Balding and bland looking, with a grand sense of his importance, Vandenberg was often exasperating. As a speaker and writer he never used one word when two, or five, would do. Before entering the Senate he had written some very bad books about Alexander Hamilton (his hero) and some very turgid short stories, and his prose, not surprisingly, didn't become more concise once he entered an institution that set no limits on how long its members could speak. To talk with Vandenberg was mostly to listen. Vandenberg loved words, but the affair was unrequited: In his speeches he was drawn to the cliché and enraptured by the florid. In full flight he could leave his listeners thumbing their dictionaries or simply scratching their heads over phrases such as "our mirific inheritances" and "marcescent monarchy." Robert Taft once instructed his wife to "butter Van up" at a dinner he held in the senator's honor. "I tried manfully," Martha Taft later wrote to her sons, "but he buttered himself so thoroughly that I really couldn't find a single ungreased spot." Vandenberg, in short, was a man that many in Washington, especially those who were not members of his party, or who traced their roots back to towns larger than Grand Rapids, found difficult to take as seriously as he always took himself.

But with all these affectations and limitations, Vandenberg played an indispensable role in winning congressional approval for each major piece of Truman's program for reconstructing Europe and containing communism: the Truman Doctrine of aid to Greece and Turkey in 1947; the Marshall Plan to rebuild the continent in 1948; and the North Atlantic Charter that created NATO, the North Atlantic Treaty Organization, in 1949. Vandenberg worked as closely with the Truman administration when Democrats controlled the Senate (1945–46 and 1949–50) as he did when Republicans held the majority (1947 and 1948). He did not agree with Truman on every issue: He resisted postwar suggestions for cooperation on atomic weapons with the Soviet Union and dissented, more ambivalently, when Truman moved to acknowledge the inevitable by abandoning Chiang Kai-shek in China. But Vandenberg made genuine efforts to find agreement wherever he could, even amid a steady pulse of criticism from conservatives in his own party.

The Truman team made extraordinary efforts to sustain the relationship too. On foreign policy, perhaps because his own views were not as long held, Truman displayed a flexibility that largely eluded him on domestic issues. George Marshall, Truman's titanic secretary of state, spent hours courting Vandenberg. Dean Acheson, Marshall's elegant undersecretary, did too, though the imperious Acheson and ponderous Vandenberg sometimes bristled at each other. The mechanics of the relationship smoothed out when Robert A. Lovett, the brilliant and amiable former aide to both Stimson and Marshall, replaced Acheson as undersecretary of state in 1947. Truman instructed Lovett to be "completely frank" with Vandenberg, and Lovett took the injunction seriously. Lovett, a nominal Republican, developed the habit of stopping off on his way home from the State Department at Vandenberg's apartment in suite 500G of the Wardman Park Hotel "with a sheaf of telegrams in my hand." Over cocktails the two men pondered the mysteries of Soviet intentions and the deeper mysteries of legislative strategy. Side by side in Vandenberg's apartment, the two in 1948 drafted a resolution that encouraged the United States to pursue new security arrangements with Europe. One month after the Senate emphatically endorsed that language, Truman began the negotiations that led the next year to the North Atlantic Treaty and NATO.

Truman offered Vandenberg not just courtesy but genuine input. Truman accepted Vandenberg amendments to his program of aid to Greece and Turkey, and the concessions helped the Truman Doctrine pass the Senate 67–23, with support from more than two thirds of the Republicans. The next year Truman accepted Vandenberg's proposal to establish an independent commission to monitor the dispersal of aid under the Marshall Plan and credited the senator with the idea during a large, bipartisan meeting with senators. During the Senate debate the administration accepted a critical suggestion of legislative strategy from Vandenberg that soothed Republican skeptics by providing Congress more control over the spending. After the plan cleared the Senate with support from nearly all Democrats and almost three fourths of the Republicans in March 1948, Truman initially wanted to name Acheson as administrator. Acheson told him to check with Vandenberg first. Vandenberg, as Acheson expected, vetoed the choice and recommended instead Paul G. Hoffman, a Republican business executive. Truman, in his diary, complained that he thought it a "silly idea" to appoint "some industrialist without experience." But in the end, to cement his relations with Vandenberg, Truman did exactly that. As a bonus Hoffman proved an excellent choice, one of Truman's most successful appointments to high office.

Truman may have courted Vandenberg so much over those two years because Republicans held the Senate majority. But the pattern of cooperation continued even after Truman's upset victory in 1948 returned Democrats to control. Acheson, whom Truman nominated after the election to succeed Marshall, convened negotiations with Connally, Vandenberg, and other senators from both parties even as he conducted the diplomatic discussions that produced NATO. In a calculation almost unimaginable today, Acheson concluded it would be unwise to try to "move any faster" with the allies "than I could move in my discussions with Senators Connally and Vandenberg, since agreement would mean little unless it carried senatorial opinion with it." When the treaty came before the Senate in 1949, Truman and Acheson accepted Vandenberg's request that the addition of any new members require Senate approval. With Vandenberg's strong support, the Senate approved the charter, 82–13. Once again, virtually every Democrat and nearly three fourths of the Republicans voted yes.

Inevitably, this partnership frayed. Personal strains between Vandenberg and Acheson intruded. The political winds shifted too. After the GOP's losses in the 1948 election, it became more difficult for Vandenberg to fend off demands from frustrated conservatives for a more confrontational Republican message on foreign policy. The tipping point inside the GOP came on February 9, 1950, when Joe McCarthy stood up before the Ohio County Women's Republican Club in Wheeling, West Virginia, and declared that he held "in my hand a list of 205" Communists in the State Department. From then on, confrontation eclipsed cooperation as the Republican strategy.

By then Vandenberg was receding from the Senate, suffering from the cancer that would kill him in April 1951. After Vandenberg stepped away Truman could never recapture the bipartisan (or "nonpartisan," as

Vandenberg often termed it) cooperation of the immediate postwar years. The Korean War shifted the foreign policy debate toward Asia and the challenge of responding to communist China, which had always divided the parties more than policy toward Europe and the Soviet Union. But Truman continued to pursue openings to the GOP, even to the extent of appointing the haughty Republican attorney John Foster Dulles as a consultant to the State Department in 1950. When the State Department first suggested the appointment of a frequently bitter administration critic who had served in the 1948 campaign as the top foreign policy adviser to Truman's Republican opponent, Thomas E. Dewey, Truman's initial reaction was understandable: "What, that bastard? Not on your life!" But Truman ultimately recognized that including a Republican like Dulles in the design of foreign policy could improve its reception among other Republicans in Congress. Once Dulles was on board, Acheson suggested appointing him to negotiate the peace treaty with Japan. This would be the equivalent, half a century later, of Bush naming a Democrat such as Richard Holbrooke, one of John Kerry's senior advisers, to manage the Middle East peace negotiations. Truman no doubt bit on his lip hard, but he gave Dulles the assignment in May 1950, three months after McCarthy signaled the outbreak of greater hostility between the parties. Dulles proved an extremely effective negotiator, not only with Japan, but between the Pentagon and the State Department, and between the Truman administration and congressional Republicans. The assignment didn't pacify Dulles; when the treaty was completed, he resigned from the State Department and undertook a speaking tour in which, undeterred by his two years of employment by Truman, he resumed his criticisms of him. But in March 1952, the peace treaty with Japan easily cleared the Senate, 66 to 10; once again, virtually every Democrat and about three fourths of the Republicans voted yes. It was a remarkable showing just eight months before a presidential election.

The outreach to Republicans from Roosevelt and then Truman, of course, wasn't the only reason Congress blessed the architecture they built for the postwar world. The two sides could not have agreed unless Truman and his advisers devised a policy that inspired broad consensus: the resistance of Soviet expansion through the steady but usually not belligerent application of American economic, political, and military strength. That vision of containment navigated between the demands from the far left for greater concessions to Soviet designs and the conflicting conservative impulses toward greater isolationism, increased focus on Asia, and later, more direct confrontation to "roll back" Soviet control of Eastern Europe. Containment did not always serve America ideally; applied too literally, and with too much emphasis on military confrontation, it inspired the debacle in Vietnam. But the strategy forged by Truman, Vandenberg, and the men around them proved flexible, practical, and acceptable enough to leaders in both parties to broadly guide American foreign policy for the next forty-five years, through the presidencies of five Republicans and three Democrats. Perhaps the greatest measure of their success is the contrast with their successors. Since the cold war's end, no president has crafted a vision of American engagement in the world that endured beyond his term. George H. W. Bush's "New World Order" and Bill Clinton's "enlargement" were quickly abandoned once their authors left office, and, by all indications, the "Bush Doctrine" of unilateral preemption against emerging threats is heading for the same fate.

It's tempting to see the bipartisan achievement of the post–World War II years as a fossil from an ancient era, the days of dispassionate wise men who placed country above party. But both Truman and Vandenberg could be fierce partisans. Each could be petty. Many Republicans found Truman cocky and hotheaded. Democrats considered Vandenberg vain and pretentious. Vandenberg did not applaud every foreign policy step Truman took. The senator found little to cheer in Truman's domestic policies. And yet through some of the most tumultuous years in American history, Truman and Vandenberg reached a series of accommodations that transformed America's place in the world. Without denying or ignoring their differences, they recognized a national interest in surmounting those differences wherever possible. Precisely because of their flaws and disagreements, they demonstrated that imperfect politicians with complex motives could collaborate in ways productive for the country.

This was the lesson from almost every major achievement during the age of bargaining, from the civil rights bills of 1957 and 1964, to the interstate highway system approved under Eisenhower, the Peace Corps passed under Kennedy, and the nuclear test ban treaty in 1963. This cooperation between the parties was never easy. Even to the participants it often seemed an unnatural act. But on regular occasions they overcame their suspicions and hostilities to reach reasonable agreements with broad appeal. Hesitation, conformity, and at times timidity all marred the age of bargaining. But at its best it encouraged—and even demanded—a level of constructive bipartisan cooperation that would well serve the nation again.

CHAPTER 4

THE AGE OF
TRANSITION

During the age of bargaining, presidents measured their progress
in Congress foot by foot, sometimes step-by-step, like generals
in the trench warfare of World War I. In the spring of 1965,
Lyndon Johnson was like a man who had been handed the keys to a tank.
In weeks he roared past obstacles that had stymied other presidents for
years. Every president since Truman had sought to provide federal aid to
education. Each one had been stalemated by intractable disputes over segregation in Southern schools and what sort of aid, if any, would flow to
parochial schools in the North. The Civil Rights Act of 1964, finally barring segregation, ended the first dispute, and Johnson's administration
negotiated an agreement between teachers' unions and Catholic groups
that resolved the second. "I want—and I intend—education to be the cor-
nerstone on which we build this administration's program and record,"
Johnson told Congress on January 11. Just over ten weeks later the House
of Representatives approved the Elementary and Secondary Education
Act. Only two weeks after that the Senate, the proud imperious Senate,
accepted the House bill word for word, as Johnson urged, so that the
two chambers would not need to hold a conference committee and then

approve the legislation again. On April 11, 1965, less than three months after his inaugural, Johnson stormed the citadel that had repelled Truman and Eisenhower and Kennedy, and signed into law the federal government's first widespread program to improve the performance of local schools.

Federal health insurance for the elderly had been a liberal priority for decades. It was the descendant of Harry Truman's failed push for universal health care in 1949. It had been on the short list of issues that John F. Kennedy asked Congress to address in the special session after his nomination in 1960. It had then become a centerpiece of Kennedy's domestic agenda as president, and the source of bitter frustration when he could not maneuver it past the conservative coalition in either the House or the Senate. Even Johnson failed to pass the program in 1964. But in the spring of 1965, the conservative coalition gave way. Medicare cleared the House on April 8 and the Senate on July 9. Johnson signed the bill into law on July 30, impulsively shifting the ceremony to Independence, Missouri, so Harry Truman could be at his side when he did.

On it went through that frenzied spring in Washington. On Capitol Hill it was as if a spigot had opened. Aid to the depressed hollows of Appalachia passed the Senate on February 1, and the House, replicating the Senate's extraordinary deference on aid to education, accepted the Senate's bill on March 3 without changing a word, so it could reach Johnson's desk more quickly. Legislation that committed the federal government to new steps to clean polluted rivers and streams passed the Senate eight days after Johnson's inaugural address, and the House exactly three months later; a bill authorizing the government to regulate the air pollution from cars and trucks followed in the Senate in May and the House in September. The monumental Voting Rights Act, which would revolutionize life in the South and politics across America by razing the barriers that had kept African Americans from the polls, passed the Senate in May and the House in July. The House approved Johnson's plan to create a cabinet-level Department of Housing and Urban Development in June, and the Senate concurred in August. The most consequential immigration reform in more than four decades, legislation that released the restrictive quotas imposed in the early 1920s and ignited the largest surge of immigration to America since the melting pot days at the turn of the twentieth century, roared through the House in August and the Senate in September. In a final flourish the Senate voted in June and the House three months later to establish the National Endowment for the Arts and the National Endowment for the Humanities.

This was more consequential domestic legislation in a single session of Congress than any president had achieved in an entire four-year term during the age of bargaining. Johnson's breakthrough marked the end of that era as a distinct historical period. In these initial years of his presidency Johnson governed in a style that harkened back to the disciplined party majorities in the era from McKinley through Franklin Roosevelt's first term. He could not sustain that level of control through his four years: Mounting discontent over Vietnam and racial unrest at home forced him on the defensive after 1966. (Johnson compressed the arc of Roosevelt's first two administrations into a single tumultuous term.) Nor would any of Johnson's successors until George W. Bush govern with the support of a congressional majority as cohesive as the one that coalesced during the first two years of the Great Society.

But after Johnson, the political system did not consistently revert to the divided loyalties and Rubik's Cube bipartisan negotiations of the age of bargaining. Instead, the period from 1964 through 1990—roughly from the Civil Rights Act to the balanced budget agreement signed by President George H. W. Bush—was an age of transition in Washington. On the surface political life in the capital oscillated between periods that resembled the age of bargaining and confrontations that foreshadowed the more partisan and polarized politics of our own time. But the underlying currents in American political life—structural changes in the allegiance of voters, the way organized interests advanced their agendas, and the rules that governed Congress—all swept away the conditions that encouraged the earlier era's more conciliatory style. Slowly but steadily the martial approach to politics that would dominate the early twenty-first century would come into focus.

DURING THE SPRING and summer of 1965, Johnson roared through the barriers that had constrained each of his predecessors through the age of bargaining. Johnson was relentless in urging action on his priorities, whose progress he followed on an elaborate chart that he wheeled into his meetings with the congressional leadership. On the telephone that spring, in the conversations with aides and legislators that he secretly recorded, Johnson does not sound like a man trying to assemble an intricate puzzle, the way presidents so often did over the previous quarter century. Gone was the plaintive president from the age of bargaining, searching for any thread of shared interest that might stitch together a fragile majority. Johnson that spring was expectant, insistent, insatiable. "For God's sakes, let's get it before Easter!" he told Wilbur Mills, when he called the Ways and Means Committee chairman to assess the progress of Medicare. "What the hell has been happening to your committee?" he demanded when he reached Adam Clayton Powell, the mercurial chairman of the House Labor and Education Committee, to discuss his aid-to-schools bill. At the moment Johnson asked that impatient question, only six weeks had passed since his inaugural address.

Like Woodrow Wilson, Johnson saw himself leading something like a British parliamentary government, where the responsibilities blurred between the executive and legislative branches. But Johnson was not as emotionally and intellectually rigid as Wilson. Throughout his congressional career Johnson had seen himself as an agent of consensus; encouraging consensus had been a central chord in his 1964 campaign message against his unapologetically ideological Republican opponent Barry Goldwater.* If Johnson expected much from Congress, he also provided it almost unprecedented input in the shaping of his agenda. Like Roosevelt at his best, Johnson drew ideas from eclectic sources and tried to invest as many others as possible in his causes. He demanded that his Cabinet officers consult regularly with the House and Senate members who held jurisdiction over their departments. Before Johnson would finalize a new legislative proposal, he insisted that his aides provide him a written statement that they had sounded out the key players in Congress. The night before he issued any major proposal Johnson invited the legislators likely to determine its

---

* Introducing a committee of prominent Republicans and business executives who endorsed him during the campaign, Johnson declared, "I did not, I do not, and I shall never seek to be a labor president, or a business president, a president for liberals, or a president for conservatives, a president for the North or a president for the South—but only President for all the people."

fate to a briefing over dinner at the White House. Johnson focused his consultations on Democrats, but did not exclude Republicans. He spoke often and easily with Everett Dirksen, the Senate Republican leader with whom he had crossed swords, and bent elbows, since the 1950s. Johnson's original conception of Medicare had focused solely on providing assistance to seniors for hospital and nursing home care. When House Republicans formulated an alternative that included help in paying routine doctor bills, Johnson quickly embraced it as his own.

This whirlwind of activity didn't eliminate all the structural obstacles that had inhibited decisive legislative action on so many issues since the late 1930s. The entrenched power of Southern Democrats dubious of most of Johnson's agenda remained a challenge. But these barriers, which had so often frustrated John F. Kennedy, were no longer impregnable; through that frantic spring, they fell before Johnson's indefatigable assault.

Partly, Johnson overwhelmed the Southern resistance because he had carried in so many Democrats from elsewhere in his 1964 landslide over Goldwater: The Democrats' overall margin (155 seats in the House, 36 in the Senate) was the largest advantage for either party since Roosevelt's day. But equally important was Johnson's success at attracting Republicans into his coalition. A majority of Senate Republicans voted with Johnson on aid for education, the Voting Rights Act, immigration reform, and the clean water legislation; just under half supported him on Medicare and aid to Appalachia. The clean air legislation attracted such broad Senate support, it passed on just a voice vote. Similarly, most House Republicans supported Johnson on clean air and clean water, the Voting Rights Act, and immigration; nearly half supported Medicare. Among Johnson's major bills, only the aid to education and Appalachian development plan drew widespread opposition from House Republicans. With the public Johnson's reach was just as broad: In the first ten months of 1965 his public approval rating in Gallup Polls never fell below 63 percent.

For a single spectacular season, Johnson had fused the best parts of the partisan era and the age of bargaining: He had passed a sweeping agenda in a manner that accommodated and respected enough interests to inspire a broad sense of inclusion, in the country and in Congress. But the moment did not last; the center did not hold. Johnson continued to accumulate legislative achievements in 1966, and even beyond. But Republican criticism of his Great Society as overly expensive and bureaucratic grew, especially after Democratic losses in the 1966 election. Race riots in Watts in 1965, and in Detroit and Newark in 1967, deepened frustration with "social engineering." Even more debilitating to Johnson's presidency was the growing alienation over the war in Vietnam. There was no easy path forward for Johnson on Vietnam, no simple solution for a war that he did not believe he could afford to lose but could not find a way to win. And yet he compounded his difficulties by abandoning the inclusive instincts that had served him so well on domestic issues. On Vietnam, Johnson closed himself off to all but sympathetic voices. He drove away those on his staff who grew skeptical of the war: McGeorge Bundy, George Ball, Bill Moyers, and ultimately Robert McNamara, the defense secretary who had led America into the morass. "Johnson was ravenous for information when things were going well," Doris Kearns Goodwin later wrote in her acute portrait, *Lyndon Johnson and the American Dream*. "Under siege, however, his operational style closed in and insulated him within the White House, where discussion was confined to those who offered no disagreement." Johnson didn't seal out only the dissenting voices on his staff. He built walls against all of those challenging his course. He told one aide that the liberal Senate critics of the war had been "taken in" by the Russians. He insisted, against all evidence, that Communists were directing and controlling the widespread antiwar movement that surged across college campuses and into the streets throughout his term. "Most of the protests are Communist-led," he told one friendly interviewer.

Johnson's increasingly insular response to Vietnam replicated the failures of other forceful presidents who could not find the means to meet new challenges. Like Woodrow Wilson with the League of Nations and Herbert Hoover during the Depression, Johnson lost the ability to hear or learn from, much less accommodate, those who disagreed with him. If anything, Johnson's failure was more profound, because he had displayed throughout his career far more ability than either Wilson or Hoover to do each of those things. Johnson in the Senate had been a great harmonizer, a conductor of men who sought to enhance his own power by braiding together diverse interests into powerful coalitions. By the end of his presidency he was instead accelerating the social and political conflicts that one historian accurately described as "the unraveling of America." The grand electoral and legislative coalition Johnson commanded in 1964 and 1965 fragmented to the point where Americans appeared united only by discontent over his leadership. His approval rating from the public, which never dropped below 60 percent in the first two years of his presidency, fell below 40 percent by the summer of 1967, and reached 50 percent only once more before he left office: in the days after his March 1968 announcement that he would not seek another term.

The collapse of Johnson's support shattered the New Deal coalition of Franklin Roosevelt that had provided Democrats a lasting advantage over Republicans, numerically if not ideologically, through the age of bargaining. Under Johnson, the enduring tensions between conservatives and liberals in that coalition finally reached a breaking point. Johnson's successes (particularly the civil rights laws that alienated white Southerners resistant to integration) ironically undermined the New Deal coalition as much as his failures (Vietnam and the excesses of the Great Society, such as the community action and model-cities programs that failed to reverse urban decay). In the backlash against both sides of Johnson's record, droves of white Southerners and socially conservative blue-collar Northerners began a generation-long migration toward the Republican Party that left both parties more ideologically homogenous and sharpened the differences between them—an evolution we'll explore more later. In partisan terms, the result was to reverse the usual advantage in the competition between the two parties for the presidency. From Franklin Roosevelt's election in 1932 through the end of Johnson's tenure in 1968, Democrats controlled the White House for twenty-eight of those thirty-six years. Republicans held the White House for twenty of the first twenty-four years after Johnson left office. Just as important for our purposes, the changes in the political system that began under Johnson would make it much more difficult for all of those successors, in both parties, to attract the remarkable bipartisan support he generated in the country and Congress during the first years of the Great Society. From its heights to its depths Johnson's presidency functioned as a hinge in history—a turn away from the muddled but consensual politics of the age of bargaining toward a new era defined by vivid ideological divisions and relentless partisan confrontation.

WHEN RICHARD M. NIXON won the White House in 1968 by defeating Hubert Humphrey, Johnson's vice president, old and new patterns continued to intermix. Like Eisenhower, Nixon had to cope with a divided government: Democrats controlled both houses of Congress throughout the nearly six years of his presidency. And like Eisenhower, Nixon's instinct was to bargain for peace on domestic issues to maximize his freedom of action on foreign policy. But Nixon faced a different Democratic Party than Eisenhower had confronted. Pressured by the social crusades that had sprouted through the 1960s—the environmental, consumer, civil rights, feminist, and antiwar movements—and energized by the arrival of waves of liberals after 1958, congressional Democrats challenged Nixon with a much more ambitious agenda than Lyndon Johnson and Sam Rayburn had pressed on Eisenhower in the 1950s. Nixon in turn was more receptive to federal activism than Eisenhower. The result was an outpouring of domestic legislation—probably the largest and most consequential example of bipartisan legislative cooperation in the twentieth century.

Nixon inverted Truman: He mostly cooperated with the opposition party on domestic policy and warred with it over foreign policy. Under Nixon, agreements between the two parties produced an extension of the Voting Rights Act, the end of the draft, the eighteen-year-old vote, the creation of Amtrak, revenue sharing for the states, the Consumer Product Safety Act, the law creating a federal agency to monitor workplace safety, and the initial funding for the federal "war" against cancer. The collaboration was especially fertile on environmental issues. Nixon was sometimes an unenthusiastic partner; he usually sought to soften congressional proposals he considered too onerous on business. But in the end he almost always provided his signature when Congress pushed further. In just five years Nixon and a bipartisan congressional coalition produced the Endangered Species Act, the law requiring the federal government to assess the environmental impacts of its major actions, the law mandating federal protection of the coastline, the 1970 amendments that significantly strengthened the Clean Air Act, an expansion of the National Park System, and the legislation that created the National Oceanic and Atmospheric Administration and the Environmental Protection Agency.

Like Kennedy, Nixon was pushed toward a deal-making presidency not only by the strength of the opposition party but by the diversity of his own. The cross pressures were evident in his appointments. His Cabinet included not only conservatives like Attorney General John Mitchell but Republicans to the left of many congressional Democrats, such as Housing and Urban Development secretary George Romney and Robert Finch, the secretary of Health and Human Services. The White House staff similarly was divided between conservatives such as Patrick Buchanan, Charles Colson, and Arthur Burns, and moderates such as John Ehrlichman, David Gergen, and even Democrat Daniel Patrick Moynihan, later a left-of-center senator from New York. Paranoia ultimately destroyed Nixon, but halfway through his first term, political schizophrenia seemed a more obvious diagnosis.

In Nixon's era the GOP demonstrated instincts just as mixed in Congress. Senate Republican moderates like Jacob Javits, Clifford Case, and Margaret Chase Smith, later reinforced by figures such as Charles Percy and Robert Packwood, constituted a formidable bloc. In 1970 more than one third of Senate Republicans voted with Democrats to terminate funding for Nixon's incursion into Cambodia; liberal Kentucky Republican John Sherman Cooper joined with Democrat Frank Church as the measure's principal sponsor. Seventeen Senate Republicans joined with Democrats in November 1969 to vote down F. Clement Haynsworth, Jr., a conservative Southerner Nixon tried to place on the Supreme Court.

The paradox of Nixon's presidency was that he pursued (mostly) conciliatory ends with (almost invariably) divisive means. He recognized that he had been elected in part because he had promised to heal the divisions, between white and black, young and old, and above all the supporters and opponents of the Vietnam War, that had torn apart the country during Johnson's final years. At a rally soon before the election a little girl in Deshler, Ohio, held a sign that expressed the anguish so many Americans felt at that polarized moment: It read "Bring Us Together." Nixon promised to take inspiration from the plea: "The one great objective" of the administration, he said, would be "to bring the American people together." His administration, he insisted the morning after his election, would be "open to new ideas . . . open to the critics."

In some ways, Nixon tried to fulfill that pledge. He offered to appoint Humphrey as UN ambassador and Henry Jackson, the hawkish Democratic senator from Washington, as his defense secretary. (Both declined.) On domestic issues Nixon usually understood the need to widen his support with sensible compromise. Late in his first term, and through his aborted second term, Nixon generally tilted toward more conservative positions. But in the early stages of his administration he accommodated the views of the opposition party as much as any twentieth-century president. Even all the legislation just noted doesn't exhaust the list. Nixon also proposed a guaranteed federal income for all lower-income Americans (drafted by Moynihan), an ambitious proposal to expand access to health insurance, the Philadelphia Plan (which laid the groundwork for federal efforts to encourage more hiring of minorities and women through affirmative action), and signed a 20 percent increase in Social Security benefits advanced by Wilbur Mills during his quixotic bid for the 1972 Democratic presidential nomination. Nixon reached plenty of domestic decisions that angered liberals: He vetoed a bill to provide free child care to the poor and touted a constitutional amendment to ban school busing. But he reached beyond the interests and priorities of his traditional Republican base on so many fronts that Patrick Buchanan, then working on Nixon's White House staff, understandably concluded in a 1971 memo, "The president is no longer a credible custodian of the conservative political tradition of the GOP."

But if Nixon's head drew him to reasonable compromise, his heart yearned for division and spite. As a matter of both personal instinct and political strategy, Nixon welcomed polarization. Nixon's overriding political aim was to peel away blue-collar voters in both the North and the South—what he called "the silent majority"—from the Democratic Party. From the outset of his presidency he dispatched his acid-tongued vice president, Spiro Agnew, to heighten cultural divisions by condemning the media, liberals, and opponents of the war. For the 1970 midterm election, he centered his election strategy on elevating sharp-edged "wedge" issues that he thought could divide the culturally conservative silent majority from a Democratic Party dominated in its leadership by social liberals. "Emphasize—anti-Crime—anti-Demonstrations—anti-Drug—anti-Obscenity," he wrote to his top aides in September 1970. "Get in touch with the mood of the country which is fed up with the Liberals. This stuff is dynamite politically." In his speeches he contrasted the "bums" on college campuses with the "kids" in Vietnam. As a near-term strategy, cultural polarization flopped: Republicans in 1970 lost seats in the House, lost governorships, and gained only two seats in the Senate, not nearly enough to threaten the solid Democratic majority. But Nixon's embrace of the wedge agenda ignited what would become one of the most powerful engines of polarization over the next quarter century: the rising prominence of issues that divided Americans along cultural rather than economic lines.

Nixon could be just as confrontational and vindictive in his dealings with Congress, but he didn't bear all the blame for the acrimony. His opponents in the Democratic Party encouraged his worst instincts by almost always failing to credit him when he moved in their direction; the typical liberal response to inventive ideas like his guaranteed annual income was that it did not go far enough. But Nixon, driven as much by personal demons as political needs, often seemed to throw rocks at the Capitol just to hear the glass break. Other presidents had occasionally claimed the right to refuse to spend funds Congress had authorized if they disagreed with the decision; Nixon (encouraged by a legal decision from Assistant Attorney General William Rehnquist) "impounded" as much as one fifth of all the discretionary spending Congress approved from 1969 through 1972. After the Senate rejected Haynsworth, his first Supreme Court nominee, Nixon told Harry Dent, his White House specialist on Southern politics, "I want you to go out this time and find a good federal judge further south and further to the right." The administration came back with G. Harrold Carswell, a Florida judge Nixon had appointed in 1969 to the Fifth Circuit Court of Appeals. Carswell, another Democrat turned Republican, was indeed more Southern and more conservative than Haynsworth, but alas, even less qualified. The nomination failed when 13 moderate Republican senators joined with 38 Democrats to reject it by

51–45, in April 1970. Only then did Nixon concede to the bipartisan majority by nominating Harry A. Blackmun, a circuit court judge recommended
by conservative chief justice Warren Burger.

Nixon's ends and means collided even more explosively, and tragically,
in Vietnam. Nixon's overall goal in Vietnam might have attracted broad
support from a country wearying of the war. His approach, building on
thinking in the Defense Department during Johnson's final months, was
to steadily withdraw American troops and shift more responsibility for the
country's defense to the South Vietnamese through a strategy he called
Vietnamization. But Nixon pursued what might have become a consensus
policy in the most inflammatory manner imaginable. He concluded that
the only way to disengage from the conflict with America's international
prestige intact was to first escalate it, often while trying to hide his actions
from the public. Hoping to disrupt North Vietnamese supply lines, he escalated bombing runs and covert raids into Laos. On the same rationale,
he conducted a secret bombing campaign in Cambodia, and in 1970
launched a full-scale invasion of that country, sparking an unprecedented
eruption of protest across America. (It was in that wave of protests that
four students were killed at Kent State.) He mined the North Vietnamese
harbor in May 1972 and unleashed a massive Christmas bombing across
the north when peace talks stalled later that year. At each step he met the
scorn of antiwar protesters and critics on Capitol Hill with scorn in return.
Nixon managed the unenviable and almost unimaginable feat of widening
America's divisions over the war even as he extricated the nation from it.

Nixon displayed his tendency toward isolation most powerfully through
his campaigns against his political opponents. Other presidents, almost
always to their detriment, had stopped listening to interests they considered hostile. Nixon went a long step further. He sought to mobilize the
government's vast resources against all those he viewed as his enemies.
Wiretaps, the White House plumbers, "enemies' lists," dirty tricks in the
1972 campaign: In all these ways Nixon gave physical expression to the
resentments against enemies real and imagined that had tormented
him throughout his political career. In the Watergate scandal, those
resentments finally consumed him. While there is little evidence that
Nixon authorized the break-in into the Democratic National Committee

headquarters at the Watergate complex on June 17, 1972, he sealed his fate by energetically enlisting in the failed attempt to cover it up.

Other presidents who had lost their capacity to speak to the entire nation—Taft in 1912, Wilson in 1920, Hoover in 1932—had been rejected, or seen their parties rejected, by the voters at the next election. Nixon didn't survive that long. Facing near certain impeachment by the House and conviction by the Senate, he resigned in August 1974. In a nod to the frequent bipartisanship of the previous generation, about one third of the Republicans on the House Judiciary Committee joined with Democrats in supporting two articles of impeachment, and senior Senate Republicans like Barry Goldwater helped precipitate the resignation by telling Nixon he could not avoid conviction in the upper chamber. No president had ever deliberately separated himself from more of America. And none ever paid a higher price for his insularity.

LIFTING THE LID

Lyndon Johnson and Richard Nixon presided over an era of politics painted in primary colors. Emotions ran high almost every day either man sat in the Oval Office. Both compiled gaudier records of legislative achievement than any president since Franklin Roosevelt's first term. And yet both, after promising to unite the country, left office with their support shattered and the nation angrier, more sullen, and more divided than when they arrived. It might have been unrealistic to expect any president (short of a Lincoln) to entirely tame the forces dividing America in the turbulent years of the 1960s and early 1970s. But Americans had a right to expect that their president would not deepen and widen those divisions, often as a matter of conscious political strategy. Johnson and Nixon, so different in so many ways, demonstrated again that while there is no single route to success for a president, the surest road to failure is to abandon the goal of speaking to, and for, all Americans. Like Taft, Wilson, and Hoover, Johnson and Nixon proved that no president can survive in a bunker.

During these tumultuous presidencies, the forces emerged that shaped the long transition from the age of bargaining to today's systemic, sustained partisanship. One of these forces slowed the change: the repeated decision of voters to divide control of government between the parties. During the age of bargaining, no matter which party held the White House or Congress, power had been divided in practice because of the differences within each party. After Johnson's presidency, voters consistently divided power between the parties in form as well. In the twenty-four years from 1968 through 1992, from Nixon's election through the defeat of George H. W. Bush, America provided one-party unified control of government only once—when Democrats held the House and Senate during Jimmy Carter's presidency. Otherwise, Americans partitioned power between Republican presidents in the White House and Democrats who controlled the House for all of those twenty-four years and the Senate for all but the first six years of Ronald Reagan's presidency.

This division of authority pressured the two sides to negotiate their disagreements, as they did frequently through the 1950s and early 1960s. To advance their agenda, Republican presidents had no choice but to attract at least some congressional Democrats. Congressional Democrats, except under Carter, could not pass their ideas without a signature from Republican presidents. Those imperatives, as we'll see, encouraged some significant bipartisan accomplishments under Ronald Reagan and George H. W. Bush.

But three other changes in the structure of American politics pushed Washington away from the conciliatory deal-making style of the previous two decades. One of these transformed the organized pressures on Congress from outside interest groups. The second restructured the rules and practices inside Congress. The third changed the nature of the politicians elected to Congress and the electoral incentives they faced in office. That third change, the great sorting out of American politics, was the most sweeping of the three, and had such profound implications, not only for Congress but also for the presidency, that it will be examined at length in its own chapter.

These three structural changes unfolded at different speeds. The great sorting out in the electorate moved like a glacier, transforming the landscape but only over a period of many years. The changes in congressional rules began in the 1970s, but their full effect was not apparent until two decades later. The first of these forces to leave a mark were the new interest groups pressing fresh issues on Washington. The moment when they emerged as a significant variable can be documented with unusual precision. It came on March 22, 1966, when James Roche, the president of General Motors, the company that symbolized the unchallenged industrial might of American business, admitted to a Senate subcommittee that the firm had sent detectives to snoop on a rail-thin, solitary, ascetic, and idiosyncratic lawyer named Ralph Nader. Nader, who had been working as a part-time consultant on auto safety to Daniel Patrick Moynihan at the Department of Labor, had established a modest name for himself the previous November when he published a muckraking manifesto called *Unsafe at Any Speed*. The book was a coruscating, exhaustively researched indictment of the auto industry for elevating style over safety in the design of its cars. But it attracted only modest attention in the press, and Nader didn't generate much more when he testified on his conclusions in February 1966 before a subcommittee of the Committee on Government Operations chaired by Abraham Ribicoff, a liberal Democratic senator from Connecticut. Only after Roche acknowledged the surveillance, and the subcommittee filled in the details (with tough questioning from Senator Robert Kennedy of New York, among others), did Nader explode into the public consciousness.

Nader's appearances before Ribicoff's subcommittee marked a new stage in a synergistic relationship between ambitious politicians and organized interests that sought to shape Washington's agenda. Ribicoff, an activist but pragmatic liberal, provided Nader a platform, and Nader provided Ribicoff a road map into a high-profile issue, as well as a magnet for press attention when GM acknowledged its gumshoe operation. Less than six months after Roche's confession, Lyndon Johnson signed the first law requiring the federal government to set automotive safety standards. The law imposed much tougher federal regulation than Johnson, much less the auto companies, preferred. But the combined effect of Nader's outside agitation, and the determined inside maneuvering of Democratic senators like Ribicoff and Warren G. Magnuson of Washington, rolled over both of them. Nothing quite like it had happened in years. It was as if Nader, Ribicoff, and their allies had demonstrated a new mathematical proof that challenged the accepted arithmetic of power in Washington.

The passage of the National Traffic and Motor Vehicle Safety Act of 1966 proved a landmark. It marked a shift in control over the terms and boundaries of political debate. After Nader's breakthrough, a panorama of other interest groups emerged, first on the left and then on the right; together they forced Washington to consider a much wider—and often more polarizing—range of issues than it had typically addressed in the first decades after World War II. The age of bargaining had been an insiders' age. Leaders like Rayburn and Johnson, to say nothing of Russell or Taft or Smith, expressed their power mostly in back rooms. The power to set Washington's agenda rested primarily with the leadership of the two parties themselves. *New York Times* reporter William S. White, in his book *Citadel*, the classic account of Senate life in the 1950s, correctly described the Senate as "indrawn and ingrown." The Senate, White declared, "walks apart, very often, from the country itself." The only outside voices that consistently penetrated into the back rooms during those years belonged to business: the oil and gas companies, the farm lobby, the American Medical Association. Organized labor functioned as something of a counterweight among Democrats. Civil rights groups demanded increasing attention through the early 1960s. But other activists promoting causes of left and right were usually no more than a muffled presence on the other side of the glass.

By all measures business enjoyed a preponderance of power among interest groups well into the 1960s. "Few issues appeared on the political agenda that threatened business prerogatives, and business exercised virtual power over the resolution of those few issues that did," concluded historian David Vogel in his definitive history of business influence in Washington. And business in those years did not seek a revolution in government policy. Much to the frustration of ideological conservatives at the *National Review*, the flagship magazine of the right, or in the Goldwater campaign, business leaders largely accepted the New Deal. Secure in their post–World War II dominance of the world economy, the largest companies had even reached something of a truce with organized labor. For most corporate executives the best news from Washington was no news: Their top priority was to prevent government from undertaking new initiatives that might threaten them with increased regulation, oversight, or taxes.

And in that they largely succeeded: Kennedy and Johnson signed into law half a dozen regulatory statutes through the mid-1960s on issues from clean water to cigarette labeling, but all were relatively weak. Although business's own lobbying efforts during these years were often unsophisticated and haphazard, industry faced such little organized resistance in Washington that most studies of power in the capital from the late 1940s through the early 1960s do not even mention citizen groups. During the age of bargaining Washington did not face big fights over the environment, government regulation, or the power of business simply because on most of these issues there was only one fighter in the ring.

Through the 1960s, that changed with incredible speed. It was as if a lid had been lifted off the capital. The causes and consequences of the decade's powerful social movements, the civil rights and antiwar crusades, and the turmoil on the campuses have inspired dozens of books and need not be debated again here. What's important for our purposes is that these movements unleashed an enormous wave of skepticism about authority in all forms, from the military to business to government.* That wave crashed into the streets, in sit-ins and teach-ins and the enormous civil rights and antiwar marches on Washington. But the same wave, less turbulently, also powered the largest reform campaign since the New Deal.

New groups dedicated to purifying government or curbing the power of business proliferated in nondescript office buildings across Washington. Between 1967 and 1971 five major new environmental organizations, including the Environmental Defense Fund, the Union of Concerned Scientists, and the Natural Resources Defense Council, opened their doors; all would become significant forces in the capital. John Gardner, Lyndon Johnson's secretary of Health, Education, and Welfare, took out full-page newspaper ads in 1970 seeking members for a "citizen's lobby" he called Common Cause; not much more than a year later, 230,000 people had signed up and the group was forcefully pushing a broad agenda of government reform. Nader transformed himself from gadfly into empire

---

* In 1964, the University of Michigan's National Election Study found that only 29 percent of Americans believed "government is pretty much run by a few big interests looking out for themselves," while 64 percent thought "that it is run for the benefit of all the people." By 1970, the percentage that believed government was in the pocket of big interests had soared to 50 percent, en route to 70 percent in 1980.

builder, constructing a "public interest conglomerate" that eventually included groups dedicated to everything from auto safety to monitoring the airlines, lobbying and investigating Congress, and challenging the pharmaceutical companies over drug safety.

The air seemed so charged with activism that launching a new group was like flying a kite in a lightning storm. In 1966, a group of feminists established the National Organization for Women; three years later they were joined by the National Association for the Repeal of Abortion Laws.* In 1974, a small group of activists dismayed by gun violence formed the National Council to Control Handguns. The list sprawled in every direction—clean air, clean water, the disabled, access to government information—rare was the cause so obscure that it could not inspire a "center," located somewhere between DuPont Circle and K Street in Northwest Washington, funded by direct-mail or foundation grants, and staffed with bright young men and women freshly minted with Ivy League degrees. Nor was the boom confined to new groups. Older organizations were reinvigorated. Membership in the Wilderness Society, the National Wildlife Federation, and the Audubon Society, three long-standing if often stodgy conservation groups, all doubled roughly between 1960 and 1970. Membership in the Sierra Club, the most venerable of all the environmental groups, increased more than fivefold.

The priorities and styles of these groups varied enormously. But in all their diversity the groups shared one quality: Each forced Washington to debate issues that rarely had been discussed during the age of bargaining. The new groups both pressured and empowered the congressional liberals who had felt marginalized during the heyday of Johnson and Rayburn and the conservative coalition. The outside and inside voices worked together in a reinforcing loop. Sometimes the groups leaned on legislators to promote their causes; sometimes legislators promoted their causes by courting the groups to adopt them. Whatever the initial tactic, the result was to propel a panorama of new issues onto the national agenda. During the 1970s Congress passed twenty-nine significant pieces of environmental

---

* The group changed its name to the National Abortion Rights Action League (NARAL) in 1973, when the Supreme Court established a constitutional right to abortion in the decision of *Roe v. Wade*.

legislation. A steady stream of consumer-related bills (tougher meat inspection, fair lending laws, community reinvestment requirements for banks) accompanied them. Social issues like abortion, the rights of homosexuals, and the status of women moved more prominently into political debate than ever before. By the 1980s gun control issues, which had flared briefly into the national consciousness after the assassinations of Robert F. Kennedy and Martin Luther King, Jr., in 1968, and then receded under fire from the potent National Rifle Association, began to push their way back onto the congressional agenda.

The debates during the age of bargaining often positioned Congress and the White House as a referee between contending business concerns. Many of the new issues placed them squarely in the crossfire between much more antagonistic interests—business and its critics, gun owners and supporters of gun control, the advocates and adversaries of the cultural changes that remade American family life during the 1960s. Finding an acceptable compromise on any of these issues was much more challenging than splitting the difference on a farm support bill or a depreciation schedule under Eisenhower and JFK. By itself, the changing nature of the debate encouraged more polarization and partisan conflict.

This surge of liberal organizing initially caught conservatives off guard. But they recovered in a countermobilization that ultimately exceeded the initial thrust from the left. The conservative response developed along three lines. One was a rejuvenation of business's presence in Washington. Business's privileged position in Washington during the 1950s and 1960s reflected more the weakness of its opposition than its own strength. As late as 1964, a *Harvard Business Review* survey found few business executives actively participating in politics. Two challenges shattered that complacency. The most visible was the rise of the environmental and consumer movements. The more subtle was a slowdown in domestic economic growth and an acceleration of the competition from foreign companies through the early 1970s. Each of these threats encouraged business leaders to press a more proactive agenda than they had during the age of bargaining, a blueprint centered on lower taxes, less regulation, and opposition to union organizing. Lewis F. Powell, Jr., a prominent Virginia attorney and former president of the American Bar Association, crystallized the case for a reinvigorated business presence in Washington in an extraordinary 1971 call to arms. Shortly before Richard Nixon nominated him to the Supreme Court, Powell wrote an epic memo to the education committee of the U.S. Chamber of Commerce urging business to mount a widespread political and intellectual counteroffensive against its critics in the proliferating "public interest" and environmental movements. "Business," Powell counseled, "must learn the lesson . . . that political power is necessary; that such power must be assiduously cultivated; and that when necessary, it must be used aggressively and with determination—without embarrassment and without the reluctance which has been so characteristic of American business."

Business responded in force. The number of corporations and trade associations with offices or lobbyists in the capital exploded. So did the number of political action committees formed by business to contribute money to campaigns. Perhaps the most significant change was the increased effort to organize broad-based business coalitions that joined interests from across industry and geographic lines. Most attention focused on the 1972 opening of the Business Roundtable, an elite group composed of the chief executive officers of the nation's largest companies. But even more significant was the steady growth of the associations that primarily represented small business, which almost always fought the regulatory agenda of the new liberal groups more fiercely than their larger counterparts. The National Federation of Independent Business, which would become the most ardent of all, doubled its membership during the 1970s. Likewise, the U.S. Chamber of Commerce doubled its membership between 1967 and 1974, and then more than doubled it again by 1980.

The business groups mostly confined their efforts to battles over economic and regulatory issues, but more ideological conservatives, focused heavily on social issues, followed quickly behind them. This was a powerful new development. Through the mid-1960s grassroots conservative organizing primarily had been the province of fringe, furtive, conspiracy-oriented groups convinced that Communists had infiltrated the highest rungs of the American government; organizations like the secretive John Birch Society (which at various points saw both Harry Truman and Dwight Eisenhower as tools of a communist conspiracy) probably did less to expand than to narrow conservatism's appeal.

That changed in the 1970s with the arrival of the groups that became known as "the New Right." Former Democrat Jesse Helms, elected as a Republican senator from North Carolina in 1972, used polarizing direct-mail appeals to build his Congressional Club into the first true nationwide grassroots conservative fund-raising machine. Antiabortion activists organized the National Right to Life Committee, which would prove one of the most enduring institutions on the right, at a meeting in Detroit a few months after the Supreme Court legalized abortion in January 1973. Phyllis Schlafly, a longtime toiler in conservative causes, formed the Eagle Forum two years later to oppose the Equal Rights Amendment prized by feminists. The National Conservative Political Action Committee (NCPAC), building on Helms's breakthrough, raised millions of dollars through direct-mail campaigns for searing television advertising blitzes against Democratic senators that began in 1978. The next year Jerry Falwell, a Baptist minister from Lynchburg, Virginia, who had started his ministry almost a quarter century earlier in an unused soda-bottling plant, launched his Moral Majority.

Down a third track, conservatives built a new intellectual architecture. Money from business and conservative foundations poured into think tanks, magazines, and university research centers. Inside Washington the effort focused on building edgier counterparts to the Brookings Institution, the pioneering think tank that analyzed public policy from a mildly left-of-center perspective. When the public interest movement erupted, the sole established Washington think tank with a conservative bent was the American Enterprise Institute. AEI had been a voice of business-oriented conservatism since 1943 (when it was known as the American Enterprise Association). AEI caught the quickening breeze and grew rapidly as an unbending opponent of the new federal regulation promoted by the consumer and environmental groups.

Even more significant was the arrival of the Heritage Foundation, which would become the most important think tank on the right. The idea for the Heritage Foundation came from Paul Weyrich and Edwin J. Feulner, two aides to Republicans on Capitol Hill, who lamented the shortage of attractive policy proposals available to right-leaning politicians. Weyrich, a former newspaper reporter and radio newscaster from

Racine, Wisconsin, took his inspiration from the new groups proliferating on the left. A turning point for Weyrich came when his boss, Colorado Republican senator Gordon Allot, who was seen as a moderate on racial issues, was invited to a coalition meeting of civil rights groups in 1969. Weyrich, who was working as Allot's press secretary, attended in his place and sat wide-eyed in the back of the room as liberal lobbyists, political operatives, think-tank scholars, and columnists divvied up responsibilities for advancing a fair housing law. One talked about organizing protests; another about filing a lawsuit; a third about advancing the release of a study documenting the problem; a fourth about timing a sympathetic newspaper column. A Russian general given a tour of NORAD would not have been more mesmerized. "Here before my eyes was the whole panoply laid out," Weyrich recalled. "I had seen the effectiveness, but I didn't know the mechanics." Weyrich left the room a few hours later with a new cause. "I said, 'Now I understand how this works,'" he remembered, "and I became maniacal in my determination to see to it that we [on the right] had a similar setup."

From that day forward Weyrich became the most energetic institution-builder in the New Right. He founded a political action committee called the Committee for the Survival of a Free Congress that supported conservative candidates (including a young history professor named Newt Gingrich) and another group called Coalitions for America to network the conservative organizations sprouting across Washington. He launched efforts to train young activists (modeled, he said, on the political training the AFL-CIO provided to union members). He played a central role in encouraging the political organization of the evangelical Christian ministers growing more active through the 1970s. (It was Weyrich, at a meeting with Falwell, who coined the term "moral majority.") Most important, he worked with Feulner to launch the Heritage Foundation.

Heritage opened its doors in 1973 with seed money from brewing magnate Joseph Coors, who had been inspired by Powell's memo and disillusioned by Nixon's accommodations with the left. Heritage approached the political debate without the tweedy pretensions that often characterized Brookings and AEI. Heritage sought to provide conservatives on Capitol Hill with sword and shield—policy proposals they could promote and crisp critiques of the ideas promoted by Democrats. When Reagan took office in 1981, Heritage presented him with a 1,093-page volume of policy recommendations called *Mandate for Leadership* that probably functioned as much as a doorstop as a road map, but nonetheless marked the flowering of the conservative intellectual network assembled over the previous decade. Heritage rumbled into the political debate like some new form of intellectual assembly line. It provided Republicans not only a steady source of new ideas, but a pool of conservative intellectuals they could hire to help implement them. And it worked relentlessly to tilt the terms of debate toward the right, systematically building support for cutting-edge conservative ideas—missile defense, the introduction of private investment accounts to Social Security, the use of health savings accounts to provide access to medical care—that almost always sharpened the contrast and the conflict with Democrats.

Liberals lacked the funding to match the scale of the new conservative groups and were somewhat complacent even in trying. But as the conservatives organized across so many fronts, a second generation of liberal activists eventually mobilized to oppose them, largely on social and cultural issues. A group initially called the Human Rights Campaign Fund organized in 1980 to defend politicians who supported gay rights against NCPAC and the Moral Majority. One year later Hollywood producer Norman Lear, the father of *All in the Family* and *Maude*, formed People for the American Way to combat the influence of the social conservatives. Reinforcements arrived on other fronts too. During the Reagan years new liberal think tanks—the Center on Budget and Policy Priorities, the Economic Policy Institute—opened to counter the growing drumbeat from Heritage, AEI, and their followers for tax cuts, deregulation, and spending reductions.

Not all of these organizations thrived or even survived. The Moral Majority (whose critics derided it as neither) closed its doors in 1989, a victim of Falwell's intemperate tongue and chaotic approach to management. NCPAC, once the most fearsome of all the New Right groups, flamed out even earlier, consumed by debts for its direct-mail prospecting. But new groups always stepped forward to replace them. After a failed bid for the Republican presidential nomination, televangelist Marion G. (Pat)

Robertson unveiled his Christian Coalition, with the cherubic but unsentimental young conservative operative Ralph Reed at the helm. (When the Christian Coalition itself foundered in the late 1990s, other social conservative groups like James Dobson's Focus on the Family supplanted them.) Grover G. Norquist, another young conservative believer, developed a taste for theatrical politics and uncompromising ideology with Reed in the College Republicans in the early 1980s, and put out his own shingle in 1985 when he formed Americans for Tax Reform.

Important differences separated the liberal and conservative interest groups that grew after the 1960s. The liberal groups were more focused on discrete issues, like abortion rights, or auto safety, or the environment; by comparison more of the conservative institutions sought to tilt policy to the right across a broad spectrum of issues. The conservatives also placed a higher priority than liberals on building institutions that offered young people training in conservative politics, and then pathways to a career in the cause. And Republicans generally seemed more successful than Democrats at encouraging the groups on their side to sublimate their inevitable disagreements to the larger cause of building a reliable right-of-center political majority. These contrasts in strategy and approach, compounded over time, eventually led to widespread, even inordinate, concern among liberals that conservatives had built a more effective "infrastructure" to support their pursuit of power.

But more important than the differences between the two sides was their common influence on the tone and content of political debate. Beginning in the 1960s these proliferating, and feuding, groups on left and right tore at the foundations of the age of bargaining from several distinct angles. The explosion of interest groups focused the voice of the core activists on each side—the true believers whom the political professionals would increasingly describe as "the base." The ideas that these groups promoted, the way they reacted to ideas from politicians, the questionnaires they distributed to presidential contenders, the grades they provided legislators on their ubiquitous "scorecards" all provided a new tangibility, a new precision, to demands that the parties line up behind a common ideological agenda. The way politicians in each party related to these groups provided an easy yardstick for the press and activists to determine where everyone stood on the ideological spectrum. To a considerable extent the groups seized from the elected officials themselves the power to define for many Americans what constituted a good Republican or a good Democrat.

They also wrestled with elected officials for control of the national agenda. The leaders of the two parties, and especially the president, retained a dominant role in determining which issues the country debated and how it viewed the available options. But politicians no longer initiated all the meaningful disputes. Increasingly after the mid-1960s they were forced to take sides in arguments sparked mostly by others. Weyrich spoke for many of the emerging activists on both sides when he said that the constellation of groups he founded was intended less to support the agenda of elected officials than to "change the agenda" they considered. The competing efforts from NARAL and the National Right to Life Committee compelled every candidate for federal office to articulate a position on abortion, an issue that might never have crossed the mind of Russell or Rayburn when they sipped their bourbon at the end of a long day debating defense appropriations or offshore oil leasing. Most Republicans in Washington and the business community were reluctant to seriously resist when President Jimmy Carter signed the treaties in 1977 surrendering American control of the Panama Canal; but a rebellion among the New Right grassroots groups (amplified by Ronald Reagan, methodically moving toward capturing the 1980 GOP presidential nomination) pressured most Senate Republicans to vote against the accords nonetheless. The supply-side tax-cutting agenda that Reagan embraced in his 1980 presidential campaign, and then drove through Congress in 1981, represented a convergence of pressure from above and below. Thinkers and publicists in the new conservative network like economist Arthur Laffer, journalist Jude Wanniski, and Representative Jack F. Kemp, the former football star from Buffalo now holding a Republican seat, spent years promoting the ideas before Reagan endorsed them. But just as important may have been the passage of California's Proposition 13 in June 1978, which demonstrated the power of a tax-cutting message in an era of economic strain. And Proposition 13, which slashed California property taxes, emerged not from a high-powered think tank but rather from the efforts of a small-time inventor and former home appliance manufacturer named Howard Jarvis with a history of commitment to obscure conservative causes. When Jarvis hit his political equivalent of a hole-in-one after a lifetime of mulligans, he turned heads all the way to the Capitol.

This was a very different political world than Washington had known twenty or even ten years earlier. In some respects it was an undeniable improvement. The age of bargaining had denied meaningful influence to many voices, in both parties; it offered a consensus built partly on exclusion. The explosion of interest groups and think tanks after the mid-1960s expanded the conversation. It compelled Washington to acknowledge a broader range of problems than it had typically discussed earlier, and to consider a wider range of viewpoints as it tried to resolve them. With the emergence of all of these organized interests, one of the great sources of power in any democracy—the power to set the nation's agenda—was decentralized. The doors to Washington's back rooms might not have been kicked down, but they were undeniably pried open. Ordinary citizens, banding together in groups of left or right, could press their concerns on the capital far more effectively than their parents or grandparents.

But if the interest-group expansion after the 1960s increased access, it also institutionalized conflict. Most of the new groups, on both sides, officially portrayed themselves as nonpartisan, and many tried to function that way. But in Washington almost all of them drew most of their support from one of the two major parties: No one had any doubt which party was more sympathetic to the Sierra Club or the National Right to Life Committee. In effect, the interest groups and think tanks and fund-raising committees that exploded after the late 1960s crystallized the most ardent elements in each party—the ideological vanguard on each side—into an enduring, tangible force, advancing relentlessly an agenda that guaranteed collisions with the other ardent interests mobilizing in the capital.

Some groups were more sympathetic to compromise than others (small-business lobbies, for instance, considered the corporate chieftains at the Business Roundtable too quick to concede ground to liberals). But the dominant ethos of the new groups was to resist compromise and often to criticize those in the White House or on Capitol Hill who pursued it. The new groups, as a rule, did not gain members, raise money, and increase their visibility by conceding that their opponents might have a reasonable point. Almost all of them saw their role as upholding principle against a political system too prone toward concessions.

No matter how committed a public official was to their cause, the commitment almost never matched the groups' own sense of what could be achieved with yet more dedication and principle. They could never be satisfied, because each gain inspired them to set a new, more demanding goal. They often bargained to reach a legislative settlement, but each agreement represented only a truce before the next confrontation. Almost all of the groups would deal when necessary. But almost all of them preferred to fight. And year after year, as they filed onto the battlefield in Washington, they pressured the parties they principally aligned with to fight as well. After the interest-group upheaval that began in the 1960s, Washington was more open, fluid, and accessible. But it was also much more polarized.

THE RISE OF interest groups challenged the traditions of the age of bargaining from the outside. Changes in Congress undermined those traditions from within.

The most gradual change came in the routines of daily life. The demands on legislators multiplied. No longer did the speaker of the House have time for an afternoon walk. As airplane travel became more common and inexpensive, pressure grew on legislators to travel home on weekends. Senators and House members were also forced to devote more time to chasing checks from campaign contributors. In 1974, the average House incumbent spent just $56,539 on his or her race; by 1984, the figure was almost five times that. Senators likewise increased their average campaign spending nearly fivefold over that single decade. The workload inside Washington grew as the number of subcommittees proliferated through the 1970s, increasing the number of issues each member needed to master. All these changes left less time for legislators to build personal relationships with colleagues in their own party, much less those from the opposition party. The older pattern of friendships that crossed party lines didn't end overnight; Tip O'Neill, the Democratic speaker from 1977 through 1986, had a close relationship with Bob Michel, the Republican leader during the same period. But such genuine personal connections became the exception. Warren Rudman, an independent-minded Republican elected to the Senate from New Hampshire in 1980, captured the new reality when he told a reporter a few years after his arrival, "I don't socialize at all. My friends are the people I left in New Hampshire. I don't see much socializing among the others either."

It's easy to overstate the role that social relationships played in greasing the deal making common during the age of bargaining; the principal reason leaders in both parties negotiated so much was that the era's diffusion of power demanded it. But personal relationships that crossed ideological lines had always been a barrier against all-out war between the parties in Congress. And as the number of cross-party friendships withered, that barrier crumbled. John Breaux, a smooth Louisiana Democrat with a zest for both cutting deals and enjoying life, watched the change unfold over a career that began with his first election to the House in 1972 and ended after three Senate terms in 2004.

"Bob Michel was a middle America, Peoria, Illinois, Republican and Tip O'Neill was an FDR-liberal, Cambridge, Massachusetts, Democrat. They didn't agree with each other philosophically on almost any issue. [But] they traveled together, they played golf together, they bet on sporting events, they went to sporting events together, they drank in the evening together, and they spoke more in one day than the current leaders speak in a year," Breaux recalled. "Now instead of having these conversations, the leaders write letters to each other, very pointed letters about whatever has happened. I've always said you can't run a country, a business, an institution unless the people in charge of running it have a dialogue and discourse between each other."

Increased media attention accelerated the change in congressional life. Capitol Hill never operated in obscurity, but through the first post–World War II decades it still faced a modest level of media scrutiny that preserved great leeway for quiet negotiation. William White had found the essence of the Senate during the 1950s in closed rooms: "[I]n so many of its critical moments, it is *smallness* that characterizes the Institution: a handful of quiet, intent men in a room now shut away from all turmoil in making a decision." Shuman, the keen aide to Senator Paul Douglas, remembered that the Capitol press in those years "was not very critical of people. They didn't report the drunks or the crooks." Even as late as the 1970s, influential Democratic representative Tony Coelho thought "nobody paid any attention" to the House. That changed as press attention intensified through the 1960s and 1970s. More investigative reporting, symbolized by the *Washington Post*'s digging into the Watergate scandal in 1972, helped dispel the clubby atmosphere that earlier discouraged tough questioning of congressional leaders or much scrutiny into their ethics.

Television opened the curtains further by allowing the public to directly view the action in Washington. Television first aimed its lights at Capitol Hill during the 1950s, with occasional coverage of flashy Senate hearings, like Tennessee senator Estes Kefauver's inquiry into organized crime or the confrontations between Joe McCarthy and the Army. In the 1960s television's presence in Washington deepened after the evening network newscast expanded from fifteen minutes to a half hour (starting with Walter Cronkite's CBS broadcast on Labor Day 1963); the dramatic daily reports on the Southern filibuster against the Civil Rights Act in 1964 from CBS correspondent Roger Mudd marked television's arrival as a permanent, institutional force in the life of Congress. In 1980, Cable News Network inaugurated the twenty-four-hour news cycle. C-SPAN opened another new window on the Capitol with live coverage of the House of Representatives beginning in 1979 and the Senate seven years later.

With congressional debate now routinely visible to the public through C-SPAN, and available to all other news programs, the parties changed the way they viewed their encounters on the House and Senate floor. The audience for floor debates changed from the members of the body itself to the public at large. And that changed the nature of the debate, from detailed arguments meant to persuade other legislators to sharper thrusts meant to move the public. Before television "the House of Representatives was a backwater; nobody knew what was happening in the House unless you were some person at home who just read the *Congressional Record* every day," recalled Gephardt, the Missouri Democratic representative, who was first elected in 1976 and rose to become the House Democratic leader before retiring after 2004. After television, he said, "the rhetoric on the floor became much more sharp and much more partisan, and much more [oriented toward] message making."

The increased attention also transformed the nature of leadership and power on Capitol Hill. During the age of bargaining the most effective leaders had been those who could build a consensus for legislation with a tap on the shoulder, or a gentle word to their colleagues, almost always out of public view. Beginning in the 1960s the parties increasingly expected their congressional leaders to shape public opinion through the media. The requirements of that new responsibility conflicted directly with the imperatives of the old. The deal-making era encouraged party leaders to minimize sharp public pronouncements to maximize their flexibility to craft private deals. The new era pressured them to deliver strong partisan messages that helped define the party to the public. The old system focused on passing legislation from the inside out, by building a consensus among key legislators. The new system increasingly assumed that the most effective way to pass legislation was from the outside in, by mobilizing opinion among the voters. The new system didn't preclude compromise on Capitol Hill. But it meant that the parties almost always preceded any agreement by first articulating positions that highlighted their philosophical disagreements with the other side. The age of bargaining, with its complex cross-party alliances, only rarely sent voters a clear cue of partisan conflict. The new system broadcast that signal unendingly.

The first signs of this change were evident as early as 1961 when the Republican leaders Everett Dirksen and Charles Halleck inaugurated a series of folksy weekly televised press conferences (which became known as the "Ev and Charlie Show") to make the Republican case against Kennedy and Johnson. But the new system, ironically, hardened into place during the decade Thomas "Tip" O'Neill ran the House as speaker. A shambling, white-haired bear of a man who held the same Cambridge-area seat that once sent John F. Kennedy to Congress, O'Neill was a throwback in style (he preferred back rooms to bright lights) and philosophy (his political thinking had never advanced much beyond a New Deal–era ward heeler's belief in government as a protector of the little guy). Like Rayburn, O'Neill's conception of the speaker's job initially focused inward, on organizing the House and managing his caucus. But he was forced out of that posture, first when Republicans used him as a symbol of a doddering Democratic Party (O'Neill, charged one House Republican backbencher, was "big, fat, and out of control—just like the federal government"), and later when Reagan's appeals to the public through television peeled away votes from House Democrats O'Neill thought would oppose the new president's tax and budget plans. The younger Democrats elected to the House in the 1970s had been the first generation to use television commercials extensively in their campaigns, and they steadily agitated for their leadership to exploit the medium more aggressively. "There was dissent or unrest with the younger people in my group coming in, because we were now the first age of television," Gephardt remembered. "We all came knowing the power of television, knowing the power of having messaging on television and believing that our leaders had to carry a message. So from that point on, the leadership in Congress assumed more of a loyal opposition [role], or just an opposition persona in the country."

O'Neill had no choice but to shift his focus outward, toward lobbying the public rather than concentrating solely on his members. Aides polished, preened, and buffed him, and sent O'Neill on television to become the face of the Democratic opposition against Reagan in a way Rayburn and Johnson had never done under Eisenhower. Ever since, congressional leaders from the party out of the White House have followed O'Neill into that role. Jim Wright, the florid Texas Democrat who succeeded O'Neill in 1987, advanced the transformation to the next level by preparing a detailed list of Democratic legislative priorities that he framed as the party's alternative to President Reagan's agenda. After Republicans seized both chambers in 1994, the new GOP speaker, Newt Gingrich, raised the bar again, presenting himself almost as a prime minister who would drive the domestic agenda, while a largely ceremonial President Clinton conducted foreign affairs and signed the legislation Gingrich's majority sent him.

Breaux shrewdly summarized how all these changes encouraged greater partisanship in Congress by attaching the institution more closely to the broader interests that gathered in each party. "What has happened over those years to a large extent is the Congress has become players on the team," Breaux noted. "The party strategists, the public relations firms, the party structure . . . provide polling information and strategy and ideas to strengthen their team, and the other side is doing the same thing. You've got this culmination of the outside interests . . . trying to coach their team into taking positions to defeat the other team. . . . The people who run the party structures have candidates who pay them to win elections, so they are constantly saying to [Members of Congress] 'you've got to do this, you've got to do that' [to improve the party's chances of winning]. I've had people in caucuses say, 'This is a Republican proposal, how do we find something wrong with it?' instead of saying, 'How do we try to nail it into something that we can both agree to?' "

Changes in Congress's internal rules further eroded the traditions from the age of bargaining. Since the late 1940s liberals had pushed for reforms they believed would undermine conservative power and allow the majority of Democrats to impose their priorities on the Congress. Through the mid-1970s the reformers achieved many of their goals. In 1975, House liberals finally broke the independent power of the Rules Committee that Smith had used to torment Kennedy, by empowering the speaker to unilaterally appoint its Democratic members without utilizing the usual party procedures for filling vacancies. Reformers also provided the House leadership with more authority to determine who would fill vacancies on all other committees. That same year the Senate slightly curbed the power of the filibuster by reducing from sixty-seven to sixty the number of votes required to end one.

The most important change undermined the power of seniority, an institution so pervasive and entrenched on Capitol Hill that White in the 1950s had described it as "an ineluctable and irresistible force." The reliance on seniority to allocate committee chairmanships had been central to the tangled politics of the age of bargaining, because it protected the members on each side who habitually supported the other. Through the early 1960s liberals made no tangible progress in their campaign to curb seniority. But they maintained their pressure through the rest of the decade, and as liberal strength increased in Congress they enjoyed some small successes. In 1965, the House Democratic caucus stripped two Southern Democrats of their seniority for supporting Goldwater over Johnson in 1964; in 1969, another Southerner suffered the same punishment for backing George Wallace over Hubert Humphrey the previous year.

In 1971 and 1973, House liberals pushed through rules changes that eroded the power of seniority by allowing critics who demonstrated enough support in the Democratic caucus to force votes on individual committee chairs. With their numbers swelled by the huge class of seventy-five Democratic "Watergate babies" elected in 1974, and support from the proliferating new liberal and public interest groups, the critics finally dethroned seniority in 1975. House Democrats agreed to require a secret caucus vote to select all committee chairmen. The critics immediately used the power to oust two elderly and conservative Southerners—Agriculture Committee chairman W. R. Poage of Texas and Armed Services Committee chairman Edward Hebert of Louisiana; age, not ideology, drove the vote to remove a third Southerner, the maverick Texas populist Wright Patman, from control of the Banking Committee. Henry Reuss, the liberal Wisconsin Democrat elevated over two other higher-ranking Banking Committee members to replace Patman, captured the sense of upheaval when he told a reporter, "From now on, the sword of Damocles will be hanging over every chairman."

In fact, the revolution unfolded more subtly and gradually. Senate Democrats and Republicans in both chambers eventually adopted similar rules ending the formal deference to seniority. But in practice, both parties used the new power rarely until the Republican takeover in the 1990s. When House liberals, supported by Nader and other outside groups, sought to depose Mississippi conservative Jamie Whitten as Appropriations Committee chairman in 1979, O'Neill helped him repel the assault. O'Neill's explanation reflected the durability of the old attitudes even amid the new rules. "A party support record," he insisted, "is no reason to run a man down." The House Democrats didn't oust another committee chairman until 1985, when eighty-year-old representative Melvin Price of Illinois was deposed from the leadership of the Armed Services Committee mostly because of his age. (Even then, Tony Coelho, a canny Democratic representative who helped to orchestrate the purge, had difficulty finding another committee member willing to buck seniority by seeking the job.) Price's successor, the brilliant but mercurial Wisconsin Democrat Les Aspin, was nearly removed the following year for supporting Reagan too often on national security votes. Later in the decade Democrats removed two other chairmen of secondary committees who many believed had grown ineffective with age.

Yet it did not take many examples to make the point. Political scientists studying House Democrats found that committee chairmen (as well as the other senior members closest in line for vacant chairmanships) voted with their party much more often by the early 1980s than in the early 1970s; even Whitten moved much closer to the Democratic mainstream after his near-death experience in 1979. Under the new system, with no guarantees of advancement, junior members felt heightened pressure too. By the late 1970s the Democratic leaders who assigned House Democrats to vacant committee seats kept track of the applicants' party loyalty scores on a blackboard in their room during the deliberations.

Even after the fall of seniority, party loyalty was never the sole factor that determined advancement in Congress; regional balancing and personal relationships also governed who moved ahead. But the move away from seniority marked a crossroads on the path from the age of bargaining to the more partisan era that followed. John Kennedy, frustrated by the obduracy of the conservative Southern Democrats, had lamented, "There's nothing that can be done about a man from a safe district. He'll vote the way he wants to." After seniority fell, no one in Congress was entirely immune from party discipline. Under the new rules, everyone was judged every day on how often they voted with their party, how much money they raised for their colleagues, and how reliably they stood with their "team" in rhetorical firefights against the other side. John Feehery saw the impact of the change when he served as a senior aide to Bob Michel, Tom DeLay, and then House speaker Dennis J. Hastert, from 1989 through 2005. "The seniority system," Feehery said, "was basically replaced with a merit system."

That shift from seniority to merit provided not only the congressional leadership but the ideological majority in each party much greater leverage to demand conformity from those in their caucus most inclined to support and deal with the other side. Only after Republicans took control of Congress in 1994—and imposed another set of reforms that further undermined seniority—would the full potential of these changes be felt. But the fall of seniority reinforced all the other upheavals in the political landscape from the 1960s and 1970s—the rise of the interest groups of left and right, the ideological sorting out of the electorate, the growing importance of television and the fading of cross-party friendships on Capitol Hill—that destabilized the age of bargaining. The replacement for that system wasn't yet visible in the 1970s; indeed it wouldn't fully coalesce for nearly another two decades. But stone by stone the foundation was being laid for an alternative political competition that would be characterized by more cohesion within the parties and more conflict between them. When seniority fell, the era of hyperpartisanship moved a long step closer.

FROM CARTER TO REAGAN: THE OLD ORDER CRUMBLES

That wasn't apparent at first. Most commentators, in fact, initially believed the internal rules changes in the 1970s had diminished party discipline and weakened the leadership on Capitol Hill. One reason was that other rule changes simultaneously multiplied the number of subcommittees in Congress and guaranteed them more independence from the full-committee chairmen. That reform tended to fragment power by providing so many junior members a platform to advance their own causes. Initially the decentralizing impact of those changes seemed to overshadow the opportunity that the end of seniority provided for congressional leaders to exert more centralized control over their members.

The larger reason commentators initially missed the implication of seniority's fall is that Jimmy Carter and the congressional Democratic leadership failed to effectively utilize the new tools after his election in 1976. A Southerner and evangelical Christian who supported civil rights and took liberal positions on most social issues, Carter offered himself as a unifying figure after the trauma of Watergate and the ferocious cultural and racial disputes of the previous decade. But as president he could not set a course that won him stable support from any source, in the Congress or the country. Carter governed with the benefit of substantial Democratic majorities in the House and Senate. But the party still could not overcome persistent ideological and regional differences that frustrated his legislative agenda on issues from energy to health care to tax reform to the federal budget. With a centrist, eclectic, and often nonideological approach that stressed fiscal discipline and management reform, Carter might have assembled legislative coalitions with moderate Republicans. But he failed to seize that opportunity consistently. Instead he persisted in a failed marriage with Democratic congressional leaders that embittered both partners. Capitol Hill Democrats accused the White House of ignorance and arrogance; the White House considered many of them parochial and hidebound. Each side could justify its portrait.

Compounding Carter's problems was the growing clout of the new conservative network that had emerged through the 1970s. The revivified business lobby soundly defeated the administration and its public interest and union allies in legislative showdowns over a federal consumer protection agency and labor law reform. The uprising from grassroots conservatives made passage of the Panama Canal treaty Carter negotiated an ordeal. The Committee on the Present Danger, a hawkish foreign policy group centered on neoconservative former Democrats, maintained an effective drumbeat against Carter's efforts to negotiate new arms control agreements with the Soviet Union. All of this narrowed Carter's support. Yet the escalating attacks from the right failed to quell the differences among Democrats. Through four painful years, Carter struggled to hold together his party's liberals and conservatives, and succeeded only in alienating both. Inflation, high interest rates, gas lines, and the inability to rescue the American hostages in Iran each deepened a debilitating image of weakness. Carter did not so much polarize the country as unite it against him: After he narrowly survived a primary challenge from the left mounted by Senator Edward M. Kennedy of Massachusetts, Carter's support collapsed from all directions in the general election. Not only conservatives but moderates abandoned him for Ronald Reagan; liberals defected in substantial numbers to independent candidate John Anderson, a moderate Republican who bolted the GOP after losing the party's presidential nomination to Reagan that spring.*

---

* According to exit polls, from 1976 to 1980 Carter's vote actually declined more among liberals (11 percentage points) than among moderates (9 percentage points) or conservatives (6 percentage points).

By the end, the question looming over Carter's presidency wasn't whether the nation could be unified; it was whether it could be governed at all. Reagan decisively answered the second question. After Nixon's disgrace, Gerald Ford's caretaker interregnum, and Carter's failure, Reagan restored the presidency to the center of American political life. On the first question, Reagan's record proved more mixed. In many ways he showed the capacity to unite the country behind an idealistic if often airbrushed vision of America as a "shining city upon a hill." In other ways Reagan unleashed ideological energies that widened the distance between the parties and escalated the conflicts between them.

Like Nixon, Reagan had a foot in the age of bargaining and a foot in the more partisan age that followed. Reagan's sweeping victory in 1980 carried Republicans to control of the Senate but left Democrats with a numerical majority in the House. To pass Reagan's tax- and spending-reduction plans through the House in 1981, the administration briefly reassembled the venerable conservative coalition, joining Southern "boll weevil" Democrats with Republicans to overwhelm resistance from O'Neill and most Democrats. In form, the vote for Reagan's economic plan resembled the sort of coalition Howard Smith and Charlie Halleck might have constructed twenty years earlier. In substance, it represented something very different. During its heyday in the first decades after World War II the alliance of Republicans and Southern Democrats had united primarily to block liberal initiatives; the alliance was conservative in the sense that it resisted lurching change. Reagan, though, reunited the coalition for a radical redirection of government policy: a three-year 25 percent reduction in income tax rates and an accompanying round of spending reductions in dozens of government programs.

It was a telling difference. Eisenhower and Nixon, the previous two Republican presidents, sought mostly to restrain government's growth. Reagan arrived in Washington determined to retrench it. The scale of his ambitions testified to the intellectual spadework completed by the new conservative network during the 1970s. Reagan entered office with something Eisenhower and Nixon never had and might not have welcomed: a set of comprehensive conservative proposals for redirecting federal policy at home and abroad. And Reagan arrived with something else his

Republican predecessors lacked: a roster of conservative potential appointees fluent in federal policy from apprenticeships in the think tanks and interest groups that had sprouted in response to the liberal mobilization of the 1960s.

This surge of conservative energy had first swelled in Goldwater's campaign. It had been nurtured in all the institutions conservatives built during their countermobilization through the 1970s. With Reagan's election it spilled over Washington as if released from a dam. The Reagan administration challenged the prevailing assumptions of liberalism more forcefully and across a far broader range of issues than Nixon's or Eisenhower's had done. Reaganites arrived determined to limit government's reach in agencies large and small—and immediately found themselves in hand-to-hand combat with the liberal public interest groups and their Democratic allies in Congress dedicated to maintaining the agencies' traditional missions. On any given day early in Reagan's presidency, the administration and its allies might be battling against the Democrats and their allies over tax cuts, spending reductions in social programs, offshore oil drilling, nuclear power, limits on federal regulations, arms control, defense spending, enforcement of civil rights laws, and whether ketchup qualified as a vegetable for purposes of the federal school lunch program. It sometimes seemed the White House felt that any administrator who was not being sued by a liberal public interest group or facing a subpoena from an angry Democratic committee in the House was shirking his responsibilities. Murray Weidenbaum, the wry economist Reagan plucked to run his Council of Economic Advisers, offered his administration colleagues puckish counsel that caught the prevailing mood: "Don't just stand there, undo something."

This broad-based challenge to the legacies of Lyndon Johnson and the liberal public interest groups marked another step away from the consensus politics of the age of bargaining. Under Reagan the country divided in ways that would become more familiar for his successors. In one early 1982 survey Gallup reported that 83 percent of Republicans approved of Reagan's performance, compared to just 20 percent of Democrats—at that point the widest gap between the parties Gallup had recorded since it began systematically measuring attitudes toward presidents under

Eisenhower. Even without polls it wasn't difficult to track the rising emotions Reagan inspired. His push for a new conservative direction produced an intense response from the left. A coalition of 150 groups fought his budget cuts. Some 700,000 people crowded Central Park in 1982 to protest his push to place new nuclear weapons in Europe. On Capitol Hill, Democrats spared no adjective in denouncing the administration as callous and hard-hearted in its support of tax cuts that provided the greatest benefits to the rich and spending cuts that imposed the greatest burdens on the poor. When Reagan traveled to Denver to address an NAACP annual convention in 1981, the group's chairwoman provided a more biblical, if less gracious, greeting than presidents usually receive when she told the crowd that his budget cuts were responsible for "war, pestilence, famine, and death."

Through the remainder of Reagan's presidency the parties continued to clash regularly over issues from aid to the Nicaraguan Contras to Reagan's attempt to place the conservative legal hero Robert Bork on the Supreme Court to the Iran-Contra scandal in his second term. Yet the full-scale ideological and partisan Armageddon that Reagan's early months threatened never arrived. If anything, over time, the scales tilted more from conflict toward cooperation. In Congress, the administration found common ground with Democrats more regularly as the months passed (often to the frustration of young, backbench, congressional conservatives led by Newt Gingrich). Reagan stressed unifying, not polarizing, themes in his 1984 reelection campaign—and was rewarded with one of the most lopsided landslide victories ever. And until the Iran-Contra scandal sent Reagan's support skidding, polls during the first two years of his second term showed him winning positive reviews for his job performance from about 40 percent of Democrats—a much greater level of support from voters in the opposition party than any of his three successors usually would enjoy.

Reagan's adjustment partly reflected necessity. During his first two years, support from the Southern Democratic boll weevils provided Reagan operational control of the House, which allowed him to pursue dramatic change. But after the Democrats added twenty-six House seats in the 1982 election, the party leadership regained a working majority in the body. (With the added numbers O'Neill and then Jim Wright also discouraged their members from supporting Reagan by more aggressively employing the tools of discipline that the reforms of the 1970s had provided them.) In the 1986 election, Republicans lost control of the Senate as well. Reagan could ignore Democrats, or advance his agenda, but he could not do both.

But more than expediency pushed Reagan away from consistent confrontation. Reagan still faced pressures from some of the same dynamics that had encouraged compromise in the decades after World War II—and his own absorption of that era's underlying political assumptions. Like Nixon and Kennedy, Reagan was forced by the continuing diversity in his own coalition to bend toward opinions more common in the other party. Pressure from traditional Republican fiscal conservatives led by Senators Robert Dole of Kansas and Pete Domenici of New Mexico compelled Reagan to accept a substantial tax increase in 1982 to reduce the deficit opened by his tax cuts of the previous year. Opposition from moderate Republican senators such as Connecticut's Lowell P. Weicker doomed a Reagan-backed constitutional amendment to overturn the legal right to abortion, and another amendment from Senate conservatives to reauthorize school prayer. Robert Stafford, the veteran Republican moderate from Vermont, fought much of Reagan's environmental agenda from his position as chairman of the Senate Environment and Public Works Committee; another Republican moderate, Charles Percy of Illinois, questioned many of his international priorities as chairman of the Foreign Relations Committee. The pattern extended into Reagan's administration. When William Bradford Reynolds, an ardent conservative at the Justice Department, mounted a crusade to roll back federal affirmative action requirements, he was blocked by William Brock and George Shultz, two Cabinet officers with roots in more centrist Republican traditions. When Reagan then tried to promote Reynolds to the Justice Department's number-three job, opposition from moderate Republican senators Arlen Specter of Pennsylvania and Charles McC. Mathias of Maryland killed the nomination in the Senate Judiciary Committee. On each of these issues the differences among Republicans pushed Reagan in directions that defused confrontations with Democrats.

When Reagan reached deals with Congress more regularly after his first few months, activists in the burgeoning conservative network angrily condemned White House aides they accused of blunting his ideological fervor—the "pragmatists" led by chief of staff James A. Baker III, his deputy Richard Darman, and Reagan's longtime image adviser Michael Deaver. "Let Reagan be Reagan," the conservatives cried. Yet Reagan's own instincts were conflicted. He expressed deeply ideological views on most issues. But his political and personal tendencies were integrative, not divisive. Unlike Nixon, Reagan wasn't personally vindictive. (For all his rhetorical collisions with the Democratic speaker, for instance, Reagan still enjoyed O'Neill's company and offered him the ambassadorship to Ireland after he retired from Congress.) And, as a labor negotiator for the Screen Actors Guild during his Hollywood days, he understood the value of compromise that moved him closer to his goals without entirely alienating anyone at the table. Reagan never hid his conservative beliefs. Yet in his political message he mostly sought not to deepen ideological or partisan differences but to transcend them in an appeal to shared assumptions (which critics often derided as myths) about individualism at home and American exceptionalism in the world. In his 1984 reelection campaign Reagan ran not as an ideological warrior but as a septuagenarian symbol of national rejuvenation. Reagan promised voters "morning again in America," not midnight for the Great Society.

These conflicting instincts produced a presidency that unfolded like a series of border skirmishes between two suspicious countries not yet committed to full-scale war. Through the Reagan years an ascendant conservatism probed for weaknesses in outwardly formidable but aging liberal defenses. Reagan smashed through the liberal fortifications at several points—in cutting taxes, increasing defense spending, and marshaling a more assertive challenge to the Soviet Union. The expansion of government regulatory power that the liberal public interest groups had inspired under Nixon and continued under Carter was slowed, and in some respects reversed.

But just as often Reagan withdrew at signs of serious resistance. His passion for slashing the federal budget dimmed after 1981, and he settled for a standoff that limited the growth in domestic programs but accepted rapid increases in entitlements such as Medicare, defense spending, and, of course, the federal deficit. After his early reversals in the Senate, Reagan offered social conservatives little more than sympathetic rhetoric. His environmental policies ignited some of the most intense conflicts of his first years, but, facing opposition from congressional Republicans as well as Democrats, Reagan largely sued for peace: When Anne Gorsuch Burford, the brusque conservative he installed as his first Environmental Protection Agency administrator, was forced out by ethics controversies in 1983, Reagan replaced her with William D. Ruckelshaus, a favorite of environmentalists who had served as the agency's first director. A few months later James G. Watt, Reagan's ardently conservative and flamboyantly confrontational interior secretary, also resigned.

Meanwhile, bipartisan agreements with Congress accumulated. In 1983, Reagan signed a Social Security solvency plan constructed by Daniel Patrick Moynihan and Alan Greenspan that sensibly balanced an increase in the retirement age with a rise in payroll taxes. In 1986, Reagan signed legislation crafted through compromises between the parties to reform the tax code, provide amnesty to millions of illegal immigrants, and expand the federal fund dedicated to cleaning toxic waste dumps. Two years later came an agreement with Moynihan on legislation reforming the federal welfare system and a sweeping rewrite of federal trade laws. In foreign affairs, Reagan followed much the same trajectory: The fierce anticommunist who condemned the "evil empire" in his first term reached a productive rapprochement with Soviet leader Mikhail Gorbachev in his second. When Reagan concluded an agreement with Gorbachev for both sides to remove their nuclear weapons from Europe, the treaty drew support from nearly 4 in 5 Americans in surveys, and 93 senators in the vote for ratification.

In each of these agreements Reagan demonstrated greater flexibility and receptivity to divergent views than he is usually credited with. Jack F. Matlock, Jr., a career foreign service officer, was near Reagan's side during most of the breakthroughs with Gorbachev, first as a senior official on the National Security Council, and then as his ambassador to the Soviet Union (a position he also held under George H. W. Bush). Matlock saw Reagan as a president whose strong beliefs did not prevent him from hearing other perspectives. "Reagan . . . kept a relatively open mind," Matlock said soon after Reagan's death. "He always was happy to listen. He consulted with many people, including people he didn't necessarily agree with, and he took it seriously. Reagan knew what he didn't know, and he liked to be educated about it. He was anything but arrogant, and he didn't close out things."

In the march from the age of bargaining's restrained partisanship to today's pointed and shearing conflicts, Reagan exerted a split-level impact. At the practical level of day-to-day politics he demonstrated that a president could hold strong ideological beliefs and yet reach reasonable agreement with others who did not share them. That proved as true in Reagan's dealings with Gorbachev as it did in his encounters with Tip O'Neill. Reagan operated with a belief system too sharp and edgy to ever describe him as a consensus figure; but his impulse toward inclusion allowed him to frame his beliefs in a manner that attracted even many Americans who did not agree with all of them. As a communicator Reagan's instinct was to seek the notes that would broaden his audience in America and the world. As a negotiator he usually preferred a deal to a debating point. He changed course (raising taxes after 1981, tempering his war with environmentalists, negotiating with Gorbachev), recognized the difference between conviction and intransigence, and routinely reached agreements with Democrats who had criticized him only the day before. He proved that a president can impose significant change without precipitating all-out political war.

But at the level of symbol, and inspiration, Reagan accelerated the key trends injecting more partisan conflict into the political system. The passions surrounding his agenda, especially in his first term, fueled the growth of interest groups and think tanks on both the left and the right; the enormous media and lobbying campaign liberal groups mounted to defeat Bork's nomination in 1987 proved a milestone in escalating the political conflict surrounding Supreme Court appointments.

Most important, Reagan inspired a generation of young activists and politicians who rose to prominence after his presidency determined to exceed him in advancing a conservative revolution at home and abroad. In the decade after Reagan left office, the ascent of those young conservatives combined with the sorting out in the electorate to reduce Republican moderates to their weakest position in the party since the 1920s. When Reagan arrived in Washington the GOP still operated as a coalition of diverse voices; by the time he left it was evolving into a chorus of like-minded ones. "Reaganism completely defeated Rockefellerism," said Grover Norquist, the conservative organizer. "This is the Bolsheviks and the Mensheviks. There aren't any Mensheviks anymore. It's over. The Bolsheviks have the whole thing. It's now called Bolshevism. Well, it's now called Reagan Republicanism. There is no alternative vision within the Republican Party." With time, the pragmatic elements of Reagan's record faded, and conservatives enshrined him as a monument to principle and purity. And with that ideal as their beacon, they worked to build a "Reaganite" Republican Party more disciplined, more uniform in its views, and more committed to a common ideology than anything American politics had seen since the distant days of Nelson Aldrich and Joe Cannon.

CHAPTER 5

★

THE AGE OF
TRANSITION II:
THE RISE OF
HYPERPARTISANSHIP

From the moment Newt Gingrich arrived in the House of Representatives in 1979, he was overflowing with ideas. Pudgy, prolix, and prematurely gray, Gingrich tossed off policy proposals (government bonuses for poor children who learn to read, tax credits to help lower income families buy computers); management theories ("There is a model I work off," he told one interviewer: "visions, strategies, projects, and tactics"); legislative strategies ("It is my tactic to confront them so hard they have to respond"); and projections of the future ("My interest is in creating a positive, dynamic, high-tech, self-governing, free-market, future") in a torrent of words that suggested either a touch of genius or Tourette's. He sometimes resembled a human PowerPoint presentation. Gingrich's whirling activity and tireless proselytizing touched on almost every conceivable subject of policy and political debate. But at its root was a simple injunction: Republicans must sharpen their differences with Democrats in every possible way and create clear, bright lines of division between the parties. "I'm tough in the House, because when I arrived, the Republican Party was a soft institution that lacked the tradition of fighting," Gingrich said years after his arrival. "You had to have somebody who was willing to fight."

With that militant vision, Gingrich began an insurrection against the viewpoint that had dominated the House GOP since the days of Joseph Martin in the 1950s. An army brat and history professor at West Georgia College, Gingrich ran strong but unsuccessful races in 1974 and 1976 as the Republican nominee for the suburban Atlanta seat held by John J. Flynt, an aging old-time Southern Democrat. When Flynt retired in 1978, Gingrich swept to Washington as the sole Republican in the Georgia congressional delegation. Gingrich was inspired by Barry Goldwater and Ronald Reagan. But from the outset he was never an ideological purist; his conservatism was leavened by a generous (and often prescient) futurism that led him to worry about such things as how technology might empower the disabled for more productive lives. What truly set him apart was his capacity to formulate a long-term plan for redefining both parties, and his willingness to pursue almost any means necessary to advance it. Even as a junior member, his ambition was boundless. "I have an enormous personal ambition," he told the *Washington Post* in 1985. "I want to shift the entire planet."

Gingrich started with one small corner of the planet, the Republicans in the House of Representatives who had not spent a single day in the majority since 1955. At the time of Gingrich's arrival the House GOP leadership resembled a sleepy family-owned company ripe for a takeover. Under the leadership of John J. Rhodes in the 1970s, and then Robert Michel after 1981, House Republicans had generally minimized their confrontations with Democrats. Instead they worked quietly to maximize their influence on the legislation Democrats advanced. Michel, a quintessentially self-effacing, midcentury mid-American who had first been elected from his Peoria, Illinois, seat in 1956, believed that collaboration was a more effective political strategy than confrontation, because it allowed the minority Republicans to share the credit for Congress's accomplishments. He was leery of ideas that veered too sharply from the accepted political mainstream. Ed Feulner, the longtime president of the Heritage Foundation, recalls being invited to a breakfast with Michel and the senior Republican committee members during the Reagan years. Michel wanted to know what Heritage was working on, and Feulner ran through the list:

tax reform, other domestic issues, Social Security. As soon as the words left Feulner's mouth, Michel reached over and squeezed him on the arm. "Ed," Michel said gravely, "we don't talk about changing Social Security in this building."

This cautious strategy also fit Michel's conciliatory personality. Throughout his career he maintained a close friendship with Tip O'Neill. During breaks in the session, Michel would sometimes drive home to Illinois in a station wagon that included Dan Rostenkowski, the bluff Chicago Democrat who would later chair the Ways and Means Committee. Michel often argued that Republicans had a "responsibility" to help the Democrats govern by reaching reasonable agreements.

Michel's approach brought tangible benefits for Republicans—an appropriation for their district here, a small change in legislative language to benefit a local interest there. But Gingrich and the allies who gathered around him considered the Michel system a formula for permanent subjugation. To Gingrich, Republicans were trading ease and intermittent influence for real power. Democrats might provide small favors to Republicans, but the majority still controlled all the big decisions on policy. Gingrich thought the GOP leadership accepted that deal because it did not really believe it could overthrow the Democrats. "If you think you are the subordinate wolf you spent a lot of time cultivating the dominant wolf," Gingrich said. "If you think you are capable of becoming the dominant wolf you spend a lot of your energy beating the dominant wolf." After the invigorating breakthroughs of Reagan's first six months, Gingrich and his allies grew more frustrated as the Republican revolution flagged through the rest of 1981 and 1982. When Reagan agreed to raise taxes in 1982, younger Republican members from the classes of 1978 and 1980 voted in large numbers against the deal. After Democrats trounced the GOP in the 1982 midterm election, a discouraged Gingrich traveled to New York to seek advice from Richard Nixon. Nixon told him that Congress was too large for any single individual to change; if Gingrich wanted to make a difference, he would need reinforcements. A few months later, with a small group that included Vin Weber of Minnesota, Robert Walker of Pennsylvania, and Judd Gregg of New Hampshire, three other shrewd Republican backbenchers, Gingrich founded the Conservative Opportunity Society.

Gingrich became the personification of the COS, but it functioned as a collaborative effort. Weber, Walker, Gregg, and Connie Mack of Florida all played large roles. The change it represented was not personal but generational. Michel, in every respect, was a creature of the age of bargaining. The young conservatives who formed COS plugged into the new currents that were transforming that system. Far more than most of their colleagues, the COS activists recognized that in the changing media environment congressional Republicans could define themselves more through the messages they broadcast on television than the commas they inserted into complex pieces of legislation. The group's goal, Gingrich recalled, was to fill "a vacuum in terms of creating a confrontational activism that was media oriented."

The COS activists also quickly built alliances with many of the new conservative institutions that emerged in the 1970s; Gingrich visited the fledgling Heritage Foundation's modest C Street office for a briefing over brown bag lunches even before his election. He considered the arrival of the groups "enormously important. It was important because you needed the intellectual resources, it was important because you needed the noise, it was important because you needed the training for younger activists who could become candidates." He encouraged Paul Weyrich, the conservative visionary who helped found the Heritage Foundation, to inaugurate a weekly Wednesday lunch with conservative groups that Gingrich envisioned as the outside equivalent to the inside maneuvering of the COS. And then Gingrich looked for issues that would allow him to activate the emerging grassroots conservative networks. One of the first opportunities came with the National Federation of Independent Business, the passionately antigovernment small-business lobby. "We had some fight under way and I called the head of the NFIB," Gingrich recalled. "I said, 'I want to start this fight.' This was 1979. He said, 'It's our issue, we're totally with you.' I said, 'What can you do for me within forty-eight hours?' He said, 'I can send out forty-four thousand telegrams'—they weren't e-mails back then—'to my most active members.' Well, it had never occurred to John Rhodes [that] if he thought of the network he could energize, rather than thinking about the resources that he owned, that the world was enormous. . . . I would look for networks that had a parallel interest to us."

The COS sought to reshape the political landscape through two strategies. Gingrich and his allies promoted an ambitious agenda that embraced the cutting-edge conservative thinking the GOP leadership had kept at a distance. In its early manifestos the COS championed a marriage of economic (balanced budget, line-item veto), social (welfare reform, school prayer), and foreign policy (missile defense) priorities that proposed to push beyond Reagan on almost every front. They spent hours debating principles, proposals, and priorities. Their ideas presented the terms for a much more ideologically polarized contrast with the majority Democrats. But the group quickly learned that the policy wish lists of junior members in the House's minority party attracted little attention.

Instead the COS made its mark primarily through its other central focus: attacks on Democrats. It was Walker who found a megaphone big enough to make them heard from the backbenches. The key was an unprecedented use of C-SPAN, the cable service that began televising House proceedings in 1979. Acting on Walker's suggestion, the COS members regularly gathered on the House floor to flay Democrats during late-night speeches that found a small, but enthusiastic, audience through C-SPAN. (Among the regular viewers was a young radio talk show host named Rush Limbaugh.) From the start, the group's hallmark was the use of flamboyant, inflammatory rhetoric. Gingrich especially reveled in barreling through the traditions of euphemism and civility that muffled congressional debate. He used adjectives like rocks. Gingrich described the House as a "sick institution" and "Tammany Hall on Capitol Hill." He scored his greatest early coup in 1984 when he used one of his evening speeches to charge that Democrats opposing aid to the Nicaraguan Contras had been "blind to communism." Gingrich's attack provoked Tip O'Neill to lash back against him on the House floor; O'Neill's words violated House rules against personal attacks and prompted a rare rebuke against the speaker. When the parliamentarian formally rebuked O'Neill for his remarks, House Republicans, celebrating a singular moment of triumph after nearly three decades of uninterrupted Democratic control, rose to applaud Gingrich. "Tip made a critical error when he took on Newt, because he elevated Newt," said Tony Coelho, the tough and savvy Democrat who first arrived on Capitol Hill as an aide in 1965, and then was elected as a representative from California in 1978. "The rest of the Republican caucus loved it, because they finally got under [O'Neill's] skin, and that's what they were trying to do."

Gingrich and his allies hurt Democrats most through a sustained campaign to portray the House as endemically corrupt. Gingrich sought to expel a Democrat who had been convicted of diverting office funds into his pocket, and urged the censure (rather than the milder reprimand) of a Democrat and a Republican who admitted sexual relationships with congressional pages. He hit the jackpot when he promoted ethical allegations against Jim Wright, O'Neill's successor as Democratic speaker, centered on Wright's lucrative contract for a privately published book. Michel kept his distance, but Gingrich pressed on, eventually filing a formal complaint with the House Ethics Committee. A long, tangled confrontation led to Wright's resignation in 1989, after an angry final blast at "mindless cannibalism" consuming the Capitol. A separate ethics dispute forced Coelho, who had ascended to the number three position in the Democratic leadership, the majority whip, to step down around the same time, too. Even those twin departures didn't stop the crusade. Gingrich encouraged younger Republicans, who hammered away at irregularities in the operations of the House Post Office and House bank. "We'd sit down and chat, and I'd say, you know, 'Be bold. Have courage. When in doubt, take risk,'" Gingrich recalled in an interview a few years later.

All of these offensives threatened Republican members as well as Democrats* and created an atmosphere of tension in the House so thick that the fights among members sometimes extended beyond words to fists. But Gingrich never wavered in his Vietnam-like conviction that saving the House required him first to destroy its credibility with the public. Soon after Gingrich's long campaign resulted in his election as speaker in 1995, he was asked in one interview how much damage he had been willing to inflict on the House to pry it from Democratic control:

QUESTION: You had to bring it down . . . to start over?
GINGRICH: Yes, I always thought that.

---

* Weber, Gingrich's brilliant but more personable ally in the COS, announced that he would not seek reelection in 1992 after his own overdrafts at the House bank were disclosed.

Gingrich and his allies focused most of their firepower on Democrats, but also targeted Republicans who resisted their vision of a party committed to contrast and conflict. After Dole drove through the 1982 tax increase, Gingrich famously derided him as the "tax collector for the welfare state." Even Reagan wasn't immune. Whenever Reagan compromised with Democrats, or sounded unifying themes, Gingrich and his allies complained. "It totally blurred all the issues between the parties," Gingrich grumbled after Reagan signed the Dole-designed 1982 bill raising taxes. "We want to delineate for the country what the real choices are." In 1984, Gingrich condemned Reagan's gauzy "Morning Again in America" campaign message: "Reagan should have prepared for [a second term] . . . by forcing a polarization of the country," Gingrich told a seminar at the Heritage Foundation. "He should have been running against liberals and radicals." The next year House conservatives joined in an insurrection that led Reagan to renounce a bipartisan agreement Dole had assembled in the Senate to reduce the budget deficit through difficult budget cuts, including reductions in Social Security benefits. The group's frustration deepened as Reagan reached agreements with Democrats more often in his second term. "The minority party doesn't win elections if there's no difference with the majority party," Weber fretted in 1987.

Most House Republicans initially kept their distance from Gingrich's uncompromising approach. Even some conservatives, like Representative Mickey Edwards, regularly criticized their tactics as counterproductive. Though Michel tried to avoid open warfare, his unease with Gingrich's strategy often slipped out. (When many House Republicans applauded Gingrich after his confrontation with O'Neill, Michel walked out of the chamber without clapping.) "While Michel wanted to be speaker," said Coelho, "he didn't want to hurt the establishment. And Newt understood [that] the only way to get there was to go after the establishment."

Through the Reagan years the balance inside the GOP conference tipped toward Gingrich. Democrats, ironically, deserved much of the credit for his success. The changes in House rules Democrats had engineered in the 1970s eroded the rationale for Michel's cooperative strategy. The greatest opportunity for House Republicans to influence legislation had come in the committees, where senior members could build close relationships with their Democratic counterparts. But those opportunities for quiet accommodations diminished after the end of seniority pressured the Democratic committee chairmen to more closely follow the wishes of their overall caucus. Under the new rules, not only junior but senior Republicans accustomed to a measure of influence found themselves excluded.

These frustrations, replicated in committees across the House after the mid-1970s, widened the audience for the COS message. The liberal reformers' fundamental goal in changing the House rules had been to provide the majority in the Democratic caucus more leverage to impose its will without resistance either from conservative Democrats or Republicans. Each step Democrats took toward fulfilling that vision rallied more Republicans to Gingrich's banner. Even many Republicans who preferred to work with Democrats concluded that they could be heard only by confronting them. In the House, a more militant and unified Republican Party was the inevitable, if often unanticipated, consequence of a more unified Democratic Party. In that sense, Gingrich was Richard Bolling's bastard son.

The cycle of action and reaction, like a gang war, spiraled toward ever higher levels of conflict. Rank-and-file Democrats pressured their leaders for a tougher response to Gingrich's escalating challenge. "Our caucus started to get more and more aggressive against our leadership, because our leadership was collegial, and [was] permitting Newt and crowd to kick the shit out of us," said Coelho. "And when [we] started pushing back . . . the caucus wanted to keep pushing."

A critical moment came in 1985, when Democrats overrode Republican objections to award an Indiana seat to Democrat Frank McCloskey, after a close and disputed race; the decision so infuriated House Republicans that they marched out of the chamber in protest. (That night, Gingrich said, there was a surge "in the number of members . . . who were Gingrich-ites.") The confrontations grew even angrier after the brusque Jim Wright succeeded O'Neill in 1987. Wright shared none of Gingrich's ideology but matched his any-means-necessary ethos. Wright's goal, in fact, was the same as Gingrich's: to advance an agenda that sharpened the differences between the parties. Far more than O'Neill, Wright used the leverage granted him by the previous decade's rules changes to tighten the screws on Republicans and dissenting Democrats. Wright threatened Democrats who resisted his proposals with loss of their chairmanships or seats on the prestigious committees. He pressured the Rules Committee to send more bills to the floor under restrictions that denied Republicans opportunities to be heard. Republicans complained that Democrats excluded them from committee deliberations on drafting key bills, such as the budget or tax legislation. Wright infuriated Republicans by bringing more bills directly to the House floor, bypassing the committees altogether. During a 1987 struggle over a proposal to reduce the deficit by raising taxes, Wright kept the vote open at least fifteen minutes past the deadline while he jawboned a Texas Democrat into switching his vote and providing the party a one-vote victory.

Wright's provocations drove more House Republicans away from Michel's congenial approach and toward Gingrich. Generational change also bolstered Gingrich. Each succeeding election brought in new Republicans inspired by Goldwater and then Reagan, and reduced the influence of the Michel generation marinated in the less confrontational traditions of the age of bargaining. The advance guard for change arrived in the 1976 election, which brought to the House twenty new Republican members, including Robert Walker, David Stockman, and Dan Quayle. In 1978, Republicans added thirty-six more new faces, including Gingrich, Dick Cheney, and James Sensenbrenner. Another fifty-two new House Republicans swept in with the 1980 Reagan landslide, including Weber and Judd Gregg. In 1982, Dan Burton and Connie Mack came on with twenty-two others, and two years after that the thirty-one freshmen Republicans elected amid Reagan's second landslide included two Texans named Tom DeLay and Richard Armey, who would help lead the Republican resurgence a decade later.

Michel still held the reins, but the party was being remade around him. "We out-recruited the other side slowly and steadily," said Gingrich. The tipping point inside the GOP caucus came in 1989, when Gingrich won election as House Republican whip. He narrowly defeated Michel's choice, Ed Madigan, a colorless but shrewd insider known as a skilled legislative tactician. The result didn't divide exactly along ideological lines. While some conservatives sided with Madigan (the young Tom DeLay for one), several leading moderates backed Gingrich. And Gingrich ran more on a platform of injecting vitality into the leadership than of lurching it to the right. But Gingrich's victory still represented a landmark for Republicans. Madigan's calling card was his ability to find the places where the two parties could agree; Gingrich was a provocateur skilled at highlighting the places where the two parties disagreed. His victory provided the first institutional foothold for the viewpoint that maintained Republicans could prosper more by fighting than by negotiating with Democrats. The first president to face the implications of that shift was not any Democrat, but the man who succeeded Ronald Reagan in 1988, George H. W. Bush.

THE PATRICIAN, courteous, and cautious George Bush offered the Democrats who controlled the House and Senate throughout his presidency the same implicit trade-off as Eisenhower and Nixon. Like them, Bush seemed willing to give ground to Democrats on domestic issues to buy freedom to maneuver abroad. With his promise of a "kinder and gentler" America, he signaled that he intended to set a less confrontational tone than Reagan at his most ideological moments. Bush viewed his role less as advancing a conservative domestic agenda, or a domestic agenda of any sort, than as slowing the advance of a liberal agenda. On domestic policy Bush placed less priority on maintaining control of the steering wheel than the brake.

That modest instinct actually produced reasonable compromises between Bush and congressional Democrats on many fronts: an extension of the Clean Air Act long delayed under Reagan; the passage of the Americans with Disabilities Act; far-reaching immigration legislation; a civil rights bill; and above all the deal he accepted in 1990 to begin reducing the massive budget deficits of the Reagan era through a combination of spending restraints and tax increases.

But Bush was unable to establish an overarching framework to explain or market his approach. Many Americans, accurately, viewed it as listless, a kind of split-the-difference shrug. It didn't help when Bush's White House chief of staff, after the 1990 budget deal, said that as far as the administration was concerned Congress could simply go home for the next two years because the president had nothing else he wanted to accomplish.

As the economy slowed, the demand for a more activist, energetic strategy grew. Bush's caution and lack of ambition on domestic issues began to be seen as indifference.

More than his own torpor led to Bush's failure. He might have been an ideal president during the age of bargaining. Instead his presidency demonstrated how little of that political system had survived after a quarter century of centrifugal pressure. The bipartisan agreements that Nixon and Eisenhower and even Reagan had forged became tougher to assemble, as the parties moved further apart. That growing distance was evident partly in the heightened appetite for confrontation among congressional Democrats determined to sharpen the differences between the two sides. Repeatedly during Bush's four years they passed legislation—an increased minimum wage, extended unemployment benefits, mandatory family and medical leave—in a form they knew would provoke a veto from him.

But the larger change was evident in the growing antagonism toward Bush's deal-making approach among conservative congressional Republicans, particularly in the House. Bush frustrated the young conservatives by presenting so few positive alternatives to Democratic proposals for new government programs. But he infuriated them, and the activist groups they aligned with, by compromising so frequently with Democrats. From small-business owners in the National Federation of Independent Business, to gun owners in the National Rifle Association, to antitax and antiregulatory activists, Bush throughout his term alienated almost every element of the grassroots Republican coalition that had emerged since the 1970s.

The discontent culminated in a full-scale revolt over the budget deal in 1990. When Bush agreed to raise taxes as part of the package—breaking his "no new taxes" pledge from his 1988 campaign—Gingrich led a rebellion among House Republicans against the agreement. Eventually almost half of the House Republicans voted against the deal. The objection from Gingrich and his allies was not only ideological but tactical. On substantive grounds, the Republican critics objected to tax increases. But they objected almost as profoundly to the idea of negotiating a solution that bridged the differences between the parties. The explicit goal of the conservative House Republicans was to make such accommodations unacceptably painful.

"The number one thing we had to prove in the fall of '90," Gingrich said later, "was that, if you explicitly decided to govern from the center, we could make it so unbelievably expensive you couldn't sustain it." DeLay, the Texas Republican who would later succeed Gingrich as the defining symbol of the pugnacious Republican congressional majority, insisted: "The only way we could take over Congress and be a party of prominence was to have a very clear distinction between the Democrats and the Republicans. The Bush administration muddied that distinction. The Bush administration wanted to work with Congress, rather than beat Congress. And so it was contrary to what we were doing."

This was more than a single policy dispute. It was a signal of a more fundamental shift. The revolt against Bush's budget from conservatives inside and outside Congress marked a triumph for the campaign against bipartisan cooperation that the COS had waged against Bob Michel and even Reagan through the 1980s. The immediate measure of the conservative victory was the opposition from every Republican in the House and Senate when Bush's Democratic successor, Bill Clinton, proposed to raise taxes in 1993. But their real success was much broader. After Clinton defeated Bush in 1992, conservatives trumpeted his defeat as proof that it was self-defeating for Republicans to pursue bipartisan agreements like the budget deal that could divide or demoralize the party's ideological base.

In fact, it was implausible to blame Bush's 1992 defeat on discontent among conservatives or any other single group. Bush's support collapsed on almost every front. Compared to his 1988 victory Bush's share of the vote declined more among independents than among Republicans, and slightly more among moderates than conservatives; he lost the campaign as much in the center as he did on the right. These facts were not ignored in the postelection analysis from GOP leaders. But after the election it was the defections on the right (almost entirely to Ross Perot, the quirky independent candidate, rather than Clinton) that many Republican leaders remembered most. And it was Bush's budget agreement with congressional Democrats that conservatives blamed above all for those defections. Over the next eight years the fear of another party split would become a powerful weapon for conservatives agitating against cooperation with

Clinton. And the desire among Republicans to excite, mobilize, and unify their conservative base would combine with Clinton's disastrous habit of provoking that base to hurtle American politics deeper into the age of hyperpartisanship.

NEW DEMOCRATS AND OLD DIVIDES

Bill Clinton offered a path toward political reconciliation that was at once more nuanced and more ambitious than George H. W. Bush's minimalism. Clinton's dozen years as governor of Arkansas, a state with little tolerance for extravagant liberalism, had instilled in him a gut-level instinct toward moderation and building consensus. Above that foundation, Clinton had devised by the 1992 presidential campaign a policy and political blueprint meant to transcend many of the traditional divisions between the parties. Clinton's "New Democrat" agenda was heavily influenced by ideas incubated at the Democratic Leadership Council, a group that party centrists had formed to increase their influence after Reagan's landslide victory in 1984 over Walter Mondale, the gray embodiment of conventional interest-group liberalism. Clinton didn't follow the DLC blueprint in all respects—he infused his message with a Southern populism and passion for racial reconciliation much more muted in the DLC version—but he shared with it two overriding goals: rebuilding a political majority for the Democratic Party and reviving a public consensus for activist government. He thought he could do both with ideas that synthesized priorities of the left and right usually considered incompatible. As a candidate Clinton pledged to demand personal responsibility and expand opportunity (for instance by requiring work for welfare recipients while also providing them more training and child care); to increase public investments and balance the budget; and to support open trade while providing workers endangered by foreign competition the training and education to find new jobs. In all these ways, Clinton promised voters during his march to the White House, he would transcend "brain-dead politics in both parties," offer "a new choice based on old values," and build "center out coalitions."

In many respects Clinton did exactly that during his tumultuous eight years in the presidency, especially after the 1994 landslide that carried Republicans to control of both the House and Senate. (As with his predecessors, Clinton found compromise with the other party more attractive when it was a necessity.) In his 1996 campaign he showed that it was possible to win a presidential election decisively with a centrist agenda that relied primarily on controlling the moderate center of the electorate. (Exit polls showed that Clinton won moderate voters comfortably, and also carried a plurality of independents.) Through his second term, even amid the chaos of the Monica Lewinsky scandal, upward of three fifths of Americans said they approved of his performance as president. Like Franklin Roosevelt, Lyndon Johnson, or Richard Nixon (on domestic policy), Clinton integrated ideas from a broad spectrum of thinkers and interests. "He was omnivorous," said Bruce Reed, his shrewd and self-effacing domestic policy adviser. "He saw his job as being a scientist in the laboratory of democracy." Clinton balanced the federal budget for the first time in nearly three decades while increasing spending on liberal priorities such as education and health care. He signed legislation ending the federal entitlement to welfare but also vastly expanded government assistance to the working poor and presided over the largest reductions in poverty, especially among children, since the boom years of the 1960s. On these fronts, often through grueling negotiations with congressional Republicans, Clinton produced policies that advanced liberal goals (expanding opportunity, rewarding work) through means acceptable to conservatives (encouraging fiscal discipline or personal responsibility). Exit polls in the 2000 election showed that even as two thirds of voters said they disliked his personal behavior, nearly 60 percent of them approved of his policies.

Yet overall Clinton failed to stop the current toward greater political polarization. In fact, whether measured by the gap between his approval ratings among voters in the two parties, the extent of party line voting in Congress, or just the general vehemence of political emotions that surrounded him, it was raging more powerfully when he left office than when he arrived. Clinton failed to stem that tide partly because he evoked such powerful emotions as a cultural symbol. The allegations of marital infidelity and draft dodging that emerged in the 1992 campaign, the succession of ethical allegations that flowered through his two terms (many of them exaggerated and distorted by his opponents), and the supreme self-inflicted wound of his affair with the chatty former intern, Monica Lewinsky, all made Clinton a flashpoint for the unresolved tensions over the social changes of the 1960s. His personal behavior drove away many of the same swing voters his policies aimed to attract, and accelerated the trend toward a political alignment that divided the nation more along lines of culture than class.

But Clinton's policy missteps, compounded by the myopia of the congressional Democratic leadership, also accelerated the trend toward polarization. By instinct and intellect, Clinton was better equipped than any recent president to establish a broad consensus with pragmatic bipartisan compromise. But in his first two years, while Democrats controlled Congress, Clinton's reluctance to confront his own party prevented him from consistently offering policies with appeal across partisan and ideological lines. After Republicans won control of Congress, Clinton steered a more reliably centrist course (no doubt partly from necessity). But by then he faced a Republican congressional majority so fired with ideological fervor and committed to a confrontational political strategy that agreement typically proved elusive, except during one extraordinarily productive window. When Clinton had greater freedom to maneuver, his commitment to a unifying agenda wavered; when his commitment to a unifying agenda solidified, his freedom to maneuver diminished.

Clinton never entirely recaptured the opportunity he had squandered in his first two years to build a durable centrist legislative and electoral coalition. If Clinton had dependably pursued his campaign promise of a "third way" approach from the outset, he might have broadened his public support and increased pressure on Democrats and moderate Republicans to follow him toward compromises that blended the priorities and preferences of both parties. Instead, his initial agenda oscillated between ideas that advanced his third way and others that stamped him as the champion of a partisan and conventionally liberal government. Even when Clinton reached out, Republicans, scarred by the backlash against Bush's decision to raise taxes and hectored by conservative leaders denouncing any cooperation, often would not reach back. In his first two years Clinton managed some important centrist achievements—a crime bill; the North American Free Trade Agreement with Mexico and Canada; a sustained effort to "reinvent" government and shrink the federal workforce—that showed the potential of his approach to bring together the parties. But these were overshadowed by hugely partisan fights, on issues from allowing gays to serve openly in the military to taxes, that divided the electorate and energized the right.

Early in his presidency, Clinton often faced the worst of all worlds, as Democrats divided over his direction and Republicans unified against him. The unity of purpose congressional Democrats generally achieved in opposition to Reagan and George H. W. Bush receded when they tried to work in harness with a Democratic president. The overall trend toward greater party unity in Congress that began in the 1970s continued under Clinton; voting statistics showed that House and Senate Democrats voted with their party more often during Clinton's first two years (about 85 percent) than they did during Carter's four years (about 67 percent). But on Clinton's top priorities—his 1993 budget, his universal health care plan, the massive crime bill, and NAFTA—the Democrats crumbled under pressure. Many Democratic liberals didn't like the crime bill or NAFTA; many moderates resisted the budget and health care plans. Neither faction sufficiently recognized its shared interest in producing a record of accomplishment to take to the country in 1994. The Democrats voted on Clinton's agenda in the way they thought would strengthen their individual positions at home; yet in the process they produced an image of ineffectiveness that hurt all of them.

Meanwhile, on all of his early priorities except NAFTA, Clinton faced unrelenting resistance from congressional Republicans and ferocious opposition from groups in the grassroots conservative network like the National Rifle Association and the National Federation of Independent Business. This was the third force that propelled polarization in the Clinton years. For many on the right, hostility toward Clinton burned like a fever. Gingrich called his administration the "enemy of normal Americans." Congressional Republicans (once they gained control of Congress in 1995) and shadowy conservative groups spent millions of dollars and thousands of hours investigating every conceivable aspect of Clinton's personal and professional life in a crusade that seemed powered as much by personal loathing as political calculation. Hillary Clinton may have indulged in hyperbole when she spoke of a "vast right-wing conspiracy" mobilized against her husband, but there was no question that by the time Clinton took office, the conservative movement seeded in the 1970s had grown into an imposing, militant force committed to massive resistance against him, the Democrats in Congress, and any Republican inclined to compromise with either of them.

The battles over the top two priorities of Clinton's first two years demonstrated how each side contributed to his initial failure to construct a new center. The first was the budget. In 1993, Clinton, somewhat reluctantly, accepted as his top domestic priority a serious campaign to reduce the federal budget deficit, which had reached record heights in the final years of George H. W. Bush's presidency. Less than a month after taking office, Clinton offered a plan to shrink the deficit in half over five years.

By itself this emphasis was a concession to the centrist and conservative priorities. Focusing on the deficit required Clinton to disappoint liberals eager to expand government spending rapidly after twelve years of Republican rule in the White House. Moreover, Clinton's proposal clearly built on the Bush package Congress had approved in 1990. It recognized that both politically and programmatically the only way to control the deficit was to both raise taxes and cut spending. Clinton tilted the balance more toward the tax side than Republicans would have done if they controlled the executive branch and Congress, but the balance was hardly lopsided. For every dollar in tax increases, Clinton proposed slightly more than a dollar in spending cuts, a reasonable approach for attacking a problem that both parties had declared a priority.

And yet no Republican voted for the bill: not when it first passed the House, not when it passed the Senate, nor when it returned from the conference and cleared both chambers by the most tenuous of margins (two votes in the House, and a fifty-fifty tie in the Senate broken only by Vice President Al Gore). Even the Republicans who mutinied a decade earlier to demand that Ronald Reagan raise taxes to reduce the deficit said no when Clinton offered a comparable remedy. Pete Domenici, the New Mexico deficit hawk who had helped lead the earlier insurrection, told

Clinton's budget director, Leon Panetta, that the Republican Senate leadership had sent a clear message warning its members to vote against any tax increase. The Republican refusal to support a budget that while imperfect still qualified as centrist testified to the pressure inside the GOP both to reject any compromise with Clinton and to maintain an unbroken line of resistance to new taxes after the revolt against the Bush tax increase. It showed that Clinton could not count on Republicans meeting him halfway even when he reached out from his foxhole.

Health care, ultimately the defining battle of Clinton's first two years, showed the opposite: that the new president could not be relied upon to consistently reach out. In his push to guarantee universal access to health care, Clinton faced the same Republican impulse toward resistance that he confronted on the deficit. Business groups and other foot soldiers in the conservative coalition spent sums estimated between $100 million and $300 million in lobbying and advertising campaigns against his plan, enough to make Harry and Louise (the fictional couple that starred in the insurance industry's television ads against the Clinton proposal) something of a household name. But on this front Clinton's mistakes tremendously compounded his difficulties.

His first error was to pick health care as his top priority after the budget. In retrospect, Clinton would have helped himself by moving first on legislation to fulfill his campaign promise to "end welfare as we know it"—an idea that might have attracted much more support from Republicans, strengthened his credentials as a centrist, and fostered a climate of cooperation in Congress. (As we'll see in Chapter 10, Clinton himself has come to this conclusion.) The substance of his health care proposal multiplied the difficulties created by the sequencing. Clinton rejected liberal demands to establish a single-payer government-controlled health care system. But the plan that emerged from a process directed by his wife, Hillary Rodham Clinton, was numbingly complex and confusing. It was so sprawling and bureaucratic (the actual legislation embodying the proposal weighed in at 1,342 pages) that Republicans and business groups opposed to it had little difficulty portraying it as a frightening government takeover of the health care system.

Given the pressure for opposition inside the GOP, and the frenzied conservative mobilization against him, there was no sure path to a health care agreement for Clinton. Bill Kristol, the brainy chief of staff to Vice President Dan Quayle during the first Bush presidency, established his name as an independent GOP strategist through a series of memos in the winter of 1994, urging Republicans to oppose any health care deal with Clinton. Gingrich echoed that message from inside the House leadership. So did many of the Republicans who had graduated from the House to the Senate, such as Phil Gramm, a slow-talking, quick-thinking former Democrat from Texas who had switched parties after House Democrats disciplined him for supporting Ronald Reagan's 1981 tax and spending plans.

Yet a deal might still have been possible if Clinton had reached for it more quickly. Through the fall of 1993, Kristol's approach had not yet achieved dominance in the GOP. More moderate Republicans, such as Senator John Chafee of Rhode Island, were touting alternative approaches intended to significantly reduce the number of Americans without health insurance; even Bob Dole, the Senate minority leader, and Republican National Committee chairman Haley Barbour initially suggested Republicans might negotiate a compromise. But Clinton, pressured by Hillary Clinton, at first discouraged talk of concessions. In his 1994 State of the Union he drew an uncharacteristic, and unfortunate, line in the sand by promising to veto any bill that did not achieve coverage for every American. By the time Clinton signaled more flexibility the next summer, it was too late. Conservatives had unified in opposition to anything resembling his original vision; Dole and Gingrich were pressuring Republican moderates to reject any agreement with the administration; and Democrats had fractured beyond repair. Picking through the wreckage, Paul Starr, a Princeton University sociologist who helped design the plan, correctly concluded: "The lesson for next time in health reform is faster, smaller." Clinton's health care proposal died without reaching a vote on the floor of either chamber.

Each side, then, had contributed to the division that marked Clinton's first two years, not only on the budget and health care, but on an array of other issues. But by the fall of 1994, these failures, missteps, and disappointments had merged like colliding storm systems to produce a hurricane of discontent aimed solely at Clinton and congressional Democrats. Republican voters and interest groups were energized in opposition to

Clinton's health care proposal, the tax increases in his 1993 budget, his efforts to allow gays to serve openly in the military, and the gun control measures he had muscled through Congress. Democratic constituencies, meanwhile, were dispirited by the failure to win health care reform, his support for free trade, and the limits on new spending demanded by Clinton's focus on reducing the deficit. Independents recoiled against the image of disarray in Washington that followed the collapse of health care reform and Clinton's abandonment (in deference to a skeptical Democratic congressional leadership) of the Perot-like lobbying and campaign finance reform agenda he had promoted as a candidate.

The storm arrived with more power than almost anyone had predicted: On Election Day Republicans gained fifty-two seats in the House, and eight in the Senate—enough to sweep them into control of both chambers of Congress for the first time since 1954. The result was not only a crushing defeat for Clinton and congressional Democrats but a milestone in the polarization of American politics.

In several distinct respects the 1994 election hurtled America toward the current age of hyperpartisanship. First it marked a huge advance in the political re-sorting that had started in the 1960s (a dynamic we'll explore more in Chapter 6). In the 1994 election conservative voters who had abandoned Democratic presidential candidates starting in 1964 and 1968 rejected Democratic congressional candidates in huge numbers. That migration reshaped the political map, especially in the South, where Republicans won a majority of the seats in the House for the first time since Reconstruction.

Second, the loss of Congress proved pivotal in preventing Clinton from building a lasting consensus within the Democratic Party for his centrist strategy. Although Democrats modestly regained seats in both chambers from 1996 through 2000, their inability to recapture either house during Clinton's two terms clouded his achievement in restoring his party's capacity to compete for the presidency. And while Clinton and the Republican majority reached several important agreements, the loss of Congress also limited his policy achievements. Both of those blemishes on his record helped liberals skeptical of Clintonism to argue for a more confrontational and partisan approach after he left office. (Al Gore's defeat in the 2000 presidential race, after a campaign in which he ran somewhat to Clinton's left but also suffered from disillusionment over the Lewinsky affair, compounded the problem, by denying Clinton a successor who likely would have solidified the Democrats' commitment to his general direction.) Clinton moved his party toward his centrist vision, but the party would have changed much more if it had not lost Congress (and then the White House) on his watch.

Conversely, the Republican takeover of Congress institutionalized in the GOP a strategy of accentuating political division to build electoral support. Before 1994, the conservatives who preferred a more ideologically unified and confrontational Republican Party had no real lever to consistently demand it. Republicans controlled the White House, except for Jimmy Carter's four years, from 1968 through 1992, but only Reagan advanced an aggressively conservative agenda, and he just intermittently. Republicans controlled the Senate in the early 1980s, but the key decision makers, Howard Baker and Dole, were old-fashioned legislators who preferred deal making to division. Gingrich's approach, as we saw, gained strength through the 1980s, but Michel still functioned as a cap on the bottle. After the 1994 landslide, the restraint was removed. When Michel retired, the new GOP majority elected Gingrich as speaker, and chose Armey as majority leader and DeLay as the party whip, the second- and third-ranking positions. With those decisions the House stood unmistakably under the control of leaders committed to a defiantly divisive vision. And while the Senate was still ambivalent about such a combative approach, Dole, as the incoming majority leader, faced rising pressure for compliance from two sources: the surge in new conservatives brought into the Senate in the 1994 landslide and his own ambitions for the Republican presidential nomination in 1996. Both forces compelled him, often against his own political instincts, to support the ascendant House revolutionaries in a strategy of saber-rattling confrontation with Clinton.

In the House, the election hit with the force of a tidal wave. The seventy-three freshmen Republicans, as determined as the Democrats who poured in after Watergate, provided a huge jolt of conservative energy. Gingrich seized the moment to complete the centralization of power in the House that liberals began by toppling seniority two decades earlier.

Gingrich engineered a change in House rules that imposed six-year term limits on all committee chairs and an eight-year term limit on the speaker. The fall of seniority had provided the party leadership more leverage to enforce party discipline by forcing members to compete for committee chairmanships. Term limits added to the leadership's strength by ensuring that there would be regular competitions for those prizes.* Seniority had created an atmosphere in the House that demanded patience but allowed independence. The new rules allowed a rapid rise to power but demanded loyalty. Tom Davis, a brainy political junkie elected as a Republican representative from suburban Virginia in the 1994 landslide, expressed the new dynamic succinctly. "It is very clear that you ascend by loyalty—loyalty to the organization which is expressed in any number of ways," Davis said. "One is votes. Another is fund-raising. And even if you are not with the leadership, if you are from a tough district taking tough votes, even if your record isn't as true as somebody else's, [you get] some credit for that."

The upheaval in House rules that began in the 1970s and culminated with Gingrich's sweeping changes in 1995 didn't make dictators of the congressional leaders. Even the most powerful party leaders could still fall from their pedestals when they lost support from their caucus, as Gingrich discovered a few years later, and DeLay a few years after that. The real impact of the changes was to strengthen the dominant ideological faction in each party. The reforms allowed the majority of each party's caucus, exercising their will through the leadership, to impose more pressure for conformity on the legislators most inclined to resist the party consensus. Seniority had protected each party's heretics—the voices most likely to seek alliances across party lines—by allowing them, with the rarest of exceptions, to rise in influence without retaliation. By eliminating seniority the ideological majority in each party effectively provided their leaders more authority to act as enforcers against the voices of dissent in each cloakroom.

Gingrich immediately sent an unmistakable signal about his willingness to use that power when he named the first House Republican committee

---

* Gingrich said his principal motivation for imposing term limits was not to increase the leadership's leverage over committee chairs but to ensure a steady flow of "new blood." In practice, the change has had both effects.

chairmen in forty years. On three committees he bypassed the senior Republican member to select a chairman he believed would be more committed to his agenda. Gingrich further tightened his control by doodling all over the organizational flow charts with task forces that eroded the authority of committee chairs, and by salting the key committees with an unusual number of freshman members, whom he considered most responsive to his aggressive vision. His lieutenants, to an unprecedented extent, integrated representatives for business and other elements of the conservative coalition into their efforts to win votes for the leadership's agenda. The Republicans inaugurated elite "Thursday Group" morning meetings for lobbyists with House and Senate leaders, and allowed even the most powerful groups in the conservative universe—the NFIB, the Christian Coalition—to attend only if they committed to work for every element of the ten-point party agenda called the Contract with America that Gingrich had proudly unveiled on the West Front of the Capitol in the waning weeks of the 1994 campaign, not just those elements that directly benefited their members. These maneuvers didn't eliminate all disagreements, or the need for relentless negotiating and hand-holding within the caucus. But they provided Gingrich and his team more powerful tools to enforce discipline and compel loyalty than any congressional leadership since the days of Joe Cannon and the Four.

The result produced a remarkable contrast to the Democratic disorder of Clinton's first two years. Within the first hundred days the Republican House approved nine of the contract's ten legislative proposals; the only measure that failed, a constitutional amendment imposing term limits on members of Congress, received a majority, though not the two-thirds vote required for passage of such amendments. On average, 98 percent of House Republicans voted with the party on each of the thirty-one key votes related to the contract. Even more striking was the Republican unity on the genuinely revolutionary federal budget that Gingrich and the party leadership assembled later that spring. The Republican budget included large tax cuts; a comprehensive restructuring of Medicare (a program that affects forty million seniors); cuts in student loans, farm subsidies, and Medicaid; reductions in dozens of programs with long-established constituencies; and the elimination of the Commerce, Education, and Energy departments. It represented a more profound change in federal policy, and arguably a greater political risk to its supporters, than the 1993 Clinton budget that nearly tore apart the congressional Democratic Party before passing by the narrowest possible margin. Yet only a single Republican House member voted against the GOP budget in the spring of 1995.

Change did not come as rapidly to the Senate after 1994. Indeed, partisan conflict had not increased in the Senate nearly as much as in the House over the previous two decades. The Senate's culture of individuality never allowed as much centralized command as the House developed after the 1970s.* Senate Democrats and Republicans had adopted rules similar to the House that abandoned the deference to seniority in picking committee chairs. But despite occasional threats, neither party had used them; punishing senators for independence still seemed less accepted than disciplining House members who strayed from their party's mainstream. "I think it's tougher to do that in the Senate," said Tom Daschle, the South Dakota senator who served as Democratic leader from 1995 through George W. Bush's first term. "Ownership of a seat on a committee is pretty well established." Other Senate traditions—civility, comity, the desire of senators to be seen as statesmen rather than partisans—further discouraged the open warfare that had erupted in the House through the Reagan years. It was as if senators were surrounded by too much marble to imagine throwing mud. Moderates from each side still routinely worked together through the early 1990s. And there was a final practical restraint on partisanship in the Senate: Ending a filibuster required sixty votes, which almost always required the majority party to attract some support from the minority.

Yet, as in the House, the decorous traditions from the age of bargaining frayed and faded in the Senate. Twice in the last half of the 1980s, the Senate convulsed in unusually ugly confirmation battles. After Democrats

---

* Differences in rules reinforced divergence in habit. A key to the House leadership's power was its ability to determine which issues would come to a vote before the full chamber through its control of the Rules Committee. Even if a bipartisan group developed a proposal that might win a majority on the House floor, they would never receive the opportunity to offer it unless the speaker opened the gate at the Rules Committee. Senators, though, had more freedom to offer relevant amendments to any pending legislation. That meant any senator could try to build his or her own ad hoc legislative coalition simply by presenting an alternative on the floor. No matter which party held the majority, that option represented a constant threat to the leadership's control of the agenda.

regained control in 1986, the Senate rejected Reagan's nomination of Robert Bork to the Supreme Court, and then denied George H. W. Bush's selection of John Tower, himself a Republican senator from Texas, as defense secretary. Senators became more likely to stand with their team against the other: The average senator voted with his or her party on contested votes about three fifths of the time in the 1970s, three quarters in the 1980s, and more than four fifths in the 1990s. And senators resorted more often to the ultimate weapon in Senate debate, the filibuster. During the age of bargaining senators had reserved the filibuster for the most epic confrontations, usually the showdowns between North and South over civil rights. Even as late as the 1960s, in each two-year Congress, the Senate on average held only about four votes seeking to end a filibuster. During the 1970s that number increased to an average of about twenty per Congress; during the 1980s, the average rose again to twenty-seven. The number soared past forty during both the final two years of Bush's presidency and the first two of Clinton's. Senate Republicans, led by Dole, mounted a successful filibuster against Clinton's first major proposal, an economic stimulus plan, and never looked back. By the end of 1994 Senate Republicans had used the filibuster against fully half of Clinton's top priorities, political scientist Barbara Sinclair later calculated. The filibuster once had been the legislative equivalent of a nuclear weapon. Now senators turned to it as routinely as a police officer might reach for his nightstick.

When Republicans regained control of the Senate after 1994, the pattern persisted. The Senate didn't change as much or as quickly as the House, but it followed in the same direction. Conservatives grumbled when the Senate, facing strong resistance from Democrats and defections from some moderate Republicans, failed to approve some of the key items in the House's contract, like a constitutional amendment to balance the federal budget. But Senate Republicans united behind a budget plan that cut taxes, reduced the growth in spending, and challenged the seemingly inexorable growth of the federal government nearly as aggressively as the blueprint approved by the young revolutionaries in the House. Not a single Republican senator voted against the GOP budget.

Clinton's 1993 budget had balanced one idea popular with Republicans (restraining spending on some domestic programs) with two elements

preferred by Democrats (raising taxes, increasing spending on other targeted programs). But the 1995 GOP plans approved in the House and
Senate aimed squarely at conservatives: They matched tax cuts with reductions in the growth of government spending severe enough to change the
character of long-established programs like Medicare and Medicaid. Senate Republicans sanded down some of the roughest edges when they met
in a conference committee to reconcile their plan with the version approved in the House. But the blueprint that emerged represented much
more of a frontal assault than even Ronald Reagan ever dared on the federal programs that Democrats had built and nurtured for a century. Not a
single Democrat in the Senate and just eight (of two hundred) in the
House voted for the final plan that June; once again, every Senate Republican and all but one in the House voted for it. The Republicans had produced a vision of the federal role in society that polarized the two parties
in the starkest possible terms.

Even more confrontational than the substance of the plan was Gingrich's
strategy for driving it into law. He crystallized the abstract conservative
demand for more confrontation with Democrats into a tangible showdown, or more precisely, a shutdown: a plan to shut down the ordinary
operations of government unless Clinton accepted the long-term Republican budget plan.

The subsequent standoff in the fall of 1995 broke the momentum of the
new Republican majority, and placed Clinton on a trajectory to reelection.
The Republicans could not sell the nation on their vision of a substantially
reconfigured federal government. More important, most Americans recoiled from a vision of partisan warfare so unconstrained that it shuttered
Social Security offices and closed national parks. Twice through the fall
and winter of 1995 the Republican Congress tried to compel Clinton to
sign their long-term budget plans by linking them to the legislation required to fund the ongoing operations of government. Twice Clinton surprised them by vetoing the bills. The Republicans expected the public to
blame Clinton when all but essential government offices shut their doors.
Instead, the cloud burst over the Capitol. The approval rating for Congress plummeted. Clinton's numbers, with hydraulic precision, rose. Dole,
watching his presidential hopes sinking in the debacle, eventually broke

ranks and pressured the House Republicans to reach a deal that reopened the government and deferred the longer-term questions about taxes and spending cuts. But from the GOP perspective, the damage was done. Clinton had reestablished his relationship with the public in a way that virtually ensured his reelection. The 1996 presidential race essentially ended at that moment; no Gallup survey ever again showed Clinton trailing Dole.

The fight, just as importantly, transformed Clinton's relationship with the Democratic Party. In his first two years he had deferred too often to the instincts of the congressional leadership. Their principal focus was maintaining unity in their own caucus. That focus had its own internal logic: It was the caucus, after all, who elected them. But it led them to consistently pressure Clinton against compromises that might have attracted moderate Republican votes at the price of alienating liberal Democrats. That approach wasn't in Clinton's interest, or even in the long-term interest of congressional Democrats, as the 1994 disaster demonstrated. Clinton first signaled his restlessness with that strategy in the spring of 1995. On the April day that Gingrich and his allies celebrated their one-hundredth day of control in Congress, Clinton spoke in Dallas to the American Society of Newspaper Editors. By then Clinton was listening closely to Dick Morris, a shadowy political consultant the president enlisted as an adviser after the 1994 landslide. Morris, who had worked for Democrats (including Clinton in Arkansas) and Republicans over a baroque career, thought Clinton could revive his presidency by transcending and ultimately reconciling both parties with a strategy Morris called "triangulation."

Morris was a manic self-promoter with a theatrical penchant for secrecy whose purpose often seemed to be validating the most demeaning stereotypes about political operatives. Yet Morris's basic insight was sound: In a deeply divided country, Clinton could do the most good, for the nation and his own political fortunes, by navigating a course between rote opposition and feeble acquiescence to the congressional Republicans. The Dallas speech offered the first sign that Clinton had accepted that direction. In it he pledged to be reasonable in dealing with the new force rising on the other end of Pennsylvania Avenue. "I do not want a pile of vetoes," he declared at one point. "Ideological purity is for partisan extremists," he said at another. But then he condemned many of the specific proposals Gingrich was driving through Congress: a repeal of the ban on assault weapons Clinton had signed in 1994; limits on his ability to commit American military forces to missions commanded by the United Nations; and, above all, the large tax cut Republicans had included in their budget plan.

It wasn't apparent at the time, but in that speech, Clinton had found ground he could stand on. It set the tone for the next two years of his presidency, the period of the most productive bipartisan deal making since Nixon's first term. Harold Ickes, a tough New York liberal who joined the White House as deputy chief of staff in 1994, echoed others on the president's staff when he concluded that the Republican takeover freed Clinton to surmount the familiar partisan arguments that had engulfed his first two years. "In a very strong sense it was liberating for him," said Ickes. That freedom, Ickes added, came "at a very high cost," but "I think he used it in fair measure to a lot of his advantage."

That became clear in the first critical choice Clinton faced after his Dallas speech. As Republicans advanced their proposal to balance the budget, most congressional Democrats wanted Clinton to create the sharpest possible contrast by opposing the GOP plan without committing himself to an alternative. But Clinton, following the framework he offered in Dallas, chose a more subtle and effective response. Over intense resistance from many congressional Democrats, Clinton in June 1995 accepted the Republican premise that the federal budget needed to be balanced. But he offered a radically different means to eliminate the deficit, and condemned the Republican approach as a threat to Medicare, Medicaid, education, and the environment, or M2E2 as the White House dubbed it. Clinton positioned himself as the one figure in Washington offering an accommodation while still promising formidable resistance if accommodation was denied. That synthesis proved much more attractive to the public than the GOP vision of unlimited warfare or the liberal Democratic approach of unconditional opposition. It also set a model for how a president committed to compromise can drive the parties toward it even in an era when most forces push toward confrontation.

The unambiguous victory for Clinton and unambiguous defeat for the House Republicans in the budget showdown over the winter of 1996 shifted the balance of power in both parties. The Senate Republican deal makers sought to climb from the rubble by reaching more agreements with Clinton before the 1996 election, and the House leaders no longer had the credibility, or the will, to resist them. At the same time, the standoff increased Clinton's ability to confront the Democratic congressional leaders resisting agreements and enlarged the number of backbench congressional Democrats willing to support his strategy.

The result was an Indian summer for the deal makers, or more precisely two Indian summers. After Dole stepped down as majority leader in May 1996 to focus full-time on his presidential campaign, his successor, Mississippi Republican Trent Lott, reached a series of agreements with Clinton that would have been unimaginable the year before.

The legislation that most clearly showed both the strength of the new deal-making impulse and its fragility was welfare reform. The issue split both parties. Republicans divided between those who wanted legislation Clinton would sign and those who wanted to send him the bill in a form that would generate a veto and provide them an issue for the November election. Democrats divided between centrists attracted to restructuring welfare and liberals who had opposed significant reform since Clinton first promised "to end welfare as we know it" in his 1992 campaign.

Clinton twice vetoed Republican welfare reform plans, including one that ended guaranteed access to health care for the poor through Medicaid, a red flag for a president who already had been frustrated trying to expand access to health care. Eventually, congressional Republicans valuing an accomplishment over a dispute dropped the provision ending the Medicaid entitlement, thus eliminating the major obstacle to a deal. Negotiating directly (or through the intermediary of Morris, who had worked for both men), Clinton and Lott narrowed many of their other differences over issues such as providing day care for welfare recipients required to work. But even with those changes, and the removal of the Medicaid poison pill, almost all liberal Democrats still found welfare reform too much to swallow. The Republican bill ended the federal entitlement to welfare and imposed a five-year lifetime limit on benefits without the guarantee of a publicly funded job that Clinton originally proposed. Many House Democrats urged Clinton to veto the bill. So did much of his cabinet when Clinton gathered them in the Roosevelt Room for a rare full-dress debate over the legislation's merits. All of this left Clinton with no doubt that he would divide his party, and generate howls of outrage from his base, by signing this version of welfare reform. And yet he signed the bill anyway.

Inevitably, Clinton's motivation was partly political: By accepting welfare reform he denied Bob Dole a potentially biting issue that could revive his moribund challenge in the 1996 election. (Republicans also felt Clinton was more willing to deal on welfare after Dole left the Senate, because his opponent could not then receive credit for any agreement.) But Clinton also concluded that the bill represented his best and perhaps last chance to fulfill his 1992 promise of remaking a welfare system that he genuinely believed trapped recipients into generations of poverty. He accepted an imperfect bill because he realized he would have no chance in the foreseeable future to impose his version of a perfect solution. The first decade of experience, at least, has mostly validated his gamble. The legislation was flawed (particularly in its harsh treatment of legal immigrants who had not yet become citizens), but it brought millions of welfare recipients into the workforce, where they could benefit from the rising economic tide of the late 1990s. By the time Clinton left office, the share of single women in poverty had fallen to its lowest level ever recorded, and the number of children in poverty had decreased by 4.1 million. During Ronald Reagan's eight years the number of children in poverty had fallen by just 50,000.

In Washington, the effects of the welfare agreement were almost as beneficial, though not nearly as enduring. Clinton's welfare announcement opened the door for rapid-fire agreements between the White House and the Republican Congress to raise the minimum wage, allow workers to more easily preserve their health insurance when they changed jobs, and help cities ensure safe drinking water. The voters then provided more incentive for compromise in the 1996 election by returning to power both Clinton and the Republican House and Senate majorities. "It was clear we were going to have to deal with each other," recalled Reed, the White House domestic policy adviser. "They had been humbled by the experience of the last two years . . . and they had to decide whether they were going to govern or not, and we recognized that we'd been vindicated [with Democrats] in our philosophy that getting things done, trying to govern from the center, was what the country wanted. And so . . . it was possible to put the pettiness aside."

The resurgent deal making reached its apex the next summer when the two sides reached consensus on a plan to balance the federal budget for the first time since 1969. The path to an agreement was smoothed by an improving economy that provided enough revenue to avoid any discussion of new taxes. Even so, the negotiations required the two parties to mesh their priorities in a way that they could not during their repeated standoffs the previous winter. Republicans won tax cuts and future restraint on Medicare spending. Democrats were pleased by the structure of the tax cuts, primarily a credit for families with children, and increased spending for domestic social programs such as education. On the spending side, the biggest winner was a plan both sides supported: a joint federal-state partnership to provide health insurance for the children in working poor families, which has proven to be Washington's most successful new social program in decades.

In Congress the budget compromise drew opposition from some Democratic liberals and Republican conservatives, each of whom, with inverted rigidity, considered it a capitulation. Yet the agreement showed even stronger bipartisan appeal than welfare reform had demonstrated the previous year: It passed the House by a margin of more than 4 to 1 and the Senate by more than 5 to 1. It showed, as clearly as any other agreement in recent times, that the parties could advance some of their most prized goals and make progress against entrenched problems by blending each other's priorities. Most important, the compromise worked: Through the remainder of Clinton's second term the federal deficit was replaced by growing surpluses; the tax burden on middle-income families declined; and states steadily enrolled hundreds of thousands, and ultimately millions, of children in the new children's health insurance plan.

With the passage of the budget in 1997, Clinton established his center-out approach, for the time, as the dominant position in the Democratic Party. The forces of polarization, while hardly extinguished, seemed on the defensive among Republican elected officials as well. Clinton mused about following the budget deal with bipartisan initiatives on even knottier problems: the long-term solvency of Social Security and Medicare. Gingrich thought the two sides might work out an agreement to create private investment accounts, not carved out from Social Security as George W. Bush later proposed, but as an addition to the system. And Gingrich brainstormed with Clinton about agreements they might reach on other issues, such as health care. ("He and I privately got along fine," Gingrich said. "We were like two graduate students hanging out.") The budget breakthrough inspired others as well. John Breaux, the smooth Louisiana Democrat, and Bill Frist, an ambitious Republican heart surgeon elected to the Senate in 1994, collaborated on proposals to reduce the cost of Medicare and increase access to health care. Reed imagined future agreements on issues like child care "where Democrats would go along because it was investment and Republicans would go along because it was popular."

Yet the budget deal proved the zenith of accommodation. Just like Bush in 1990, congressional Republican leaders faced a ferocious backlash from conservative leaders for reaching a budget compromise with the other party. Some prominent conservatives (especially those, like Grover Norquist, personally close to Gingrich) supported the agreement. But Bill Kristol's new *Weekly Standard* magazine denounced it as "a capitulation . . . to fear." The Heritage Foundation issued a similar verdict. At an early gathering of Republican activists auditioning potential contenders for the party's 2000 presidential nomination, Dan Quayle, the former vice president, complained that the "Contract with America" had devolved into a "contract with Clinton."

A more tangible expression of discontent came from a group of about twenty conservative House members. Frustrated partly by the leadership's concessions to Clinton, they met to plan a coup against Gingrich even as he helped to negotiate the final details in the budget agreement. The plot collapsed when it was revealed, but it represented a clear warning to him against further deals with Clinton—especially because, by some accounts, both Armey and DeLay had participated in various stages of the talks. Discontent with Lott never reached such a point in the Senate, but he faced similar grumbling from conservative groups as the agreements accumulated with the White House.

The recoil against the 1997 budget deal from conservative activists revealed attitudes with implications far beyond these specific tax and spending decisions. On both policy and political grounds many conservative critics rejected not only this particular deal, but the very concept of agreements that required substantial concessions from each party, a category that encompassed just about any possible arrangement with meaningful bipartisan support. From one angle, the critics denounced the deal's political implications. Gingrich, slipping into Bob Michel's old shoes, defended the budget deal as necessary to prove to voters that Republicans could "take responsibility for getting things done." "I used to tell my members, 'if [Clinton] runs in and says I'll sign it, why are you complaining?' " Gingrich recalled. "You're not going to turn [an idea] into law unless the president signs it. It is not a defeat to have your bill signed." But many conservatives lashed Gingrich with the same arguments that he had wielded against Michel, Dole, and Reagan in the 1980s: They insisted the budget deal was politically counterproductive because it clouded the distinctions between the parties. "We're fudging the differences between Republicans and Democrats, and when we do that, we hurt ourselves," said Tom Pauken, the staunchly conservative chairman of the Republican Party in Texas.

Just as telling were the conservatives' substantive complaints about the agreement. The deal did not include the tax increases that had ignited the firestorm against Bush's 1990 budget package. But many conservative commentators still faulted it for not cutting spending or taxes enough. When Republican "leaders say this budget realizes their dreams," the *Wall Street Journal* complained in an editorial, "it's time for Republicans to look for people with bigger dreams." These assessments testified to the scale of the conservative ambition to remake Washington and retrench government regulatory and safety-net programs that traced back from the Great Society through the New Deal, and in some cases to the Progressive Era. The widespread criticism of the budget agreement was a signal that many conservatives harbored goals that could not easily fit into agreements with almost any Democrat.

The gales of conservative discontent over the 1997 budget quickly changed the climate on Capitol Hill. "After the balanced-budget agreement, the conservatives just had had it making deals with Clinton," said Bruce Reed. "It was clear that we'd run out of things to agree on." On almost every front the watchword changed from accommodation to annihilation. That fall, Senator Jesse Helms (R-NC) single-handedly derailed Clinton's nomination of Republican William Weld as ambassador to Mexico, and the Republican majority on the Senate Judiciary Committee blocked NAACP Legal Defense Fund lawyer Bill Lann Lee as assistant attorney general for civil rights. After conservative groups complained that the Senate was approving too many of Clinton's judicial nominees, confirmation of his choices for the federal courts "slowed to a trickle." House and Senate Republicans passed legislation blocking Clinton's top education reform priority, a plan to create voluntary national tests in math and reading that could provide a benchmark for state progress. Dueling filibusters from Republicans and Democrats smothered campaign finance reform legislation in the Senate. Dissension among congressional Democrats chafing at the centrist deal making of the previous year compounded the sense of confusion. Dozens of House Democrats joined with Republicans to sink Clinton's education plan, partly, Reed felt, to signal their discontent over the White House's frequent deal making with Republicans. Even more House Democrats bolted to prevent him from obtaining enhanced authority to negotiate more trade deals like NAFTA. While all these legislative initiatives crashed, the Senate Governmental Affairs Committee spent over $2 million on thirty-two hearings from July to October exhaustively searching for misconduct in the frenetic fund-raising for Clinton's 1996 reelection campaign. In the House, seventeen impatient Republicans went one better: They filed a resolution formally requesting that the House investigate whether Clinton's actions in the campaign finance controversy provided grounds for impeachment.

And then Clinton provided the forces of polarization the weapon they needed to end any thoughts of further cooperation.

In some ways the scandal that surrounded Clinton's affair with Monica Lewinsky was not a contributor to, but an outgrowth of, the polarized atmosphere. The relationship became public in January 1998 only through the intersecting machinations of Kenneth Starr, the zealous special prosecutor investigating Clinton's Whitewater business investment; the conservative legal team advising Paula Jones, an Arkansas woman suing Clinton for sexual harassment; and Linda Tripp, an embittered former White House aide who had improbably befriended Lewinsky. All of these swirling circles testified both to the depth of conservative antipathy toward Clinton, and the barrage of investigations that his opponents directed against him.*

Clinton's mistakes unshackled the dissenters from accommodation who had been suppressed for the previous eighteen months. The Lewinsky scandal reinforced the sense on the right that Clinton was fundamentally illegitimate as a president and a man, and thus strengthened the hands of those demanding that congressional Republicans reach no policy deals that could enhance his credibility. The scandal shifted the balance of power on the Democratic side even more emphatically. Clinton could not risk deals with Republicans that alienated the left while he needed those same legislators to protect him against possible impeachment and removal from office. He abandoned his earlier talk of restructuring Social Security and other entitlements. The window for a grand compromise, always narrow, slammed shut.

The next object that came toward Clinton was shaped more like a guillotine. Just before the 1998 midterm election, House Republicans formally began the process of impeaching him, despite substantial misgivings from many House GOP moderates and polls showing overwhelming public opposition among Democrats and independents, and majority support only from Republicans.† The push for impeachment rumbled past all obstacles. In a clear signal of the country's uneasiness with the Republican course, Democrats gained five House seats in the November 1998 election—the first time a president's party had gained House seats in the sixth year of his tenure since Andrew Jackson. But the House Republicans continued to move forward. Even the successive resignations from Congress of both Gingrich (who faced widespread discontent over his mercurial style and

* It's difficult to avoid the conclusion that investigating Clinton was the strategy congressional Republicans used to mollify the portions of their base demanding absolute war against him while they courted the center of the electorate through policy agreements with the administration.
† Just before the House impeachment vote, ABC/*Washington Post*, CNN/*USA Today*/Gallup, and CBS/*New York Times* surveys all found that at least 58 percent of independents and 84 percent of Democrats opposed impeachment. In each survey, by contrast, about two thirds of rank-and-file Republicans supported it.

the GOP losses in November) and his successor, Bob Livingston (felled by his own sexual indiscretions), didn't slow the train. With DeLay tirelessly greasing the tracks, in the House all but four Republicans voted for at least one of the four articles of impeachment (two of which passed). Even in the Senate, where the leadership did not apply as much direct pressure, fifty of the fifty-five Republicans voted to convict Clinton and remove him from office on at least one of the two articles the House approved.

That left Republicans far short of the two-thirds vote needed to remove him, since not a single Democrat voted with them. But even after the end of Clinton's ordeal, the momentum of 1996 and 1997 could not be recovered. In the aftermath of impeachment, Washington was a changed place. "We were impeaching each other," said Breaux, who saw the ideas he had formulated with Frist consumed on the pyre. "It was not a climate suitable for compromise." Achievement dwindled largely to the annual budget bill that allowed each side to fund some of its priorities. Impeachment had detonated like a nuclear bomb. Its fallout was so toxic that nothing grew in the crater.

The lessons of the Clinton years were both sobering and encouraging about the possibility of reversing the trend toward polarization and promoting more compromise in American politics. The failure of Clinton's 1994 health care plan, and then Gingrich's budget revolution the next year, clearly demonstrated the political danger of seeking to impose sweeping change in a closely divided country without bipartisan consensus. Each man's frustration validated an aphorism of Thomas Jefferson: "Great innovations should not be forced on a slender majority." If those two failures had shown the risks of confrontation, the bipartisan agreements from the summer of 1996 through 1997 had shown the promise of cooperation: The agreements demonstrated that it was possible to win broad public support for significant changes when both parties linked arms to present them to the country as a reasonable compromise. In polls at the time the welfare reform agreement drew support from more than three fifths of Democrats and four fifths of Republicans; similarly, almost two thirds of Americans from both parties said they supported the budget agreement reached the following summer. And the policies that generated such broad support produced genuine progress on real problems: The welfare bill prompted a social revolution that moved millions of single women into the workforce, and the budget agreement helped to produce four consecutive years of federal budget surpluses for the first time since the 1920s.

In all these ways the climate of cooperation that warmed Washington through the Indian summer of deal making demonstrated that agreement could provide each side tangible policy and political benefits. But it also demonstrated that those benefits were insufficient to suppress the forces, especially in the Republican coalition, demanding more conflict in American politics. After the budget deal Washington almost immediately fell back into a spasm of partisan confrontation that culminated in the virtually party-line vote to impeach Clinton in December 1998. The hallmarks of the impeachment fight—unrelenting partisan confrontation, and the explicit rejection of any compromise that could unite the parties and the country (such as a resolution of censure)—proved a far better predictor of the politics that would follow than the agreements over welfare and the budget.

Indeed, the House vote to impeach Clinton may mark the final, full transition into the political era in which we now live. Certainly many congressional Republicans, like millions of other Americans, were genuinely offended by Clinton's behavior. But impeachment also drew momentum from a political calculation among congressional Republicans that elevated the demands of their hard-core base (which supported impeachment) above the overall current of public opinion (which decisively opposed it). It demonstrated too the increasing capacity of the congressional leadership, especially in the House, to pressure wavering members to support the dominant party position. On impeachment, the vast majority of congressional Republicans concluded that maintaining party unity—in their caucus and with their party's hard-core supporters—mattered more than aligning themselves with majority opinion in the country overall.

THIS WAS A POLITICS John F. Kennedy or Dwight Eisenhower or even Richard Nixon could not have imagined. It was a politics that only became possible after the ideological and geographical bases of the parties had grown so distinct and adversarial that political leaders could hold support inside their own core coalition for a course of action that alienated virtually everyone else. Conceived, endorsed, and executed almost entirely by a single party, and more precisely, by a single faction of conservatives within that party, impeachment provided a sudden and stark demonstration of how a generation of political realignment had changed the incentives in American politics. Clinton had handed his opponents a sword with behavior that validated their darkest assumptions about his character. But whatever their moral indignation, in an earlier era Clinton's opponents probably would have feared the electoral consequences of wielding that sword. The force that dispelled their fear was the arranging of the parties into more disciplined, ideologically coherent, and culturally homogenous coalitions. It is that process, the most powerful engine of polarization in American politics, we turn to now.

CHAPTER 6

★

THE GREAT
SORTING OUT

In the tumultuous spring of 1968, two ambitious young men took the
first important steps of their political careers.

In Pascagoula, Mississippi, a recent graduate of the University of
Mississippi law school named Trent Lott packed his wife Tricia and all of
their belongings into a 1968 Pontiac and drove to Washington, D.C. Lott
was on his way to begin a job as administrative assistant for Pascagoula's
longtime representative, the staunchly conservative Democrat William
Colmer.

Around the same time, in South Bend, Indiana, a Notre Dame student
named Ralph G. Neas, Jr., volunteered for the Republican presidential
campaign of New York governor Nelson Rockefeller, who was making a
late bid to deny the GOP nomination to Richard Nixon. Neas devoted
most of his spring and summer to Rockefeller's quixotic cause. At the Republican convention in Miami Neas joined a contingent that mounted
such an enthusiastic floor demonstration for "Rocky" that they were evicted
from the convention hall.

Neas and Lott both began their political careers in the parties of their
parents. Lott was born in October 1941 to Chester and Iona Watson Lott

in Grenada, Mississippi, and spent his early years in small, poor, rural counties north of the state capital in Jackson. Mississippi in those years was classic "Yellow Dog" Democrat country, the sort of Southern state that it was said would vote for a yellow dog before a Republican. The year before Lott's birth Franklin Roosevelt won 96 percent of the vote in the state; in 1944, he won 94 percent. Lott's family had little money. His father worked as a sharecropper, and later at a shipyard in Pascagoula, and his mother taught school. But relatives on both sides of his family were active in the state's one-party Democratic politics. As a young boy Lott was fascinated by their political gossip and lore, sitting up late under the porch of his house to hear them swap stories and settle arguments. The men who gathered on those sultry evenings lived in a political world virtually without Republicans, who were still tainted as the party of the North in the Civil War. In his memoir Lott says that he doesn't remember his parents ever disagreeing about politics until 1952, when his mother voted for Dwight Eisenhower and his father voted the party line for Adlai Stevenson and the Democrats, as he had done for his entire life. The Democrats' hold on Mississippi loosened during Lott's adolescence, as the party became more closely identified with the cause of ending segregation and extending civil rights to African Americans. Colmer had pointedly refused to support John F. Kennedy in 1960. In 1964, amid the white fury over the passage of that summer's seminal Civil Rights Act, Barry Goldwater became the first Republican to carry Mississippi since Ulysses S. Grant in 1872. Yet, even so, when Lott pointed his Pontiac to Washington that spring of 1968, Democrats still held both of Mississippi's Senate seats, its governorship, and all five of its House seats.

The political environment that shaped Neas wasn't as suffusing. He was born in 1946 in Brookline, the affluent suburb outside Boston, lived briefly in Connecticut, then spent the rest of his younger years in St. Charles, Illinois. St. Charles, located about forty miles west of Chicago, stood at the far edge of suburbia, on the border of rural Illinois. It was quiet, pretty, overwhelmingly white, and mostly Republican.

Neas's father, Ralph G. Neas, Sr., was a vice president for a brass company, and firmly conservative in his politics, a committed Republican and Goldwater admirer. The younger Neas found himself pulled in a different direction, mostly by his admiration for the civil rights movement that blossomed during his high school years. In high school Neas wrote an essay praising Harry Truman's decision to integrate the armed forces; at Notre Dame, over his father's objections, he participated in a fair housing march in Chicago in 1966. "He certainly evolved before he died in 1998, but I remember in 1966 Dad getting so mad, [saying], 'Don't do that again,' " said Neas.

Neas's involvement with the civil rights movement, and the growing skepticism he felt about the Vietnam War after he left Notre Dame (where he served as a lieutenant colonel in the ROTC) for the University of Chicago law school, made him recognize that he didn't share his father's conservative ideology. But he felt much less conflict about sharing his father's partisan identification. In college Neas considered himself to be an independent. But he found that the politicians he most admired were often moderate and liberal Republicans. "I've always found liberal Republicans immensely appealing," Neas said. "Remember the two places where I'm from: Chicago and Boston. When I was growing up there were city machines that were corrupt and the Republicans were the reformers. The real good government types, the courageous politicians were many times the liberal Republicans."

At the top of the list for Neas was Nelson Rockefeller, New York's dynamic, big-spending Republican governor. "I fell in love with Rockefeller," Neas said. "He was great on civil rights issues and he was trying to find a way out of the war." After Nixon defeated Rockefeller, Neas that fall cast his first presidential vote for Hubert Humphrey. But he was not drawn toward abandoning the Republican Party. When he finished law school Neas settled in Washington, where he took a job in 1971 as a legal researcher and writer for the Congressional Research Service. After a short stint at Fort Benjamin Harrison in Indiana to fulfill his military responsibilities, Neas returned to Washington and received job offers from Bella Abzug, the flamboyant liberal Democratic representative from New York, and Edward W. Brooke, the erudite, African American Republican senator from Massachusetts. By then Neas understood that his political views placed him to the left of center. Yet he felt no hesitation about expressing those views as an aide to a Republican senator. "For me it was Edward

Brooke, historic figure, first African American popularly elected to the Senate, leader on civil rights issues," Neas said. "It was the easiest decision I ever made." Sometime after joining Brooke, Neas switched his registration from independent to Republican.

Lott's political evolution is a bit more opaque, though in many ways it represented the flip side of the historic forces that moved Neas away from his father's conservatism. Race was once again a triggering factor. In interviews over the years, and in his memoirs, Lott portrays himself as aloof from the civil rights revolution that rattled Mississippi through his youth. Lott seemed largely indifferent when James Meredith, a young black Air Force veteran, sought to integrate the University of Mississippi in fall 1962. As Mississippi's governor Ross Barnett escalated his opposition to Meredith, Lott, by his own admission, was more concerned about his fraternity and the Ole Miss football team. "I confess that I was in the ranks of the clueless," he wrote in his memoir. When attempts to register Meredith provoked a riot on the university campus that forced the intervention of federal troops, Lott's principal interest was to keep his Sigma Nu fraternity brothers away from the violence—a reasonable, if narrow, focus. In an interview years later Lott acknowledged that he shared the support for segregation widespread among Mississippi whites at the time, but there's no evidence he felt any personal animus toward African Americans or any passionate attachment to the old racist order; he simply felt no urgency to challenge it.* Disconnected from the moral issues involved, Lott drew an eccentric conclusion from the crisis on his campus: He seemed more disillusioned by the federal effort to support Meredith than the violent resistance against him. "I felt anger in my heart," he wrote years later, "over the way the federal government had invaded Ole Miss to accomplish something that could have been handled peacefully and administratively."

In Washington Lott stood at the elbow of a man who shared those views, and then some. William Colmer, then seventy-eight, was an archetype of the old one-party South, an unwavering segregationist skeptical of the expansion of federal power on almost any front. For years Colmer had

---

* In his memoirs Lott wrote that he recognized that the defense of segregation was doomed and that integration's "time had come."

joined with Chairman Howard Smith and the four Republicans on the House Rules Committee to block civil rights and other liberal legislation. (Sam Rayburn, recall, initially tried to break the conservative coalition's hold on the Rules Committee in 1961 by stripping Colmer of his seat for opposing Kennedy, until a rebellion among other Southern Democrats forced him to abandon the plan.) When a primary challenger ousted Smith in 1966, Colmer succeeded him as the Rules Committee chairman and steered the same reliably conservative course (though the enlargement of the committee Rayburn and Kennedy had engineered diluted his power).

A shrewd young man, Lott quickly noticed the obvious: Though Colmer labeled himself a Democrat he voted more often with House Republicans like Gerald Ford and H. Allen Smith, the ranking GOP member on the Rules Committee, and seemed closer to them in every way. The power that Colmer's connection to the Democratic Party provided him as chairman of the Rules Committee made it impractical for him to align his partisanship with his ideology by switching parties. Lott felt no such constraint. He edged away from his inherited Democratic loyalties when he founded a bipartisan group of congressional conservatives. He felt the final break one day when he sat in on a meeting of Democratic Senate staff members known as the Young Burros Club. Lott listened with mounting frustration as a Democratic congressman and Democratic National Committee chairman Larry O'Brien, the former Kennedy and Johnson congressional liaison (who had helped manage the 1961 campaign to shatter the conservative hold over the Rules Committee), delivered boilerplate party speeches. Walking back to the House Lott elbowed a friend who had attended the luncheon with him. "I don't agree with a single word I heard today," Lott said with a mixture of revelation and amazement. "I'm not a Democrat."

Lott later said that that was the day he "crossed the Rubicon and became a Republican." When Colmer stepped down in 1972, Lott surprised no one by announcing he would seek to replace him. But he stunned Colmer, and almost everyone else, by announcing he would do so as a Republican. At the moment fewer than one in every ten of the district's voters were registered as Republicans. But Lott had correctly gauged the shift in the winds. Thousands of voters across Mississippi, and millions across the South, were beginning the same journey to align their partisan label with their ideological orientation. Lott won the seat with 56 percent of the vote, and never looked back. He was reelected seven more times and quickly rose to the leadership of the young conservatives in the House, winning election as minority whip. When John Stennis, the aging, ailing segregationist Democratic senator, finally stepped down in 1988, Lott won his seat. Rising quickly again, Lott won election as Republican whip after the GOP takeover in 1994; when Bob Dole stepped aside in 1996 to focus on his presidential campaign against Bill Clinton, Senate Republicans picked Lott to succeed him as Senate majority leader. The vote signaled more than Lott's personal ascent. With Newt Gingrich serving at the time as House speaker, Lott's victory meant Southern Republicans—a species that virtually did not exist in Lott's youth—held the two top positions in the congressional GOP. The wave that Lott had seen building a quarter century earlier had not only transformed the South, but remade the Republican Party itself.

This new Republican Party was more amenable to views like Lott's but less congenial to those like Neas's. Even so, Neas's attachment to the party of his youth dissolved only slowly. He worked happily for Brooke until 1978, when the senator lost to a Democrat in the general election after fighting off a challenge from a conservative in the Republican primary. Even after Brooke's defeat, Neas went to work for another moderate Republican, Minnesota's David Durenberger. Neas's career, and nearly his life, was derailed in 1979 when he was paralyzed with Guillain-Barré syndrome, also known as French polio. He spent nearly six months in the hospital, totally incapacitated, unable to move, breathe, speak, or even remove his own wastes. Then the plague lifted, and Neas slowly recovered. When he resumed his career he still felt most comfortable operating in Republican circles. He returned to Durenberger's office, and nearly went to work for the Reagan administration until congressional conservatives lobbied to kill his proposed appointment to the top civil rights job at the Department of Housing and Urban Development.

It was an eye-opening moment for Neas. In 1981 he took his first step out of the GOP by accepting the job of executive director of the Leadership Conference on Civil Rights. The conference, an alliance of nearly two hundred groups, drew support from moderate Republicans as well as Democrats for many of its efforts. But its principal causes—civil rights for minorities and women, access to abortion, gay rights—all inspired the most enthusiasm among Democrats and liberals. In his new position Neas dueled almost daily with Republican conservatives in Congress and the Reagan and Bush administrations through the remainder of the 1980s. When Reagan nominated Robert Bork to the Supreme Court in 1987, Neas stood at the center of the massive grassroots and lobbying campaign that helped defeat him.

But through it all Neas retained his registration as a Republican. Expediency partly explained the decision: Neas, and many of the key figures at the conference, thought his connections to Republican leaders like Dole and Howard Baker benefited their cause. But Neas also believed his worldview still had a place in the GOP. His closest friends in Congress remained moderate pro–civil rights Republicans like New York representative Hamilton Fish or Maryland senator Charles McC. Mathias. "It was certainly an issue in the 1980s," Neas recalled, "but I really loved Ham Fish or Mac Mathias. Even until the early 1990s, if you had Ham Fish in the House you had forty Republican votes. At the time, naively, I thought there was still a chance that wing of the party could be resurrected."

Neas finally abandoned that hope only after the Republican landslide in 1994. The conservative forces he had opposed in so many legislative disputes since the 1970s suddenly controlled both chambers. And as their confrontations with Clinton culminated in the government shutdown of 1995, Neas felt his last connections to the GOP vanishing. "I realized [that] there was a slim chance in my lifetime that moderate Republicans would play a real role," Neas said. "The people I'd been battling since '73 were totally in control of the House and the Senate." On October 15, 1996, at age fifty, Ralph Neas for the first time registered as a Democrat.

Two years later Neas ran unsuccessfully as a Democrat for Congress from the Maryland suburbs. After a short interlude of writing and teaching, Neas became president of People for the American Way, the pugnacious liberal group founded two decades earlier by television producer Norman Lear to combat the influence of religious conservatives. With that appointment Neas completed his odyssey: He now directed an organization that fought congressional Republicans and the conservative movement as tenaciously and unabashedly as any institution on the left.

Traveling along their mirror-image trajectories, Lott and Neas occasionally crossed paths. Lott accumulated one of Congress's most consistently conservative records on civil rights, regularly voting against the measures Neas promoted. In December 2002, the two men finally collided head on. At a ceremony honoring Strom Thurmond on his one-hundredth birthday, Lott ignited a firestorm by praising Thurmond's 1948 Dixiecrat campaign for president—which Thurmond ran, of course, on a platform of defending segregation. It was difficult to imagine Lott was really pining for a return to Jim Crow. But the incident blew up because Lott had used racial innuendo and coded language so many other times before. Neas quickly moved to the front of the line of those demanding Lott's ouster. "Lott's continued leadership of the Senate is an embarrassment to the nation," he charged. When Senate Republicans removed the former Mississippi Democrat as their leader, few were more pleased than the onetime Rockefeller Republican from Massachusetts.*

THE VOTERS RE-SORT

Neas and Lott have probably hardened somewhat in their views since the 1960s. But mostly their youthful beliefs have not changed. What changed is the party they found most compatible with those beliefs. To remain constant in their convictions, both concluded they needed to change their parties. With that decision each joined in a great migration. Over roughly the past forty years, millions of other Americans made the same journey as Lott and Neas to realign their partisanship with their ideology. Millions of younger Americans, when they entered the electorate for the first time, followed their tracks to identify with the party they considered most hospitable to their broad ideological beliefs.

This massive, generation-long process produced the great sorting out in American politics. In this political re-sorting liberals like Neas have become much more likely to identify with the Democratic Party and

---

* Lott completed a remarkable comeback when Republicans elected him their minority whip after losing control of the Senate in the 2006 election.

conservatives like Lott have become much more likely to identify with the Republican Party. The views that Lott and Neas championed in the parties of their youth have been marginalized on each side. The differences within the two parties' electoral coalitions have narrowed, but the distance between the two sides has widened. This ideological realignment has been accompanied by a re-sorting of the parties on cultural and geographical lines that has reinforced their differences. In the process American politics has been transformed. No other single factor has contributed more than the great sorting out to the decline of the deal-oriented politics of the age of bargaining, and to the rise of the fierce political conflict that marks our own period of hyperpartisanship.

During the age of bargaining each party was an ideological jumble not only in Congress but in its electoral coalition. Polling on the attitudes and beliefs of the two parties' supporters was not nearly as thorough in the 1950s and 1960s as it is now. But the best evidence is that in those years both parties drew support from voters with a wide range of views. Opinions diverged within the parties' coalitions and overlapped between them. Americans might pick their party because of the customs in their family (like Neas), or the traditions where they lived (like Lott), or a general sense of where they stood on the class ladder, but the evidence suggests relatively few believed that they were enlisting behind a detailed set of shared beliefs.

Three researchers at the University of Minnesota—Herbert McClosky, Paul J. Hoffmann, and Rosemary O'Hara—conducted perhaps the most comprehensive study of attitudes within the parties during these years. In 1957 and 1958 they designed an ambitious split-level survey. On one track they surveyed thousands of leaders in the two parties—everyone from governors and senators to local officials and members of the parties' national committees. Then they measured attitudes among the parties' rank-and-file supporters through an exhaustive national poll administered by Gallup.

The leaders of the two parties divided in a pattern that would be familiar today. On the twenty-four domestic and foreign policy issues the survey measured, the Republican and Democratic leaders expressed significantly different views on twenty-three. And the differences aligned in the expected way, with Republican leaders predominantly taking the more conservative position for lower taxes, less government regulation, less government spending, less reliance on the United Nations or international military alliances, and Democratic leaders lining up behind the contrasting liberal positions.

But the lines were much less distinct among the parties' followers. Not surprisingly, the study found the clearest differences on the bread-and-butter disputes that had dominated American domestic politics since the New Deal. More rank-and-file Democrats than Republicans wanted to increase the minimum wage and farm price supports and to raise taxes on the wealthy; more Republicans wanted to increase regulation of trade unions and reduce government regulation of business. But on each of these choices the differences between the rank-and-file members of each party were not nearly as large as the distance between their leaders. And on most of the twenty-four issues the survey measured, only small differences emerged in the views of Democratic and Republican voters. The two groups expressed similar views on economic concerns, such as raising taxes on business or increasing federal aid to education; on most social issues, such as the level of immigration and the extent to which the federal government should enforce integration; and on foreign policy choices that ranged from reliance on the UN to the amount the United States should spend on defense and foreign aid. "Whereas the leaders of the two parties diverged strongly, their followers differ only moderately in their attitudes toward issues," McClosky and his collaborators concluded. "Little support was found for the belief that deep cleavages exist among the electorate . . ."

Two other encyclopedic studies of public opinion in this era—*The American Voter*, published by four University of Michigan political scientists in 1960, and *Public Opinion and American Democracy*, a 1961 book by the great political scientist V. O. Key, Jr.—reached similar conclusions. Both books relied on the national election studies (NES), national opinion surveys conducted by the University of Michigan since 1948. Like the University of Minnesota researchers, Key and the authors of *The American Voter* found the two parties' supporters divided most consistently on the central issue in the partisan debate since Franklin Roosevelt—the size and scope of the federal government. But while Republican voters generally favored less government activism and Democratic voters more, the differences were modest: In 1956, significant shares on both sides thought the federal government was doing about the right amount to cope with problems like housing and unemployment. On noneconomic issues such as foreign policy, or the federal responsibility to ensure school desegregation, the NES surveys found almost no differences in opinion between rank-and-file Republicans and Democrats.

This muddled electoral alignment reinforced the temperate political strategies of the age of bargaining. As we saw in Chapter 4, many of the era's key figures, from Eisenhower and Kennedy to Lyndon Johnson and Sam Rayburn, were personally inclined toward consensus. But to the extent voices in each party wanted a more confrontational and purist politics they lacked the electoral base to support it. With both parties relying on such a diverse range of voters, each stood to lose at least as much as it might gain from polarizing the electorate with a sharply defined ideological message. Both parties were drawn to the center because their electoral coalitions sprawled across it.

In the 1960s, the electoral underpinnings of this system began unraveling, like a rope that frayed from both ends. On a series of divisive issues the parties took positions that transmitted more ideologically consistent signals to the voters. Over time the voters responded to those signals by sorting themselves between the parties in a more ideologically consistent manner. As the parties became more ideologically cohesive, they increasingly elevated politicians who sent strong ideological signals, accelerating the cycle of change. Like the forces that sustained the age of bargaining, the dynamic that destroyed it fed on itself.

The impetus for the change came partly from each party's ideological vanguard, which had seen its priorities jointly suppressed since the late 1940s. In 1964, Republican presidential nominee Barry Goldwater offered voters a much more conservative agenda than Nixon or Eisenhower proposed. "Extremism in the defense of liberty," Goldwater declared, "is no vice." Lyndon Johnson presented himself as a conciliator against Goldwater, but in 1965 Johnson embraced (and advanced) the domestic agenda of the left far more than Kennedy had. When Nixon finally won the White

House in 1968, he compromised broadly with Democrats on a wide range of issues but systematically solidified the Republican identification with conservative positions on social disputes like crime and busing. In 1972, Democratic presidential nominee George McGovern stamped his party with a leftist perspective on foreign policy and defense that it has still not entirely escaped more than three decades later.

In all of these ways the strategies pursued by Democratic and Republican leaders in the 1960s and early 1970s sharpened the ideological differences between the two sides. But events were more important than any of those choices in separating the parties. The extraordinary social, economic, and foreign policy challenges that converged on America during those years repeatedly forced the two parties to pick sides in disputes that powerfully divided the country. The civil rights movement that culminated in the mid-1960s finally compelled the two sides to take stands on an incendiary issue that both had tried to suppress for decades. The Vietnam War forced them to clarify differences over national security and America's role in the world that had been moderated by the bipartisan commitment to containment for the first two decades after World War II. The Supreme Court's 1973 decision legalizing abortion required both parties to take positions on an issue that few politicians had even publicly discussed until a few years earlier. New strains in urban life pushed forward highly emotional issues like crime and school busing. The drive for the Equal Rights Amendment during the 1970s—and the conservative backlash against it—crystallized disagreements over the changing role of women. The new liberal interest groups that emerged after the late 1960s ignited conflicts with business over the environment, occupational safety, and consumer protection. The conservative groups that arrived a few years later agitated for action on tax cuts, abortion, and other social issues like school prayer, and resisted rising demands from homosexuals for protection under civil rights laws.

Both parties experienced at least some internal divisions on these issues. But over time each party became predominantly identified with one side in the disputes. And on almost every one of them—first on civil rights, or remaining in Vietnam; and later on busing, crime, abortion, and taxes—the center of gravity among the leaders in the Democratic Party drifted to the liberal side of the argument, while the center of opinion among the leaders in the Republican Party migrated to the conservative side.

The result of all these upheavals was to trigger the great sorting out in American politics. Over the next generation the parties' electoral coalitions were reshaped. They acquired the ideological coherence they had lacked in the age of bargaining. In their basic philosophic orientation toward the choices America faced at home and abroad, the electoral coalitions that supported the two parties became more distinct and more antagonistic.

By itself, the great sorting out didn't change the absolute level of disagreement in society. In fact, it's an open question whether Americans are more divided in their views today than twenty or forty years ago. The concept itself is slippery at best. And the evidence that might measure it is mixed. Certainly on many practical questions facing Washington—whether the best strategy for invigorating the economy is to cut taxes or reduce the national debt; whether to amend the constitution to ban gay marriage; whether the United States should work mostly with allies or act alone to defend its interests in the world—polls often show the country split almost exactly in half. But on many other issues surveys show a growing consensus for social tolerance. Compared to twenty or thirty years ago, there is a wider consensus among Americans today that accepts interracial dating, rejects the idea that a woman's place is in the home, and agrees that homosexuals should have equal rights for job opportunities.

Whether all of this means there is more or less disagreement in society than a generation ago is, to a large extent, in the eye of the beholder. What's indisputable is that the differences that do exist are now organized more consistently and coherently in the political system. We can't trace the process in detail until 1972, when the University of Michigan's NES studies first asked Americans whether they considered themselves liberal, moderate, or conservative. But there's strong circumstantial evidence to suggest the big bang that began the ideological sorting out was the 1964 race between Johnson and Goldwater, especially amid the Southern backlash against the civil rights law approved that summer that ended state-sponsored segregation. Goldwater's breakthrough in winning five Deep South states left little doubt that millions of white conservative Southerners who had voted Democratic for generations took a first tentative step into the GOP.

But Johnson's dominant performance almost everywhere outside the South also suggested that many moderate to liberal voters who traditionally supported Republicans simultaneously took a step in the opposite direction. In 1964, to a greater extent than under Eisenhower or Kennedy, ideology aligned with partisanship.

Over the next four decades the connection between ideology and party loyalty deepened, producing a Republican Party dominated by voters who consider themselves conservatives, and a Democratic Party increasingly influenced by liberals. The key to the process has been the growing alignment between ideology and partisanship, not a change in the ideological balance of the country itself. In fact, the NES surveys show that the ideological balance among voters has changed relatively little since it first asked Americans to place themselves on a left-right scale in 1972. The table following tracks the share of Americans who identified themselves as liberals, moderates, and conservatives in NES surveys over the past four decades.*

This table shows much more continuity than change. Conservatives have consistently outnumbered liberals since the 1970s, but the gap between them has not changed much over time: It stood at twelve percentage points in the 1970s and fifteen percentage points in the most recent measure. Both

IDEOLOGY BY DECADE

Decade	Liberal (%)	Moderate (%)	Conservative (%)
1970	26	36	38
1980	24	34	41
1990	25	33	43
2000	28	29	43

Source: Calculated from National Election Studies by Alan Abramowitz, Emory University. Columns may not add up to 100 percent because of rounding.

* These figures exclude voters who could not identify themselves along the ideological spectrum. That group stood at about 3-in-10 during the 1970s and has shrunk to about 2-in-10 now. In this, and in the tables that follow, the 1970s include elections from 1972 through 1980; the 1980s include the elections from 1982 through 1990; the 1990s include the elections from 1992 through 2000; and the current decade includes the elections of 2002 and 2004.

ideological camps have gained ground at the expense of moderates, but again the change is only modest (seven percentage points). Neither of those findings suggests significant movement in the country's underlying ideological balance. Nor does another result from the NES research (not reported in the table): Since 1972 there has been essentially no change in the share of voters who call themselves extremely conservative (up from 1 percent then to 3 percent in 2004) or extremely liberal (1 percent then, 2 percent now). Both groups together add up to little more than a rounding error. All of these findings justify the verdict of veteran Republican pollster Bill McInturff when he concludes, "There is no evidence to my mind that we are more ideological or more divided than fifteen or twenty years ago."

Yet over these same years, the country's partisan balance clearly changed. In NES surveys during the 1950s and 1960s, Democrats outnumbered Republicans by about 3-to-2. Today NES surveys show Democrats with only a slight lead, and other polling organizations at various points in the Bush years found the two sides virtually tied in allegiance. (Democrats reestablished a larger advantage as President Bush's popularity collapsed in his second term, but given the long-term trends, it seems unlikely the party can sustain a lead of that magnitude once Bush fades from the scene.) The exact numbers from survey to survey are not that significant; the important point is that a wide variety of measures now find the two parties more closely balanced than a generation ago.

The great sorting out is the reason the country's partisan balance has changed while its ideological balance has remained stable. Though the number of voters who consider themselves liberal or conservative hasn't shifted much over the past generation, the partisan allegiance of those voters has changed dramatically. The key to the GOP's growth has been an exodus of conservative voters, especially in the South, from the Democratic Party. A migration of liberal voters from the Republican Party has mitigated, but not nearly offset, that loss for the Democrats.

With fewer conservatives identifying as Democrats and fewer liberals identifying as Republicans, each party's electoral coalition has grown more ideologically uniform. That change is evident both in the way voters describe their partisan loyalties, and the way they actually vote on Election Day. Let's look at the loyalties first.

The tables following report the way voters who identify as Democrats or Republicans described their ideological views in NES surveys since the 1970s:*

IDEOLOGY OF DEMOCRATS

Decade	Liberal (%)	Moderate (%)	Conservative (%)
1970	35	39	26
1980	36	38	26
1990	43	35	22
2000	52	32	17

IDEOLOGY OF REPUBLICANS

Decade	Liberal (%)	Moderate (%)	Conservative (%)
1970	9	29	63
1980	10	25	65
1990	6	22	72
2000	6	18	77

Source: Calculated from National Election Studies by Alan Abramowitz, Emory University. Columns may not add up to 100 percent because of rounding.

These results underscore two important points. One is that Democrats remain more of an ideological coalition than Republicans. Liberals are the dominant group among Democrats, but they don't comprise nearly as large a share of the party's overall support (52 percent) as conservatives do among Republicans (77 percent). In terms of their supporters' underlying ideological inclinations, Democrats face more conflicting, and moderating, pressures than Republicans.

The second point qualifies the first. Though the Democratic base is not as ideologically homogenous as the Republican base, the clear trend on

---

* The figures exclude voters who could not identify themselves on the ideological spectrum.

both sides is toward greater uniformity. During the 1970s there were two Democrats who considered themselves moderate or conservative for every one who called himself a liberal. Today, among voters who identify as Democrats, liberals (slightly) outnumber moderates and conservatives combined. A parallel tilt is evident in the GOP. Among Republicans in the 1970s there were almost two liberals and moderates for every three conservatives. Today in the GOP, conservatives outnumber liberals and moderates combined by more than 3 to 1. In each party the dominant ideological tendency has increased its strength at the grassroots.

These party loyalties tell only part of the story. Not every voter who identifies as a Republican or Democrat, of course, supports all of their party's candidates on Election Day. But those actual voting decisions, as reported in NES surveys since the 1970s, also show a solidifying link between ideology and partisanship. The share of liberals voting for Democratic candidates is rising. The share of conservatives voting for Republican candidates is increasing even more. The two tables following track the change:

PERCENT OF LIBERALS VOTING FOR DEMOCRATIC CANDIDATES BY DECADE

Office	1970 (%)	1980 (%)	1990 (%)	2000s (%)
House	75	79	79	83
Senate	73	76	83	86
President	74	77	91	89

PERCENT OF CONSERVATIVES VOTING FOR REPUBLICAN CANDIDATES BY DECADE

Office	1970 (%)	1980 (%)	1990 (%)	2000s (%)
House	59	60	71	78
Senate	62	65	74	80
President	81	79	76	90

Source: Calculated from National Election Studies by Alan Abramowitz, Emory University.

These tables show that in both parties the re-sorting has gained momentum over the past three decades. Liberal support for Democratic House, Senate, and presidential candidates was already high in the 1970s, but it has increased in close parallel since, as if ascending on an escalator. Conservative support for Republican presidential candidates started high, dipped some under Bill Clinton, and then peaked in George W. Bush's 2004 reelection. The larger change has been the growing parallel between conservatives' preference for president and their choices in House and Senate races. Conservatives began dating the GOP to spend time with right-of-center presidential candidates like Goldwater, Nixon, and Reagan; but from these numbers it is clear that the vast majority of them have now entered into a lasting relationship with the party.

REPUBLICANS ARE WINNING more votes from conservatives all across the country. But the biggest shift in the allegiance of conservatives occurred in the South. Indeed, the forty-year transformation of white Southern conservatives like Trent Lott from Yellow Dog Democrats to reliably Republican voters probably has been the single most significant force in the ideological re-sorting of the parties. By removing conservatives from the Democratic coalition, the shift has tilted that party's balance of power toward liberals. And by adding conservatives to the Republican coalition, it has reduced the relative influence of moderates and liberals in the GOP.

White Southern conservatives abandoned their ancestral loyalty to the Democratic Party for many reasons. The white backlash against the landmark civil rights laws of the 1960s opened the door for the GOP in the region, and in the years that followed many Republican candidates implicitly or explicitly exploited lingering racial tensions around issues such as affirmative action, busing, and crime. Debates over taxes, the size of government, and national security that placed the national GOP firmly to the right of the national Democratic Party during the next two decades helped Republicans consolidate the breakthrough. Since the 1980s the GOP's identification with conservative social causes such as opposition to abortion or gay marriage has probably been the central factor in its Southern ascendance.

Together these factors have virtually obliterated support for Democratic candidates among Southern conservatives. As recently as the 1970s, the NES surveys show, about half of Southern conservatives still voted for Democrats in Senate races and more than three fifths supported Democrats in House contests. But, as the table following makes clear, Republicans have overrun those defenses.

SUPPORT FROM CONSERVATIVE SOUTHERNERS FOR REPUBLICAN CANDIDATES BY DECADE

Office	1970 (%)	1980 (%)	1990 (%)	2000 (%)
Representative	38	47	74	77
Senator	52	51	76	84
President	79	75	76	87

Source: Calculated from National Election Studies by Alan Abramowitz, Emory University.

The GOP's gains among Southern conservatives have been essential to its modern strength. But the right-leaning messages that helped Republicans in the South weakened the party's support elsewhere. As recently as the 1970s Republican House, Senate, and presidential candidates still won support from nearly 3-in-10 liberal voters outside the South, the NES surveys found. But that support has almost vanished. In the 2002 and 2004 elections Republican House candidates won votes from only about 1-in-6 liberals outside the South. Republican Senate candidates won support from only 1 of every 10 liberal voters outside the South. In 2004, Bush attracted just 1 in every 9 of those voters. In all, liberals outside the South are now voting for Democrats at rates even higher than conservatives are voting for Republicans in the South.

Over the same period moderate voters have shifted their allegiance in ways that compound the sorting out. Republicans have *improved* their per-

formance among Southern moderates since the 1970s in House and Senate
races (while slightly losing ground in presidential contests). But as the next
table shows, the GOP consistently has lost ground among moderate voters
elsewhere.

SUPPORT FOR REPUBLICAN CANDIDATES AMONG MODERATES IN STATES OUTSIDE THE SOUTH, BY DECADE

Office	1970 (%)	1980 (%)	1990 (%)	2000 (%)
Representative	46	40	42	40
Senator	47	43	42	33
President	59	53	36	47

Source: Calculated from National Election Studies by Alan Abramowitz, Emory University.

After all these changes the parties now divide the electorate in much
sharper and more consistent patterns than they did a generation ago. Voters who identify as conservatives now overwhelmingly favor Republican
candidates not only for the White House, but for the Senate and House of
Representatives as well. Voters who identify as liberals are voting just as
heavily for Democrats up and down the ticket. In each party the preponderant ideological group has grown more dominant since the 1970s. Liberals constitute a larger share of the Democratic coalition than thirty-five
years ago; conservatives represent more of the Republican coalition. The
great regional anomaly in American politics has been eliminated. Conservatives in the South now favor Republican candidates as decisively as conservatives from the rest of the country. Meanwhile, liberals in states outside
the South now support Democrats with majorities even greater than
Southern conservatives provide Republicans. Even moderates have polarized. Inside the South they have moved toward the GOP. Outside the
South they are tilting more toward Democrats.

The parties are not monolithic even today; each still contains diverging
and sometime conflicting opinions. But they now enter each debate repre-

senting coalitions much further apart in their basic philosophic assumptions than half a century ago.

THE PICKET FENCE DIVIDE

This separation between the parties has been reinforced by a second form of re-sorting over the past three decades, one that has reconfigured the electorate around lifestyle choices and cultural attitudes. The principal glue for the parties in the middle years of the twentieth century was class. The New Deal, the Depression, and Franklin Roosevelt cemented an image of the Democrats as the party of the "little guy" and the GOP as the party of the rich and business. "At least since the invention of polling techniques," V. O. Key concluded in 1961, those "differential images of the Republican [Party] and of the Democratic Party have prevailed." In 1959, when Gallup asked Americans from different occupations which party best represented their interests, business executives and professionals picked the Republicans over the Democrats by nearly 4 to 1. Both skilled and unskilled workers picked Democrats over the Republicans by more than 3 to 1. These distinctions, of course, were never absolute. Each party drew significant support from beyond its expected class stronghold. But through the first six decades of the twentieth century, Americans typically aligned with the party they believed would defend their *interests*.

Class hasn't vanished as a factor in American politics. Bill Clinton, Al Gore, and John Kerry all won handily among voters earning less than thirty thousand dollars a year. George W. Bush in 2000 and 2004, and even hapless Bob Dole in 1996, carried most voters earning over one hundred thousand dollars a year. But class distinctions don't separate the parties as reliably, or as powerfully, as they once did.

Starting in the late 1960s, and accelerating under Reagan, Republicans carved into the Democratic advantage with blue-collar workers. Beginning in the 1970s, and then accelerating under Clinton, Democrats have increased their support among affluent and college-educated professionals and suburbanites. The two trends are intertwined. Republicans weakened the links between Democrats and white working-class voters by stressing conservative positions on racially tinged disputes like crime, welfare, and busing (especially in the 1970s and early 1980s), opposition to taxes, hawkish messages on foreign policy, and culturally traditional positions on social issues like abortion and gay rights. But the Republican identification with the conservative side of those arguments opened the door to Democratic gains in the suburbs around messages of tolerance on social issues and international cooperation on foreign policy (especially after Clinton's centrism reduced the Democratic vulnerability with upscale voters on issues like federal spending, crime, and welfare).

The difference between the two closest presidential elections of our time is revealing. Whether measured by income or occupation, Al Gore performed better in 2000 than John F. Kennedy in 1960 with upscale groups and George W. Bush ran better than Richard Nixon with blue-collar and middle-income voters. The result was to flatten the class distinctions. In 1960, the NES polls found, Nixon won almost three fifths of professionals and white-collar workers, while Kennedy carried more than three fifths of blue-collar workers; in 2000, the widest margin for either candidate in any of those groups was 53 percent to 47 percent. Nor is the class attachment to the parties as consistent as it once was. Nixon in 1972 and Ronald Reagan in 1984 carried most blue-collar workers; Clinton twice carried most professionals. Since 1980, according to the NES studies, white-collar workers have voted, in order, for Ronald Reagan twice, George H. W. Bush, Clinton twice, Gore, and George W. Bush.

These numbers tell us that while class still matters in American politics, its relative influence is diminishing. We are moving from a politics based primarily on class to one that revolves principally around culture. Increasingly, Americans are aligning with the party they believe will defend their *values.*

Arguments over values, as opposed to interests, aren't new in American politics. In the nineteenth century Protestants and Catholics feuded over public support for parochial schools. In the early twentieth century prohibition divided the South from the Northeast, evangelical Protestants from Catholics, and the countryside from the city. Slavery is probably the best example of an issue that engaged millions of Americans not because it affected their interests but because it affronted their values.

But the number and variety of issues that divide Americans along cultural lines is running at an historic high tide. Since the mid-1960s, social rather than economic concerns have ignited many of the most incendiary arguments in American politics: AIDS, school prayer, abortion, partial-birth abortion, public funding of abortion, the Equal Rights Amendment, gay marriage, gays in the military, gay adoption, stem cell research, the regulation of pornography, the teaching of creationism, or the display of the Ten Commandments. These values questions are defining the parties far more than they did a generation ago. The best evidence suggests that voters classify themselves as liberal or conservative less by their attitudes on material questions such as taxes, trade, or social spending than by their views on cultural issues and other nonmaterial concerns, like the use of force in foreign policy.

Stanley B. Greenberg, the veteran Democratic pollster who worked for Bill Clinton in 1992, Al Gore in 2000, and John Kerry in 2004, speaks for many political strategists in both parties when he says, "The meaning of liberal and conservative has changed." A former Yale University political scientist who retains an owlish, scholarly air, Greenberg has spent the past two decades studying the ways Americans make political decisions. And over that period he's seen Americans increasingly view their vote as a means of expressing their values rather than of advancing their material interests. "I've looked, over time, at what are the predictors of being liberal or conservative," Greenberg continues. "And since I ask all the time, I ask about ideology, and a whole variety of [questions] measuring attitudes on different institutions. There is almost no material issue or institution that correlates with ideology. Attitudes toward the market, toward corporations, toward unions don't correlate with ideology. Same thing is true on trade. What it is correlated with are cultural issues, and security issues, like the Iraq War. You have cultural issues reinforced by security issues driving out economic issues."

Today the most important boundary in American politics may be the picket fence. The GOP has become the party of Americans who live the most culturally traditional lives: marriage; kids; Sunday morning in the pews; probably in a suburban, exurban, or rural community. The Democrats run best with the groups that don't fit into those cultural archetypes: singles; seculars; gays; nonwhites; and those people (including married couples) who feel comfortable living closer to the racial and ethnic diversity of urban centers. In effect, the electorate has sorted between the parties not only in the priorities they declare on issues, but in those they express in their daily lives. Married and single voters now diverge in their political choices. Even larger is the political chasm between Americans who attend church regularly and those who don't.

Neither of those distinctions affected voting behavior during the age of bargaining. In the 1950s and 1960s, Eisenhower and Nixon actually ran better with single voters than with married couples; Stevenson and Kennedy and Johnson ran as well with those who attended church once a week or more as with those who attended less often or not at all. But since the 1970s Republican presidential candidates have performed substantially better with married than with single voters. Religious practice has become an even more powerful electoral force. In every election since 1972 the Republican presidential candidate has won significantly more support from voters who attend church at least once a week than from those who don't, according to the NES studies and media exit polls. This phenomenon extends across denominational loyalties. For most of the twentieth century political allegiance divided along lines of religious belief: Catholics and Southern evangelicals leaned toward the Democrats, Northern Protestants were reliably Republican. Now the most important divide is religious practice. In every major denomination—Catholic, mainline Protestant, evangelical Protestant—Republicans run better with those who attend church most regularly. Even Jewish voters, who are more difficult to track because of their smaller numbers, appear to follow the same pattern. The table following tracks the widening gap between the Republican presidential vote among those who attend religious services once a week or more, and those who visit less frequently or not at all.

Since the age of bargaining the parties' coalitions have dispersed along other demographic dimensions as well. The first important change was the racial re-sorting of the electorate. Through the 1950s both parties effectively competed for the votes of Northern blacks; but since the civil rights

RELIGIOUS ATTENDANCE
AND GOP PRESIDENTIAL VOTE

Elections	once a week or more (%)	less than weekly (%)	gap (%)
1952/1956	59.2	59.1	0.1
1960/1964/1968	45.8	45.8	0
1972/1976/1980	60.8	53.4	7.4
1984/1988	58.6	53.1	5.5
1992/1996	51.6	33.7	17.9
2000/2004	56	43.3	12.7

Source: Calculated in 2006 by John Green, University of Akron, from NES data for this book. The figures represent the Republican share of the two-party vote in presidential elections and exclude votes for third-party candidates such as John Anderson in 1980, Ross Perot in 1992 and 1996, and Ralph Nader in 2000.

era, African Americans have moved overwhelmingly into the Democratic Party. Gender followed next. Women and men didn't differ much (or consistently) in their support for Republicans and Democrats through the 1970s. But the gender gap—the tendency, depending on your viewpoint, of men to vote more heavily Republican than women, or women to vote more heavily Democratic than men—has appeared in every presidential election since 1980. Differences between the city and countryside are a more enduring feature of American politics, but they, too, are running at an especially high level. The past two elections have produced a huge divergence between voters based on place, with Democrats running best among urban voters, Bush dominating rural and exurban communities, and the two sides battling closely in the suburbs.

These social differences, of course, are not absolute. Each party attracts votes from millions of people who fit the predominant cultural profile on the other side. And there is reason to believe these divisions need not be as wide as they are today. But, for now, each party holds a commanding position on the opposite side of racial, gender, marital, geographic, and religious divides. That has added a deeper dimension to their separation.

At the heart of each party is a group of voters—married churchgoers for the GOP, singles and seculars for the Democrats—who differ from the other side not only in their political philosophy, but also in their reaction to the most basic social changes of the past generation, and in the choices that shape their personal lives. John Edwards, the Democratic vice presidential nominee in 2004, spoke about "two Americas"—one struggling economically, the other economically comfortable. It is more relevant politically to say the two Americas divide between those who mostly embrace the changes in sexual, family, and social mores of the past forty years and those who mostly resist them. And after decades in which millions of Americans re-sorted their partisan loyalties, each side in that argument now holds the dominant position in one of the two major political parties.

THE PARTITIONING OF AMERICA

In a moment of exuberance during the waning weeks of the 1996 presidential campaign, Bill Clinton scheduled a campaign rally in Birmingham, Alabama. He arrived on a beautiful late October day to find ten thousand people waiting for him under crystalline blue skies at Birmingham Southern College. The crowd buzzed with enthusiasm and optimism. One supporter held a sign that read "Democrats are Christians."

Clinton's presence in Alabama testified to the opportunities he believed he had created with his New Democrat centrism. No Democratic presidential candidate had carried Alabama since Kennedy in 1960. With Ross Perot siphoning away conservative votes, Clinton in 1992 performed better in Alabama than most recent Democrats, but still lost the state to George H. W. Bush by about 114,000 votes. Under the warm sunshine, before the excited rows of supporters, Clinton seemed to imagine he might reverse that result in 1996. "It is such a beautiful day, and the crowd is so large," Clinton declared, "maybe Alabama is going to come along with me."

Alabama didn't come along with Clinton. A few weeks later on Election Day, Clinton reduced his deficit slightly from four years earlier, but still lost the state by a decisive 106,000 votes to Bob Dole. Even with the gains Clinton registered among culturally traditional voters in 1996, Alabama was still a bridge too far for the Democrats.

Eight years to the week after Bill Clinton visited Alabama, George W. Bush pointed Air Force One to Evesham Township, New Jersey. New Jersey wasn't quite as inhospitable territory for a Republican as Alabama was for a Democrat. Nixon (twice), Ford, Reagan (twice), and George H. W. Bush, in fact, had carried it in each of the six presidential campaigns from 1968 to 1988. But New Jersey's leafy upscale suburbs were filled with the socially liberal professionals who had migrated toward the Democrats in the cultural re-sorting between the parties after the 1970s. New Jersey voted narrowly for Clinton in 1992, then provided easy double-digit victories to him in 1996 and Al Gore four years later. Bush's team believed the trauma of September 11 provided an unusual opportunity to reverse the trend. As the 2004 campaign neared its end, the president, in fact, was showing unusual strength all around the New York metropolitan area, where memories were most vivid of his firm response to the attack. And in case anyone had forgotten, Bush in his New Jersey appearance made sure to remind them. "On September the eleventh, from places like Hoboken and Jersey City, you could look across the Hudson River and see the twin towers burning," he said in his speech. "We shall never forget that day, and we will never forget our duty to defend America."

New Jersey clearly hadn't forgotten that day. When voters there went to the polls a few weeks later, Bush significantly improved his performance from 2000. But like Clinton eight years earlier in Alabama, Bush still fell way short. John Kerry beat him in New Jersey by more than 240,000 votes.

The disappointments for Clinton in Alabama and Bush in New Jersey show the extent to which the ideological re-sorting of the electorate has triggered a geographic re-sorting as well. Even with formidable assets— the strong economy for Clinton in 1996, the memories of 9/11 for Bush in 2004—both failed to capture a prized target in the other side's stronghold. That frustration has become a common experience. As Republicans have deepened their hold over voters who consider themselves conservative, especially on social issues, they have solidified their control over the most ideologically conservative states, across the South, the Plains, and the Mountain West. As Democrats have strengthened their hold over voters who consider themselves liberal, and even moderate (outside the South), especially on social issues, they have fortified their control over the Northeast, mid-Atlantic, and West Coast, and improved their position in the upper Midwest. The geographic competition between the two parties looks far more settled, polarized, and even rigid than it did during the age of bargaining.

One measure that marks the change is the stability of voting in presidential elections. The 2004 general election between Bush and John Kerry started earlier than any presidential campaign in modern times. The two sides spent gargantuan sums (roughly $700 million between them, plus hundreds of millions more through the national parties). And yet after all that effort, only three states switched hands. Two states that narrowly voted for Gore in 2000 (Iowa and New Mexico) narrowly backed Bush in 2004. New Hampshire, which tilted toward Bush in 2000, bent toward Kerry in 2004.

A deeper measure of the division is the pattern of loyalties in the past four presidential elections. Fully 34 states, or about two thirds of the total, have voted for the same party in each presidential election since 1992. That level of consistency has not been common since the highly partisan period that stretched from McKinley through Franklin Roosevelt. In the four presidential elections the GOP won from 1896 through 1908, 33 states (or 73 percent of the 45 states in the union for all 4 elections) voted the same way each time. An incredible 38 of the 48 states (79 percent) voted the same way in each of the three Republican victories from 1920 through 1928. Franklin Roosevelt's victory in 1932 shattered that system but imposed a new one that proved just as durable: In his four victories from 1932 through 1944, 33 of the 48 states (69 percent) voted the same way all four times.

But through the age of bargaining, as partisan lines blurred and the parties traded control of the White House more frequently, states did not align as consistently with one side. From 1948 through 1960, just 11 states voted the same way each time. Just two states voted the same way in each election from 1964 through 1976; even dropping 1964 from the list to eliminate the influence of Lyndon Johnson's landslide increases the total only to 22.

These numbers portray a political system during the heart of the twentieth century in which relatively few states were entirely beyond either party's reach for extended periods. But after the ideological and cultural re-sorting of the electorate, the number of states that reliably tilt toward one side or the other is again increasing. In the presidential elections from 1976 through 1988, 25 states voted the same way all four times. Leaving out Carter's 1976 victory and looking solely at the triumphs of Reagan and George H. W. Bush in 1980, 1984, and 1988, the number soars to 39.

The point isn't that states are locked so permanently into one camp that they cannot be dislodged by a big enough earthquake. In 1992, Clinton won twenty states that voted three times for Reagan and Bush (though the number might not have been so high if Ross Perot had not siphoned away so many ordinarily Republican votes). A few of the states that voted the same way four times since 1992 have been consistently competitive (such as Wisconsin and Pennsylvania). And enough states remain in play to provide either party a competitive opportunity to win the White House. But with all that said, in the past quarter century the parties have established more lasting advantages in more states than at any point since the first half of the twentieth century.

Another measure underscores the hardening of these loyalties. The number of states that divide closely between the parties in presidential races, while still enough to tip a tight election, is running at a historically low level. It is most revealing to compare highly competitive elections. Measured by the overall popular vote, the 2000 election between Al Gore and Bush was nearly as close as the 1960 race between Kennedy and Nixon. In 1960 the two contenders finished within ten percentage points of each other in thirty-four states. In 2000 the two men finished within ten percentage points of each other in just twenty-two states. Similarly, the 1976 race between Jimmy Carter and Gerald Ford, measured by the candidates' shares of the overall popular vote, was only slightly closer than the 2004 race between Bush and John Kerry. But in 1976 Carter and Ford finished within ten percentage points of each other in thirty-one states. For Bush and Kerry the corresponding number was just twenty-one.

This trend toward solidifying state loyalties is unhealthy. It encourages each party to write off entire regions in the presidential election. That reduces the pressure on the parties to craft messages or nominate candidates with an appeal that transcends geographical and ideological boundaries. There may be reason to hope that over time demographic and political changes—the migration of blue-state social liberals to fast-growing outer South red states; the tension between Mountain West libertarians and a GOP colored by Southern evangelical social conservatism; the Republican efforts to improve their performance among churchgoing African Americans in big cities—might break down these barriers and allow both parties to genuinely compete in more of the country. But for now each side views much of the political map as immutable. When Republican presidential nominees can't contemplate a serious bid for California, and Democrats can't give even a passing glance to Georgia, the parties take another discouraging step toward functioning as the champions of one group of Americans against another.

The effect of this re-sorting is compounded by a parallel trend. More voters are aligning their votes for Congress and president. As we saw earlier, liberals and moderates outside the South are voting more consistently for Democrats in congressional as well as presidential elections; conservatives, especially in the South, are voting more reliably Republican. That ideological re-sorting has struck with devastating force against the largest groups of swing votes in Congress: the moderate Republicans (most of them from the Northeast, the upper Midwest, and the West Coast) and the right-of-center Southern Democrats.

The moderate Republicans and Southern Democrats did not always agree. From the 1940s through the 1960s they often aligned on opposite sides of major issues in the four-party congressional politics of the era. Yet even then both functioned as bridges between the parties (albeit at different bends along the river). And their purposes converged more after the 1960s, when the changing nature of Southern politics nudged the post–civil rights generation of Dixie Democrats like Louisiana's John Breaux or Georgia's Sam Nunn closer to the center than their segregationist predecessors. (With Southern Republicans attracting the most conservative whites, the remaining white Southern Democrats increasingly built their electoral coalitions around African Americans and moderate whites, which required them to offer more centrist stands on issues.) In the years roughly from Richard Nixon through Bill Clinton's first term the Northern Republicans and Southern Democrats constituted a formidable centrist block in both the House and Senate. Each exerted a steady moderating influence on their party in Congress. And each was the first group a president from the opposite party would target when trying to assemble a bipartisan alliance.

Today, a president reaching for either of these groups would find few hands left to reach back. The Northeast and mid-Atlantic always provided the most reliable stronghold for the moderate Republicans. But over the past half century, as the ideological identity of each party hardened (especially on social issues), Republicans have been routed in these states. In 1951 Republicans held two thirds of the Senate seats and nearly three fifths of the House seats in the eleven states from Maryland to Maine. By 2006 the proportions had flipped: Republicans held only one third of the region's Senate seats and less than two fifths of the House seats. And then in the 2006 election, the bottom fell out for Republicans in the East. With exit polls showing that only one third of Eastern voters approved of George W. Bush's job performance, Republicans lost eleven more seats in the House across the region and two more in the Senate. After the election Democrats held seventeen of the region's twenty-two Senate seats (including independents Bernie Sanders of Vermont and Joe Lieberman from Connecticut, both of whom caucused with the party) and nearly three fourths of its House seats. In the six New England states House Republicans were virtually exterminated: They were reduced to just the single Connecticut seat held by moderate Chris Shays, a frequent critic of Bush.

In the South the parties' sharpening ideological definitions had the opposite effect. The South was the stronghold of first the conservative and then the moderate congressional Democrats. But their numbers have dwindled amid a relentless Republican advance. In 1951, Democrats held all 22 Senate seats in the 11 states of the old Confederacy, and 98 percent of the House seats. After 2006 Republicans held 17 of the South's 22 Senate seats and almost three fifths of its 131 House seats. The number of Southern Democratic representatives stood at just 54 after 2006, and nearly a third of those were African American members, several of them quite liberal.

Both parties, especially Democrats, still elect moderates from else-where. But overall, after the decline of the Northeastern Republicans and Southern Democrats, both chambers now contain fewer centrists than they did in the age of bargaining. Graphs that measure the voting records of representatives and senators on a liberal-to-conservative axis used to show much of the Congress crowding in the middle, with many Demo-crats finishing slightly to the right of center and many Republicans placing slightly to the left. Now the graphs look like lines of boys and girls plas-tered to opposite sides of the gymnasium at a sixth-grade dance. Almost all congressional Republicans reliably line up to the right of center. Almost all Democrats stand to the left. Fewer legislators from either side gather near the intersection of the two sides. In Congress, the midpoint of the two parties has become an abandoned neighborhood.

These changes exacted a particularly heavy toll on the moderate Senate Republicans, who had constituted a powerful and productive force for compromise from Eisenhower through Reagan. One way to track the change is to look at what has happened to the seats of the fifteen moderate GOP senators who voted most often against the coalition of conservative Republicans and Southern Democrats in 1970. This was a moment of high tide for Republican centrists in Congress. Their roster included figures of long-standing influence like Jacob Javits of New York, Clifford Case of New Jersey, John Sherman Cooper of Kentucky, Hugh Scott of Pennsyl-vania (the Republican Senate leader at the time), and George Aiken of Vermont, as well as younger members beginning careers that would make a vivid imprint over the coming years: Charles McC. Mathias of Mary-land, Edward W. Brooke, the African American from Massachusetts, Mark Hatfield of Oregon, and Charles Percy of Illinois. These were fig-ures of independence courted by both parties and reliably controlled by neither.

But in the years that followed the centrist Senate Republicans were squeezed between contradictory forces generated by the electorate's ideo-logical sorting out. On the one hand the sorting meant they faced more uniformly conservative electorates in Republican primaries. On the other it meant that over time many of their states tilted more toward the Demo-crats in general elections. The combination proved lethal for the GOP centrists. Some (such as Case and Javits) were ousted by conservative challengers in primaries. Others (Brooke, Percy) lost to Democrats in states evolving away from the GOP. Still others (Mathias, Aiken) saw Democrats take their seats when they retired. In all, eleven of the seats held by the fifteen most moderate Senate Republicans in 1970 have now moved into Democratic hands. Only in two cases have relatively moderate Republicans succeeded the GOP centrists of 1970: in Oregon, where Gordon Smith holds the seat once represented by Mark Hatfield, and in Pennsylvania, where Arlen Specter has succeeded Richard Schweiker. A conservative Republican held one other, in Kentucky. The final seat from the 1970 group is still held by Alaska's Ted Stevens, who probably leaned as far to the right as any of the original centrists, and has tilted further in that direction since.

After the 2006 election the proud Senate tradition of Northeastern moderate Republicans was reduced to a remnant of three members: Olympia Snowe and Susan Collins of Maine, and Arlen Specter of Pennsylvania. (The other two Eastern Republican senators were conservatives from New Hampshire.) In the Bush years the Republican Senate caucus retained a handful of moderates, or at least maverick conservatives, from other parts of the country—John McCain of Arizona, Lindsey Graham of South Carolina, George Voinovich of Ohio, Gordon Smith of Oregon on some issues. But they were neither as numerous nor as moderate as the earlier generations of Republican centrists like Javits or Mathias. And the influence of the Republican moderates, ironically, was further marginalized by the fall of the Southern Democrats. With only a few exceptions, the Republicans who replaced the Southern Democrats in the Senate have been among the most conservative voices in the chamber. Their arrival in the Senate has moved the center of gravity in the Republican Senate conference appreciably to the right.

Senate Democratic centrists have maintained a stronger position than their Republican counterparts. Even with their decline in the South, Democrats, as we'll see below, still elect more senators from states that lean toward the GOP in presidential elections than Republicans elect in states that usually prefer Democratic presidential candidates. Those "red state" Senate Democrats share a powerful electoral incentive to pursue a moderate course. Yet most of these modern Democratic moderates, like James Webb of Virginia or Ken Salazar of Colorado, approach debates with beliefs much further away from mainstream Republican thinking than the Southern Democrats who defined their party's right flank during the age of bargaining, and even as late as the Reagan years. Even at their closest points in Congress, the parties today are more distant than a generation ago.

The ideological and geographic re-sorting of the electorate has played the largest role in driving the parties apart in both the House and Senate. But a second factor has deepened the polarization in the House: the trend in the way states draw the lines for congressional districts. After the 2000 census in particular, many states drew maps that protected incumbents from both sides by packing their districts with voters from their party.

The construction of so many districts that lean so securely toward one of the two parties has created perverse incentives for much of the House by significantly reducing the risk of defeat in general elections and (somewhat) increasing the danger of a challenge in primaries. Even accounting for the upheaval in the 2006 election, the number of close House general election races has fallen dramatically since the age of bargaining. (For more detail see note on page 442.) This decline in competition has increased the electoral security for most House members but reduced their motivation to cooperate across party lines. Members in highly competitive seats, like the nineteen Democrats elected in 2006 from districts that Bush carried only two years earlier, gravitate toward compromises attractive to the swing voters who typically decide their fates. But most members now represent districts tilted toward one party. In districts that lean so heavily to one side, ardent ideologues that excite the party base almost always have an advantage over moderates in winning party nominations. And because the districts are so lopsided, ideologues can usually stay in office without reaching much beyond that base. Appealing to swing voters, much less partisans of the other side, by pursuing centrist policies or compromises across party lines is rarely a priority for them, because they don't need much support from those voters to win. In districts designed that way, the greater risk for House members is that compromising with the other party will expose them to uncomfortable complaints from supporters or donors; in the most extreme cases, which are, as we'll see later, growing more common, they can face primary challenges fueled by the charge that they are collaborating too often with the enemy. For these legislators, flexibility and bipartisan cooperation is often more politically dangerous than absolutism. "If you've got to listen to both sides to get elected, and sometimes vote [with] the other side to stay elected, it's a very different conversation than if you've got an 80 percent Democratic district, where you just have to stay alive and you get elected," said Dick Gephardt, the longtime Democratic House leader. "Your only threat is a primary, possibly, and if you do it right, you're never going to have that."

SPHERES OF INFLUENCE

The fall of the Southern Democrats, the decline of the Northeastern Republicans, the division of the states into more stable patterns in their preferences for president, and the segregation of the House into districts that herd Republican or Democratic voters into like-minded ghettos are all pieces of a larger picture.

After the ideological re-sorting of the electorate, both the Democrats and Republicans have integrated and deepened their hold on the portions of the country that lean in their direction, particularly on cultural issues. Each now controls a commanding majority of the House and Senate seats in the states they consistently win in presidential elections. Both have partitioned the country into what amounts to competing spheres of influence that they dominate up and down the ballot in federal elections—from the House, through the Senate, to the presidency. The rigidity of that system has reinforced the hyperpartisanship of our time.

The best way to understand the dynamic is to divide the states into three categories that measure their contemporary attachment to the two parties: those that voted for Bush in both 2000 and 2004; those that voted against Bush in both elections; and those that split their vote.

In the first category are 29 red states that Bush carried in both 2000 and 2004, most of them in the South, the Mountain West, and the Plains. Republicans held most of the House and Senate seats from those 29 states before Bush first appeared on the national ballot in 2000. But in the three elections from 2000 through 2004, Bush's ability to unify and mobilize Republicans, and his strong appeal to culturally conservative voters, powered Republicans to further gains from those states in both chambers. After Bush's reelection in 2004, Republicans held 44 of the 58 Senate seats in those 29 states (76 percent), and 141 of the 216 House seats (65 percent).

Democrats have established a comparable advantage in their sphere of influence. Eighteen blue states voted against Bush in both 2000 and 2004. Democrats, in contrast to their retreat in the red states, gained Senate seats in those states from 2000 through 2004 and maintained their strength in the House. After Bush's reelection in 2004, Democrats held 81 percent of the Senate seats in the 18 blue states (29 of 36)* and 60 percent of the House seats (125 of 209), figures comparable to the GOP's strength in its regional strongholds.

In the third category stood only New Mexico, New Hampshire, and Iowa, the sole three states to switch their votes between the 2000 and 2004 presidential races. Those states provided the final margin of the Republican congressional majority during Bush's first six years: after 2004, the GOP held eight of their ten House seats, and four of their six Senate seats.

What these numbers show is that under Bush the vast majority of the country reliably enlisted into two competing camps, one that tilted strongly and consistently toward the Republicans in federal elections, the other toward the Democrats. Like many of the political trends shaping our age, the division of the country into these spheres of influence represents a reversion to a pattern not seen since early in the twentieth century—the period we've called the age of partisan armies. In those years the same states that provided a president the backbone of his Electoral College majority also provided his party huge majorities in the battle for control of Congress. That overlap encouraged that era's strong partisan discipline, and its sharp partisan conflict. Almost everyone in Congress from the president's

---

* That figure includes Senator James Jeffords, the independent from Vermont, who caucused with the Democrats after 2001.

party knew that the same voters who had elected them also voted for the man in the White House.* There was a consistent line of partisan preference from the voters through Congress to the White House that bound the winning party in common purpose—and also left the governing majority with little need to solicit support or compromise with the minority party.

That line blurred in the middle of the twentieth century. Through the age of bargaining and well into the transition years that followed, more states split their loyalties in voting for Congress and the White House. The mismatch was especially pronounced under Republican presidents because their victories in Southern states didn't translate into significant gains for GOP House and Senate candidates in the region. But the disconnection between congressional and presidential voting during the middle years of the twentieth century extended far beyond the South. After the 1956 election, for instance, Democrats held both Senate seats in six states outside the South that twice voted for Eisenhower; as recently as 1985 the Democrats still held both Senate seats in ten states that twice voted for Reagan, including seven states outside of the South.

Such mismatches were possible because many voters routinely backed presidential candidates from one party and congressional candidates from the other. Through the 1970s and 1980s the share of voters who reported splitting their tickets between the two parties in their votes for the presidency and House or Senate races peaked in NES surveys. Political scientists primarily interpreted the rise in split-ticket voting as an indication of loosening attachment to the parties. But it also reflected the lag between the ideological sorting out in races for Congress and the White House. Many conservatives (particularly in the South) who started voting Republican in presidential races during the 1960s maintained their Democratic loyalties in congressional races until the 1980s. For liberals the reverse was true. But in the years since, as we saw above, more liberals have voted Democratic and more conservatives have voted Republican not only in presidential but also congressional contests. As a result, the share of voters

---

* Before the Seventeenth Amendment in 1913, senators were elected by majorities in the state legislature, but the same principle applied.

who report splitting their tickets between the parties is declining. (It's now at the lowest point since the 1960s.) And that is reviving the connection between the votes states cast for president and the legislators they send to Congress.

The table that follows documents the strength of that connection early in the twentieth century, the way it wavered after World War II, and its revival since the 1990s. The table examines periods in which one party has held the White House for (at least) two terms. It tracks the number of states that party won in both of those successful presidential campaigns, and then lists the share of House and Senate seats it won in those same states. Effectively it measures the degree to which the party in the White House has consolidated its control over House and Senate seats in the portions of the country that provided its Electoral College majority. It establishes what we might call the partition index in American politics.

These numbers show the country today sliding back into patterns of allegiance that McKinley, Wilson, and Theodore or Franklin Roosevelt would recognize. After 2004 Republicans controlled a higher percentage of House and Senate seats in the states that voted twice for Bush than Republicans did in the states that voted twice for Reagan, Nixon, or

THE PARTITION INDEX

Elections	Winning Party	States won twice	Senate seats (%)	House seats (%)
1900/1904	R	28	96	89
1912/1916	D	30	73	78
1924/1928	R	30	70	77
1932/1936	D	40	89	80
1944/1948	D	23	76	75
1952/1956	R	38	58	55
1960/1964	D	19	74	71
1968/1972	R	32	50	50
1980/1984	R	44	55	43
1992/1996	D	29	67	53
2000/2004	R	29	76	65

Eisenhower, or Democrats did in the states that voted twice for Clinton. The GOP's commanding position in the red states meant that the vast majority of Republicans in both the House and Senate were elected by constituencies that also voted for Bush.* Just as in the days of McKinley or Theodore Roosevelt, that alignment provided the electoral underpinning for the extraordinary unity congressional Republicans achieved through much of Bush's tenure, a pattern we'll explore in Chapter 7.

The modern twist in this old pattern is that the party out of the White House has also solidified its control over a significant portion of the country. This is a development without exact modern precedent; through the twentieth century, the party out of the White House had rarely established a stronghold that reliably supported its candidates for Congress and the presidency. (The closest parallel was the one-party Democratic control of the South in both congressional and presidential races until the 1950s.) The new pattern first surfaced under Bill Clinton in the 1990s. Sixteen states voted for both George H. W. Bush and Bob Dole against Clinton; after the 1996 election, Republicans held 81 percent of the Senate seats and 61 percent of the House seats from those states. After 2004, as noted previously, Democrats held a similar percentage of House and Senate seats in the eighteen states that voted for Gore and Kerry. This meant congressional Democrats had the same incentive for party loyalty in their dealings with George W. Bush as congressional Republicans, only in reverse: The vast majority of Democratic senators and Democratic House members were elected by constituencies that voted against the president.†

The resounding Democratic gains in the 2006 election accelerated this pattern on one side of the ledger and moderated it on the other. In the states that voted for Gore and Kerry, Democrats gained 13 seats in the House (raising their total to 138 of 209) and 2 in the Senate (raising their number to a stunning 31 of 36). After these advances the Democrats held an

* The most precise way to measure the correlation between support for Bush and support for Republicans in the House is to look at the presidential vote by congressional district. In 2004, all but 18 of the 232 House Republicans were elected from districts that Bush also carried. Forty-four of the 55 Republicans in the Senate after 2004 came from states that supported Bush both times.
† Again, looking at the vote by congressional districts, 161 of the 202 Democratic House members after 2004 were elected in districts where Kerry defeated Bush. After 2004, 28 of the 44 Senate Democrats, plus Jeffords, the Vermont independent who caucused with them, came from states that rejected Bush both times.

iron grip on the blue states, controlling two thirds of their House seats and fully 86 percent of their Senate seats.* Perhaps even more impressively, Democrats also reversed their Bush-driven decline in the red states; Democrats in 2006 captured 4 Senate and 14 House seats in the states that twice voted for Bush. Those breakthroughs dented the Republican dominance of the red states, but they did not dislodge it: Even after the Democrats' 2006 gains, Republicans still held about 60 percent of the House seats in those states (127 of 216), and 70 percent of their Senate seats (40 of 58).

Only future elections will tell whether the Democrats' red-state gains of 2006 were a temporary incursion registered at a peak of voter discontent or a lasting change in the landscape. Seen from the longer perspective of the past generation, the bigger story is the trend toward each party controlling more House and Senate seats in the states that also usually support its presidential nominees. This simultaneous consolidation by both parties reinforces the pressure for party loyalty in Washington and accelerates the trend toward partisan polarization. The legislators with the strongest motivation to encourage compromise between the parties often have been those who come from states that split their loyalties between one party for the House or Senate and the other party for president. Now only a smaller number of such cross-pressured legislators survive. (Although the number of Democrats in that circumstance increased after the party's red-state gains in 2006, the number of Republicans dwindled after their rout in the blue states.) In the end, Congress is an institution of individuals, and when the number of bridge builders in it declines, so does the number of bridges that are built.

STABILITY, RIGIDITY, AND RISK

In all these ways American politics over the past three decades has become something of a lab experiment. We've learned how most Americans will respond if presented with a political debate that highlights the country's

---

* That figure includes Bernie Sanders of Vermont and Joseph Lieberman of Connecticut, the two independents who caucused with the Democrats as 2007 began.

fault lines rather than its points of common ground. The critical question for the future is how many Americans are weary of participating in that experiment. Would voters in the two parties express such vehement disagreements if their leaders framed the choices in a more conciliatory way? Do most Americans want to remain locked into a political system that presents the options so starkly and sorts out the country so profoundly?

Some of the generals in the battles that shaped the current system think the answer to those questions is no. Matthew Dowd, the senior strategist and pollster for Bush's two presidential campaigns, and Stanley Greenberg, the veteran Democratic strategist for Kerry, Gore, and Clinton, use almost identical language to describe many if not most Americans as reluctant conscripts in the hyperpartisan wars of roughly the past two decades. "Parts of the electorate are locked in," says Dowd. "But at the same time, the view of both parties is at its lowest levels in forty-something years. . . . I think there is this vast chunk of the society that feels left out of the conversation. Because the things that are getting talked about in Washington or Austin or wherever don't speak to them. So they are [saying], 'I agree with this guy on this, but this makes me uncomfortable, this doesn't seem to be the right thing'; and so they feel more and more disconnected to what both parties are saying."

Greenberg notes the same slippage in polls measuring the public's attitudes toward both parties and reaches the same conclusion. "Public esteem for the parties and the system is declining," he says. "The parties are following each other down in public esteem. All of the evidence is that people don't like these polarized parties."

It's important to remember that even after the great re-sorting neither party has achieved complete unanimity among its supporters. The Pew Research Center for the People and the Press, a nonpartisan group in Washington that studies public opinion, conducts what is generally considered the most thorough examination of the consistency of opinion in both parties. Every few years since 1987 Pew has produced a detailed survey that measures Americans' opinions not only on specific policy questions but also on broader social and political attitudes, such as whether it is necessary to believe in God to lead a moral life and whether people can still get ahead if they work hard. From correlating the answers to dozens of such probing questions, Pew produces a typology that divides Americans into distinct categories of shared beliefs.

The last time Pew performed this exercise, in 2005, it identified three distinct groups within the Republican coalition, three within the Democratic one, and three others not firmly attached to either party. In each camp the three groups did not agree on all fronts. The Republican groups (not surprisingly) coalesced around conservative positions on social issues and foreign policy, but divided on the role of government. The upscale, mostly male, uniformly conservative group Pew identified as "enterprisers" staunchly opposed government intervention in the economy, but government activism to constrain the power of business or strengthen the social safety net was welcomed somewhat more by the middle-income "social conservatives" and considerably more by the downscale "pro-government conservatives." The three Democratic groups (not surprisingly) supported an activist government, but the working-class, religiously oriented "social conservatives" leaned much more toward conservative positions on cultural issues and hawkish approaches on foreign policy than the upscale and secular "liberals." The low-income, heavily alienated, "disadvantaged Democrats" consistently placed between the two groups on social and foreign policy issues.

Pew identifies a final set of three groups, representing about a quarter of the electorate which did not consistently align with either party. Political strategists fiercely disagree about whether the number of people truly neutral between the parties is that large; many, especially in the Bush camp, believe the number is much smaller. But to some extent that argument is mostly about terminology. Even those who believe that there are few true independents left in our polarized system acknowledge that many Americans remain soft partisans, conflicted ideological "mutts" (as Dowd calls them), or just conscientious objectors in the partisan wars. The share of voters who might shift allegiance between the parties from election to election may be 15 percent or 20 percent, or 25 percent, but even if it was only 10 percent it would be enough to tilt the balance of power in a country where the two sides' core coalitions are so evenly matched. (As we'll see in Chapter 8, it was just such a sharp movement among independent voters that carried Democrats to control of the House and Senate in 2006.) Even after the great sorting out there is no reason to believe that the electorate's cultural and ideological realignment is completely irreversible, or that some voters now in one camp could not be moved, with the right candidate and the right message, into another.

That is the opportunity for the future we'll discuss more in the final chapters. Today, though, the parties are still moving in the opposite direction. All of the electoral trends we've explored in this chapter are dissolving the political incentives that encouraged more cooperation between the parties from the 1940s through the 1980s.

Politics through the age of bargaining and well into the period of transition that followed was messy, untidy, and sprawling. Each party, as we've seen, relied on voters who shared views with large numbers of voters in the other party. Each won elections in states usually considered strongholds of the other. Each sent to Washington members of the House and Senate whose opinions probably fit more comfortably in the other party than their own. Each saw large numbers of its usual supporters occasionally cross over to vote for candidates from the other side. In all these ways each was the sort of "umbrella party" political scientists said lacked "organizational or programmatic coherence."

Compromise between the parties in Washington has never been easy, but the very instability of this political order facilitated it. The fluidity in the political alignment during the first decades after World War II discouraged absolutism. Presidents needed a broad appeal because they usually competed for support in almost all regions of the country (especially after the GOP became competitive in the South). In Congress, Northeastern Republicans, with much more moderate constituencies than their colleagues elsewhere, were receptive to compromises with liberal Democrats. Southern Democrats, with much more conservative constituencies than their colleagues elsewhere, were receptive to agreements with conservative Republicans. From the 1940s through the 1980s significant numbers of legislators in each party represented voters who often preferred presidential candidates from the other party. That provided them a powerful incentive to reach agreements across party lines, especially when a president from the other side held the White House.

But the ideological and cultural sorting out of the past quarter century has diminished each of these incentives. The parties are more distinct in their geographical basis of support. Their voters are more uniform in their beliefs. Each party, in one sense, has become more of a true national party, with fewer of the regional variations that once differentiated, say, Southern from Northern Democrats or Northeastern from Midwestern Republicans. But, simultaneously, each party has been weakened to the point of debilitation in entire regions of the country. The space between the parties, both ideologically and geographically, is more cleanly defined, and less porous.

The process of ideological and geographic re-sorting has produced a unified and streamlined political system that provides enormous opportunity for one side to impose its agenda, but also virtually guarantees a mounting sense of disenfranchisement among those excluded from the ruling coalition. The age of bargaining was an era in which no faction in either party won exactly what it wanted, but none was entirely excluded from influence either. The new rules are producing more of an all or nothing politics.

That's partly because the re-sorting has changed the nature of bargaining between the two parties. The ideological sorting of each party's electoral coalition has made it more difficult for either to engage the other in bipartisan agreements without provoking a backlash from their core supporters, as the congressional Republicans learned after their budget deal with Bill Clinton in 1997. Many elected officials are now more concerned that critics will accuse them of cooperating with the other party too much, not too little.

The sorting out also has changed the nature of bargaining within the parties in a way that further marginalizes the party out of power and its supporters. For most of American history even unified one-party control of Washington has been a form of coalition government because opinions in the parties were so diverse. When both parties harbored a diverse range of views, opinions from across the ideological spectrum, even in diluted form, could still be heard no matter which party held the initiative in the capital. When Democrats controlled Washington, Republican conservatives knew that the Southern Dixiecrats would champion a version of their views. When Republicans held power, first the progressive and then the moderate Republicans raised arguments more commonly heard among Democrats.

The great exception to this pattern was the intensely partisan years between McKinley and Franklin Roosevelt, when the ruling parties conceded little even to the minority view in their own coalition (much less sentiments in the other party). But later in the twentieth century, presidents trying to mollify diverse opinions within their own party were often pressured toward positions that also narrowed their disagreements with the opposition. We saw that pattern with Kennedy's design of his tax plan, Nixon's appointments to the Supreme Court, and Reagan's decision to raise taxes after 1981 and retain federal affirmative action programs.

But after the great sorting out the range of opinion within the parties has narrowed even as the bargaining between them has diminished. The transformation has been much more dramatic among Republicans than Democrats, who continue to rely upon a more diverse coalition both in Congress and the country, but the direction has been the same on both sides. The parties' electoral coalitions have each grown more ideologically uniform and more consistent in their views on almost every major issue. The same pattern is evident in Congress after the decline of the Democratic conservatives and Republican moderates.

After this re-sorting, unifying a party today doesn't mean what it did for Lincoln or Franklin Roosevelt, or even for Kennedy and Nixon. Holding together a party now requires less coalition building than it did before; even the balancing act Democrats face in trying to accommodate so many moderate new House members elected from conservative-leaning districts in 2006 paled beside the challenge of managing a party that included Hubert Humphrey and Richard Russell. Among Republicans the change has been even more profound. From 2001 through 2006, George W. Bush and congressional Republicans repeatedly assembled congressional majorities, often by achingly narrow margins, for an agenda that on most issues conceded little to the demands not only of Democrats but even of moderate Republicans. Republican divisions grew more pronounced, and at times debilitating, in Bush's second term. But the driving force in Bush's presidency has been the priorities of one faction of one party, in this case the conservative wing of the GOP. One wing of one party has exercised that level of control before, but almost always when it held a decisive majority in the country and in Congress—as conservative Republicans did under William McKinley in the 1890s or Coolidge and Hoover in the 1920s, or liberals did early in the presidencies of Franklin Roosevelt and Lyndon Johnson. Until the voters raised a red flag in 2006, the Bush presidency produced something unique: domination by a single faction of a single party at a point when the country and the Congress were closely divided. That is the story we turn to next.

CHAPTER 7

THE PRESIDENT
OF HALF OF AMERICA

The backdrop made the promise more memorable.

The date was June 14, 1999. The place was the small town of Bow, New Hampshire. The occasion was Texas governor George W. Bush's inaugural trip as a presidential candidate to the state that hosts the critical first primary in the race for the White House.

Even before he arrived in New Hampshire Bush's famous name and the endorsements he had collected from prominent Republican fund-raisers and elected officials had already established him as the commanding favorite in the GOP race. The most eloquent testimony to his status was the huge media throng that followed him throughout his visit. When he stopped at the small local firehouse in Bow, the press corps was so large that it sprawled into the street outside.

Bush's staff chose to stop in Bow because the local fire department had traveled to Texas a year earlier to help fight a dangerous outbreak of wildfires. Bush seemed genuinely pleased to mingle with the firefighters. He shook hands enthusiastically and genially placed a fire hat on his head when one of the men handed it to him. For a moment, while ceiling fans whirred in a futile effort to dispel the heat and a row of photographers clicked their shots, Bush stood quietly with a lopsided grin, staring out at the supporters and reporters squeezed into the firehouse so tightly they could barely move. Then he broke the silence. "Now that I got you here and you're captured," Bush said, "I'm running for president."

For the next few minutes Bush ambled through the first version of the campaign speech he would hone and refine for the next seventeen months. In a soft voice he championed a familiar list of conservative priorities: cutting federal tax rates; reducing regulation; encouraging free trade; and strengthening the military. But he also talked about improving education to provide more opportunity for children in poor neighborhoods. And then he finished his short speech with a ringing promise to soothe the partisan conflicts in Washington. "I've learned to lead," Bush said. "I know you can't lead by dividing." It was an unusual confluence of setting and meaning: In a firehouse Bush was promising to extinguish the firefights between the parties in the capital. "I'm a uniter," Bush said finally, in a pledge he would repeat countless times on his march to the White House, "not a divider."

FOR THOSE WHO had watched George W. Bush in Texas that claim hardly seemed implausible. In Texas Bush had reconciled and soothed the state capital after four years of the incandescent but mercurial Democratic governor Ann Richards. Bush began courting Texas Democrats even before he defeated Richards in November 1994. Twice before Election Day Bush quietly visited the home of Bob Bullock, the irascible, larger-than-life Democratic lieutenant governor. In Texas the lieutenant governor steers the State Senate, and Bullock at the time was generally considered the state's most powerful politician. Bush, who had grown up around politics but never before won public office, launched a concerted effort to win his support. The first time he came to Bullock's house the two men spent hours sitting over the family's kitchen table. "Bob doesn't pass out compliments easily; nothing or nobody impressed him . . . and especially because [Bush] was the son of a president and had never been in an elected position, Bob was leery," recalled his widow, Jan Bullock. "But when he left Bob said, 'I really like him. He's got his head in the right place.' "

After Bush's election he continued to seek connections with Democrats. He surprised Paul Sadler, a brilliant young Democratic representative from East Texas, by inviting him to his office for lunch soon after his inaugural. As an expert on education Sadler had often delivered the Democratic case on school reform at campaign events where Bush also appeared. But when Sadler sat down with Bush for box-lunch sandwiches to discuss education reform, the new governor instantly put him at ease by thanking him for avoiding partisan attacks during the race. Every Wednesday during the state legislative session Bush met for breakfast with Bullock and Pete Laney, the Democratic speaker of the state House of Representatives. And he routinely popped in unannounced to Bullock's office to discuss legislative strategy, or just to trade gossip, something the somewhat imperious Richards had never done.

For the next six years, until his election as president, Bush worked with statehouse Republicans and Democratic leaders like Bullock, Laney, and Sadler (who chaired the State House Committee on Public Education throughout Bush's time as governor) to create an unusually productive climate of compromise and accommodation in Texas. Bush's outreach didn't eliminate all partisan conflicts; at various points he collided with Democrats over spending, regulatory, and social issues. And in a right-of-center state Bush compiled a record that clearly placed him to the right of center himself. But although Bush's compass pointed to the right, he routinely adjusted his course to bring others along. Almost always he preferred a deal to a debating point. In each of his three Texas state legislative sessions, Bush presented a relatively focused list of priorities and concentrated his attention on those issues. Each time he accepted compromises that tilted the debate in his direction, but gave enough ground to broaden support for his ideas. In his first session Bush made significant concessions to critics on all of his top four priorities: juvenile justice, welfare reform, a rewrite of the state education code, and legislation to limit lawsuits against business. In his second session he publicly supported Sadler and House Democrats as they fundamentally rewrote a tax reform plan he had proposed, moving it much further toward Democratic priorities. In his final session he accepted a tax cut significantly smaller than he had proposed, more spending on education than he originally offered, and safeguards sought by Sadler and other

Democrats for students who might otherwise be forced to repeat a grade under his plan to end "social promotion" in Texas schools.

Through all of these legislative skirmishes, and dozens of others, Bush worked closely with legislators in both parties to untangle knots and find reasonable compromises. Over his six years he developed a reputation on both sides as accessible, open-minded, and pragmatic. In his dealings with Republicans and Democrats alike, Bush demonstrated day after day that he viewed building consensus as an indispensable component of his job. "To the extent people want to work together, and want to seek solutions," Sadler said, "he can build consensus." Most Texas legislators from both parties reached similar verdicts.

Large forces in Texas politics pushed the two sides toward this cooperative relationship. Bush was encouraged to deal with Democrats because they controlled both the state House and Senate in his first two years as governor, and maintained control of the state House even when Republicans captured the Senate during his final four years. The Democrats were motivated to deal with Bush because the GOP's steady gains up and down the ballot left no doubt about the direction of the state's partisan leaning. And the two sides could come together in part because they did not begin as far apart as Democrats and Republicans did in most states: The Texas Democratic Party, though influenced by a contingent of minority and liberal members, still revolved around a powerful business-oriented bloc that preferred a centrist, and even a conservative-leaning, agenda.

Yet even with all of these factors encouraging cooperation, Bush's pursuit of a strong working relationship with Texas Democrats was not without cost. "Some of our Republicans are much less inclined to compromise than he is," said Bill Ratliff, a powerful state Senate Republican after Bush's final legislative session. The Texas Republican Party chairman, a combative former Reagan administration official named Tom Pauken, publicly condemned Bush's 1997 tax reform plan. The *National Review* suggested that based on Bush's "solid, if uninspiring, record of moderate conservatism" in Texas, conservatives should hold out for a more ardent alternative if he ran for president.

But despite these repeated warning shots from the right, Bush never abandoned his conciliatory course as governor. Sadler was struck by the depth of Bush's commitment to that strategy even during his final legislative session in 1999, when he was already under scrutiny from the national media and Republican activists as the party's presidential front-runner. "In the end . . . the thing that has made Bush different to me than other Republicans is, he is comfortable with making a decision that is not a staunchly conservative Republican decision, and yet defending it," Sadler said a few weeks before Bush's visit to Bow. "I think he seems to have a fairness about him that, once you explain it, and if he agrees with you, he is not afraid of advocating it, even though it may be different from the hard party line."

IN SOME WAYS, Bush the presidential candidate was noticeably more partisan and ideological than Bush the governor. His agenda at the national level—a large tax cut, the introduction of personal investment accounts into Social Security, a reconstruction of Medicare that would push seniors to rely more on private insurance for their health care—leaned more to the right than his proposals in the state. He courted socially conservative voters more overtly than he had in Texas, memorably declaring Jesus his favorite philosopher at one early Republican presidential debate, appearing at fundamentalist Bob Jones University (which forbade interracial dating) at a crucial moment during the Republican primaries, and typically ending his speeches with his promise to restore honor and dignity to the Oval Office, a barely veiled reference to Bill Clinton's affair with Monica Lewinsky. And his team demonstrated a tolerance for bare-knuckled politics, with a whispering campaign of personal allegations that helped to sink Arizona senator John McCain, his principal rival for the Republican nomination during the decisive primary contest in South Carolina.

Yet Bush, as a presidential candidate, also reaffirmed many of the centrist themes he had stressed as governor. He proposed greater partnerships between government and religious charities to confront entrenched social problems like teen pregnancy. He identified education reform as one of his top priorities, challenging conservative resistance to federal involvement in the schools by proposing mandatory national tests to measure the progress of students in reading and math. In fall 1999, when congressional Republicans sought reductions in a tax credit that benefits the working poor, Bush denounced them. "I don't think they ought to balance their budget on the backs of the poor," he said tartly.

He also reaffirmed his determination to reach across party lines. Bush often cited his relationship with Texas Democrats as a model the parties should emulate in Washington. (To underline the point he sometimes brought Democrats from the Texas state legislature on the road to testify to his commitment to bipartisanship.) At a Republican fund-raising gala in spring 2000, Bush accused Clinton and Gore of offering "the most relentlessly partisan administration in our nation's history," but then criticized congressional Republicans for responding in kind. "Americans have seen a cycle of bitterness: an arms race of anger, and both parties share some of the blame," Bush lamented. He promised an inclusive presidency open to viewpoints all across the political spectrum. "I will listen to the best ideas from my fellow conservatives and moderates and new Democrats," he pledged, the final phrase a reference to the centrist movement associated with Bill Clinton. "I will bring Americans together."

Throughout the campaign Bush presented himself as a candidate who could surmount not only partisan but also ideological divisions. He described himself as a "different kind of Republican" in an unmistakable echo of Clinton's 1992 self-description as a "different kind of Democrat." And Bush raised eyebrows among many on the right by calling himself a "compassionate conservative"—a label that subtly distanced him from the militant brand of conservatism identified with the Republican Congress. "I heard it to mean conservatism is compassionate, which I believe to be the case," said Grover Norquist, the ubiquitous conservative organizer. "Some people thought they were apologizing for the hard-edged Republican House guys [as in], 'We're for compassionate conservatism, as opposed to what?' "

In the final two months of the general election campaign against Al Gore, Bush dialed down the volume on the compassion and amplified the conservatism in his message. Reverting to more conventional Republican themes, Bush insisted that his agenda would arm individuals with more opportunity while Gore would expand government with wasteful new spending. Yet even as Bush critiqued his opponent in more traditionally ideological terms, he never wavered from his promise to bridge the ideological and partisan divides that had opened between Clinton and the Republican Congress since 1997. That was the central message of Bush's closing statement at his pivotal first debate with Gore in early October 2000. And it was the theme Bush stressed when he addressed the nation on the evening of December 14, just a few minutes after Al Gore conceded the presidential election following the Supreme Court's decision to stop the statewide recount of disputed ballots in Florida.

Bush decided to deliver his address from the chamber of the Texas House of Representatives and to have Pete Laney, the Democratic speaker of the House, introduce him. Laney, plainspoken and modest, praised Bush for reaching out to both parties as governor. Bush, following him, promised to do the same as president.

> Tonight I chose to speak from the chamber of the Texas House of Representatives because it has been a home to bipartisan cooperation. Here in a place where Democrats have the majority, Republicans and Democrats have worked together to do what is right for the people we represent. . . . The spirit of cooperation I have seen in this hall is what is needed in Washington, D.C. . . .
>
> Our nation must rise above a house divided. Americans share hopes and goals and values far more important than any political disagreements . . . I know America wants reconciliation and unity. I know Americans want progress. . . . Together, guided by a spirit of common sense, common courtesy, and common goals, we can seize this moment and deliver.

Bush seemed nervous, even a bit overwhelmed, as he spoke to the country that night, but his setting spoke as loudly as his words. In that chamber Bush had functioned as a "uniter, not a divider." He had changed the tone of politics in Austin. Now, in his first address to Americans as their president-elect, he reaffirmed his promise to do the same in Washington.

FROM AUSTIN TO WASHINGTON

As Bush approached, and then settled into, the presidency he conspicuously reprised some of the inclusive and conciliatory approaches he had
used in Texas. Before his inauguration Bush invited John Breaux, the
deal-making Louisiana Democratic senator, to Texas, and in a gesture of
reconciliation offered to appoint him as energy secretary; Breaux, prefer-
ring the independence of the Senate, turned him down. (Breaux also
recognized that Bush's offer wasn't entirely altruistic: Since the Senate
was divided fifty-fifty after the 2000 election, if Breaux accepted the job
Louisiana's Republican governor would have appointed a successor that
provided the GOP with a fifty-one–forty-nine majority.) During his transition Bush also traveled to Capitol Hill to meet privately with congressional leaders, including Missouri representative Dick Gephardt, the top
Democrat in the House, and South Dakota senator Tom Daschle, the
Democratic leader in the evenly divided Senate. At Daschle's request
Bush even paid a courtesy visit to a meeting of the full Democratic Senate
caucus. "Basically," Daschle recalled, "his message was, I want to work
with you."

Bush immediately fulfilled that pledge on one issue. Administration
officials quickly began intensive negotiations over the president's education reform bill with leading Democrats, particularly two venerable liberals, Senator Edward M. Kennedy of Massachusetts and Representative
George Miller of California. Kennedy found the process responsive and
inclusive. Kennedy enjoyed easy access to Bush's top aides on education,
his domestic policy adviser Margaret Spellings, Education Secretary Rod
Paige, and Sandy Kress, a Dallas Democrat who had advised Bush on
school policy in Texas. With all of them, Kennedy said, there was an "ability to communicate and get an instant kind of response." Most important,
Kennedy found the president willing to dive into the details of the complex legislation and emerge with reasonable compromises. "When we had
issues and questions we went down to see the president," Kennedy recalled. "And he made the calls. So people who cared about the particular
issues felt you were carrying their issue to the top. You weren't always go-

ing to get the right answer, but we got a lot of answers that were worked out decently." Kennedy described a process that looked and sounded very much like Sadler's productive experiences with Bush in Texas, and it produced a similar outcome: an education reform bill that won majority support from both parties in both chambers.

Bush's conspicuous praise of the liberal icon Kennedy, his outreach to Daschle, and his collaboration with Democrats on education reform all fit with one set of priorities for his political staff after the agonizing 2000 election. In 2000, Bush became only the fourth president ever to lose the popular vote and win the White House; his disputed Electoral College majority of 271–267 over Gore was the second narrowest ever. The extended recount in Florida, which left many Gore supporters questioning Bush's legitimacy, added to the fragility of his victory. Emerging from that harrowing experience, Bush's political advisers juggled complex calculations. On the one hand, Bush's team initially considered it a top priority to broaden his appeal wherever they could, largely by convincing Americans he would fulfill his campaign promise to reach across party lines and change the tone in Washington.

In the beginning, said Matthew Dowd, the former Democrat who served as a senior strategist in both of Bush's presidential campaigns, the president's team largely believed the path to reelection "was to build consensus on issues with the Democrats and continue to show that he could do what he did in Austin. That was a huge part of the mantra, and what was wanted to be done [was to show] that we could reach across the aisle . . . to show that Washington could get stuff done, and Washington doesn't always have to be this way. . . . There wasn't this idea that, 'Okay, the electorate is polarized, and therefore we are just going to appeal to this [conservative bloc].' Because we knew [that] if all you did was that, you would end up with 40 percent of the vote, or a third of the vote."

But other considerations always qualified that assessment. Dowd and the other key members of Bush's political team also believed that the sorting out of the electorate had left very few independent voters genuinely uncommitted to either party. Further, they believed that Bush's personal style and persona made it difficult for him to convert large numbers of the voters who had resisted him in 2000. Given those constraints on Bush's potential support, his White House team believed from the outset that motivating his conservative base would be unusually important to his success.

Those calculations pushed Bush away from the bipartisanship he had practiced in Texas, and their imprint was evident from the beginning of his presidency. During the transition some observers speculated that Bush might seek to emulate John F. Kennedy, who had attempted to promote reconciliation after his close election by offering several of his top cabinet jobs to Republicans (including Eisenhower's undersecretary of state, Douglas Dillon, who became Kennedy's treasury secretary). But after Breaux rebuffed Bush's freighted overture, Bush brought into his cabinet only one Democrat, former California representative Norman Mineta, in the second-tier post as transportation secretary.

Bush and his top advisers reinforced the implicit message of that decision in public and private comments. On *Face the Nation* Dick Cheney ridiculed the idea that the dead-heat election required the new administration to produce a more conciliatory or bipartisan agenda. "[T]he suggestion that somehow because this was a close election, we should fundamentally change our beliefs," Cheney sniffed, "I just think it's—is silly." Shortly before the inauguration Karl Rove told a private gathering of conservatives convened by Paul Weyrich, the veteran organizer on the right, that Bush intended to govern as "a philosophically driven president who is a conservative." An even stronger sign came from Bush himself when he met with Nicholas E. Calio, his first White House director of congressional affairs. Calio, a smooth Washington insider who had held the same job for Bush's father, remembers that many people were telling the son that his narrow victory demanded widespread compromises with Democrats. "He didn't see it that way," Calio recalled. Bush, he said, was determined to "defy conventional wisdom" by governing as if he had received a clear mandate. "He consistently [said] he did not want to play 'small ball.'" Calio remembers an early meeting where he presented Bush with a variety of changes he might have to accept to win congressional approval for the sweeping tax cut he had proposed in the campaign. Bush cut him off. "He looked at me," Calio remembered, "and said, 'Nicky, we will not negotiate with ourselves, ever. . . . People will move toward us and will continue moving toward us.'"

If education reform embodied Bush's early desire to reach out, the drive for his tax cut demonstrated the harder edge of his initial strategy. On taxes Bush displayed almost none of the flexibility or inclusiveness he had shown on school reform. That decision proved an early fork in the road for his presidency. If Bush had reduced the size of his proposed tax cut and devoted more of the anticipated federal surplus to reducing the government debt, as well as on new spending in areas such as education and health care, he might have assembled a grand coalition similar to the majorities in both parties that supported Clinton's 1997 budget agreement. Such a deal also might have drained away some of the bitterness from the disputed 2000 result.

But Bush never sought such an agreement. He firmly resisted even smaller changes in his proposal. When a bipartisan group of centrist senators sought a slightly smaller tax cut, the administration initially refused to negotiate with them; it came to the table only after three Republican defectors joined with Senate Democrats in April to pass an amendment to the budget that reduced his tax cut by more than a fourth. Through the final stages of the legislative maneuvering the White House worked with sympathetic Republicans to push the final number back in Bush's direction. Eventually Bush signed into law a substantial $1.35 trillion tax cut that won support from every Republican in the House and all but two in the Senate. The price was opposition from three fourths of Democrats in the Senate and more than five sixths of Democrats in the House.

Bush's experience on taxes lent itself to two possible interpretations. One was that he had unnecessarily divided the parties by resisting compromise until he had no other choice. "The president could have gotten a substantial portion of what he's hoping for with bipartisan support," Indiana senator Evan Bayh, a moderate Democrat, said at the time, "but he chose to make the $1.6 trillion figure almost a talisman." The other interpretation was that by standing firm and unifying congressional Republicans Bush had achieved more of his goal than seemed possible when he took office. In reality, the tax fight had demonstrated both of those propositions. It showed that in a polarized era staunch party discipline could allow Bush to achieve significant changes in policy despite a narrow division of power in Congress and minimal support from Democrats. But it also demonstrated that that approach could reinforce the underlying spiral of polarization by deepening feelings of disenfranchisement among Democrats in Congress, and ultimately the country as well.

Through the spring and summer of 2001 confrontation steadily eclipsed compromise in Bush's relationship with congressional Democrats. In May, Democrats gained a one-seat majority in the Senate when Republican James Jeffords of Vermont, disillusioned over Bush's initial direction and feeling increasingly isolated in a more monolithically conservative party, left the GOP to declare himself an independent. Conflict quickly mounted between the new Democratic majority and the White House. The policy goals Bush unveiled week after week demonstrated a commitment to conservative causes with little appeal for most Democrats. From his abandonment of the Kyoto negotiations on global warming, to his appointment of prominent conservatives to the federal bench, to the limits he imposed on federal funding for stem cell research, Bush advanced a succession of proposals that divided the parties. With their new majority, Senate Democrats in turn approved a "patient's bill of rights" for patients in health maintenance organizations that the White House opposed, and began formulating sharply contrasting alternatives to Bush's proposals on energy and prescription drugs for seniors.

As disputes over these issues accumulated, each side pulled away from the other. Congressional Democrats saw Bush renouncing any pretense of bipartisanship. By the summer Daschle felt the White House had abandoned the thought of negotiating with the Democratic congressional leadership to reach broad bipartisan agreements (as they did on education), and instead had committed to a strategy of picking off a handful of Democrats here or there to build a slim legislative majority for Bush's priorities.

The White House saw relations moving in the same direction, but along a very different track. Some bristled from the outset when Daschle, just days after Gore conceded defeat, charged that Bush would divide the country by attempting to pass his full tax cut and urged him to scale it back. Through the spring and summer aides watched Bush's approval rating among rank-and-file Democrats sink and attacks on his agenda from Democratic leaders in Washington rise. (That July Daschle violated an unwritten rule of Washington civility, and marked a new milestone in conflict between the two sides, by criticizing Bush's performance on foreign policy while the president was leaving for a foreign trip.) Karl Rove, the most partisan of Bush's major political advisers, reached the most militant conclusion. He quickly came to believe congressional Democrats were determined to deny Bush a chance to establish his legitimacy. "The mind-set of too many people at the head of the Democratic Party in the aftermath of the 2000 election was that 'they stole it, he doesn't deserve to have the job, I'm going to keep him from doing anything,'" Rove said. Six months into Bush's presidency his conciliatory speech from the Texas House of Representatives seemed as dated as a daguerreotype.

The September 11 terrorist attacks interrupted the spiral of partisan confrontation. Faced with a real enemy, the two parties found their own conflicts less urgent. Voters from all points on the ideological spectrum rallied behind the president. And despite skirmishes over some issues— particularly a heated dispute over whether the new federal agency established to control airport security should be staffed with private or public employees—the two parties worked swiftly and smoothly in Congress to pass a broad array of legislation in response to the tragedy. (The two sides worked together so briskly, in fact, that some liberals and conservatives alike would later accuse Congress of failing to ask tough questions about the USA Patriot Act, which expanded government's ability to monitor suspected terrorists.) The invasion of Afghanistan to overthrow the Taliban government sheltering Osama bin Laden generated overwhelming support from both parties in public opinion polls and nearly unanimous agreement in Congress. For a few months in the fall of 2001 the two parties demonstrated (as they did between 1996 and 1997) that all the forces encouraging polarization in American politics could not preclude consensus when the incentive for agreement was powerful enough.

But the moment did not last. The cooperation ended when Bush proposed a post-9/11 economic stimulus package centered on tax cuts, and Democrats countered with a plan focused on extended unemployment benefits and health care for displaced workers; after the two sides fought to stalemate, Congress could approve only a bare-bones alternative.

That was a turning point. Through the remainder of Bush's presidency there was never another sustained period of legislative cooperation between Republicans and Democrats. The two parties intermittently found common ground on other issues: corporate reform after the Enron scandal; extending elements of Bush's 2001 tax cuts aimed at middle-class families (such as the children's tax credit); reform of the intelligence agencies recommended by the independent commission that investigated the 9/11 attacks. But these were the brief pauses in years of legislative warfare. Week by week, month by month the lines in Washington hardened, until the coming together after September 11, or even the cooperative spirit on education reform, seemed an improbable memory.

In Congress a deep and persistent divide opened between the parties. Cohesion within the parties reached levels not consistently seen, according to the most authoritative long-range study, since the dawn of the age of partisan armies. But conflict between them soared. More and more congressional votes saw the two parties confront each other with almost military precision. During Bush's first four years congressional Republicans voted together at a rate that vastly exceeded the level of party unity achieved under George H. W. Bush or even Ronald Reagan. Bush occasionally faced small uprisings of Republican dissent. Resistance from a handful of moderate Senate Republicans, as we saw earlier, required Bush to shrink his 2001 tax cut, and opposition from Senate fiscal hawks George Voinovich of Ohio and Olympia Snowe of Maine compelled him to reduce his proposed tax cut again in 2003. But on most of his key priorities Bush enjoyed overwhelming support from congressional Republicans. During Bush's first term the House cast 12 major votes on tax cuts. On average, Republican House members supported them by a vote of 215–3. On the 8 major tax cut votes during Bush's first term, Senate Republicans on average voted 47–2 with the president. Just 6 of 221 House Republicans and only Rhode Island moderate Lincoln Chafee among the 49 Senate Republicans voted against the use of force in Iraq. No more than one Senate Republican voted against Bush's budget in any of his first four years; no more than 12 House Republicans (and as few as 2) ever opposed his budget. Nearly 90 percent of both Senate and House Republicans voted for a constitutional amendment to ban gay marriage. About 95 percent of Republicans in both chambers backed Bush's proposal to limit patient awards in medical malpractice cases.

At times the White House also drew sizable support from congressional Democrats either attracted to its proposals or, more often, fearful of opposing them. Bush's education reform plan drew broad, substantial Democratic support, and his first tax cut (after the Senate vote to reduce it) made some inroads. In the aftermath of the 9/11 terrorist attacks almost all Democrats backed Bush on the Patriot Act, and many (about 40 percent in the House and nearly 60 percent in the Senate) supported the resolution authorizing the use of force in Iraq. On issues where business or regional interests divided the Democrats (such as the energy bill that provided lucrative tax subsidies for oil companies or legislation restricting bankruptcy filings), Bush sometimes attracted respectable levels of support from the party.

But most of Bush's domestic priorities provoked substantial Democratic opposition. Just seven Democrats in the House and two in the Senate, for instance, supported Bush's 2003 tax bill. No more than four Senate Democrats supported any of his controversial first-term appointments to the federal appellate courts. Bush's first-term annual budgets never drew support from more than a handful of congressional Democrats. After Republicans regained control of the Senate in 2003, filibusters supported by virtually every Democrat blocked Bush proposals to limit medical malpractice and class action lawsuits. Overall, in Bush's first term, Democrats voted together in the House more often than they did under Clinton; in the Senate, Democrats equaled the unprecedented level of party unity they had achieved under Clinton.

In the country as well the fissures around Bush widened. His approval rating among Republicans hovered at astronomical levels through his first term, consistently running at 90 percent or above in national polls. Those were extraordinary numbers, higher even than Ronald Reagan's. But independents and Democrats grew steadily more alienated. By the first half of 2004 Bush's approval rating among independents, which had peaked at nearly 90 percent after September 11, had fallen back below 50 percent in Gallup surveys, and it sank further through that summer, occasionally dipping to 40 percent and below. Among Democrats Bush's approval rating plummeted below 20 percent by late January 2004 and never again exceeded that level through the election that fall. By 2004, the gap between

Bush's ratings among Americans in his own party and those in the other routinely ran at seventy percentage points or more, by far the largest disparity Gallup had recorded for any president. "It's almost," Dowd wrote halfway through Bush's first term, when the chasm wasn't even as large, "as if we are operating in two political worlds."

Even the staggering division in opinion surveys didn't capture the depth of emotion Bush evoked. He divided communities, congregations, even households. Even in the most peaceful surroundings Bush quickened pulses. I saw the effect in the summer of 2004 at the beautiful, sun-splashed Colonial Church in Edina, Minnesota, a quiet, comfortable suburb just west of Minneapolis. A Congregationalist church housed in an elegant brown clapboard building that looked as if it were imported from New England, Colonial stressed unity and acceptance. Yet when fifteen parishioners gathered after services to discuss Bush one Sunday morning, the differences between them were deep and sharp. Bush's open expressions of religious faith inspired some ("I'm glad to know he has a faith, that he gets down on his knees before a higher power and doesn't see himself as the highest power," one woman said), but grated on others ("A lot of times I react negatively because I feel it's usually in the context that he has an understanding of what God would or wouldn't bless," said one man). Bush's certitude and decisiveness, his unflinching descriptions of the Iraq war and the struggle against terrorism as a confrontation between good and evil, stirred Andy Fronek, a mutual funds salesman. "I like the directness," he said. "I think . . . we need a leader that is strong, and he is strong. In a changing situation all the time, it is reassuring to me that he has some faith behind him and some direction." The exact same qualities in Bush repelled Megan Fronek, Andy's pregnant wife, who was outraged over the war and the Abu Ghraib prison scandal. She planned on voting against Bush as "my only way to communicate with the rest of the world and say, 'I'm sorry for our lack of humility and our self-righteous pushing [of] our opinions on someone else.' "

So it went, across the country. Bush sent people into opposite camps even with his style of walking, a loping gait with his arms hanging loosely toward his hips that seemed modeled on Hollywood's portrayal of a gunslinger. He was refreshingly plainspoken to some, painfully inarticulate to others. His tendency to present choices with either-or finality—you're

with us or against us—struck supporters like Andy Fronek as morally brac-
ing and critics such as his wife as dangerous and simplistic. (He divided
the country into two camps over whether it is appropriate to divide the
world into two camps.) To his supporters Bush was resolute; to his critics
he was stubborn. He crystallized all the stereotypical virtues of small-
town, religious, and heartland America while also fulfilling cosmopolitan
America's worst stereotypes about the defects of those same places. When
the nonpartisan Pew Research Center for the People and the Press asked
Americans for one-word descriptions of the president in spring 2004, the
most common five responses included "honest," "good," and "leader" on
one side of the ledger, and "incompetent" and "arrogant" on the other.
Even Bush's victory in 2004, as we'll see in Chapter 8, divided the country
more closely than any successful presidential reelection in American history. And by Bush's second term, as we'll also see, the chasms over his performance grew so wide that they virtually swallowed his presidency.

FROM A UNITER TO A DIVIDER

How did it come to this for the man who pledged to govern as "a uniter,
not a divider"?

The polarization of American politics, as all the history in this book
demonstrates, didn't begin with George W. Bush or Bill Clinton or any
single one of their predecessors. Forces larger than any president—the rise
of interest groups of left and right, the changes in the rules and practices
of Congress, and above all the ideological, cultural, and geographic re-
sorting of the electorate that began in the 1960s—have all moved political
life toward greater conflict. Beyond those strains, Bush faced a new source
of centrifugal pressure. The September 11, 2001, terrorist attacks and the
ongoing threat of violent Islamic extremism forced on Bush momentous
life-and-death decisions whose gravity and consequence inevitably stirred
more emotional responses from Americans than the choices government
ordinarily faces in times of peace and prosperity.

These are forces beyond the control of any political leader. The relevant
question for political leaders is how they respond to these forces.

During the Bush years both parties responded in ways that intensified partisan and ideological conflict and divided, rather than united, America. During Bush's presidency, as we'll see in Chapter 9, the center of gravity in the Democratic Party moved away from Bill Clinton's centrist deal-making philosophy toward a mirror image of the highly partisan strategy that Democrats saw Bush and Rove implementing.

But the president more than any other figure sets the tone for his time. He frames the choices facing the nation. The tone Bush set, and the choices he framed, intensified the underlying current of polarization. His presidency, though initially successful in achieving many of its objectives, deepened and sharpened the divisions he inherited. After his few initial gestures toward compromise with Democrats, Bush approached the White House in a forceful, even belligerent, style inimical to his conciliatory approach as governor of Texas. Just over halfway through Bush's first term as president, Sadler, the Texas Democrat, said he no longer recognized the man he had worked with so closely in Austin. "Almost all of us who had dealt with Bush, who were chairmen of committees or worked with him in Texas, have noticed the difference," Sadler said from his law office in a small East Texas town. "There has not been that collaborative spirit. I don't know if he's changed since Texas or the Democrats are different in Washington, or maybe it's both. But he is not the centrist as president that he was as governor."

The change in environment from the state to the national level explained part of the difference. Governors did not deal with as many inherently polarizing issues as federal officials (which was one reason why each party usually won more governorships than Senate seats in the other side's geographic strongholds). In Texas specifically, the strong strain of business-oriented moderation (and even conservatism) among Texas Democrats meant the two parties converged on many issues. Since Texas had become a competitive two-party state in the 1970s, there was also a strong tradition of bipartisan cooperation in the state legislature. In Congress the two parties began with greater differences and less inclination to surmount them.

But Bush also was a different politician in the White House than in the statehouse. In Washington Bush emulated his Texas style in one important respect: He usually avoided personal attacks on individual Democrats. He generally did not question the motives, especially the patriotism, of his critics (though his supporters were not always so punctilious). But in almost every other respect, Bush pursued a much more partisan and polarizing governing strategy as president than as governor. The contrast was visible along five distinct dimensions. Let's consider them in ascending order of importance.

RELATIONSHIPS

In Texas, Bush's personal relationships with Democrats in the state legislature built a level of trust that helped him broker agreements on difficult issues. Bush never established similar connections with Democrats in Congress. When arguments over policy flared, neither side could draw on a well of personal goodwill to help douse the flames.

On that basic assessment both sides agreed. As usual, they disagreed over the cause. Rove placed the blame partly on institutional differences between Texas—where Bush lived in a governor's mansion down the street from the statehouse and the legislature met for just over three months every two years—and Washington, where the pomp and circumstance of the presidency made every human interaction more cumbersome. "There is just a physical difference when you live 150 yards away from the capitol, and when members are there for 140 days every two years, and when you get to see them in a nonconfrontational environment," Rove said. "Members would come to Austin all the time, and he would see them when the legislature was not in session, so you had a chance to build [a relationship] outside the confines of the legislature." Mostly, though, Rove blamed Democrats in Washington. In Texas, Rove said, the leading Democrats looked for places they could reach agreement with Bush once the election ended. In Washington, he said, the "permanent campaign" made such discussions almost impossible: "I can't tell you how many Democrats have said to me, 'I wish I could work with you, but Harry [Reid] or Nancy [Pelosi] won't let me talk to you. I'd be dead.'"

There's no doubt that Democrats and Republicans in Washington, shaped by all the electoral forces encouraging greater ideological conflict between the parties, were more partisan and confrontational than their counterparts in Texas. But there's also no question that Bush devoted less energy to building personal ties with the opposition party as president than he did as governor. Democrats saw that lack of effort, not any institutional restraint, as the key to their distant personal relations with the president. At one meeting with Daschle shortly after Democrats gained control of the Senate in 2001 Bush asked the new Senate leader what he could do to establish the rapport with Democrats he had enjoyed in Texas. Daschle suggested to Bush that the president invite the Democratic leaders to the White House for regular meetings the way Eisenhower had with Lyndon Johnson and Sam Rayburn. "I said, 'I think it all comes down to familiarity and a relationship that has a lot more to do with chemistry than issues,'" Daschle recalled. "If we have chemistry we can work through the issues. But if we don't have chemistry, which only came from a lot of interactive experience, it's just not going to happen." The suggestion went nowhere. Bush did invite Daschle and his wife to one private dinner in the White House. But the president did not meet regularly with Democratic leaders until after September 11—and then only as part of meetings with congressional leaders from both parties focused mainly on security.

And once those meetings faded, personal interaction between Bush and the leading congressional Democrats dwindled even further. Harry Reid of Nevada, the Democratic Senate whip in Bush's first term and the Democratic Senate leader in his second, said that he had had only one personal conversation with Bush during his first six years in office: a brief phone call after Democrats selected him as their leader following Daschle's defeat in the 2004 election. "That's it," Reid said. "Never had a call on anything else." Reid said that his only other dealings with Bush came in the irregular and highly structured meetings between the president and congressional leaders from both parties that survived as descendants of the gatherings after September 11. Sitting in his Capitol office, the shades lowered against the searing sun of a late summer day, Reid described those meetings with undisguised contempt: "The breakfasts are like this," he said. "The meeting lasts one hour. There's Pelosi, there's me, there's [Bill] Frist, there's the speaker, and there is the Republican [House] leader. And then you have [Bush's] chief of staff and Cheney. . . . And then he [Bush] starts off with the name dropping. He does a lot of first names. I've talked to Vladimir [Putin], that kind of stuff. Vladimir. Talks for half an hour on what's going on in the world. Or Iraq: We're on the road [to success], it's going great. Then we each get to ask a question; that's what it amounts to. That's it. It's a good breakfast, off we go."

Reid seemed bewildered by his lack of interaction with the president in less formal settings. "It would seem to me, if I were running a business, a country, I'd say, 'That Reid is such a pain in the ass, why don't we see what we can do to neutralize him a little,'" he said. "Why don't we have him over to watch a movie at the White House? Why don't we invite him to a state dinner? . . . Why don't you have him come down and see me some afternoon?' That's what Clinton's style was. That's what Reagan's style was. That's what his dad's style was." Only after Reid's Democrats recaptured a Senate majority in the 2006 election did Bush invite him for White House meetings. Reid's habit of denouncing Bush's performance in vitriolic terms understandably might have diminished the president's enthusiasm for deepening their acquaintance. But that never stopped Ronald Reagan from spending time with Tip O'Neill. And the lack of personal contact between the White House and congressional Democrats meant that when new conflicts emerged there was no ongoing line of communication that allowed senior congressional Democrats and the White House to quietly assess whether they could reach agreements that preempted a full-scale confrontation. When a controversy erupted the two sides usually addressed each other first at press conferences, through confrontational statements written by aides steeped in years of partisan warfare.

Some in Bush's orbit worried about his lack of personal interaction with the other side. One Bush adviser, who watched him in Texas as well as in the White House, lamented his lack of social outreach in Washington. "We have no social presidency," said the adviser. "We have no presidency that says we can invite Democrats to Camp David and sit around and build relationships that are unrelated to issues. The fact that we don't do state dinners, we carry [that] about like a badge of honor, and we wonder why the perception is [that] we don't have people in. We don't use the White House, we don't use Camp David, we don't use Air Force One, we don't use all the symbolism of the presidency to build community and connection with people on the opposite side, so when it comes time to talk to the issues, we [would] have relationships. We have none of that."

Even when Bush did sit down with congressional Democrats, their interaction was more stilted and guarded than his conversations in Texas. Sadler, the shrewd Texas Democrat who repeatedly forged agreements with Bush on complex education and spending issues, said that as governor Bush would routinely convene legislators from both parties and ask the pragmatic, bottom-line questions of a deal maker. What will it take to reach an agreement? What do you need to get this done? "That was constantly our conversation," Sadler said. But in Washington, a succession of senior Democrats said they never had such a straightforward discussion with Bush. Bush told Calio that he would not negotiate with himself, but as his presidency unfolded, it seemed to senior Democrats that he was determined not to negotiate with them either.

In interviews, leading congressional Democrats described discussions with Bush that, except for the early encounters on education, bore almost no resemblance to the candid sessions Sadler described. In Washington, they said, Bush in private mostly repeated the arguments he raised for his policies in public. Bush was unfailingly cordial and respectful. But almost never, several Democrats said, did they feel Bush was genuinely considering their arguments and engaging them in a search for a middle ground. Sometimes it seemed to them that the conversations might have been no different if they had been conducted before the press at the White House podium.

Daschle appeared especially frustrated by his private dealings with Bush. There was, he said, "a window of about two months post-9/11 when everything was different," and the president engaged in productive, problem-solving discussions with the congressional leaders. "The rest of the time," Daschle said, "it was 'here's what we've got to have.' It was him telling me this is what we are going to do. There was no sense of how we can figure out a way to do this together. It was his very dictatorial expressions of willingness and interest in doing something, but there was no negotiation about it."

Representative Richard Gephardt of Missouri, the Democratic leader in the House during Bush's first two years, portrayed similar experiences. Gephardt described his personal meetings with Bush as "completely different" from his private conversations with Ronald Reagan and George H. W. Bush. "[The younger] Bush is truly a product of what is happening [in Washington]," Gephardt said. Bush's father, "because of the age he came from, knew he had to work with the other side, and to get a deal you had to put everything on the table. Reagan, same thing: It wasn't so much from his experience, but he listened to Jim Baker [the smooth centrist White House chief of staff] and his other advisers, and they said, 'You've got a big deficit, you've got to raise taxes, you've got to talk to Tip [O'Neill], you've got to do Social Security.' This guy [George W. Bush] just doesn't do that. It's not in the cards. It's not going to happen. They're not interested in that. . . . He never would engage, he never would talk, . . . there never was a dialogue."

Such assessments may sound jaundiced coming from Daschle and Gephardt, whose senior positions required them to lead Democratic criticism of Bush. But John Breaux, the moderate Louisiana Democrat whom the White House often courted as a potential ally in legislative disputes, expressed just as much frustration about trying to engage Bush in discussion. "We'd go over there in the leadership meetings with Daschle and Harry [Reid] and me and a couple of others, and he basically asked everybody's opinion, but he didn't really engage them in helping to find solutions as much as I thought," Breaux said. "He listened to your opinion, but I don't know you ever felt you were making a lot of progress."

Calio, Bush's first legislative affairs director, said Bush retained such distance from Democrats in these talks as part of a White House strategy to preserve his options in negotiation. "That was part of the plan," Calio said. "He would talk, he would listen, because it would inform his thinking. . . . But he kept himself once removed from the actual negotiating, because that kept more options open for us and more territory for us to operate in to get the results we wanted."

Such calculations may have influenced Bush's posture in his private interactions with Democrats. But overall the evidence suggests that Bush was so opaque in his private meetings with members of Congress less because he wanted to maintain negotiating freedom than because he had so little enthusiasm for negotiating with them in the first place. Leading

Democrats generally did not find the White House staff much more responsive to their concerns than the president himself. "We got the impression from the president that there was very little negotiating room, and that was confirmed with our meetings with the staff," said Daschle wryly. "There was no good cop. . . . for them there was really no middle ground; it was their position or none at all, even on little things, petty things."

Moreover, Bush typically was not much more forthcoming in private meetings with Republicans, around whom he presumably could let down his guard. Tom Davis, the politically astute Republican representative from Virginia who chaired the National Republican Congressional Committee and then the House Committee on Government Reform under Bush, said that the president often did little more than recount his public arguments even in private meetings with Republicans. "I don't think the president has been as good in the one-on-ones with members as Clinton," Davis said. Nebraska senator Chuck Hagel, a Vietnam veteran who served on the Foreign Relations and Intelligence committees, was one of the few elected Republicans to publicly raise alarms about the trajectory of the Iraq War before the 2006 election. Bush, he said, never invited him to privately discuss his concerns. Nor, Hagel said, did the administration see much value in his suggestions that they try to build a broader consensus for their direction by consulting more with legislators from both parties, especially on national security issues:

> You've seen it with the style of this administration the last six years in foreign policy, in everything. Because of September 11 they had a tremendous amount of leverage up here, starting with the fact that the Congress was of the president's party, so he had a very willing Congress to go along with him for political reasons. But they never ever reached out for accommodation or inclusion or consensus building. They shortcut that. They never ever made any effort to do that, or take the time to do that. Call members down and spend time. The secretary coming up here. The national security adviser bringing people down there. It was just a waste of time [to them].

Alone among the members of Congress interviewed, Richard Lugar, the soft-spoken Indiana Republican who chaired the Senate Foreign Relations Committee during most of Bush's presidency, said he had participated in a meeting when Bush appeared to change his mind in response to arguments from others in the room. (The occasion, Lugar recalled, was a conversation between Bush, Senate majority leader Bill Frist and other senators, and humanitarian groups over how to structure the administration's initiative against AIDS in Africa.) But Lugar agreed with Hagel that Bush ultimately did not place a high priority on building congressional consensus. Especially in the administration's early years, Lugar said, there was "very little desire to have debate" with legislators over Bush's national security decisions. "There was conviction on the part of those who were involved that they were on the right track of history and they simply wanted congressional *support*," Lugar said. "My feeling all along has been essentially that the president is not entrapped by his advisers, but on the other hand, he hasn't really wanted to reach very far beyond whatever the inner circle was at the time."

Would Bush's presidency have unfolded differently if he spent more time openly engaging with members of Congress, especially the Democrats who became such bitter adversaries? It is possible that even if Bush reached out more to Democrats they might not have reached back. After the ideological re-sorting of the electorate, congressional Democrats faced heightened pressure from their liberal base to vote against Bush (just as Republicans faced greater pressure from their conservative base to vote with him). But the testimony of Democrats as diverse as Daschle and Breaux suggests that even in private Bush made at best minimal effort to discover where the two sides could agree. Even Kennedy, whose deliberations with Bush on education in 2001 marked a high point in the president's outreach to Democrats, said the two men never achieved such a level of candor and cooperation on any other issue. "There's been nothing that's really been similar," Kennedy said. "There's just been a lot of missed opportunities." Congressional Democrats might have been too constrained by the politics of their own coalition to meet Bush halfway on most issues. But he made it easy for them by so rarely offering to move anywhere near that far in their direction.

TACTICS

That doesn't mean Bush never gave ground. Bush may not have liked to discuss compromise, but that doesn't mean he never accepted it. Like any president, Bush sometimes made tactical concessions to advance his strategic goals. And, like all his predecessors, Bush sometimes conceded defeat to overwhelming pressure, especially on issues at the periphery of his concerns, such as when he signed the legislation from Senators John McCain and Russell Feingold reforming the campaign finance system despite his reservations, because it had attracted preponderant support in Congress.

But on his priorities Bush was typically much less flexible. On his core concerns Bush almost always negotiated, either with Congress or other nations, only if opponents demonstrated the power to stop him from moving in the direction that he preferred (as was the case on his first tax cut in 2001). He responded to power, not argument. When Bush had the leverage to advance his agenda he did, whether or not he had established a consensus for his course. Bush never went as far as Margaret Thatcher, the conservative icon and former British prime minister, who once publicly declared that "consensus is the absence of leadership." But his actions made clear he did not view consensus as a priority. It was not an end with inherent value, but valuable only when it advanced the goal of implementing his ideas. In Bush's first term one of his senior political advisers briskly summarized the prevailing philosophy in the White House. "This is not designed to be a 55 percent presidency," he said. "This is designed to be a presidency that moves as much as possible of what we believe into law while holding fifty plus one of the country and the Congress."

On issue after issue Bush validated that assessment. In his congressional strategy he consistently demonstrated that he would rather pass legislation as close as possible to his preferences on a virtually party-line basis than make concessions to reduce political tensions or broaden his support among Democrats. He preferred to impose a conservative change in policy by a small margin than a more moderate change by a large margin. Bush exhibited a fundamental continuity between his tactics with other countries and with Democrats in Congress: He would move with others if possible, but alone if necessary.

After the outreach of his initial months Bush and his White House aides rarely expressed much concern about his level of opposition among congressional Democrats or devoted much effort to diminishing it (at least until Democrats regained control of Congress in 2006). Even moderate congressional Democrats complained that the White House made virtually no attempt to solicit their support or to hear their concerns. "In January [2001] I remember coming to work thinking, 'Well, they are going to call,'" said Democratic representative Ellen Tauscher, who represented an affluent district northeast of San Francisco and served as a leader of Clinton-like New Democrats in the House. "He said he's going to be a uniter, not a divider; he said he is going to work in a bipartisan way; the majority [in Congress] was very narrow. And then nothing happens. And after three or four weeks, and three or four months, we were pretty convinced that things were going to be radically different, that they were not going to do any outreach."

Instead the White House centered its legislative strategy on maximizing unity among Republicans. Bush and congressional Republicans would accept Democratic votes but not pursue them at the price of offering concessions that might drive away Republican legislators or constituencies. The administration's usual strategy was to support House Republicans as they produced legislation that tilted sharply to the right, then make tactical concessions to move the idea through the Senate (where the filibuster provided Democrats more leverage); and then move the final product back as far to the right as possible when the House and Senate met in a conference committee to reconcile their alternative approaches. Over time, on issues from energy to the Medicare prescription drug plan, congressional Republicans, abandoning Capitol Hill tradition, simply excluded all or most Democrats from the discussions that shaped the final bill in conference.

At times it appeared that the White House, and even more so the Republican congressional leadership, preferred policies that separated the two parties to create sharper contrasts for election campaigns. Ted Kennedy, for instance, became convinced that such calculations shaped the maneuvering over the legislation establishing a prescription drug benefit under Medicare in 2003, one of Bush's key first-term legislative achievements. With an endorsement from Kennedy providing the critical stamp of legitimacy, the Senate that year passed a bipartisan prescription drug bill with support not only from four fifths of Republicans, but more than three fourths of Democrats. That consensus shattered, though, when negotiators gathered in a conference committee to reconcile the Senate plan with the much more conservative version the House had approved. (Compared to the Senate approach, the House bill tilted heavily toward the needs of the insurance and pharmaceutical industries, both major Republican donors, by providing them rather than government the dominant role in administering the new benefit.) Republicans set the tone for the conference negotiations by flatly excluding all Democrats except Senators Max Baucus of Montana and John Breaux, whom they considered sympathetic to their approach. Inevitably, the conference moved the plan much closer to the House version. Watching the proceedings, Kennedy concluded the White House and congressional Republicans were calibrating the final product to minimize the number of Democrats who could support it so that the GOP could claim sole credit for the program. And indeed, when the final legislation returned to the Senate, the vote among Democrats flipped: While three fourths of them supported the original Senate plan, three fourths opposed the more conservative final legislation. "[By] making some adjustments and changes, this thing could have passed overwhelmingly," said Kennedy, who faced criticism in his own party for negotiating with Republicans so extensively. "But they wouldn't do it; they wanted an all-Republican bill."

The same tactics were applied to House Democrats even more roughly. DeLay often preferred to lace bills with poison pill provisions so unpopular with core Democratic groups that even Democrats sympathetic to the overall legislation could not vote for them. House Republicans used the tactic so often, on issues from the prescription drug bill to trade, that the centrist Democrats developed a name for it—"the olive pit in the jelly donut." The aim was to force moderate Democrats to vote against powerful constituencies, usually business interests, in their districts so that Republicans could later use the votes to organize opposition against them. Not just Democrats recognized this pattern. "It seems over the last couple of years [that] if something can come to the floor and you can pass it with a bipartisan majority, . . . or if you can bring it to the floor in a way that you can just get Republican support and use it as a political issue against the Democrats, we have chosen the latter every time," said Republican representative Jeff Flake, an ambitious and eclectic conservative from Arizona first elected in 2000. In Tom DeLay's House, division was not considered a cost of legislative success; it was viewed as a measure of it.

ELECTORAL STRATEGY

One of the most enduring rules in presidential politics is that the White House is won in the middle of the electorate, among independent, moderate, and less partisan voters. Bush's first presidential campaign largely shared that assumption. Just as he did in Texas, Bush in 2000 devoted enormous effort to convincing swing voters that he would govern as a "compassionate conservative." In Bush's first White House bid the campaign targeted about three fourths of its money toward the persuasion of undecided and loosely committed voters. "In 2000, everything was about persuading," said Ken Mehlman, who served as the campaign's national field director. "In 2000 we assumed the environment . . . was a squishy environment. It was the age of the Clinton. It was about persuading people [Bush] was a different kind of Republican, all of that stuff."

Once Bush entered the White House, as we saw earlier, the effort to reach out to new constituencies on issues like education reform coexisted with doubts among his political advisers about the administration's ability to convert many of the voters who had opposed him in 2000. As his presidency unfolded, those doubts deepened.

Mehlman, who joined the White House as political director under Rove, remembers being struck by Bush's inability to expand his support in polls even after the early legislative breakthroughs on taxes and education. In a Gallup survey that concluded on September 10, 2001, Bush's approval rating stood at just 51 percent, an unusually weak number for a president so early in his first term; while nearly 90 percent of Republicans cheered him, only 27 percent of Democrats and 44 percent of independents applauded his performance. "You can argue that before 9/11, the notion of being a Clinton-type consensus guy had reached its limits," Mehlman said. "I certainly worried that summer. We had done education reform, we had done a tax cut, and look at the numbers!"

One reasonable inference from Bush's inability over his first months to attract consistent support from Democrats on Capitol Hill, or to expand his base in polls, might be that he had formulated an agenda aimed too narrowly at the priorities of conservatives. But Bush's advisers reached the opposite conclusion. They viewed Bush's equivocal position as evidence that the political divisions that split the country almost exactly in half in the 2000 election remained immutable. "We thought there was very little pliability in [the electorate]," Rove recalled.

Rove in particular grew convinced that the great sorting out had left behind very few independent voters genuinely uncommitted to either party. He saw little prospect for either side to win a significant number of voters who identified with the other party, and he believed most people who called themselves independents were in fact closet partisans who just didn't want to wear their team's jersey. "The swing [vote] . . . between the two parties dissipated over the course of the 1980s and 1990s," Rove said. "People of faith have become more Republican; people who are secular have become more Democrat. People who had been, in the 1950s, and particularly the 1960s and early 1970s, up for grabs, have made a decision."

These assessments carried important implications. They hardened the belief among Bush's top advisers that he was unlikely to shatter the fifty-fifty divide of his first election by building a broad and diverse coalition of support. "We really thought the real share of the electorate that we could ultimately get on Election Day [in 2004], that really was available to us, was basically around 53 percent," said Dowd. "That was a landslide. Honestly. From early on [we believed that]."

From that conclusion Bush's political brain trust steadily tilted their political strategy toward energizing the president's base and encouraging turnout among Republicans. When Bush's political team conducted a detailed "after-action review" of the 2000 campaign, it identified three top priorities for 2004. Only one was primarily a task of persuasion: improving Bush's performance among Hispanics. The other two goals focused on mobilization: turning out more conservatives and energizing more loosely committed Republicans.

The Bush advisers were encouraged in those conclusions not only by their long-term analysis of the electorate but by their immediate experience in 2000. In Bush's circles there was a widespread suspicion that the disclosure, in the campaign's final days, of an old drunk-driving citation against Bush depressed turnout among the core Republican constituency of religious conservatives. From the outset Rove and the others focused intently on ensuring that those voters would turn out in overwhelming numbers in 2004.

These priorities didn't leave Bush's team entirely fatalistic about their ability to court voters who had resisted him in 2000. "You are kidding yourself if you don't think there is constant reaching out," Rove said. Throughout Bush's first term, the outreach occurred both at the level of broad policy and rifle-shot interventions. Bush's team hoped his support for immigration reform would improve his performance among Hispanics, and his signing into law the Medicare prescription drug benefit would produce better results with seniors. As journalists Tom Hamburger and Peter Wallsten detailed in their book, *One Party Country*, the White House courted not only white evangelical ministers, but also conservative African American religious leaders, through grants distributed under its program to increase government partnerships with religion-based charities. The administration pursued hunting and outdoors groups—the "hook and bullet crowd"—as an alternative to the conventional environmental groups. It sought to build ties with the International Brotherhood of Teamsters, the most conservative of the major labor unions.

But this list of political priorities is as revealing for what it does not include. Nowhere on it was significantly improving Bush's performance among the voters who had been the principal political target for his predecessor, Bill Clinton: independents and others loosely attached to either party. Clinton had operated on the traditional calculation that presidents expand their coalition mostly by capturing voters floating between the parties. The Bush advisers, even with all of their targeted outreach, increasingly rejected that assumption. To the extent that they sought to expand Bush's coalition, it was more through a strategy of accretion than persuasion—targeting precisely focused appeals at narrow niches within the population rather than seeking to realign the overall electorate through a message and agenda with broad appeal across partisan and ideological lines. And expanding their coalition by reaching out to groups that resisted Bush, by whatever means, was never as great a priority as enlarging the coalition by squeezing more advantage from the groups that already preferred him. Deepen, not broaden: These were the watchwords that guided Bush's political strategy. "We were left going into '04 with a couple of things, not the least of which was that there was nothing we could say or do for a huge chunk of the country to move them to us," said Dowd. "Nothing. They had made up their minds, they knew who he was, we couldn't move them. . . . It was impossible. They knew him, and it wasn't good."

Bush's advisers did not talk openly about the policy implications of this political analysis, but it was difficult to miss: In such an ossified environment there was little incentive for a president to make substantive concessions across party lines. At best such compromises were unlikely to generate much support from voters in the opposition party. At worst they could divide and demoralize the president's traditional supporters—the way George H. W. Bush's deal with Democrats to raise taxes in 1990 had done. As inspiring a massive Republican turnout grew more important to the president's team, Bush's personal proclivity to seek dramatic change—to reject anything he viewed as "small ball"—was increasingly reinforced by the political imperative of advancing bold ideas that could mobilize his base.

Vision

The willingness to accept narrow, party-line legislative victories as a matter of course; the reluctance to negotiate with Democrats; the resigned acceptance of high levels of opposition from Democrats and even independents in polls; the political strategy that minimized the importance of converting skeptical voters: All offered clues to the distinctive philosophy of leadership that Bush applied to the presidency. Bush gave every indication that, like Woodrow Wilson, he believed a president's principal responsibility was finding what he believed to be the "right" solution to a problem and then driving the debate in that direction, even at the price of heightening division at home or around the world.

That vision of leadership downplayed the importance of attracting others to the leader's agenda. Bush did not quarrel with the idea that voters could judge his decisions on Election Day: He famously described his 2004 reelection as an "accountability moment." But he often suggested that he did not see much relevance in the public reaction to his decisions between elections, whether measured by polls, attitudes in Congress, editorial comment, or anything else. Bush dismissed doubts about his direction by arguing that contemporaries could not really judge a president's impact. In several interviews Bush raised what might be called the George Washington defense. He noted that while in office he had read several biographies of Washington, and that historians two hundred years later were still adjusting their assessment of the man. "[T]he people are gonna say what's on their mind at the moment," Bush told one interviewer in 2006. "But I read three histories of George Washington last year. The first president of the United States is still being analyzed by historians, which oughta say to this president and future presidents: 'Do what you think is right, and eventually historians will figure out whether it made sense or not.' "

That answer was easy to admire in one respect: It demonstrated a depth of conviction and a reluctance to be swayed by short-term shifts in public opinion. Those are qualities Americans often say they prefer in their president. But Bush's response also suggested how he could apply those virtues to a degree that they became defects. By describing contemporary opinion as only transitory and ephemeral ("what's on their mind at the moment") Bush offered a rationale for ignoring whether his course united or divided the country. It was unremarkable for Bush to note that history repeatedly revises its judgments on presidents. But the conclusion he reached from that observation was striking: Because history's ultimate verdict is inscrutable, a president is left with only his own instincts to guide his actions. In Texas, all evidence suggests Bush had viewed himself as part of a collaborative effort to solve problems. But Bush's words and actions both suggest that in the White House he came to see political leadership less as an interactive process between leaders and followers than a solitary responsibility. Rather than adjusting his course to bring along as many of his fellow citizens as possible, a president's highest obligation was to be true to his own principles—to "do what you think is right." In the end, by Bush's logic, a president operated with a constituency of one: his own conscience.

All the factors discussed in this chapter help explain why Bush adopted such a different view of leadership in Washington than in Texas: more personal confidence after more time in office; different political calculations; the strains of responding to 9/11; and differing responses from Democrats all probably contributed. But if the reasons for the change were complex, the impact on Bush's thinking was singular: By all evidence he hardened in the belief that the leader's highest obligation to the governed was to be true to his own mind, and the corresponding conclusion that resolve and conviction trumped values like flexibility and curiosity.

On some fronts Bush appeared genuinely reluctant to divide the country. On issues with racial overtones he generally recoiled from polarizing actions or language. He never mounted a frontal assault against affirmative action programs for minorities. On issues relating to illegal immigration, his tone was even more striking. As a presidential candidate in 2000 some of his most impassioned moments came in defense of illegal immigrants, whom he often described empathetically as moms and dads trying to create a better life for their children; on the eve of the Senate debate over immigration in 2006 he cautioned all sides to consider the impact of their words. "[W]e've got to be careful about the language we use when it comes to debating this important subject," he said. "People should not pit neighbor against neighbor, group of people against group of people in our country." On each of these concerns he clearly appeared to recognize that bringing together the country was part of the president's job description.

That simply did not appear to be part of his analysis on most other issues. So long as his core supporters stood behind him, Bush rarely appeared to mind generating intense opposition from others outside his coalition. If anything, Bush sometimes suggested that he saw strong opposition as a sign that he was doing his job properly by making tough decisions. "I fully understand that when you do hard things, it creates consternation at times," he told one interviewer.

Over time Bush's advisers portrayed the polarization that swirled around him as an acceptable, even inevitable, cost of leaving a bold imprint on history. In the White House analysis sharp division over Bush's course was not evidence of political failure—an inability to establish consensus—but proof of political success: a willingness to challenge conventional approaches with bold proposals that transformed the terms of debate. In their eyes, the ardor of opposition reflected the boldness of Bush's conception. Rove expressed that sentiment through the vehicle of a short essay he wrote for *Time* magazine about Theodore Roosevelt. Rove clearly had Bush as much in mind as TR when he wrote: "The rough-and-tumble of the political arena didn't bother him. 'If a man has a very decided character, has a strongly accentuated career,' Roosevelt said, 'it is normally the case of course that he makes ardent friends and bitter enemies.' T.R. had both. So did F.D.R. So did Lincoln. So did Reagan. So do all consequential leaders." Bush himself accepted a bitterly divided society so readily he left the impression he viewed it as a natural phenomenon entirely out of his control. Will Marshall, president of the Progressive Policy Institute, a centrist Democratic think tank whose ideas Bush praised in his 2000 campaign, captured Bush's attitude in a memorable phrase: "He is much too comfortable being president of half the country."

Bush displayed his attitudes toward leadership most vividly, and with the greatest consequence, in the war against Iraq. In his dealings with both Congress and other nations before the war Bush sought not to construct a consensus for a common direction on Iraq, but rather to obtain acquiescence for the undeviating direction he had charted in his own mind. Although no critic has demonstrated that Bush deliberately misled the country before the war, the extensive journalistic excavation of his decision making has left little doubt that he used intelligence claims about Saddam Hussein's capabilities and intentions less to shape his choices than to justify them. The policy process inside the administration always pivoted more on building a case for war than objectively assessing the need for it. In the last months before the invasion Bush went through the motions of consultation with Congress and at the United Nations, but he left no real question of his conviction that only war could resolve the threat he perceived from Iraq, or that he believed he possessed the authority to act with or without consent from others; Bush's final steps toward Baghdad unfolded in the spirit of a marketing campaign, not a dialogue. Not since James K. Polk maneuvered the United States into the Mexican-American War in 1846 had American troops been sent into combat as directly as the projection of a single man's will.

As Bush marched toward the invasion in 2003, he drew encouragement from his supporters at home and some firm allies abroad, led by British prime minister Tony Blair. And in the United States congressional Democrats, intimidated by Bush's still-imposing approval ratings and the approaching midterm 2002 election, failed in their obligation to ask tough questions before authorizing him to use force against Iraq. (So, in many cases, did the mainstream media.) But even so there was evidence in all directions that an invasion also faced substantial resistance. Right until the eve of the war public opinion polls showed America deeply divided over the prospect of an invasion without broad international participation. In one national survey, completed just three days before the invasion, only one third of independents and less than one fourth of Democrats said they would support an attack without agreement from U.S. allies; only a majority of Republicans endorsed the idea. Polls showed substantial majorities of the population in almost every major European, Asian, and Arab nation opposed an invasion. The international doubts were underscored when Bush failed to win a second United Nations resolution explicitly authorizing the attack. Bush himself recognized that the war could unleash powerful and contentious emotions. "If we have to do what is being talked about in Iraq," the president told Rove at their first meeting in January 2003 to discuss the reelection campaign, "it will be a tough and divisive election."

In all these ways the events of early 2003 showed that Bush had not convinced much of America, and the world, that all alternatives to war had been exhausted. The polling strongly suggested that America was likely to divide along party lines if the war did not go as smoothly as the administration predicted. Yet Bush still invaded Iraq, secure in the unshakable personal conviction that he was operating to safeguard America and transform the Middle East. In the months that followed Iraq buckled under first a violent insurgency against the American presence, and then roaring storms of sectarian violence that amounted to civil war. Many of Bush's prewar assumptions (that Americans would uncover stocks of weapons of mass destruction; that Iraqis would greet the foreign forces as liberators; that the reconstruction of Iraq would pay for itself; that the establishment of a democratically elected government in Iraq would undermine extremists across the Middle East) collapsed. But Bush gave no hint that those momentous events ever caused him to waver in his conviction.

Bush acknowledged difficulty but never doubt about either his initial decision or the ultimate outcome he expected. So decisive in launching the war, Bush often appeared frozen in obsolete optimism when the occupation lurched off course. As conditions in Iraq deteriorated he sealed himself off from the war's critics in Congress—not only Democrats gradually recovering their voices, but as Chuck Hagel noted, even Republicans. (Skeptics inside the government, as the reporting of Bob Woodward and others has shown, felt just as isolated.) Until Bush reached his lowest ebb in 2007, he ignored suggestions by allies ranging from Senator Joe Lieberman to neoconservative Bill Kristol, the editor of the *Weekly Standard*, to solicit ideas even from the Democrats most supportive of the war.* Even after the Republican losses in the 2006 election Bush flatly dismissed the major recommendations for a new direction from the bipartisan Iraq Study Group chaired by James A. Baker III, his father's secretary of state.

Bush often appeared to delight in not only rebutting but provoking his critics. When a chorus of retired generals denounced Defense Secretary Donald Rumsfeld's handling of the war, and called for his resignation in spring 2006, Bush sweepingly dismissed their complaints with the memorable neologism: "I'm the decider, and I decide what is best. And what's best is for Don Rumsfeld to remain as the secretary of defense."† Bush echoed that language again ("I'm the decision maker," he insisted) when he decided in early 2007 to deploy 21,500 troops to Iraq despite overwhelming opposition from public opinion, almost all congressional Democrats, many congressional Republicans, the bipartisan Iraq Study Group, and skepticism from his own military and the Iraqi government. Harry Reid, the Democratic Senate leader, sometimes spoke in partisan hyperbole, but he did not exaggerate when he concluded, "In choosing to escalate the war, the president stands alone."

---

* By the time Bush proposed in January 2007 to establish a bipartisan congressional group to consult with him on Iraq, Democratic opposition to the war had hardened to the point where the group served little function.

† Bush finally dismissed Rumsfeld the day after Democrats, riding a wave of discontent over the Iraq war, captured their majorities in the House and Senate in November 2006.

Blame for the Iraq tragedy could be fairly apportioned to all of those who had failed to sufficiently question Bush's arguments and optimistic assumptions—congressional Democrats in the early stages; the mainstream press; the internal administration skeptics like Colin Powell; much less the congressional Republican majority that, as we'll see, renounced its institutional responsibility to monitor the execution of the war. But it was Bush who drove the nation into Iraq, and Bush who bore the ultimate responsibility for the unraveling there that followed. What his advisers once hoped would be a symbol of bold and transformative leadership instead became a monument to the dangers of a governing style that stressed the leader's obligation to his personal vision; interpreted resistance as proof of boldness; and prized decisiveness over inclusiveness. At each step Bush would have better served America, Iraq, and his own fortunes if he had sought to harvest rather than discredit ideas from critics at home and abroad who urged him to allow more time for inspections before invading; to provide more troops to ensure order once he did invade; to delegate more authority over the occupation to the United Nations; and later to make earlier efforts to involve Iraq's neighbors, including Iran and Syria, in its stabilization and to increase pressure on Iraq's political leaders to share power and control sectarian violence. Circling the wagons proved no way to win a war.

Like Woodrow Wilson on the League of Nations, Bush's commitment to his course in Iraq hardened as his support in the country and the Congress softened. And like Lyndon Johnson and Richard Nixon during Vietnam, he lost the capacity to hear, much less learn from, dissenting voices. Bush's solitary vision of leadership seemed to compel him to dig deeper whenever the ground around him crumbled. His determination inspired those who shared his faith in his direction, but among his skeptics it added to the sense that he viewed stubbornness as the highest attribute of leadership. By standing in place Bush moved the country further apart.

GOALS

Amid all of the factors that widened America's divisions during the Bush years one loomed largest: As president, Bush mostly pursued policies that were not conducive to broad consensus. It was his ends, even more than his means, that produced such a polarizing presidency. His agenda aimed primarily at the priorities of one faction: the conservative wing of the Republican Party.

Bush governed in a more consistently conservative manner than Reagan. Reagan accepted a tax increase (albeit reluctantly) in 1982 after his initial tax cuts opened a large federal deficit. Bush responded to the deficits that followed his 2001 tax cuts with his proposal in 2003 to cut taxes another $726 billion over eleven years. If the struggle against terrorism after September 11 constituted a war, as Bush argued, his proposal in 2003 marked the first time any American president proposed to significantly cut taxes during wartime. Each year after, Bush proposed to cut taxes again.

Bush sought much more fundamental changes than Reagan ever proposed in Social Security and Medicare, the central cords of the federal safety net for the elderly. He also pursued a focused series of regulatory and legal proposals that would have had the effect of weakening Democratic constituencies and strengthening Republican-leaning ones. Legal reforms such as his proposed limits on class action and medical malpractice lawsuits bolstered business groups that supported the GOP and threatened trial lawyers, a major source of funds for Democrats. On environmental, occupational safety, and labor law issues, Bush's appointees consistently sided with business interests against union and environmental groups also closely allied with the Democratic Party.

Those groups also viewed almost all of Bush's judicial appointments as a threat to their causes—as did abortion rights and other socially liberal groups aligned with the Democrats. Bush challenged those groups on other fronts as well. He signed into law a ban on so-called partial-birth abortions, allowed the ban Clinton signed on assault weapons to lapse, and promoted a constitutional amendment to ban gay marriage. Bush's approach to federal funding for stem cell research (which he defended during his second term with his first veto when Congress sought to loosen it) leaned more toward social conservatives looking to restrain the research than toward scientists and medical groups hoping to expand it.

On energy issues Bush sided mostly with oil and mineral companies seeking more production rather than environmentalists aiming to reduce consumption and accelerate the development of alternative energy. Though he tilted his balance more toward conservation and alternatives in his second term, he staunchly opposed the mandatory reductions in carbon dioxide emissions that many considered the key to promoting a transition away from fossil fuels.

In foreign policy Bush pursued equally emphatic changes. Even before September 11 he moved to increase America's unilateral freedom of action while reducing reliance on traditional allies and international institutions. In the invasion of Iraq he sought to enshrine a principle of confronting rogue nations through preemptive or preventive war. In his second inaugural address he presented the promotion of democracy across the globe, and especially in the Muslim world, as the principle that should guide American foreign policy for a generation. He repeatedly pushed to the edge in expanding federal power to monitor, detain, and deny conventional legal protections to suspected terrorists.

There were places where Bush's agenda overlapped with Democratic priorities (spending more to combat AIDS overseas, increasing the federal role in measuring student progress, providing a path to legalization for illegal immigrants). After Democrats won control of Congress in 2006 Bush reached out to Democrats with new initiatives on improving automotive fuel economy and modestly expanding access to health care. He also challenged his conservative base by supporting sensible immigration reform. But these conciliatory ideas were almost completely eclipsed by his stunningly confrontational decision to send more troops to Iraq and his subsequent resistance to Democratic efforts to set a timetable for ending America's role in the war. Moreover, his gestures toward Democrats came after public disillusion over his presidency had sapped virtually all of Bush's ability to drive Washington's agenda. He was like a man who extended his hand only after he had fallen down a well.

DURING THE DEFINING years of Bush's presidency, most of what he sought to achieve had very little appeal to most Democrats, in Congress, and in the country. Of all the factors unique to Bush, that simple fact probably contributed more than any other to the unstinting partisan conflict that defined his time. No matter what else he did, no matter how he adjusted his legislative tactics or his speaking style, or even the way he walked, Bush was unlikely to create significantly more consensus in the country unless he embraced ideas that offered more to voters and interests outside of his core coalition. And that was something Bush only rarely felt compelled to do. Instead, he echoed the presidents from the age of partisan armies at the turn of the twentieth century—the line of chief executives from McKinley through the three conservative Republicans of the 1920s—in seeking to maximize unity in his own coalition while minimizing concessions to the other. Nelson Aldrich and Joe Cannon would have felt entirely at home at the elbow of Karl Rove.

Bush's determination to govern in a manner that harkened back to the intensely partisan strategies of McKinley and his successors moved America much deeper into the age of hyperpartisanship. That approach carried Republicans to a succession of legislative and electoral victories through the first half of his presidency. But through Bush's second term the downsides of his direction, for the party and the country itself, grew more apparent. If his first term frequently demonstrated the political benefits of embracing polarization, his second repeatedly illustrated the costs. The strategies Republicans used to profit from polarization, and how those strategies eventually imploded at great cost to Bush's presidency and the country, are the subjects we explore next.

CHAPTER 8

THE 51 PERCENT SOLUTION: REPUBLICAN STRATEGY IN THE BUSH YEARS

The Republican Party that George W. Bush inherited in 2001 rallied to the ambitious and intensely polarizing style of leadership he brought to the White House. The great sorting out of the electorate from the 1960s through the 1980s had homogenized and streamlined the GOP even more than the Democratic Party. By the time of Bush's election the percentage of Republican voters who considered themselves conservatives was much larger than the share of Democrats who called themselves liberals. In both the House and Senate conservatives constituted a larger share of Republican members than liberals did among Democrats. Conservative interest groups exerted more consistent and coordinated pressure on GOP politicians than liberals did on Democrats. And to a greater extent than in the Democratic Party the grassroots activists shared a common vision of the future with party leaders, especially the vanguard conservatives in the House like Newt Gingrich and Tom DeLay. The vast majority of conservative leaders inside and outside of government united around long-term goals breathtaking in their ambition: lower taxes and the eventual replacement of the progressive income tax, either with a flat tax or national sales tax; less regulation; the transformation of the social safety net to rely more on the private market and less on government assistance; a social order that reduces access to abortion and rejects the moral equivalence of homosexual and heterosexual lifestyles; more defense spending; and an aggressive projection of American power in the world, with or without support from traditional allies. On all of these fronts conservatives sought not incremental but revolutionary change.

For conservatives inspired by those possibilities, Bill Clinton's eight years in the White House had been agonizing. When Bush arrived the reigning conservative forces inside the GOP saw the opportunity to unleash their ambitions. Over the course of Bush's presidency conservatives complained about some of his decisions, particularly the level of domestic spending he accepted. The collapse of his public support in his second term inspired a different wave of conservative grumbling about White House incompetence or arrogance. Yet many conservatives recognized in Bush a kindred soul, not only in ideology, but more importantly in temperament. Because their goals were transformative rather than incremental, conservative activists could not be entirely satisfied with the give and take, the half a loaf deal making, of politics in ordinary times. Only confrontation could satisfy many on the right, because consensus could never achieve change of the magnitude they desired. In Bush they found a leader who shared that conviction and who demonstrated, over and again, that in service of his goals he was willing to sharply divide the Congress and the country.

Bush, the Republican Congress, and the grassroots conservative movement each encouraged the other toward the battlements. Bush and his allies bet that with only a narrow advantage in Congress and a slim electoral majority they could impose the galvanizing change that had almost always been accompanied by preponderant support in Congress and the country. That ambition required the GOP to perfect strategies that mobilized every available asset in the party's coalition into a disciplined force. On Capitol Hill Republicans deepened the culture of party loyalty that allowed them to consistently win achingly close votes with only minimal support from Democrats. At the White House Bush's political team developed a campaign plan intended to reelect Bush more by exciting his core supporters than by converting swing voters. On both fronts Republicans gambled that they could unify their party enough to survive levels of resistance from legislators and voters outside of their coalition that other presidents might have considered insurmountable. In the struggle for political supremacy, the GOP approach amounted to a 51 percent solution.

Under Bush and his chief political adviser, Karl Rove, the Republican policy, legislative, and electoral visions fit together crisply. They formed a closed circle. It's a fruitless exercise to ask whether Bush's political and legislative strategy of consolidating his base demanded a policy agenda consistently centered on conservative priorities or vice versa. Each reinforced and enabled the other.

This high-risk approach allowed Bush, in the first half of his presidency, to pursue, and to a considerable extent achieve, significant change without amassing a commanding margin in either of his two campaigns for the White House. He walked with substantial success along a very thin ledge for a very long time. The price was to greatly accelerate the spiral of polarization in American politics, at great cost to the country, and ultimately to his fortunes. Bush ignited volcanic levels of opposition from his critics. Over time that opposition slowed his advance, and then forced him into grudging but irreversible retreat through a grueling second term that saw his approval rating plummet and the GOP lose control of Congress in 2006 amid public anguish over the disintegration of Iraq.

The collapse of Bush's second term led more Republicans to openly question whether the party could thrive with a political strategy that provoked such a high level of division even on its best days. "They were clearly right in many, many respects," the veteran Republican pollster Bill McInturff said of Bush's team. "Clearly they've done a terrific job affecting turnout. But [their approach] is ahistoric. It's not this country's political history. So I believe the winner in 2008 is the person who breaks all of this." Some of the contenders for the Republican presidential nomination, as they began their campaigns early in 2007, also subtly distanced themselves from Bush by emphasizing their commitment to working across party lines. And Bush's refusal to change direction in Iraq prompted growing anxiety in 2007 among Republicans who feared another electoral debacle if a large number of American soldiers still remained trapped in the quicksand of the war by 2008.

Yet even so, the most striking aspect of the Republican reaction to Bush's decline was the absence of a loud call for the party to change course. Even after the resounding Republican losses in 2006 most party strategists and elected officials rejected the idea that the GOP needed to pursue a more centrist and inclusive direction. Many Republicans, as we'll see, even argued that the party had lost ground because it had not held to conservative principles steadfastly enough. Karl Rove defiantly insisted that the path he and Bush had charted still pointed Republicans toward lasting political dominance.

To understand the choices Republicans face at the end of the Bush presidency, we must first understand not only how his governing model declined, but how it rose. In its heyday the system demonstrated an enormous capacity to control the political debate and compel loyalty from all segments of the Republican coalition. But in Bush's dizzying descent almost all of the system's strengths became liabilities. The GOP's direction after Bush will likely pivot on which part of this story the party chooses to remember.

THE REPUBLICAN LEGISLATIVE MACHINE

The extraordinary cohesion that congressional Republicans generated for Bush's legislative agenda through most of his presidency culminated a transformation that began long before his arrival. After winning control of Congress in 1994, the Republican congressional leadership, especially in the House, sought to impose an unprecedented level of centralized direction not only on the party's legislators but on the interest groups aligned with them. This ambitious, even visionary, Republican project was born as much in feelings of weakness as of strength. When Republicans first won control of Congress they felt surrounded and contingent. Although the GOP had controlled the White House for twenty of the previous twenty-six years, and held the Senate for six years during that span, they still believed that Democrats and liberals dominated the capital's permanent institutions, the bureaucracy, the lobbying community, the press. "We had no one to talk to that would take our view of the path forward," said Don Fierce, the director of strategic planning at the Republican National Committee during the 1994 election, and later a top GOP lobbyist and adviser to congressional Republicans. "We knew that 80 percent of journalists were Democrats, we knew 80 percent of lobbyists were Democrats, we knew 80 percent of the bureaucracy was Democrats . . . so we had to look at, how do we fundamentally change Washington?"

Throughout the 1990s Republicans looked to leverage their control of Congress into greater influence over the capital's permanent institutions. That effort proceeded with mixed success. Congressional Republicans had little ability to influence the bureaucracy while Bill Clinton held the White House. With the establishment press, the new GOP majority mostly pursued a strategy of encirclement rather than direct confrontation. Through the Clinton years Republicans and their allied groups experimented with new forms of communication (the National Rifle Association was among the first political organizations to effectively use the Internet) and built alliances with the emerging voices of overtly conservative media, particularly talk radio. After the 1994 landslide freshman Republicans held a dinner to honor Rush Limbaugh, the most widely distributed conservative voice, as their "majority maker." When media magnate Rupert Murdoch founded the Fox News Channel just before the 1996 election, congressional Republicans quickly embraced it as a conservative alternative to the broadcast networks and CNN, which they believed tilted toward the Democrats.

The most combative Republican assault on permanent Washington came through the heralded K Street project—an effort initially launched by conservative activist Grover Norquist in 1989, and later adopted in a different form by GOP legislative leaders such as Tom DeLay and Pennsylvania senator Rick Santorum, to pressure lobbying firms and business trade associations to hire more Republicans. Republicans saw the K Street project as a corrective to decades of hiring decisions that favored Democrats. They grumbled that during the Democrats' nearly unbroken forty-year run of congressional control, business groups that should have supported the GOP's small-government philosophy instead tried to court Democratic leaders, by hiring their former aides as lobbyists. That frustration peaked in the 1980s as Tony Coelho, the able House Democrat, effectively pressed business to increase its support for Democrats, then seemingly in permanent control of the chamber. Coelho saw his effort as ensuring balance; conservatives like Norquist viewed it as a form of blackmail.

Norquist began the effort to reverse the tilt toward Democrats with reports systematically cataloguing the political background and campaign contributions of newly hired lobbyists, and with letters urging corporate executives to hire Republicans in their Washington offices. As an independent gadfly Norquist lacked the leverage to take his crusade very far. But when Republicans won control of Congress, the new majority applied a heavier hand. Senior GOP leaders like DeLay made it clear that groups that wanted access to Congress needed Republican hands to knock on the doors. "If you want to play in our revolution," DeLay insisted, "you have to live by our rules." In the most egregious cases DeLay and other House Republicans threatened interests such as the Investment Company Institute and Electronic Industries Alliance, who had hired Democrats for senior positions. But rarely were threats required. Top congressional Republicans instituted regular meetings with lobbyists where the two sides discussed pending legislation, the impending job openings on K Street, and Republicans, usually Hill aides, who might fill those openings. Often the lobbyists took the hint. "It was a very smart, very organized, strategic move to control the opposition [and] it worked brilliantly," said Steve Elmendorf, a former senior House Democratic aide who became a leading party lobbyist during Bush's second term. "Virtually every trade association in Washington is now headed by Republicans."

The placement of more Republicans in top lobbying jobs added several important pieces to the emerging Republican legislative machine. The most obvious was to help shift more of business's financial contributions from Democrats to Republicans. Even the business groups most sympathetic to the GOP's small-government, antiregulatory ideology felt compelled to preserve access by also contributing to the Democrats while they controlled Congress. Once Republicans seized the majority, ideology and self-interest aligned to tilt business further toward the GOP, a process the congressional leaders hoped to accelerate by installing Republicans in the key decision-making positions at the business groups. Organizations that still hesitated received less subtle reminders. During meetings with lobbyists after the Republican takeover DeLay famously displayed a book on his desk in which he kept track of how the largest four hundred political action committees divided their contributions between Democrats and Republicans.

All these factors converged to produce a dramatic shift in corporate giving patterns. During the 1994 election business split its contributions between Democrats and Republicans almost exactly in half. Just two years later the Democratic share of business contributions plummeted to 40 percent. Industries heavily affected by federal decisions registered even more dramatic changes: In just those two years, the Democratic share of contributions fell from 59 percent to 32 percent among defense firms, 40 percent to 26 percent among agricultural interests, and 43 percent to 27 percent among energy and natural resource firms. Through 2000, the Democratic share of overall business contributions never again exceeded 42 percent. With the K Street project the new majority tried to institutionalize its control by securing a permanent source of campaign funding, while starving its opponents.

Installing more Republicans on K Street encouraged closer ties with the business community in another respect: It helped the GOP leadership absorb those interests, to an unprecedented degree, into its own vote counting and lobbying operations. The House Republican leadership, as we saw in Chapter 5, set the mold in 1995, when it restricted access to its coveted Thursday morning meetings to interest groups that committed to lobby for all ten planks in the Contract with America, not just those that directly benefited the groups. In the years that followed Republican leaders (first DeLay, and the late Paul Coverdell in the Senate, and then successors like Senator Rick Santorum of Pennsylvania and Representative Roy Blunt of Missouri) consistently pressed business to lobby for GOP priorities and discouraged them from cooperating with Democrats. Business was too diverse, divided, and driven by self-interest to ever become a wholly owned subsidiary of the GOP machine; it always remained an independent force reluctant to participate in fights that stretched too far from a cold-eyed calculation of its self-interest. Yet when business's interests converged with the interests of the congressional majority—which, given the Republicans' ideological commitment to shrinking government and reducing regulation, was often—the two sides partnered with increasing intimacy. "On the issues where we are putting our shoulders in," said Bill Miller, the political director of the U.S. Chamber of Commerce, "they are putting their shoulders in."

The demands from congressional Republicans on business captured a larger change in thinking. On the one hand, as Democrats and government reform groups complained, the Republicans provided business lobbyists enormous access in shaping and even writing legislation. But the GOP leaders did not see themselves as simply taking dictation: In return for their support they expected the business community to enlist more unreservedly in defense of their congressional majority—supporting their legislative priorities, hiring the Republican aides ready to leave Capitol Hill, contributing to their candidates, and mobilizing their employees or members in campaigns. This approach, like so many things about the emerging Republican legislative and electoral machine, rested on logic that Nelson Aldrich or Joe Cannon easily could understand: The Republicans sent a clear signal that they would deliver for interests that delivered for them. The key to the system, as Fierce recognized, was creating a "process where elected officials drive the game, not the unelected elite power structure that was in place."

The irony is that Republicans applied central planning to the mission of liberating business from government oversight. Inside Congress they operated with the same vision. The message was more freedom for Americans. The method, especially in the House, was less freedom for legislators. After 1994, as we saw in Chapter 5, Gingrich reduced the deference to seniority and tied advancement in the House to support for the party agenda. Republican legislators, like the constellation of interests allied with the party, faced steady pressure to view themselves less as the voices of distinct and divergent constituencies and more as members of a centrally directed team.

No one—not even Gingrich, the closest thing to a guiding intelligence in the construction of this system—ever braided all these strands into a single manifesto. But the system did revolve around a central principle, which could be summarized simply as "self-sufficiency." The overall goal of the Republican legislative machine was to allow Republicans to pass their priorities, elect their candidates, and preserve their majority with as few concessions as possible to Democrats and their allies; the interlocking goals were to unify Republicans and marginalize Democrats. GOP leaders would accept Democratic votes in Congress for their proposals, but whenever possible they would not rely on them; they would solidify their ties to business and grassroots ideological groups sympathetic to their philosophy, while shunning the principal Democratic constituencies (labor unions, environmentalists, abortion- and gay-rights activists, trial lawyers); and they would try to reach their voters increasingly through overtly conservative media and direct forms of communication such as Web sites and e-mails rather than a mainstream press they considered biased against them. Gingrich, ever the visionary, still looked for ways to divide Democrats and co-opt elements of their constituency. But those ambitions almost never extended to the point of risking collisions with the core interests in the GOP coalition, the way Clinton had confronted Democrats over welfare or Nixon confronted Republicans on the environment. Outreach dwindled even further as a goal after Gingrich left Congress in 1998. Throughout the 1990s the key figures in the GOP placed the highest priority on building a system that united Republicans and their allies in a cycle of mutual advantage while isolating Democrats and their allies in ways that steadily diminished their ability to overthrow the entire structure.

Gingrich and his successors laid strong foundations for this system during the 1990s. But they faced a fundamental obstacle: Bill Clinton's presence in the White House. Clinton proved an able competitor for control of the national agenda and the allegiance of business. His skillful maneuvering meant that after the budget shutdowns in 1995 and early 1996, congressional Republicans could move their priorities into law only by reaching agreement with Clinton and the interests he defended. That meant compromises, which inevitably provoked divisions among Republicans in Congress and dissent among the groups they hoped to harness. In the Clinton years Republicans could never become entirely self-sufficient, because they could never erase the influence of the White House.

Once Bush succeeded Clinton the system's last piece clicked into place. From the start the GOP leaders in Congress made the critical decision to align with Bush more unreservedly than Democratic leaders had allied with Clinton. The feeling, recalled Tom Davis, the Virginia Republican, "was, he's our leader, let's get behind our team leader." To a far greater extent than Democrats during Bill Clinton's first two years, Republicans came out of the blocks behind Bush unified on a common course. "They thought," said Nick Calio, the director of legislative affairs during Bush's first years, "that his success would be their success."

Throughout Bush's presidency the Republicans never held a majority of more than fourteen seats in the House or five in the Senate (which, of course, reverted to Democratic control for part of Bush's first term when Vermont Republican James Jeffords quit the party). In another era, those narrow margins almost certainly would have required the president to deal extensively with the minority party. But, as we saw in Chapter 7, the historic level of cohesion produced by the Republican legislative machine allowed Bush to pass much of his agenda—from his tax cuts, to his annual budgets, to the creation of the Medicare prescription drug bill—without attracting consistent support from Democrats or, for the most part, offering the compromises that might have brought it.

By holding together so effectively under Bush, Republicans achieved the self-sufficiency that the Gingrich generation had sought, and demonstrated the power of the machine they had constructed. The more Republicans sustained their strength by maximizing unity within their own coalition the less pressure they felt to consider perspectives outside of it. And the more benefits they delivered for the constituencies aligned with them, the more those constituencies provided them the contributions that helped them sustain the power required to deliver yet more benefits. At times in Bush's first four years it appeared Republicans had discovered the political equivalent of a perpetual motion machine.

The costs of this system, as we'll see, would grow in Bush's second term. But as Congress efficiently processed and approved the key elements of his first-term agenda, Bush often seemed less like the harried manager of the disputatious and disorganized legislative coalitions that have characterized most of American history and more like a prime minister presiding over the sort of smoothly synchronized majority found in the most effective parliamentary systems abroad.

TOOLS OF CONTROL

It wasn't just the historic level of congressional Republican support for Bush legislative initiatives that inspired the comparisons to parliamentary systems. Almost as important, the vast majority of Republicans in both chambers rarely questioned Bush's first-term performance and priorities in public. Under Bush, Republicans almost completely avoided the debates over the party's direction common among Democrats under Clinton. Through Bush's first term the GOP legislative machine spoke with just a single voice—the one set predominantly by the president and his advisers.

The White House, as Tom Davis noted, "came in and . . . assumed a parliamentary system" where congressional Republicans would follow their lead. The congressional leaders sometimes bridled at that assumption; personal relationships were often strained between the White House and more independent legislative leaders like DeLay and Trent Lott, the Senate majority leader when Bush won election. (The president enjoyed better personal relations with House speaker Denny Hastert, and Senate majority leader Bill Frist, who replaced Lott after 2002 in a coup most considered countenanced, if not conceived, by the White House.) Vin Weber, a founding member of the Conservative Opportunity Society who became a premier GOP lobbyist after retiring from the House of Representatives in 1992, remembers that throughout the Bush years he "always heard a lot of grumbling on the Hill. And it was probably beyond the normal tension and complaining that you expect back and forth between the legislative and executive branch." Republican legislators groused that the White House was too high-handed or imperious, focused too much on the president's needs and not on theirs. Many echoed Tom Davis when he said, "They are always dictating, trying to tell you what to do."

Yet through Bush's first term congressional Republicans essentially accepted their role as supporting players in an American approximation of a parliamentary system. The GOP leaders on Capitol Hill merged their interests with the White House so completely that they blurred Congress's identity as a distinct and independent branch of government.

This attitude was manifest most plainly in the virtual abandonment of Congress's institutional responsibility to conduct oversight of the administration. While Clinton held the White House the Republican congressional majority had besieged his administration with investigations and subpoenas. One panel alone, the House Government Reform Committee, barraged the Clinton administration with more than 1,000 subpoenas, collected more than 2 million pages of documents, and summoned 134 administration officials to hearings investigating alleged wrongdoing. No subject was too trivial: The House, as the *Boston Globe* later reported, conducted 140 hours of sworn testimony on whether Clinton used the White House Christmas card list to prospect for Democratic donors.

In stark contrast, no congressional committee ever subpoenaed the White House while the Republicans controlled the House for the first six years of Bush's presidency, and the Senate for all but about eighteen months during that period. The sole congressional subpoena served on the White House during those years came from the Senate Governmental Affairs Committee in the brief interregnum when Democrats controlled the chamber.

The Republican majority abandoned oversight most conspicuously on national security questions. The Senate and House committees on armed services and foreign relations sometimes went more than six months without a public hearing on the Iraq War. Under pressure from Democrats the Senate Intelligence Committee in February 2004 agreed to investigate whether the Bush administration had misused intelligence information in making its case for the war. But Republican senator Pat Roberts of Kansas, the committee chairman and a close White House ally, publicly disparaged the inquiry and moved so slowly toward completing it that he called to mind Penelope secretly unraveling her father's burial shroud every night in the *Odyssey*; the study was still not finished when Republicans lost control of the chamber in November 2006. Indeed, Roberts had not even required senior administration officials to testify under oath in the investigation.

Perhaps most revealing was the congressional response to the Abu Ghraib prisoner abuse scandal that surfaced in late April 2004. The House Armed Services Committee, under the chairmanship of Republican representative Duncan Hunter of San Diego, another close White House ally, held a single hearing on the reports in May 2004. Hunter did not convene another public hearing until September, and called that only to receive the Pentagon's own investigations of the allegations. The Senate Armed Services Committee initially set a more aggressive course. Its chairman, Virginia Republican John Warner, a former navy secretary, had established a more independent and critical relationship with the administration than Hunter, and closer working ties with Democrats on his committee. Over twelve days in May, Warner's committee held three highly publicized hearings on the scandal. But Warner quickly came under friendly fire. Senators James Inhofe of Oklahoma and John Cornyn of Texas, two Republican conservatives on the committee, both publicly called on Warner to stop the hearings. Hunter, the House committee chair, in an unusual breach of congressional etiquette, pointedly charged that Warner and the Senate committee members had become "mesmerized by cameras." By summer, with the Pentagon balking at the committee's information requests and complaints from conservatives continuing, Warner was compelled to retreat. "We're not in a position to try to have an independent investigation at this point," he acknowledged. The Senate committee maintained a more skeptical eye than its House counterpart, but echoed the House in meeting again only to consider the Pentagon's own multiple investigations into the scandal.

The partisan conflict over the war that steadily intensified throughout the 2004 presidential campaign probably contributed to the collapse of oversight. Vin Weber believed congressional Republicans resisted oversight on the Iraq War and national security largely because they believed Democrats would use any information unearthed to attack Bush rather than to improve the war effort that many had voted to authorize. But other Republicans acknowledge that the parliamentary mind-set, in which the congressional majority saw itself less as an independent branch of government than as a junior partner to the president, also discouraged congressional Republicans from asking questions that might embarrass the White

House. "I think in the early days of this administration the Congress abdi-
cated its oversight responsibility, and I think it was a purely political reason," said Senator Chuck Hagel, the Republican from Nebraska who
questioned the war from early on. "I think there are some [Republicans in
Congress] who absolutely believe it is disloyal.

> I've been accused of being disloyal by my constituents, and by Republi-
> cans and others. I've never had any of my colleagues say that to my face.
> [But] I know I make some of them very uncomfortable. [They think],
> "Your job is to support the president no matter what, you're a Republi-
> can, therefore act like a Republican, therefore vote like a Republican,
> therefore whatever the president says you should do," [that] kind of
> thing. . . . [With] this administration putting so much emphasis on
> terror and fighting terror, and Iraq being the centerpiece of that, [people
> felt that] if you stray from that, then that opens up a whole valley of
> questions here in the political world and to a certain extent it starts to
> invalidate and erode and undermine the president's point, that we have
> to stick together here. So [the feeling was], don't get into oversight be-
> cause that will start to undermine what we're doing. And don't ask too
> many questions, because if you ask too many questions, this thing starts
> to come unraveled.

Republicans who pushed for more answers often faced resistance from
both the administration and the party's base. Richard Lugar, the thoughtful Indiana Republican who chaired the Senate Foreign Relations Committee, and stood as perhaps the most respected foreign policy voice in the
chamber, said administration officials repeatedly refused his requests to
testify before the committee about Iraq. "Our problem throughout
this . . . was that people from the administration did not want to testify,"
Lugar said. "If we were able to get somebody, this was an unusual day."
Lugar, who hoped to retain influence with Bush by avoiding confrontation, chose not to issue subpoenas, and instead convened hearings with
outside experts. But even those generated complaints from other Republicans after John Kerry and John Edwards, in debates with Bush and Cheney
during the 2004 presidential campaign, each quoted some of Lugar's

derogatory conclusions about the management of the Iraqi reconstruction. "This, of course, brought great resentment from Republicans around the country," Lugar recalled. "They would say, 'how in the world could you try to undercut the president in the middle of a campaign by such criticism?' " Although Lugar distributed regular letters to other senators on developments in the war, and maintained more critical independence than most of his colleagues, his committee never emerged as a major force in the debate over the administration's performance or alternatives in Iraq, a record he viewed with some regret as Iraq disintegrated.

House Republicans, if anything, deferred even more abjectly. Representative Chris Shays, a Connecticut Republican, chaired the only House panel that conducted sustained and serious oversight on the war: the Subcommittee on National Security, Emerging Threats, and International Relations of the Government Reform Committee. (It was surely no coincidence that Shays and Tom Davis, the full committee chairman, were both centrist Republicans in swing districts who maintained more independence from the White House than almost all of their colleagues.) Shays convened a succession of serious hearings that summoned midlevel administration officials and outside analysts to grapple with questions like the risk of civil war, the administration's plans for success, and the role of contractors in Iraq. He sometimes seemed incredulous that other, more prominent committees did not follow his tracks, but he also understood the thinking that deterred them.

"We ended up functioning like a parliament rather than a Congress," Shays said. "We confused wanting to get through a joint agenda [with the White House] with not doing the kind of oversight. . . . The argument, subtly, without being spoken, is, 'why do we want to embarrass the administration?' "

The ruling Republican majority demonstrated as little concern for maintaining the process by which Congress exercises oversight on itself. Both parties had contributed to a deterioration of the ethics process in the House in the 1990s, when each side informally agreed to a moratorium on the filing of ethics allegations. After a Democratic representative broke that misguided truce by filing charges against Tom DeLay, the House Ethics Committee issued a report in 2004 that admonished the powerful majority leader for a series of violations. House speaker Denny Hastert responded by pushing through, on a party-line vote, a series of rules changes making it more difficult to launch and prosecute ethics cases. Under intense criticism, House Republicans rescinded the rules in April 2005. But Hastert sent an unmistakable signal by ousting from the Ethics Committee the chairman and two other Republicans who had supported the DeLay investigation and replacing them with three members considered more loyal to the leadership.

HASTERT'S PURGE OF the Ethics Committee was a reminder that the remarkable Republican unity of the Bush years relied not just on persuasion but on coercion. The unrelenting pressure to pass proposals that divided the parties so sharply through a Congress divided so closely regularly required Republican legislative leaders to resort to tough tactics. Many of the GOP techniques were targeted against Democrats: an ever-increasing reliance on closed or restricted House rules that limited the Democrats' ability to offer alternatives to Republican proposals; votes that extended beyond the usual time limit (like the one used to pass the Medicare legislation); and the unabashed exclusion of some or all Democrats from House-Senate conference committees on issues such as energy or the prescription drug bill. Though these tactics recalled the Democratic maneuvers against Republicans after the mid-1980s, they often exceeded them. All of them infuriated Democrats, and as we'll see in Chapter 9, encouraged them to respond with hardball maneuvers of their own that escalated the cycle of conflict in the capital.

But Republican dissidents also faced rougher treatment from party leadership and conservative activists increasingly impatient with dissent. In the House, Gingrich's successors sharpened the tools of control that he had forged after the Republican takeover in 1994. House leaders sent clear signals that legislators who toed the party line would receive more favorable treatment in the distribution of earmarks. Loyalty weighed even more heavily on the opportunities for advancement within the House. Compared to the Gingrich years, House Republicans in the Bush era moved further toward a system that elevated "merit" over seniority in choosing committee chairs and allocating favorable assignments. In 2001, when the committee chairmen first chosen by Gingrich in 1995 reached their six-year term limits, Republicans needed to select new chairmen for thirteen House committees. In selecting them the GOP leadership passed over the members with the most seniority on six of those thirteen committees. In 1995, Gingrich had bypassed the most senior Republican on half that many committees.

Support for the party agenda was not the sole criterion in allocating committee chairmanships during the Bush years. Those who wanted to chair committees were also rated on their success at raising money to help maintain the GOP majority. The need for regional balance still affected decisions. And sheer talent counted, as when California representative Bill Thomas, a prickly but brilliant legislator, was chosen over more traditionally conservative alternatives to chair the House Ways and Means Committee. But there was no question that Republicans who dissented too often from the party consensus, particularly moderates, faced a ceiling on their prospects. In 2001, 2003, and 2005 Republicans repeatedly passed over moderates such as Tom Petri of Wisconsin, Marge Roukema of New Jersey, Shays, and Ralph Regula of Ohio to select less senior but more conservative colleagues to chair key committees. In 2005, GOP leaders removed Representative Chris Smith of New Jersey as chairman of the Veterans' Affairs Committee, though he had not reached his three-term limit, because he had angered them by seeking more money for veterans programs. All of these decisions told House Republicans that in their careers they could choose between independence and advancement.

The Senate, as always, resisted such overt pressure. The process of instilling party discipline there still revolved more around "intimacy than intimidation," as one leadership aide put it. Earmarks were allocated more through the personal caprice of irascible Appropriations Committee chairman Ted Stevens of Alaska than as any leadership-driven incentive for loyalty. And although the Senate had followed the House in ending the formal deference to seniority in choosing committee chairs, and then in imposing term limits on the chairs once chosen, Senate Republicans had never taken the step so common among their House colleagues of actually rejecting the most senior committee member in picking a chairman.

Despite occasional rumblings from younger conservatives, senators still derived enough benefits from a seniority system that protected their autonomy to defend it.

Yet just like their House counterparts, Senate Republicans faced rising demands, from the White House, their leadership, and the activist core of the GOP coalition, to reliably stand with their team against the other side. The incident that most clearly captured the changing climate came immediately after the 2004 election. At the time the term-limit rule for committee chairs forced Utah Republican Orrin Hatch, a reliable conservative, to step down as chairman of the powerful Senate Judiciary Committee. After winning reelection Arlen Specter, the Pennsylvania moderate, was next in line of seniority to chair the panel. But at a postelection press conference Specter, who supports legalized abortion, said that the Senate was unlikely to approve "judges who would change the right of a woman to choose."

Those words enraged conservatives. Leading social conservative groups like the Family Research Council, Focus on the Family, and Concerned Women for America mobilized their members to insist that Senate Republicans block Specter from the chairmanship. Radio talk shows and the Fox News Channel fanned the flames. Specter insisted that his words were misinterpreted, but calls and e-mails from angry conservatives flooded Senate Republican offices. As the furor continued it became clear that more than Specter's remarks on abortion sustained it. The critics' fundamental argument was that a Republican Party dominated at the grassroots by conservatives should award such important positions only to dependable conservatives. "The problem is that he's a liberal," conservative talk show host G. Gordon Liddy declared on one Fox program. "What the people deserve in a chairman up there is a chairman who will enthusiastically and skillfully push through the president's nominees."

Enough Senate Republicans agreed to force Specter into an unprecedented campaign to salvage his chairmanship. Specter was reduced to virtually groveling for his gavel. For two weeks he lobbied colleagues and conducted more than two dozen television interviews in which he repeatedly pledged to move quickly on Bush's judicial nominees. In the final act Specter was compelled to defend himself at back-to-back ninety-minute meetings, first with Republicans on the Judiciary Committee and then with the Senate GOP leadership. And even then Republicans agreed to Specter's ascension only after he produced an extraordinary written statement in which he promised not only "quick committee hearings and early committee votes" for Bush's judicial nominees, but also not to use his position to block other bills conservatives favored, including limitations on personal liability lawsuits.

In one sense this episode demonstrated the durability of the Senate commitment to seniority and the independence for senators it protected. Yet it also showed how much the insistence on loyalty inside the GOP had eroded that tradition. "We feel like a message was sent," a lobbyist for the Family Research Council said after Senate Republicans awarded Specter the chairmanship. And in fact, Specter's behavior over the next two years suggested a message was received: He smoothly shepherded both of Bush's Supreme Court nominees, John G. Roberts Jr. and Samuel A. Alito, through his committee, subjecting them only to restrained questioning about their views on abortion. Specter never fell into line with the White House or GOP leadership as reliably as most of his colleagues, but at critical moments he almost always pulled back from positions that might genuinely threaten their interests; as one senior Senate Democrat ruefully put it, Specter broke with his party and stood with Democrats "whenever we don't need him."

Specter's hazing underscored the fact that the pressures for loyalty on House and Senate Republicans came not just from their leaders or the White House. Groups in the conservative movement maintained unflagging vigilance for signs of defection from their agenda. At times those groups operated in concert with Republican leaders to squeeze rank-and-file members questioning the party priorities. Much of DeLay's ability to twist arms, for instance, came from the close ties with the conservative movement that allowed him to call in pressure on recalcitrant members from activist groups, like an infantry commander summoning air strikes.

Just as often the groups took an independent course to the same destination. Republican legislators faced a maze of questionnaires, scorecards, and pledge requests from activists determined to secure their commitments to a conservative agenda. Republicans sometimes groused about the demands. ("If I signed every pledge given to me, I might as well not be here to vote," said Lindsey Graham, the Republican senator from South Carolina, "I would have given away my vote.") Yet most fell in line. The most famous pledge, from Grover Norquist's Americans for Tax Reform, committed those who signed it to oppose any increase in marginal tax rates. That position virtually ruled out any compromise with Democrats to reduce the federal deficit or close the long-term financing gap for entitle-ment programs; but, by 2005, all but nine Republicans in the Senate and eleven in the House had signed it.

Norquist saw this as a process of gently steering elected Republicans toward the path most conservative activists preferred. "I see it more as cor-ralling," he said. "You build a fence: Don't raise taxes. You build a fence: Don't steal guns. And you herd them in." But elected Republicans who jumped the fences built by conservatives often felt the sting of right-leaning blogs, activists, magazines, and talk radio hosts. A typical example came when Graham, who spent six years on active duty as an Air Force lawyer and remained a member of the Air Force Reserve; John McCain, a former Navy pilot and prisoner of war in Vietnam; and John Warner, the former Navy secretary who chaired the Armed Services Committee, joined almost all Democrats in resisting Bush's proposal for trying suspected terrorist sus-pects just before the 2006 election. The trio faced blistering attacks from conservatives, who accused them of threatening the country's defenses. In one mailing a group called the Center for Individual Freedom stuck on them the label conservatives applied only to the objects of their deepest dis-dain: RINOs, or Republicans in Name Only. "RINO Senators," the mail-ing screamed, ". . . believe that captured terror suspects should be treated with kid gloves." The *National Review*, ordinarily among the most sober and circumspect of the conservative media outlets, ran a full-page cover photo of Graham over a stark one-word headline: WRONG. Even Jim DeMint, the more reliably conservative Republican elected to the other South Carolina Senate seat two years after Graham, publicly declared that his senior colleague's ideas "at this point are almost dangerous."

The prospect of such unflattering attention was never far from the minds of Republicans who considered compromise with Democrats on a major issue. Graham said that even the possibility of being labeled by the media as a maverick or a gadfly discouraged dissent among Republicans. "If you do step out in the middle, not only does the media seize on what you're doing, they are going to try to put you in a light where you're different," he said. "And a lot of politicians want to serve, but they don't need to serve with a neon sign on their back saying 'Hey, I'm different.' Because then you become a target for everybody."

Graham understood that dynamic all too well. He arrived in the Senate in 2003 with impeccable conservative credentials, including service as a House manager in the impeachment case against Bill Clinton. But his willingness to question Bush and seek agreements with Democrats on issues from judicial nominations to the rules for trying terrorist subjects exposed him to ever louder charges of collaborating with the enemy. "What's happened in politics is slowly but surely you are being defined not by whether you agree with a particular special interest on the subject matter, but will you publicly hate the people they hate," Graham said with evident frustration one steamy afternoon in 2006. "It's a new test. Ninety percent agreement is no longer the test. You've got to be in lockstep when it comes to punishing those who disagree." The complaints had reached the point, Graham said, where he expects conservatives to try to organize a primary challenge against him when he comes up for reelection in 2008. That wasn't just paranoia: Within weeks of Graham's remarks, one South Carolina GOP official launched an effort to draft a more conservative Republican to run against him.

The prospect of a primary challenge was the ultimate tool of control against dissenting Republicans, and it loomed as a much greater threat than it had a generation ago. That was largely because of the emergence of a conservative group called the Club for Growth. Since the election of 2000 the Club has functioned as an ideological enforcer on economics, unabashedly trying to punish Republicans who strayed from the mantra of less spending, less regulation, and lower taxes. Officially the group does not take positions on foreign policy or social issues; in practice, by targeting the Republicans most willing to consider tax increases, it also has gone into battle against many of the party's most moderate voices on those other questions as well.

The Club traced its roots back to an organization founded in the early 1980s, by investor Richard Gilder and other conservative New York City money managers, to meet with candidates and direct their political giving. The group, called the Political Club for Growth, was informal and eclectic. But the organization, somewhat surprisingly, lost momentum even as the Republicans advanced on Capitol Hill through the 1990s. It was revived when an affable young conservative ideologue named Stephen Moore, who had worked as a budget analyst for the Heritage Foundation and Cato Institute, approached Gilder with a proposal to convert the Club into a national organization that would raise money across the country to systematically promote conservative candidates. When Gilder signed on after the disappointing Republican losses in the 1998 election, Moore stowed his budget charts to become the Club's president.

Moore's critical insight was to conclude that the group could shape the political debate more by shifting the balance of power within the Republican Party than the balance between Republicans and Democrats. With redistricting producing more House seats that safely leaned toward one party or the other—and the tendency of more states to lean reliably red or blue producing something of the same effect in the Senate—Moore concluded that the most cost-effective way to increase the number of antitax votes in Congress was to intervene for the most fiscally conservative candidates in Republican primaries.

Moore pursued that goal mostly by supporting conservatives seeking Republican nominations to challenge an incumbent Democrat or to contest an open seat. But the Club generated more shock waves with its second approach: It also promoted primary challenges to moderate Republican incumbents. The first test came in 2000 in New Jersey, where moderate Republican representative Marge Roukema faced a primary rematch against Scott Garrett, a conservative state assembly member, whom she had held off by a narrow margin two years earlier. The Club invested heavily in Garrett's campaign. When Roukema again defeated Garrett in another close contest, Moore was devastated. Yet the reaction confounded his expectation. Far from growing discouraged, Moore's donors and conservatives on Capitol Hill were energized by the race, especially after Roukema retired and allowed Garrett to succeed her rather than face another challenge in 2002. Moore feared that the Club would be seen as ineffective. In fact, Roukema's close call rattled windows all across Capitol Hill.

Over the next three elections the Club followed the mold Moore had cut in 2000 (even after he left the organization in a power struggle following the 2004 election). The Club spent most of its energy helping conservatives in open primaries, but also financed a succession of primary challenges against moderate Republican incumbents, ranging from Maryland representative Wayne Gilchrest to Arlen Specter and Lincoln Chafee, the moderate Republican senator from Rhode Island. On the surface the Club's strategy of challenging incumbents showed few results. Though several of its challengers came close, none of them actually ousted an incumbent until the summer of 2006, when the Club helped a conservative win a primary against a first-term Republican representative from Michigan, Joe Schwarz. The primary challenges also provoked a steady stream of public criticism from Republican leaders, who accused the Club of diverting resources better directed against Democrats and unnecessarily weakening GOP candidates. (That latter complaint escalated in 2006 after Chafee, having survived the primary challenge, lost the general election to Democrat Sheldon Whitehouse.)

Yet other measures suggested a different verdict. Although almost all of the group's challenges fell short, a nationally financed primary challenge was an experience no incumbent relished. On Capitol Hill Republican moderates reacted as if they lived on the block where one of their neighbors had fought off an attempted mugging. The fact that the mugger was driven away didn't make them feel much more secure. House moderates regularly pressed the GOP leadership to discourage the group from mounting challenges, a dynamic the Club took as evidence of their effectiveness. Officially the congressional leadership condemned the internecine strife. But especially in the House, GOP leaders also saw the group as a useful means of promoting party discipline; many moderate House Republicans even suspected that DeLay quietly encouraged its activities. "It definitely affected how people voted," said John Feehery, who served as the press secretary to both DeLay and Hastert. "The moderates tended to be much more careful in their voting. As a disciplinary tool, it was very effective." Among the many tools of control congressional leaders possessed to discourage Republican dissension, the Club for Growth literally represented the club in the closet.

NEITHER THE CLUB for Growth nor Norquist's antitax pledge, nor DeLay's vote-counting skills, nor any other single factor could claim the principal credit for the remarkable Republican unity in Congress during Bush's first term. The dazzling party cohesion, unmatched since the height of the age of partisan armies, testified instead to the overall environment Republican leaders and their allied groups created over Bush's first four years. At every turn, as we've seen, congressional Republicans faced penalties for dissent and rewards for loyalty.

But in truth, most of those Republicans did not need much cajoling to stay in line. The vast majority of congressional Republicans enlisted willingly behind a White House agenda aimed primarily at uniting conservatives while drawing bright lines of distinction with Democrats. At the core of the congressional Republican support for Bush's agenda through his first term, Karl Rove believed, there was the simple fact that "it was things they were for."

That convergence was largely a product of the great sorting out. After the ideological and geographical reshuffling of the parties, most congressional Republicans relied on a base of voters that, like Bush's national coalition, tilted firmly to the right. In both chambers as well, the preponderant majority of Republicans were elected by constituencies that had also voted for Bush. The remaining handful of moderate GOP legislators like Chafee or Shays, who did not fit into either category, sometimes complained that too much of Bush's direction and tone alienated their voters. But after the parties' re-sorting they lacked the numbers to meaningfully affect the GOP's direction. Most congressional Republicans were comfortable with Bush's course because the same electoral incentives that shaped his direction also influenced their own.

Yet there was a more immediate reason so many congressional Republicans provided Bush the votes month after month to pass his agenda and suppressed any concerns about his decisions: As a political strategy, uniting with the White House appeared to work. "Yes, their fate was intertwined with him, but it was not a grudging marriage," said Vin Weber. "They thought they were in good hands. They may not have liked the way they were treated by the White House, but at the end of the day they thought these guys were smart, Rove is smart, Bush has shown himself to be a skillful politician, he beat Ann Richards, he got himself elected over the incumbent vice president of the United States. They thought they were in good hands."

That faith developed partly because the legislative machine hummed smoothly through Bush's initial four years, passing bills and generating financial and organizational support from business and grassroots conservative groups. But even more important was the success of the White House political strategy. Bush and his key political advisers, led by Rove, developed a pathbreaking new theory of how Republicans could build an enduring electoral majority. And for four years most congressional Republicans remained convinced that the White House strategy they had committed to support was carrying them, slowly but steadily, toward lasting dominance over the Democrats.

A NEW PATH TO POWER

Bush inherited from Gingrich and his successors the machinery to squeeze historic levels of support from congressional Republicans. Bush's most distinctive addition was to develop an electoral strategy that applied the same principle to Republican voters. The Bush White House's unique approach to building a lasting Republican political majority rested on a simple but radical premise: More than any of their predecessors, Bush's political advisers accepted a deeply polarized country as an ineradicable given. Rather than trying to reverse the centrifugal currents in American political life, they built their political strategy around profiting from them.

That decision required the Bush team to build a new electoral model designed for the age of hyperpartisanship. It shifted the core of its strategy from changing the preferences of the electorate to changing the composition of the electorate. The key to success would not be attracting Democrats or moderate independents, but overwhelming them by increasing the share of the vote cast by Republicans and the conservative independents that identified with the party in all but name. Matthew Dowd called those voters "passive Republicans" and said they were a "huge imperative" for the Bush campaign—"the main imperative. . . . because we knew we couldn't go get those other folks."

Almost from the outset Karl Rove likewise saw increasing turnout among Republicans and other conservative constituencies as the key to Bush's success. Putting the most favorable spin on the dead-heat finish between Bush and Gore in 2000, Rove viewed the result as evidence the country was almost evenly divided, with a slight advantage toward the GOP. Just as important to him was another number: Only about 55 percent of eligible voters participated. Nonvoters, Rove recognized, did not look much different in their political views or demographic characteristics from those who did vote. That meant Bush could increase his vote by mobilizing a huge pool of nonvoters who already agreed with his positions. The "tactical" question, Rove said, was how to motivate them to the polls: "How do you return to an individually oriented democratic politics that generates higher turnout?"

Recounting these deliberations years later, Rove explained the answer he reached by pointing to a small portrait of Abraham Lincoln on the wall in his West Wing office. "It's to be found in this guy right there—[in] 1840, Mr. Practical Politician," he said. From memory, Rove then recounted (with almost word-for-word accuracy) Lincoln's advice to his allies in the Whig Party on how to turn out the vote for that 1840 election: "Make a perfect list of all the voters . . . [and] ascertain with certainty for whom they will vote. . . . [K]eep a constant watch on the doubtful voters, and from time to time have them talked to by those in whom they have the most confidence, . . . and on election days see that every Whig is brought to the polls."

In that long injunction, Rove continued, "the critical phrase" was Lincoln's advice to ensure that undecided voters were spoken to by those "in whom they have the most confidence." That meant finding volunteers who would make the case for Bush to their neighbors, friends, family, and coworkers, and then help to turn out on Election Day those on their list who supported him. After 2000, Rove said, he concluded Bush won "in large measure" because the campaign's volunteer effort "allowed us to expand the number of people who were working on our behalf." Once in the White House Rove was determined to improve and expand the effort. Following a detailed review of the campaign's turnout operation in 2000, the Republican National Committee launched what it called its "72-Hour Project" to improve the party's capacity to mobilize its supporters on Election Day.

The effort's first big test came in the 2002 midterm campaign. In the previous century no president except Franklin Roosevelt in 1934, at the zenith of the New Deal, had added seats in both chambers during his first midterm election. Bush broke that pattern. With his approval rating still soaring in the afterglow of his response to September 11, and the national debate dominated by the possibility of war with Iraq, Republicans gained seats in the House and the Senate, and also won several high-profile gubernatorial races.

How the Republicans won was as revealing as what they won. Swing voters didn't break toward the GOP in 2002: The best postelection survey found that independents split evenly between the two sides in their votes for the House and Senate. Nor did Republicans attract more defections from Democrats than they had in 1998, the previous midterm election. But Republican turnout in 2002 swelled enough to tilt the election in their direction. In 1998, the exit polls found that Democrats slightly outnumbered Republicans among the voters, as they usually did in midterm elections and always did in presidential years. But in 2002, the postelection survey found that Republicans slightly outnumbered Democrats.

The 2002 results demonstrated something powerful in its simplicity: Where Bush was strong, he was very strong. The result testified to the depth of his connection with voters in the Republican coalition. And it solidified the Bush advisers' belief that they were on the right course in building their reelection plan around an effort to transform the electorate with millions of new Republican voters. That vision was the heart of the campaign plan Rove carried to Crawford, Texas, in January 2003 for his first meeting with Bush about the reelection. "When I went down to

Crawford . . . to lay out the plan," Rove recalled, "that was the critical part of it."

The focus on expanding Republican turnout led the Bush team to a heretical decision: It spent three fourths of its money in 2004 on motivating Bush supporters and just one fourth persuading uncommitted voters, a reverse of the proportions in 2000. That shift rested on the campaign's bedrock assumption: The ideological re-sorting of the electorate over the previous generation, and the particularly strong emotions that Bush evoked in supporters and opponents, made it more cost-efficient to increase turnout among nonvoters who already supported him than to try to convert large numbers of the active voters who resisted him. "We did the analysis in '03, driven by this imperative that we [believed we] can only get to 52 or 53 percent of the vote, and asked, 'So how do we get there?' " Dowd said. "If a dollar is spent on motivating a passive Republican, what's the return on that versus a dollar spent on trying to persuade somebody? And you could quickly figure out that your dollar was better spent efficiently for motivating a passive Republican and go from there. . . . All tactical decisions [derived] from that: How do we design our TV buy, what do we do on our mail, and how do we do our field? All was driven from that imperative." Dowd set a straightforward but ambitious goal: reshaping the electorate enough so that the number of Republicans casting ballots on Election Day would equal the number of Democrats, something that had not happened in the history of modern polling.

The campaign launched three massive, cutting-edge initiatives to bring more Republicans to the polls. The first was a sophisticated new means of finding voters who sympathized with Bush. The project essentially married political data with consumer data to try to identify, on a person-by-person basis, the partisan allegiance of as much of the nation as possible. The Republicans collected all available data on voting participation: who was registered to vote; who voted in primaries; who voted in general elections. Then, the RNC, in a gargantuan computerized database it called the Voter Vault, attached to each individual as much other information about him or her as they could find. Did they own a gun? Had they contributed to candidates or political causes? Did they belong to a church? Using commercial databases, they also accumulated as much information as they

could about individuals' consumer preferences: what magazines they sub-
scribed to; what car they owned; what beer they liked.

This vast database allowed the RNC to match partisan preferences
with the consumer information they had accumulated and find the corre-
lations between the two. Those matches revealed clear patterns between
the products and the parties people preferred. Bourbon drinkers tended to
vote Republican; vodka drinkers liked Democrats. Lincoln Continentals,
BMWs, and American SUVs were more likely to have Republican stickers
on their bumpers; Volvo and Subaru drivers preferred Democrats. The
lists of connections ran for pages. It was the literal expression of the electorate's vast cultural re-sorting: What people bought, in many cases, better
predicted how they would vote than what they earned.

Once the RNC had established the connections it could apply them to
voters whose partisan preference was not apparent from the data (either
because they registered as independents or lived in states that did not register voters by party). It could then target people whose consumer preferences most closely matched voters the RNC already knew to be Republicans.
Or it could aim at people who contributed money to conservative groups,
or owned guns, or sent their children to Catholic school. The data allowed
Bush's team to sift through the electorate from every possible angle. In
2004, they sorted with two goals. One was to unearth swing voters they
believed might favor Bush. But the heart of the effort was a drive to discover and motivate Republicans and conservatives who did not always
vote.

Through this Voter Vault the Bush campaign could target its efforts
not at the level of groups but at individuals, a process it called "microtargeting." Microtargeting made it affordable for the Bush campaign to pursue sympathetic individuals within generally unsympathetic groups—often
with messages derived directly from what the campaign knew about their
interests and concerns. It could find the exceptions to the rule in groups
that Democrats dominated—the black business owner who liked Bush's
tax cuts, the Jewish retiree drawn to his stand on Israel. Rather than writing off entire blocks of potential supporters—the Republicans, for example, in a heavily Democratic urban neighborhood—microtargeting allowed
Bush's camp to say "I am going to find the needle in the haystack because

you are looking at the hay not as a bushel but as individual strands," as Mehlman put it. Microtargeting provided the map the campaign used to find millions of Republicans who had not voted four years earlier.

The campaign's advertising strategy represented the second piece of its plan for mobilizing Republicans. Through one prong of the plan the Bush campaign used commercial data services to track the political leanings of the audiences for specific shows in individual markets. Then it tilted its buying away from swing voters (the usual target for presidential campaigns) toward shows with audiences that attracted large numbers of Republicans, especially the "passive" irregular Republican voters it prized.* The plan's other element became evident through the summer of 2004 in places such as Sioux City, Iowa, Ft. Smith, Arkansas, Yakima, Washington, rural Missouri, and the Florida panhandle around Pensacola. Voters in each of these media markets reliably supported Republicans, so much so that Democrats either wrote them off entirely when deciding where to air their television commercials, or made only small purchases. Yet the Bush campaign pounded all of these markets, and several more that fit the same description, with heavy buys of its campaign ads. That was an unusual and perhaps unprecedented decision by a presidential campaign, but it fit the Bush team's belief that increasing Republican turnout was more important, and cost-efficient, than converting the typical swing voter in places like the Philadelphia suburbs.

The campaign's massive volunteer operation comprised the final component of its plan to reach Republicans. Building on their operations in 2000 and 2002 the Bush campaign and RNC constructed an intricately organized network of volunteers that it deployed both to register new Republicans through the election year, and then turn out Bush supporters on Election Day. The network constituted the physical expression of Rove's desire to "expand the number of people who were working on our behalf." Ultimately, Rove said, some 1.4 million Bush supporters participated in the system, which linked volunteers into a pyramid that stretched from the precinct to the county to the state to the region to Mehlman's office at the Bush

---

* That focus led to some surprising decisions. In many markets the Bush campaign bought ads on the gay-themed NBC sitcom *Will and Grace* because the research said many "passive" Republican women watched it.

headquarters in Arlington, Virginia. It might have been the most elaborate grassroots operation any presidential campaign ever assembled.

All of this campaign machinery, the database, the huge advertising budget, the vast chain of volunteers was like a giant engine. The fuel in the engine was the intense emotion Bush generated. Even the most sophisticated operation could not generate the turnout the Bush campaign needed without a candidate who inspired a passionate connection with the party base. For four years Bush had done exactly that. The tactics his staff devised for his reelection campaign complemented his intensely partisan and polarizing approach to governing, and vice versa. "The technology matched with the evolution of the political environment," said Mark McKinnon, the former Texas Democrat who directed the Bush campaign's advertising operation. "The environment was more partisan, and so it was more important to motivate the partisans, and technology allowed us to do that." Bush might have governed as president of half the country, but he maintained a powerful hold over his half.

The cost to Bush was the antipathy he inspired in much of the other half. The resistance to Bush fueled a Democratic campaign in 2004 comparable in scale to his own enormous effort. Most political experts, and the Bush campaign itself, expected the president to dwarf the Democratic nominee in fund-raising. But an unprecedented torrent of contributions from small donors, much of it over the Internet, allowed John Kerry to match Bush almost dollar for dollar.* Money and volunteers poured in as well to liberal groups such as MoveOn.org, the Internet-based activist group, and America Coming Together, which constructed a get-out-the-vote operation in targeted states that rivaled the Bush system in its reach. The amount of money available for the campaign against Bush appeared almost bottomless. Probably not since Vietnam, and possibly not ever, had so many liberal donors, small, large, and in between, contributed so eagerly to a cause.

The Bush campaign accepted much of this antagonism as inevitable—the price both of his desire to pursue bold change as president and the

---

* According to Federal Election Commission figures compiled by the Center for Responsive Politics, Bush raised $367.2 million for his 2004 campaign, while Kerry collected $326.2 million.

longer-term ideological re-sorting of the parties. But it did not write off all of those skeptical of Bush. The campaign aimed at swing voters, too, but less through a message focused on issues than one centered on personal contrasts between Bush and his opponent. With relentless discipline the Bush campaign sought to convince persuadable voters that the president could be trusted to offer strong, decisive leadership, while Kerry was weak and indecisive, a "flip-flopper." McKinnon, as he helped to formulate the campaign's ads, considered the personal contrast between Bush and Kerry the key to expanding the president's coalition enough for victory:

> As we looked at the election, we were clearly under 50 percent. Less than 50 percent of the electorate supported the president, less than 50 percent supported his policies, less than 50 percent approved of the job he was doing. So based on all that, we had to convince voters who didn't like the president, didn't like his policies, and didn't like the job he was doing. That was a pretty big challenge. So how do we convince those people? And what we ultimately determined was that if we convinced them that even if they disagreed with him and didn't like him, that if they thought he was a strong leader, that they could trust him and he shared their values, we could move enough people across the line. And so everything we communicated from an advertising point of view and a message point of view, that's what I was thinking about. . . . And once again, we were blessed by our opposition because Kerry reflected weakness on all three of those.

The emotions that crackled around Bush for four years culminated in an electric confrontation on Election Day. Over 122 million Americans voted in 2004, almost 17 million more than just four years earlier. That was the largest increase from election to election in American history. Kerry won nearly 59 million votes, almost 8 million more than Gore had attracted in winning the popular vote against Bush four years earlier. But Bush won nearly 62 million votes, over 11 million more than he had won in 2000. "We had plenty of energy, we had plenty of turnout," Stanley Greenberg, the Democratic pollster advising Kerry, said later. "But they had more."

From many angles Bush registered a solid, even decisive, victory. He increased his share of the popular vote from 47.8 percent in 2000 to 50.6 percent. That made Bush the first presidential candidate since his father in 1988 to win more than half of the popular vote. Bush significantly improved his showing with Hispanic voters, capturing more than 40 percent of their votes. He also increased his margins with married women, the so-called "security moms," who responded to his promise of strong leadership against terror. And with the help of the microtargeting program he also ran significantly better than in 2000 among voters who lived in big cities.

But the election also testified to the stability of the resistance to Bush. He triumphed more by solidifying than expanding his coalition—more by deepening than broadening his support. The exit polls conducted by both the Edison/Mitofsky consortium and the *Los Angeles Times* found that Bush actually *lost* ground among independent voters between 2000 and 2004. In 2000 he carried independent voters by two percentage points; in 2004, he lost them by a single point. Bush also lost Democratic voters by a slightly larger margin in 2004 than he had in 2000. He won the popular vote in 2004 by generating more support from Republicans. Bush increased his share of the vote among Republicans (from 91 percent in 2000 to 93 percent four years later). More important, he increased the share of Republicans in the electorate. In 2000, the exit polls found that Democrats outnumbered Republicans by 39 percent to 35 percent. Four years later Dowd met his goal: The exit polls found that Republicans equaled Democrats at 37 percent of the voters.

The conservative surge to the polls consolidated the Republican hold on the portions of the country where the party was already strongest. In almost all of red America, Kerry never got off the ground. Bush won twenty-nine states twice; in 2004 he held Kerry to 43 percent of the vote or less in twenty-one of them. Even more impressively, the huge turnout Bush inspired helped Republicans to a net gain of six House and five Senate seats across the red states that he carried twice. In every way red America could not have expressed its endorsement of Bush's direction more emphatically.

But Bush made much smaller inroads into blue America. He reduced the Democratic margin in eleven of the twenty states he had lost in 2000.

But he only captured two of them. Iowa and New Mexico, which tilted narrowly to Gore in 2000, tilted narrowly to Bush in 2004. At the same time New Hampshire, which Bush had carried narrowly in 2000, fell narrowly to Kerry. Almost all of the big white-collar suburban counties outside the South that had shifted from the Republican to the Democratic party during the cultural re-sorting under Clinton stayed with Kerry (as they had with Gore). On other fronts, Bush's microstrategy of targeting specific Democratic constituencies conflicted with his macrostrategy of tolerating intense antagonism among Democrats. Exit polls, for instance, showed that Bush slightly improved his share of the vote among African Americans from 8 percent in 2000 to 11 percent in 2004 (which actually represented only a return to the GOP average from 1980 through 1996). But Bush's small gain in the *share* of votes cast by blacks was overwhelmed by the increase in the total *number* of votes blacks cast. Because blacks turned out at such high levels, Bush's deficit in the African American community, measured by the total number of votes cast, was actually 30 percent larger in 2004 than in 2000. (An endnote on page 451 explains the calculation.) One final measure underscored the limits of Bush's reach into blue America: As we saw in Chapter 6, Democrats emerged from the 2004 election holding three fifths of the House seats and four fifths of the Senate seats in the eighteen states that voted for both Gore and Kerry.

All of this produced an election that looked decisive from some angles but from others appeared much more equivocal. By any standard the surge of turnout Bush inspired was a historic achievement. But on several key indicators Bush's victory ranked among the narrowest ever for a reelected president. Measured as a share of the popular vote, Bush defeated Kerry by just 2.5 percentage points (50.6 to 48.1 per cent). That was the smallest margin of victory for a reelected president since the formation of the modern party system in 1828. Bush's margin in the Electoral College told a similar story. In 2004, Bush won 53 percent of the 538 Electoral College votes available. Of all the chief executives reelected since the Twelfth Amendment separated the vote for president and vice president—a group that stretches back to Thomas Jefferson in 1804—only Woodrow Wilson in 1916 (at 52 percent) won a smaller share of the available Electoral College votes.

These numbers all pointed to the same conclusion. Bush, Rove, and their team had brilliantly charted a path to victory in a divided country. But they had not transcended those divisions. They had mastered a political house divided. But the question of whether a house so divided could stand would grow more urgent and vexing for the White House almost as soon as Bush took the oath of office for the second time.

THE LIMITS OF POLARIZATION

Everything seemed possible for George W. Bush when he bounded into Room 450 of the Executive Office Building on the morning of November 4, 2004, for his first press conference since his reelection. The contrast from four years earlier was unmistakable. In his speech from the Texas House of Representatives after Al Gore finally conceded the election of 2000, Bush was cautious and conciliatory. On this morning he overflowed with confidence. No questions of legitimacy hung over his reelection. Bush had won Ohio, the last disputed state, by a margin that left all but the most die-hard conspiracy theorists sputtering. John Kerry had conceded the election the day before. For the second consecutive campaign under Bush, Republicans had gained seats in both the House and the Senate. He was the first Republican president since William McKinley in 1900 to win a second four-year term and carry with him Republican majorities in both chambers of Congress.

White House aides say it is rarely difficult to read Bush's mood, and this morning was no exception. His optimism and self-assurance radiated through his needling exchanges with reporters. He was friendly and funny, but his jokes often carried a barb, as if he intended to leave no doubt with anyone in the room about who was in charge. Even more telling was the ambitious agenda he spread out before the press. Legal reform, more education reform, streamlining of the tax code, a restructuring of Social Security, the successful completion of the war in Iraq: All this and more Bush promised to push forward in his second term. "You asked, 'Do I feel free?' " Bush said in response to one question. "Let me put it to you this way: I earned capital in the campaign, political capital, and now I intend to spend it."

Bush was hardly alone in his expectations. The four-year expanse of

Bush's second term beckoned to conservatives on Capitol Hill as an unparalleled opportunity to finally reshape Washington. "My fellow conservatives, we have waited our entire lives for the chance the American people have given us in the next two years," Tom DeLay declared shortly after the election. "I pledge to each and every one of you, we will seize it."

In a few ways the next two years fulfilled those expectations for Bush and the Republican majority on Capitol Hill. But in only a few. The disciplined, intensely partisan legislative strategy that Republicans perfected in Bush's first term churned out several additional victories in his second that carried the political benefit of bonding the GOP more closely with key constituencies (like small businesses or gun owners) and weakening groups associated with the Democrats (such as trial lawyers). Bush's two Supreme Court nominees moved smoothly through the Senate to confirmation. And at least through the 2006 election he demonstrated a continuing ability to drive the national debate over issues directly related to the struggle against terrorism.

But mostly Bush spent his second term in retreat. His central domestic legislative priority, his proposal to restructure Social Security, collapsed without ever coming to a vote in the House or Senate. The decision he made with the Republican congressional leadership in early 2005 to intervene in the case of Terry Schiavo, a brain-damaged Florida woman, ignited a widespread public backlash. Bush's halting response to Hurricane Katrina later in 2005—when the federal government at points seemed not only unsteady but paralyzed and even indifferent—astonished and dismayed legislators in both parties and tarnished his central political asset: his image as a strong leader in a time of crisis. Scandal coursed through Capitol Hill and lapped at the door of Bush's administration, as Republicans faced tough questions and ongoing investigations into their relations with disgraced GOP lobbyist Jack Abramoff. Caught in that web, and indicted by a Texas prosecutor in the controversy stemming from his fundraising in the 2002 Texas state legislative races, Tom DeLay surrendered his majority leader position and then resigned from Congress only nineteen months after his confident promise to seize the opportunity created by the 2004 election. A sex scandal involving Republican representative Mark Foley of Florida and male House pages rocked the GOP just weeks before the 2006 midterm election. Above all these other troubles loomed Iraq.

With violence unstinting, order elusive, and American and Iraqi casualties unrelenting, Bush confronted sharpening opposition from congressional Democrats, increasing uneasiness among congressional Republicans, and spreading disillusionment among voters about the course of the war. "This is an exhausted administration," a senior analyst at the libertarian Cato Institute, a group usually aligned with the president, concluded little more than a year after Bush's reelection.

Bush's second-term troubles were rooted in problems that extended far beyond the distinctive political strategy he had brought to the White House. Almost all two-term presidents, starting with George Washington, came to grief after reelection: 1600 Pennsylvania Avenue is a dangerous neighborhood, and bad things invariably happen to anyone who stays there long enough. Bush's second term also exposed weaknesses in his management style, which stressed bold, big-picture decision making over careful implementation. The federal failure after Hurricane Katrina demonstrated the limitations of that approach. So did the agony in Iraq: The administration never entirely recovered from its failure, before it launched the war, to develop a clear strategy for rebuilding the country after the invasion.

All of these large forces buffeted Bush in his second term. Yet on almost every front, the intensely partisan political and legislative strategy Bush had adopted compounded his difficulties. Throughout his first term polarization usually worked for him because it helped generate enormous levels of legislative and electoral support from Republicans. Congressional Republicans and the White House avoided the narcissism of small differences that afflicted Democrats while they held unified control during Bill Clinton's first two years. Republican conservatives and moderates alike accepted elements of the Bush plan they disliked in the interest of accumulating a joint record of legislative success, something Democrats had pointedly failed to do under Clinton. The result was that Republicans under Bush ran on a firm agenda, and then moved with machinelike precision to pass it, succeeding more often than they failed. They provided voters both clear choices and an unambiguous direction.

But in Bush's second term the limitations of this system became more glaring. It was efficient but exclusionary; it generated (partisan) unity at the price of (national) division. The formidable Republican legislative and political machine was undermined by its own insularity. Self-sufficiency, its great strength, became an insurmountable weakness in Bush's second term as the party increasingly lost the ability, and even the inclination, to reflect the perspectives of Americans outside of its core coalition. In more than half a dozen distinct respects the second act of Bush's presidency demonstrated the dangers of governing in a manner that placed so little emphasis on consensus and divided so much of the country into irremediably antagonistic camps.

Bush's second term quickly demonstrated one of the principal risks of such a polarizing approach. Because Bush's governing strategy, as we've seen, placed such emphasis on maintaining unity among Republicans, it usually produced policies that aimed squarely at the priorities of conservatives while offering relatively few concessions to other perspectives. That left Bush vulnerable to an obvious problem: confusing consensus in his coalition with consensus in the country.

The case that first crystallized that danger came shortly after Bush's second inaugural address. In March 2005, the Republican congressional majority, with Bush's active support, passed legislation to intervene in the complex, heartrending case of Terry Schiavo, the brain-dead Florida woman whose husband, over the objections of her parents, sought to turn off the feeding tube used to keep her alive. The decision to intervene fit with Bush's mobilize-the-base political strategy: Schiavo's case was a cause célèbre for social conservatives, who sought to link her to a seamless "culture of life" that opposed both abortion and euthanasia. But the move by Bush and the GOP majority to provide a new federal course of legal action for the woman's parents against her husband inspired a backlash from the overall public notable both for its breadth and intensity. Most Americans seemed horrified by the prospect of politicians intruding into such an intimate and agonizing decision. The federal action drew widespread condemnation in polls. In some surveys even decisive majorities of Republicans, conservatives, and white evangelical Christians opposed the intervention. There was a thin line between the buoyant optimism Bush expressed at his postelection news conference and hubris. The Schiavo case demonstrated how easy it was for Republicans to stumble across that line at a moment of high tide for the party. It began Bush's second term on a misstep from which he, and congressional Republicans, would never entirely recover.

Bush's push to restructure Social Security revealed the same threat with far more consequential results. Bush's drive to remake Social Security symbolized both the profound sense of possibility among Republicans after 2004 and his own determination to make a mark as a transforming, visionary leader. Even Ronald Reagan and Newt Gingrich had considered it impractical to fundamentally challenge the design of Social Security, the proudest achievement of twentieth-century Democratic governance. Bush sought to impose on Social Security the most fundamental changes in the program since its adoption in 1935.

Bush proposed to allow workers to divert part of their payroll taxes into individual investment accounts that they could invest in the stock market. In return, the guaranteed public benefit they received from Social Security at retirement would be reduced. Such a shift carried profound economic and political implications. As Bush often argued, it provided Americans more control over their retirement by allowing them to direct their own investments. But it also exposed them to more risk if those investments did not perform.

On Social Security Bush confronted the same problem, on a far greater scale, that he did with Terry Schiavo. Diverting payroll taxes into private investment accounts was a long-standing priority of conservative thinkers and activists. But there was a reason no Republican leader before Bush had seriously pushed the idea: It always provoked heated resistance outside of the core Republican coalition. Polls through the 1990s and Bush's first term often found general support for the notion of allowing workers to divert part of their payroll taxes into investments they could control. But that support always dwindled when Americans were told that the price of those investments was a reduction in their guaranteed Social Security benefit.* At a time when private guarantees of retirement benefits had

---

* Bush's proposal, and all serious private investment plans, required such a reduction in guaranteed benefits. That's because Social Security is a pay-as-you-go system: The taxes today's workers pay fund the retirement benefits for today's retirees. If future workers can divert part of their taxes into private investment accounts, less money would be available to fund benefits for future retirees. The only way to keep the system stable would be to reduce the guaranteed benefits. Advocates of partial privatization argue that future retirees could make up the difference, and then some, through their private investments. But critics note that there is no guarantee of that; the only certainty is that retirees would receive less in their monthly check from the government.

eroded, the notion of a secure public pension, sheltered from the gyrations of the stock market, turned out to retain much more enduring appeal than the White House expected.

That was apparent from the first public polling as Bush began his campaign for his plan. When Gallup asked Americans in January 2005 whether they would support private investment accounts coupled with a reduction in guaranteed benefits, only 40 percent said they considered it a good idea. A clear majority—55 percent—said they viewed it as a bad idea. Support for the idea was largely confined to Republicans: three fifths of GOP partisans liked the proposal but nearly three fifths of independents and more than three fourths of Democrats said they considered it a bad idea. Once again, by aiming his agenda so squarely at the desires of Republicans Bush had embraced an idea that generated widespread skepticism from voters outside of his core coalition.

Over the next six months Bush and his allies in the business community engaged in a mammoth struggle with congressional Democrats and their allies, primarily labor unions, to shape public opinion over Social Security. Each side mounted large advertising and organizing campaigns. Each accused the other of demagoguery and misrepresenting the facts. Bush undertook a sustained speaking campaign, centered on "town meetings" where carefully chosen supporters testified to the benefits they expected from his proposal.

And when the guns stilled, remarkably little had changed. If anything, the White House had lost ground slightly. In public polls conducted by a wide variety of media organizations the share of Americans who favored Bush's idea fell over the course of these exchanges. When Gallup measured opinion on the plan again in April 2005, the percentage of Republicans who supported it had declined slightly since January, while the level of opposition had jumped to two thirds among independents and nearly nine in ten among Democrats. Despite a public relations campaign mounted with the full force of the White House and all its business allies, Bush failed to broaden support for the idea beyond the partisan Republicans who had stood with him from the beginning. On Social Security Bush was like a general who had established a beachhead on hostile terrain but never advanced beyond it—and was soon struggling not to be thrown back into the sea.

The inability to attract rank-and-file Democrats, or even many independents, to support his Social Security plan exposed a second danger in Bush's polarizing political strategy: a feedback loop of antipathy from grassroots and congressional Democrats that hardened both against him. The widespread opposition to Bush that roared from polls of grassroots Democrats made congressional Democrats hesitant about endorsing such a central aspect of his agenda. Conversely, Bush found it more difficult to soften opposition to his plan among the Democratic rank-and-file because he could not convince any prominent Democrats to endorse and validate his proposal. Each failure seeded the other.

Initially, Bush's advisers and allies believed that his strong performance across the red states in 2004 would make House and Senate Democrats from those states reluctant to oppose him on Social Security. "There was some assumption that if you lived in a red state, if you were a red state Senate Democrat, working with the president was going to be part of your reelection campaign, it was going to be important . . . not to be an antagonist to the president," said Terry Nelson, the field director for the 2004 Bush reelection campaign and a consultant to COMPASS, the principal business group that had mobilized in support of Bush's Social Security proposal. "That certainly was part of the thinking that went into the strategy." Much of the lobbying campaign from the White House and its allies targeted those red state Democrats, especially the ones facing reelection in 2006, such as Ben Nelson of Nebraska, Bill Nelson of Florida, and Kent Conrad of North Dakota. Harry Reid, newly elected as Democratic leader after Tom Daschle's defeat in 2004, remembers being "scared to death" that Democrats from conservative states would bolt to Bush on Social Security. But with the plan, and Bush's overall performance, facing such overwhelming opposition among Democratic voters, none ever did. Only one House Democrat, Allen Boyd of Florida, ever endorsed private investment accounts funded through the payroll tax, and he never signed on to Bush's specific version.* No Senate Democrat endorsed Bush's pro-

---

* Boyd, in fact, later concluded that Bush's failure to include or negotiate with Democrats during his first term left him without the relationships and earned trust to attract meaningful numbers of them on such an explosive issue as restructuring Social Security. "It was a casualty of the way they had governed over the previous four years," Boyd said.

posal; all of them except Ben Nelson signed a letter declaring that they would not negotiate with Bush over Social Security until he withdrew his proposal to create private accounts funded through the payroll tax. And even Nelson rejected the core of Bush's vision, the private accounts funded by diverting revenue from the payroll tax; in his 2006 reelection campaign, Nelson denounced his Republican opponent for promoting the idea.

Bush's failure to win Democratic support on Social Security undermined his position in a final, ultimately fatal, respect. His model for advancing his agenda routinely required congressional Republicans, especially in the House, to pass legislation by narrow margins on a virtually party-line basis. But in Social Security the White House finally encountered an issue on which congressional Republicans were unwilling to move without at least some support from Democrats to provide political cover. When Bush could not attract those Democrats, congressional Republicans refused to restructure Social Security on their own. In that way the Social Security fight demonstrated a critical limit of a legislative strategy built around polarization: It did not work on the issues that Republicans feared to address on a purely partisan basis. When his party would not act alone Bush could not act at all, and the highest legislative priority of his second term died without coming to a vote in either chamber.

Immigration reform, the other great legislative failure early in Bush's second term, demonstrated the opposite risk. In this instance, Bush's focus on unifying his party limited his options to reach beyond it. On illegal immigration Bush offered a much more conciliatory and inclusive proposal than on Social Security. Indeed, Bush's approach to immigration represented his most important effort to reach beyond his party's base since the education reform plan of 2001. Bush insisted on a comprehensive response to the challenge of controlling the borders and dealing with the estimated twelve million illegal immigrants in the United States. After initially hesitating, Bush embraced a bipartisan Senate plan that attacked the problem from every angle: tougher enforcement at the border and in workplaces; a guest worker program that would reduce the incentive for illegal crossings by allowing more foreign workers to enter the United States legally; and a path to legal status for the millions of illegal immigrants already in the

United States. That comprehensive approach offered not only the best chance to control the problem but the only hope for establishing a broad political consensus that included business, labor and immigrants rights groups, Republicans, and Democrats.

In May 2006 the Senate passed a plan embodying those principles with sixty-two votes and Bush's support. Hardly anyone in either party doubted that the Senate proposal had enough support to pass the House as well. But the House, which had earlier passed immigration reform that focused solely on tougher enforcement, never considered it. The problem wasn't the number of House members willing to vote for comprehensive immigration reform; it was the composition of the members who backed the idea. The plan's potential majority in the House was built on support from most Democrats and probably a minority of Republicans. (Exactly such a coalition had passed the legislation in the Senate.) And that violated the rule that House speaker Denny Hastert had established to consecrate the party's overwhelming emphasis on partisan unity.

The speaker, fittingly enough, first articulated what became known as the Hastert Rule in November 2003, at a Library of Congress conference commemorating the one-hundredth anniversary of Joe Cannon's ascension to the speakership. Hastert declared that one of the principles that guided his leadership was "to please the majority of your majority." "The job of the speaker," he added, "is not to expedite legislation that runs counter to the wishes of the majority of his majority." In practice that meant Hastert would only bring legislation to the floor if he believed it had support not only from a majority of the House, but also a majority of House Republicans. That approach granted a veto over House decisions to the conservatives who comprised a majority of the House Republican caucus. Gingrich, during his years as speaker, had committed to a similar goal, but remained relatively flexible about deviating from it, for instance by allowing a vote on raising the minimum wage he thought would help moderates in 1996.

To a point, the Hastert rule was nothing more than self-preservation: Any legislative leader who routinely pushed bills opposed by most of his members would not be a legislative leader for long. And empowering the majority of the majority to drive decisions in the House had been the goal of rules reformers since Richard Bolling, the brilliant Democrat. But like many aspects of the Republican legislative machine developed in the 1990s, the rule was carried to excess under Hastert, DeLay, and Bush. After the 2004 election, in an especially blatant elevation of partisan over national interest, Hastert used it to force the renegotiation of important intelligence reform legislation that troubled some House conservatives but attracted such broad bipartisan support that it passed the Senate 96–2.

The Hastert rule doomed comprehensive immigration reform. It allowed House conservatives who opposed any pathway to legalization for illegal immigrants to block any plan that included it. Since no plan without such a pathway could pass the Senate, and no plan with it could attract a majority of House conservatives, Congress could not act. Bush might have broken the logjam if he publicly pressured the House GOP leadership to allow the comprehensive plan he supported to come to a floor vote it was almost certain to win. But Bush refused to confront his conservative base so directly, even though polls consistently showed most Americans supported the comprehensive approach. He uttered hardly a word of complaint as congressional GOP leaders buried the comprehensive plan; when they instead sent him legislation focused solely on tougher enforcement, particularly the construction of a seven-hundred-mile fence along the Mexican border, Bush signed the bill at the White House surrounded by the congressional Republicans who had killed his broader plan.

The episode dramatized how the focus on party unity and constantly "feeding the base" limited Bush's options. Comprehensive immigration reform was the centerpiece of his effort to court the Latino voters whom strategists like Rove and Dowd considered crucial to the party's future fortunes. It was also Bush's best chance for an important second-term legislative achievement after the collapse of his Social Security plan, not to mention an opportunity to make substantive progress against an entrenched problem. But Bush's overriding priority on unifying Republicans prevented him from achieving any of those goals. Instead he was left with an immigration policy built solely around enforcement and symbolized by an exclusionary fence, an approach many Latinos saw as punitive and even racist. And for that Bush paid an immediate price: support among Latino voters for Republican House candidates plummeted from 44 percent in 2004 to just 29 percent in 2006. If Republicans cannot reverse that damage, the long-term consequences for their political coalition will be severe.*

Similar ideological constraints prevented Bush from responding effectively to other challenges. Throughout his presidency the American health care system fell back into the debilitating spiral of rising costs and declining access that it had experienced in the early 1990s. As health insurance premium costs increased, the number of uninsured Americans soared, from just under 40 million in 2000 to nearly 45 million in 2005. Yet Bush's unwillingness to consider responses that might expand government's role, or to confront health care interests aligned with the GOP, like the insurance and drug industries, left him unable to do much more than gesture at the problem with peripheral proposals such as limiting medical malpractice lawsuits or expanding tax-free accounts families could use to pay their health care expenses. On the economy, where strong overall growth and low unemployment had not eliminated concern about stagnant median incomes and rising levels of poverty, Bush limited himself almost solely to a single lever, tax cuts. On energy issues, Bush and congressional Democrats matched each other in rigidity. Each blocked the ideas most favored by the other (more production on the one hand, and more conservation and promotion of alternative energy on the other), yielding energy legislation in 2005 that did virtually nothing to wean America's dependence on foreign oil. Well into Bush's second term the number of Americans in poverty and the total without health insurance was significantly higher than when he took office; the median income was slightly lower; and the nation's dependence on foreign oil was greater.

Washington's inability to produce more progress against these challenges chilled public attitudes toward *both* parties during Bush's second term. But Bush and congressional Republicans, as the party in power, bore the brunt of public discontent. And as dissatisfaction with the nation's direction mounted after 2004, it exposed another inherent limitation of Bush's polarizing strategy: A president who attracts only a narrow majority of support on his best days can sink to dangerous depths on the days that

---

* Bush confronted conservatives over immigration more forcefully in 2007, but his weakened standing diminished his leverage; moreover, Democratic enthusiasm for reform wavered by the time Congress returned to the issue.

are less than his best, which come around more often at the White House than any administration prefers.

As we've seen, except in the immediate period after the 9/11 attacks, Bush never built a broad coalition of public support. His margin of victory over Kerry in 2004 was the smallest ever for a reelected president. In Gallup surveys his approval rating during the traditional postreelection honeymoon peaked at 55 percent; every other reelected president since World War II reached at least 62 percent. Bush's approval rating fell back below 50 percent in Gallup polls less than a month into his second term, faster than any of his predecessors in the history of modern polling.

All of this meant that Bush had very little margin for error when events turned against him—as they did with a vengeance through 2005. The combination of his own miscalculations (Schiavo, Social Security) and missteps (particularly the mishandling of Hurricane Katrina), and the relentless flow of bad news from Iraq, placed enormous strains on Bush's public standing. And because he had failed to build broad support at his highest points, Bush had little goodwill to draw on when he stumbled. Through 2006 and well into 2007 Bush never again attracted support from half the country in Gallup surveys; indeed, after Hurricane Katrina he often drew support from less than 40 percent, and at his lowest points, less than 35 percent of Americans. Even deeply controversial presidents like Lyndon Johnson, Ronald Reagan, and Bill Clinton had never fallen that far. Those numbers placed Bush in the uncomfortable company of failed presidents who unambiguously lost the country's confidence, such as Nixon, Jimmy Carter, and his own father, George H. W. Bush.

To a remarkable extent Republican voters stayed with the younger Bush; even on his darkest days, three fourths or more of Republicans in public opinion surveys usually said they supported him. But by Bush's second term less than one third of independents typically said they approved of his performance. His second-term approval rating among Democrats frequently fell into the single digits; at one point, just 4 percent of Democrats said they approved of his performance. These numbers were lower than Richard Nixon's ratings among Democrats at the height of Watergate, Jimmy Carter's ratings among Republicans at the nadir of his presidency, or Bill Clinton's showing among Republicans during his impeachment. They were, in fact, the lowest ratings any president had received from Americans in the opposition party in the half century of modern public opinion polling.

This decline in Bush's public support inevitably eroded his strength in Congress. It hardened Democrats in their opposition to him and lured more Republicans toward dissent. During Bush's second term Republican conservatives revolted against his immigration plan and his effort to place Harriet Miers, his White House counsel, on the Supreme Court. Republican moderates recoiled against his decision to restrict federal funding of stem cell research and his drive to allow drilling in the Arctic National Wildlife Refuge. The iconoclastic trio of John McCain, John Warner, and Lindsey Graham, over Bush's dogged objections, forced through limits on the use of torture against detainees in the war on terror. The vast majority of congressional Republicans still stood with Bush on most issues. But through the first two years of his second term enough Republicans opposed him on enough important issues to loosen his grip on Congress and regularly frustrate his agenda.

The fall in Bush's public support and the weakening of his hold on Congress fed on each other, thus demonstrating still another danger in his governing model. As Nick Calio, Bush's insightful first legislative director, recognized, the more Bush's approval rating declined, the more congressional Republicans saw it in their interest to separate from him. And as they separated they denied Bush legislative achievements that might have reversed (or at least slowed) his decline. "It's a downward spiral that people can't break out of," Calio correctly observed.

More than anything else, Iraq was the issue that drained Bush's public support during his second term. The political damage inflicted on him by the war demonstrated yet another danger in his polarizing approach. Any president would have suffered for the bad news that confronted Americans day after day from a war that confounded almost all of Bush's optimistic expectations. But Bush was especially exposed to the danger because he had so indelibly stamped Iraq as *his* war. He had denied congressional Democrats, or even skeptical Republicans, any meaningful voice in shaping his strategy. He had injected the war into the heart of the 2004 presidential campaign, raising it as the defining symbol of his leadership and his determination to make tough decisions to protect the United States. In his appearances for Republicans in the final weeks of the 2006 campaign, Bush doubled his bet with searing attacks on Democrats as "the party of cut-and-run" in Iraq. "However they put it," Bush insisted, "the Democrat approach in Iraq comes down to this: The terrorists win and America loses." (Vice President Cheney showed the same arsonist's impulse a few months later, when he insisted that Democrats pushing to end the American commitment in Iraq would "validate" Al Qaeda's belief "that . . . they can break our will.") And, of course, early in 2007, Bush raised his commitment yet again by rejecting the recommendations of the bipartisan Iraq Study Group and sending more troops to Iraq over intense opposition from Democrats, and even from many Republicans, as well as a clear majority of the public.

Bush's refusal to reconsider his direction during Iraq's long descent into chaos did not serve America (or Iraq) because it allowed him to remain locked into a "stay-the-course" strategy long after events on the ground had rendered it obsolete, if not meaningless. It did not even serve Bush's political interest, because it left him alone to bear the mounting public discontent over the conflict. Because Bush had not moved to co-opt any of his critics by adopting (or even soliciting) their ideas for salvaging the war, in the public mind he stood exposed as the sole architect of the debacle as conditions deteriorated through 2005 and 2006. He also denied himself fresh thinking that might have allowed him to avoid, or at least ameliorate, the catastrophe that Iraq became. When Bush rejected the Iraq Study Group's recommendation to begin moving toward withdrawal, and instead insisted on sending more troops into Iraq, he obliterated his last chance at achieving any consensus over the war—or, in all likelihood, reviving any momentum for his crippled presidency.

The decision by congressional Republicans to virtually ignore oversight on the war for fear of embarrassing the White House or providing ammunition to Democrats eliminated another potential source of constructive pressure on Bush to reassess Iraq as the disaster deepened. In that way their deference demonstrated still another flaw in a governing strategy focused so heavily on party unity. The Republican majority elevated its partisan interest (to bolster Bush) over its institutional responsibility (to act as an independent check on the executive branch). But in the end it served neither the country nor its own cause. Because congressional Republicans exerted so little pressure on Bush to change direction in Iraq, or even to justify the direction he had set, they made it easier for him to dig in despite the steady deterioration on the ground. His refusal to adapt then devastated Republicans in the 2006 election, as voters dissatisfied with the war's direction flocked to the Democrats. More oversight from Congress on Iraq would have generated more pressure on Bush to seek new approaches, or even just to acknowledge mounting difficulties, before that wave crested. To compound the damage, Democratic challengers in 2006 effectively used the absence of oversight to portray the GOP majority as a "rubber stamp" for a president and a war both sinking in popularity. From every angle the parliamentary-style suppression of oversight proved counterproductive. In a conversation a few days after the election Chris Shays, the only Republican from New England elected to the House in 2006, ruefully reckoned the cost:

> If we had done better congressional oversight it clearly would have been better for the country, it would have been better for Congress; ironically, it even would have been better for the president. The best example of this is [Hurricane] Katrina. We had tough oversight of that . . . and the response of the administration was to come back with over a hundred recommendations of things they could and should do better. That's when the system works best. That's the way our founding fathers designed it. It is understandable that we would want to implement the policies the White House wanted . . . what got caught up in that, which was a mistake, was that Congress didn't do the kind of aggressive oversight that it would normally do. It really hurt the presidency; it obviously hurt Congress; and it hurt our country.

The same could be said of Congress's approach to exercising oversight on itself. The decay of the ethics process that culminated in Denny Hastert's dismissal of three Republicans on the Ethics Committee who admonished DeLay in 2004 reflected the leadership's priority on closing ranks and punishing dissent. But, like the abandonment of oversight on the executive branch, it proved enormously counterproductive. The public dismantling of the ethics process broadcast a retreat in oversight that bred scandal. As Fred Wertheimer, the veteran political reformer and former president of Common Cause, put it, "If everyone thinks there is no sheriff in town, you wind up with the Wild West." Republicans limped into the 2006 election besieged by an astonishing array of scandals that ranged from questionable ties to the disgraced lobbyist Jack Abramoff to allegations of choking a mistress and steering lobbying contracts to family members. Criminal investigations or convictions forced the resignation of no less than four Republican members in the first Congress of Bush's second term.

By the fall of 2006, troubles rooted in Bush's polarizing political strategy pressed in on Republicans from almost every direction. The disconnect from centrist voters evident on Terry Schiavo and Social Security; the declining approval ratings for Bush driven by widespread disillusionment among independents and Democrats; the mounting chaos in Iraq and the sharpening partisan divisions over the war at home; Congress's failure to maintain an identity as an independent, even if supportive, monitor of the president's performance; the greasy tide of scandal on Capitol Hill: All of this threatened the gains the GOP had registered in Bush's first term. Since taking office Bush had accepted intense opposition as the price for mobilizing passionate support. But as his party prepared to face the voters in 2006, that strategy showed every sign of crumbling. The election loomed as a referendum not only on the performance of Bush and the Republican Congress, but on their bet that with enough support from their political base they could survive almost any conceivable level of discontent among everyone else.

THE RECKONING

A few months before voters evicted Republicans from control of both the House and Senate in November 2006, Karl Rove sat in his White House office on a sweltering summer morning and coolly proclaimed his plan for building a lasting Republican majority firmly on track. He waved away the idea that the divisions surrounding Bush had left the GOP with too narrow a base of support to establish an enduring advantage over the Democrats. America might be divided fifty-fifty today, or tilting fifty-one–forty-nine toward the Republican Party, but Rove said he could envision the GOP securing the lasting allegiance of 55 percent of the voters or more. "I think that is the potential over the next several years," he said.

Rove saw two broad keys to building a stable Republican majority co-alition. One was continued progress in his effort to peel away narrowly targeted groups within the Democratic coalition. "I think there are a lot of people left as behavioral Democrats who are really weakening in their ties to the Democratic Party," he said, with his unique blend of bubbly enthusiasm and cold-eyed precision. "I mean the young Hispanic who served in the military; the African American who goes to church on a regular basis; the young Asian American entrepreneur. All of these are people who are ultimately persuadable by the Republican Party." The other key was progress on Bush's agenda. To Rove's eye, that stretched beyond immediate challenges such as stabilizing Iraq, locking in Bush's tax cuts, and winning the confirmation of conservative judges, toward gains on more fundamental goals, such as restructuring government programs like Medicare to increase their reliance on market forces; creating an "ownership society" through measures like the administration's stalled plan to create individual accounts under Social Security; and advancing a "compassionate conservative" agenda centered on improving public schools. If Republicans followed Bush's direction on all of these questions, Rove argued, they would expand their coalition and widen the edge over the Democrats that they enjoyed as he spoke. "All of these things we launched down in 1999 and 2000—I think there is plenty of room to grow on those," he said.

In all, Rove suggested, more targeted poaching of Democratic constituencies and commitment to Bush's course offered Republicans the opportunity to re-create the lasting dominance the party enjoyed in the three decades after 1896—and without sanding off their ideological edge or targeting more of their agenda at moderate and independent voters. In the electorate, Rove argued, Republicans could grow primarily by attracting more of the voters most similar to those already in their coalition ("the young Hispanic who served in the military; the African American who goes to church on a regular basis . . ."). In Congress they could extend their majorities primarily by solidifying their control over seats from the red states that backed Bush for president. Just holding the places Bush won in 2004, he noted, would provide the GOP more comfortable majorities in presidential elections after 2010, when those states, with their growing populations, are expected to gain votes in the Electoral College. Like Gingrich, Rove was too much a visionary to abandon the goal of expanding his party's reach both geographically and demographically. But he made clear that he believed the Republican coalition could survive, and even thrive, without fundamentally bridging the underlying divisions in society that Bush's presidency so starkly exposed. Asked which party would benefit if the political environment remained so polarized, Rove seemed surprised by the question. "Well, the side that is winning," he said after a moment. "The side that is winning has got the upper hand." He left no doubt which party he believed that to be.

Rove's tone changed remarkably little after the sweeping Democratic gains in the 2006 election. "The Republican philosophy is alive and well and likely to reemerge in the majority in 2008," he insisted. Republicans were on their way to recovery, he argued, until the Mark Foley sex scandal forced them back on the defensive. Without the proliferation of scandal accusations against GOP members and mistakes by other incumbents who had failed to build strong enough campaigns to survive a difficult national climate, Republicans would have held the House, he declared. As it was, Rove argued in a one-page document distributed after the election by his aides, the Republican congressional losses roughly tracked the average for the elections during a president's sixth year since World War II.

In the weeks after the voting many leading Republicans and conservatives struck similar notes. Many insisted that the election provided no mandate for Democrats. Others declared that the problem was not that the GOP had moved too far away from voters in the center, but that it had broken faith with those on the right by supporting too much spending, or by failing to sufficiently defend conservative social values. "There must be a counterculture to the culture of spending," Representative Roy Blunt of

Missouri, the outgoing House Republican whip, declared in a speech two days after the balloting. "And we must respond, directly, forthrightly, and confidently to the attacks on our traditional values." Combative conservative talk show host Hugh Hewitt went further yet: Republicans had lost the majority, he insisted, because they had compromised with Democrats *too often*. (After the election Hewitt helped establish a new conservative group that aimed, in the spirit of the Club for Growth, to stiffen party discipline by pressuring what he called "White Flag Republicans," as well as Democrats, who broke from Bush on Iraq.) Even John McCain, while bemoaning an increase in partisanship, maintained that the election offered no "affirmation of the other party's program," and if anything validated the GOP's direction. "Nor do I believe Americans rejected our values and governing philosophy," he declared. "On the contrary, I believe they rejected us because they felt we had come to value our incumbency over our principles."

Many of the Republican assessments of the 2006 result contained valid insights. There was no evidence that the election amounted to a widespread endorsement of Democratic ideas. Elections during a president's sixth year are usually difficult for his party. And the Foley scandal undoubtedly hurt Republicans. But there was also much in the Republican analysis that amounted to wishful thinking, and even willful denial. Blaming scandal for the defeat, for instance, ignored the role of the GOP governing strategy under Bush in allowing scandal to spread. Most fundamental, the rosy assessments ignored the scale and composition of the party's defeat in 2006, and the way Bush's polarizing approach to governing contributed to the result. Few in either party seriously believed that the election signaled a lasting realignment of voter allegiance to the Democratic Party. But the results undermined the claim of Bush's advisers that the elections of 2002 and 2004 had signaled the emergence of a lasting *Republican* majority. Just as importantly, the outcome raised enormous doubts about whether Bush's focus on mobilizing and consolidating the conservative base was, as Rove asserted, leading the GOP toward such a secure advantage. The 2006 election was a reckoning for Bush's belief that he could govern the country without assembling a broad coalition of support. Before the 2006 results Bush and Rove maintained that they were building a narrow but stable majority. After the results that concept seemed more than ever a contradiction in terms.

In several distinct respects the outcome stood as a powerful repudiation of Bush and his governing strategy. One was the *depth* of the GOP defeat. To regain control of the Senate, Democrats defeated six incumbent Republican senators. Only three times in the past half century had so many sitting senators from one party suffered defeat. The Democratic increase of thirty seats in the House was less dramatic by historic standards, but their gains were suppressed by redistricting plans that tilted so many seats so heavily toward one party, and the ability of the Republican National Committee's sophisticated turnout operation to win most of the very closest races. But the actual popular vote in House races moved toward the Democrats in emphatic proportions. When political analyst Rhodes Cook cumulated the results in all 435 districts he found that Democrats in 2006 won 53 percent of the popular vote and outpolled the GOP by some 6.4 million votes. In each case the Democratic showing exceeded the Republican performance during the historic 1994 election, when they had gained fifty-two House seats. In Senate races the Democrats won the popular vote in 2006 by nearly twice as large a margin as Republicans had in 1994. Two other measures framed the picture of Democratic dominance. Not a single Democratic House or Senate incumbent was defeated. And the party made broad gains as well in governorships and state legislatures.

The second revealing measure was the *breadth* of the Republican defeat. Democrats, as we saw in Chapter 6, consolidated their hold over the blue states most skeptical of Bush. With the defeat of Republicans Rick Santorum in Pennsylvania and Lincoln Chafee in Rhode Island, Democrats reduced the GOP to just five of the thirty-six Senate seats in the eighteen states that twice voted against Bush. In the Eastern states that stretched from Maryland to Maine, Democrats won so many House seats that their overall margin in those eleven states exceeded the Republican House majority in the eleven states of the Old Confederacy. But Democrats also, as we saw, reversed their decline in the red states where Republicans had consolidated their advantages under Bush. Democrats won big margins in white-collar, socially moderate suburbs not only in states where they have been strong, like Michigan and Pennsylvania, but also in places like Colorado and Virginia that Republicans until recently considered part of their base. In all of those diverse places Republicans faced crippling defections from voters who had once been open to them but felt excluded from the rigidly ideological definition that Bush and the congressional leadership had imposed on the party.

Those results pointed to the third and most telling measure of the Republican defeat: the nature of the coalition that had assembled against them. Although most of the Republican commentary after the election attributed the loss to an abandonment of conservative principles, the party's problem in 2006 was not a decline in support among its core conservative voters. According to exit polls Republicans cast almost as large a share of the vote in House races in 2006 (36 percent) as they did in 2004 (38 percent), and they voted for Republican House candidates at almost exactly the same rate as they had two years earlier. (In 2004, 93 percent of Republicans supported Republican House candidates; in 2006, the number was 91 percent.) Likewise, from 2004 to 2006, the share of the vote for Republican candidates slipped only by small margins (four percentage points or less) among such core Republican groups as conservatives, evangelical Christians, and regular churchgoers.

But in this election the base was not enough to save the GOP. Part of the party's problem was that Democratic voters, deeply hostile to Bush's direction, turned out in large numbers too, and supported their party's candidates at levels even slightly higher than Republicans. More important, the election demonstrated that the White House had been premature in declaring the demise of the swing voter. The 2006 election showed that there was still a persuadable center in American politics—and that no matter how effectively a party mobilized its base, it could not prevail if those swing voters moved sharply and cohesively against it. Across the country Republican candidates in 2006 faced deficits among independent voters much too large to overcome simply by turning out more of their core conservative supporters.

Republicans buckled under the cumulative weight of governing in a manner that offered so little outreach to voters outside of their coalition. In the 2004 election, exit polls found Republican House candidates trailed

Democrats among independent voters by just three percentage points (just as Bush only slightly trailed Kerry with those voters). But in the 2006 House races independents backed Democrats over Republicans by a crushing margin of 57 percent to 39 percent. Similarly, the exit polls showed that independents preferred Democrats in nine of the eleven most closely contested Senate races. (The sole exceptions were Rhode Island and New Jersey, where Republicans ran their most moderate candidates.) Democrats won all but one of those eleven races. Some of the advantages for Democratic Senate candidates with independents reached staggering proportions. In Ohio, Democrat Sherrod Brown won almost two thirds of independents en route to his victory; in Pennsylvania, Democrat Robert Casey, Jr., won nearly three fourths of them while routing Rick Santorum. These were overwhelming, indisputable, insurmountable margins, a roar of discontent that extended far beyond dissatisfaction with the war toward a deeper loss of faith in the direction Bush and his congressional allies had set. In one Election Day survey conducted by a Republican pollster, 63 percent of independent voters said their opinion of the GOP had deteriorated over the previous two years.

Everywhere dissatisfaction with Bush loomed heavily over the results. Nearly three fifths of the voters in 2006 said they disapproved of Bush's performance, and they preferred Democrats in the House races by 82 percent to 15 percent. (Those who approved of Bush's performance backed Republicans by 84 percent to 14 percent, but they represented only about two fifths of the voters.) The foundation of the Republican governing system—the sturdy alliance between Congress and the White House—became more like a sinkhole as voters soured on the president. In red states Democratic candidates promised to act as an independent check on the president and accused Republican incumbents of functioning as a "rubber stamp" for Bush. In blue states such as New Jersey, Connecticut, New York, Pennsylvania, and Maryland, Democrats won campaigns by convincing voters to view their Republican opponents less as individuals with often temperate views than as potential votes for Bush's hard-edged agenda. "It's one of the first votes a senator makes," an announcer intoned in a Democratic ad that helped seal the doom of the moderate Rhode

Island Republican Lincoln Chafee. "Will they support a U.S. Senate controlled by the Republicans or the Democrats?"

Rove's defiant comments after the election set the tone for the Republican reaction. Only a handful of Republicans faced these trends more squarely. Ken Mehlman, the outgoing national party chairman, also tended to minimize the scale of the defeat, but forthrightly acknowledged that if the party did not show more tolerance for dissenting views it risked becoming a regional and "minority party, one that could never win an election, much less govern a great and diverse nation." On election night the Republican Main Street Partnership, the premier group of Republican moderates, issued a statement concluding, "Tonight the American people made it clear that our party's decision to ignore the middle of the American electorate was a disastrous one." In an editorial after the vote the *National Review* wondered if the party had placed too much emphasis on unity at the price of outreach. "These election results should cause Republicans to rethink a strategy in which the president and the congressional leadership joined," the editors wrote. "A less partisan strategy may . . . have made it possible to build an ideological majority including some Democrats."

These dissidents remained a strict minority in the Republican reaction to the election despite polls through 2007 showing that the independent voters who rejected the GOP in 2006 remained intensely disenchanted with Bush and the party. Yet enough doubts surfaced among party leaders to raise the possibility that Republicans might approach the 2008 campaign, both at the presidential and congressional level, with at least a somewhat more inclusive message and agenda than Bush. The party's top-tier presidential candidates sent mixed signals through the 2008 nominating race. John McCain, Mitt Romney, the former governor of Massachusetts, and Rudolph Giuliani, the former mayor of New York City, all carried the potential of appealing to a broader audience than Bush, and each conspicuously broke from Republican orthodoxy in ways that could attract less partisan voters. (McCain did that on immigration and global warming; Romney by supporting universal health care in Massachusetts; and Giuliani with liberal positions on social issues such as abortion.) But the steady move to the right on social issues by McCain and Romney, Giuliani's pledge to appoint staunchly conservative judges, and the unyielding support for the Iraq War from all three men showed that each remained committed to placating the party's conservative base in ways that could limit their reach beyond it. Republicans displayed similarly divided instincts in Congress. Surprisingly large numbers in both chambers stood with Bush as he sent more troops to Iraq against overwhelming public opposition early in 2007. But at the same time a large number of Republicans, especially in the House, crossed party lines to support initiatives Democrats highlighted in their initial legislative thrust, such as an increase in the minimum wage and a loosening of Bush's restrictions on federally funded stem cell research. With their words, few Republicans publicly questioned Bush's confrontational governing strategy; but in their actions more of them (including McCain, the eventual nominee) appeared to edge away from it.

The most intriguing proponent of a more inclusive course was Matthew Dowd, the former Democrat who served as one of the principal architects of Bush's election and governing strategy. Cerebral, soft-spoken, and reflective, Dowd wallowed in introspection with as much energy as Bush avoided it; if Bush was the decider, Dowd was the deliberator. Though Dowd still advised the RNC, he watched Bush's second term unfold with mounting disillusion. Dowd's alienation grew as the White House and Republican Congress, aiming to energize their base once again, scheduled votes on incendiary social issues through the summer of 2006, including renewed efforts to pass constitutional bans on gay marriage and flag burning. All sides knew those amendments did not have enough support to succeed; they were the political equivalent of a Civil War reenactment, a staged battle designed solely to trigger predictable emotions. Over breakfast one morning that summer Dowd nearly sputtered with outrage over the White House's turn to these ritual confrontations:

The gay marriage stuff, I can understand [voting on] when there are rulings going on in Massachusetts and [marriages] going on in San Francisco. But all of a sudden, a proposal now—where is this coming from and why is this happening? All it is going to do is divide people. There's a part of the Republican Party on the immigration thing that is offensive to somebody like me. So is scheduling votes on flag amendments. . . . People are worrying about the cost of health [care] and whether or not they are going to have a job in the twenty-first century, and their kid's education, and whether it is going to keep up with all the changes, and we're scheduling votes on flag amendments? What are we doing?

It was a question Dowd asked himself more and more. He had helped design a strategy that won reelection for Bush primarily by identifying and energizing his most ardent supporters, but now Dowd feared that too many people in both parties took the wrong lesson from that success. That may have been the most viable strategy for Bush, but it wasn't the only way to win, Dowd said. It wasn't even the most desirable way to win. "Part of the success of democracy and politics is the ability to build large coalitions," Dowd said. "I don't think a series of very close elections is good for the body politic. . . . In a society and world that is dynamically changing, we're operating on a razor's edge. And I don't think that is good." Americans, he predicted, would flock to a presidential candidate who sincerely sought to bridge the country's partisan and ideological divides. "I think people in this country want something that brings them together, not something that separates them," he said. "I think people want that sense of community, they want that sense of connection."

Dowd seemed almost physically pained by the implications of his words. After eight years working with Bush and Rove, it was clear he felt that their Republican Party had too little room for him, or for other moderate voters he liked to call ideological mutts. He seemed equal parts angry and adrift. "Honestly, where do people go?" he said plaintively. "I'm one of those people. I was a Democrat. I switched parties, primarily because of the personal thing for Bush and what I thought he could do, and all that sort of thing—bridge the gaps [between the parties]. And then you see what's happened in Washington, and you're like, 'Where do I go?' Somebody like me: Where do I go? To a degree, both parties don't speak to me . . . and I think there are a bunch of people in this political environment that are in the same place as I am."

In the months leading to the 2006 election, Dowd's search for a political home carried him further away from the path taken by his friends in the White House. He coauthored a book (with a former senior aide to Bill Clinton and an Associated Press reporter) extolling the importance of building community in politics, religion, and business. He helped found a Web site together with veterans of the John Kerry and Al Gore presidential campaigns intended to promote more dialogue and consensus between Americans disenchanted by Washington's partisan warfare.

Dowd made the cleanest break from the White House approach by signing on to advise the 2006 reelection campaign of California governor Arnold Schwarzenegger. The former movie star had improbably won election as a Republican in that heavily Democratic state after voters recalled the hapless Democrat Gray Davis in 2003. Schwarzenegger immediately derailed his administration by igniting a series of Bush-like partisan confrontations with Democrats in the state legislature and their allies in organized labor. Schwarzenegger hit bottom in 2005 when voters resoundingly rejected four conservative ballot initiatives he had proposed.

But he surprised, and eventually disarmed, many of his critics by reversing course. After 2005, Schwarzenegger governed almost as the anti-Bush, an ideological hybrid committed to bipartisan cooperation wherever possible. He appointed a Democrat as his chief of staff. He made deals with Democrats in the state legislature to raise the minimum wage, lower prescription drug prices, and launch an ambitious public works program. His soothing new style came with one large cost: Schwarzenegger, carrying the avoidance of conflict to an extreme, abandoned too much of his initial instinct to reform and streamline California's government. But he showed genuine vision in forging pathbreaking agreements to combat global warming and promote alternative energy. He occupied so much of the center that he squeezed his Democratic opponent in 2006 to the margin. In a year when Republicans were routed almost everywhere, Schwarzenegger cruised to reelection in the biggest blue state of all, winning a majority of independents and a quarter of Democratic voters along the way.

It was easy to see Dowd's work with Schwarzenegger as a form of penance for his role in shaping Bush's far more divisive approach to governing—a modest political analogue to Robert McNamara's effort to atone for Vietnam by fighting poverty at the World Bank. In the final days before the 2006 election Dowd seemed stupefied that Bush was ending the campaign on such a shrill note, lashing Democrats in his speeches and labeling them the party of "doubt and defeat" in foreign affairs. "This whole politics of division is exactly the wrong thing," Dowd said on the phone shortly before the vote. "It should be a message of inclusion."

Smart politicians considering the 2008 presidential campaign, Dowd continued, would learn more from Schwarzenegger's conciliatory approach than from the bruising White House tactics. "The victories that people should focus on are the people who were able to bridge the divide and build a broad-based coalition," Dowd said. "That should be the takeaway from this election: The people who built a broad-based coalition and won breaking down divisions." And his old colleagues in the White House, the political team that had spent six years trying to establish lasting political dominance with a strategy that accepted division as the price of mobilization, what should they take away from the wave about to crash over the Republican Party on Election Day? "What they need to take out of it," Dowd said simply, "is that they have yet to build a majority coalition."

CHAPTER 9

THE OPPOSITION
IN AN AGE
OF POLARIZATION

The Bush presidency shook the Democratic Party to its foundations. Probably at no point since the 1920s had the party felt so embattled. The generally centrist presidencies of Dwight Eisenhower and Richard M. Nixon never dented the widespread belief among Democrats that they represented the country's natural majority party. Ronald Reagan presented a greater threat to Democratic priorities than Eisenhower or Nixon, but throughout his presidency Democrats held a majority of the House, and they recaptured the Senate before he left office. Under George H. W. Bush Democrats controlled both the House and the Senate. Even after Republicans overthrew both those majorities in 1994, Democrats still had Bill Clinton in the White House to defend their interests.

But for almost all of Bush's first six years Democrats faced unified Republican control of the House, the Senate, and the White House. And in that weakened position they confronted a coordinated effort from the GOP to solidify their advantage and marginalize Democratic influence. No other Republican president had challenged Democrats in such a systematic manner; Reagan and James Baker, much less Nixon and H. R. Haldeman, had not worked nearly as hard as Bush and Karl Rove to build a self-sustaining political machine aimed at perpetually excluding Democrats from power.

Perhaps most ominously, Democrats faced a crisis of confidence about their ability to repel that challenge. Even through the Reagan years most Democrats, pointing to their continuing strength on Capitol Hill and in state governments, believed they represented a majority of opinion in the country. The Republican congressional takeover in 1994 shook that conviction, but Democrats consoled themselves in the belief that the country divided almost exactly in half between the parties throughout the rest of the decade. Under Bush, though, many Democrats echoed Karl Rove in concluding that the GOP had established a narrow but significant advantage. For the first time since the New Deal large numbers of influential Democrats viewed the GOP as the nation's majority party, if only by a slim margin. Emerging young Democratic leaders like Markos Moulitsas Zuniga, the ringleader of the immensely popular Web site Daily Kos, counseled that the first step to recovery for the Democrats was to acknowledge that they "really are a minority party."

In the Bush years the fear of fading into lasting minority status transformed the Democratic Party from the grassroots to Capitol Hill. It tilted Democrats away from Bill Clinton's consensus-oriented third-way centrism toward a much more partisan approach that mirrored the Republican vision. Under Bush Democrats sought to replicate the strengths of the Republican governing model. Democrats stiffened party discipline in Congress, solidified their ties to the interest groups in their coalition, built new institutions dedicated to warring with conservatives, and watched—sometimes with enthusiasm, at other points with anxiety—the emergence of a grassroots activist base animated to ferocious exertion by hostility toward Bush. In all these ways Democrats during the Bush presidency molded themselves into an increasingly effective opposition party—one that shrewdly utilized many of the same political and legislative strategies employed by the majority they opposed.

But in the process Democrats absorbed some of the Bush model's critical weaknesses. The fatal flaw in Bush's governing strategy was his willingness to operate primarily as the champion of a single faction—essentially the conservative components of the Republican coalition—while making little effort to speak to, and for, the entire country. Democrats, in their resistance to that approach, ironically moved closer to it. Because Bush centered his governing strategy on satisfying the needs of his core coalition, he intensified the pressure on Democrats to function simply as the champion of those excluded from Bush's circle rather than drawing a more encompassing circle of their own. The narrowness of Bush's vision distorted the Democratic vision. They too often defined their purpose as simply resisting his purposes.

In the Bush years the Democrats turned inward, mobilizing to protect their core constituencies against a relentless challenge from the White House and the Republican congressional majority. In the process the Democrats' ability, and even desire, to speak for the whole country also diminished. Their thinking became more rigid and doctrinaire on issues like trade and entitlement reform; their willingness to demonize interests associated with the Bush coalition (such as big business) grew; their tolerance for independence and dissent in Congress diminished. Like Republicans, Democrats during the Bush years became more responsive to the concerns of their political base and less willing to challenge that base to achieve agreements across party lines. As we'll see, that may have been a rational, even inevitable, response to the combative, intensely partisan environment that Bush and the congressional GOP had established. And Democrats, for reasons we'll also explore, never moved as far toward a factional vision as Bush and his congressional allies. But the Democratic Party was a different institution as Bush's presidency concluded than it was when he took office. Democrats emerged from the grueling conflicts of the Bush years with new leaders, new strategies, and new priorities, hardened and scarred like soldiers returning home from a bloody tour at the front.

THE RISE OF THE INTERNET RESISTANCE

The message was difficult to miss.

Shortly after the 2002 midterm elections Mark Mellman, a longtime Democratic pollster working for John Kerry, conducted a national survey to measure early attitudes among Democratic voters about the 2004 presidential race. Predictably, he found that Democrats were angry at President Bush. But they were even angrier at the national Democratic leadership, who many felt had wilted before the challenge from Bush during his first two years. "Their major criterion [for the 2004 party presidential nominee] was someone who would stand up to Bush more strongly," Mellman recalled. "That's how much they detested him: The most important thing to them was standing up to him."

This indictment against the party leaders was overstated. Congressional Democrats had fought Bush to a standstill on energy and health care policy, blocked his most conservative judicial nominees, and voted almost in unison against his budgets. But a substantial majority of congressional Democrats had worked with Bush on education reform, a measurable minority had backed the final version of his 2001 tax plan (after Senate Democrats had succeeded in reducing the plan's size), and most important, large numbers in both chambers voted in October 2002 to provide Bush the authority to invade Iraq. In the 2002 election the party had run a cautious, muddled campaign that deliberately avoided discussion of Iraq, relied on moldering arguments about protecting Social Security and Medicare, and succeeded only in losing seats in both the House and Senate. As Mellman discovered, there was a substantial Democratic constituency ready to rally around a leader committed to bolder resistance to Bush.

This new force in the party publicly announced its arrival through the presidential campaign of former Vermont governor Howard Dean. Initially viewed as an irascible long shot, Dean rocketed to the top of both opinion polls in the early primary states and, even more important, the fund-raising competition among the 2004 Democratic contenders as the single-minded tribune of those who believed Democrats had surrendered too often. Dean's appeal to disaffected grassroots activists allowed him to raise more money than any presidential contender had ever attracted from small donors over the Internet. His innovative, unconventional campaign staff, led by a rumpled and visionary Democratic organizer named Joe Trippi, constructed a national network of supporters by brilliantly exploiting the Internet's capacity to enable like-minded people to find each other at low cost. In the incandescent swirl it appeared that not only a star, but a movement, had been born, virtually overnight.

Like most overnight sensations, the Dean campaign was the product of years of work. In this case the critical foundations were laid not by Dean, or even by his campaign staff, but by a diverse assortment of Democratic activists united in the belief that their party was failing to meet the.challenge of an ascendant conservatism. In this larger movement the pivotal event was the day in September 1998 when Joan Blades and Wes Boyd, a married couple who worked in the computer software industry, went to eat at a Chinese restaurant not far from their home in Berkeley, California. Blades and Boyd had founded a company, Berkeley Systems, best known for its "flying toaster" screen-saver. A year earlier they had sold the company to another firm for $13.8 million, and they were formulating plans for their next business venture. But as they sat at their table they heard people around them lamenting the drive by Republicans in the House of Representatives to impeach Bill Clinton over charges arising from his affair with Monica Lewinsky, a subject that infuriated them as well. "We were hearing people talking, yet again, about how crazy this obsession with Monica Lewinsky and the scandal was," Blades later recalled. "And we realized that we could do something."

The something was to compose a one-sentence petition, urging Congress to "immediately censure President Clinton and Move On to pressing issues facing the country." When they completed the petition the couple sent it to fewer than one hundred friends and family members and asked them to forward it to their own friends and family. "Obviously," Joan Blades recalled, "people must have gone wild sending it out." Within days they had hundreds of thousands of responses in their in-box; by the end of the impeachment struggle they had collected half a million names.

Those names provided the first evidence of something that would be demonstrated repeatedly over the next several years: A substantial liberal-leaning audience would respond enthusiastically to calls for heightened resistance against the Republican agenda. But Boyd and Blades seemed uncertain how to harness the energy they had unleashed. Both had liberal views, but neither had been particularly involved in politics. Initially, they did not envision establishing an ongoing organization. "We were . . . fully prepared and anxious to get back to our lives, really," Boyd remembered. Only after the group had raised more than $3 million over the Internet for Democratic candidates in the 2000 election did the couple decide to maintain what had become known as MoveOn.org as a permanent institution.

Even then the group drifted through the first months of the Bush presidency with a small staff and no clear direction. The next step in MoveOn's development came after the September 11, 2001, terrorist attacks. In this instance the key figure was a young man a continent away named Eli Pariser. The son of 1960s activists who had founded an alternative high school in Maine, Pariser had recently graduated from college (at age nineteen) and was working for a nonprofit organization in Boston when the twin towers fell. After the attack he went home to his apartment and composed a short message urging President Bush to resist a military response to the tragedy. Pariser created a Web site for the message, and then e-mailed a link to about thirty friends, who forwarded it to their own friends and family. Within a few days Pariser joined forces with David Pickering, a recent University of Chicago graduate who had posted a similar petition on a campus Web site. Pickering agreed to place his petition on the Web site Pariser had established. The combined petition urged "moderation and restraint" in response to the attacks, and called on Bush and other world leaders "to use, wherever possible, international judicial institutions and international human rights law to bring to justice those responsible for the attacks, rather than the instruments of war, violence or destruction."

The petition ignited the same sort of chain reaction Boyd and Blades had with their campaign against Clinton's impeachment. "The next Monday I checked my e-mail and there were three thousand messages in my in-box," Pariser later recalled. "Then the BBC called. They said 'We've been hearing a lot about this. Who are you?' [I said], 'I'm twenty years old; I don't know who I am.'" By October 9, the two young men had collected more than 500,000 names on their petition, from people in 190 different countries. Boyd and Blades, meanwhile, circulated their own petition at MoveOn entitled "Justice, not Terror." That effort similarly asked members to write their members of Congress, urging them "to counsel patience as we search for those responsible" and to "ensure that our actions reflect the sanctity of human life everywhere."

Neither the petitions from MoveOn nor Pariser and Pickering explicitly opposed military action in Afghanistan. But both left no doubt that they believed a military response would be counterproductive, and that the United States would better serve its interests through nonmilitary means to pursue Al Qaeda. That was hardly a common sentiment at the time: Polls showed most Americans supported the attack on Afghanistan, and only a single member of Congress voted against authorizing it. The fact that Pariser and MoveOn could generate such a passionate response for a position with such limited public support was a testament both to the energy surging on the left in response to Bush's presidency and the Internet's power to tap those emotions efficiently. But for Democrats watching closely, the episode also offered an early example of the danger of viewing even such a large Internet uprising as an accurate measure of overall public opinion. On the Internet, intensity of support counted more than breadth; MoveOn built its audience not by seeking to find a consensus among the broad range of Democrats (much less in the country at large) but by providing an undiluted voice for those Democrats committed to the most militant resistance to the Republican agenda, not only when it faced public opposition (as on impeachment), but even when it generated support (as in invading Afghanistan).

Like Boyd and Blades after the impeachment fight, Pariser initially had no idea what to do with the names he had collected. But he was a member of MoveOn himself, so he contacted the group and offered to join forces. Boyd and Blades accepted, and in late 2001 Pariser brought his 500,000 names to MoveOn, nearly doubling the group's e-mail list overnight. Pariser joined MoveOn as the director of its international campaigns. He quickly proved a political prodigy, the equivalent of a baseball player who makes the major leagues without ever stopping in the minors. Over the next year Pariser directed the group's growing opposition to Bush's steps toward war with Iraq. After Congress nonetheless voted to authorize the use of force just before the 2002 election, MoveOn quickly raised nearly $2 million in campaign contributions for Democrats who voted against it in a campaign it called "Reward the Heroes."

Fueled by grassroots Democratic hostility to Bush and the approaching war, the group continued to expand. In January 2003, its members provided the funds to air an updated version of the famous Lyndon Johnson "daisy" television commercial from 1964 in which it suggested that a war with Iraq could escalate into "the unthinkable," a nuclear catastrophe. The next month it joined in worldwide demonstrations against the war and organized a "virtual march on Washington" in which members deluged congressional offices with phone calls and e-mails. When MoveOn posted a request for members to contribute twenty-five thousand dollars for an ad in *The New York Times* urging Bush to "Let the Inspections Work," it collected instead four hundred thousand dollars, enough to also fund television and radio ads and billboards.

This was an extraordinary level of activity for an organization with no office (the principals worked from their homes), little structure, and just four paid staff members. By the time the Iraq War began it was clear to many political strategists in both parties that MoveOn had built the first true political institution of the Internet age. Before the Internet one of the most debilitating hurdles for any political organization was the high cost of finding people who agreed with its position, through direct mail, door-to-door canvassing, phone calls, or advertising. Using the Internet, though, MoveOn had assembled a giant list of supporters at virtually no cost. Reversing the historic relationship, those who agreed with the group's positions had found it. And once the group had captured those names it could organize them to raise money or write letters for further campaigns at minimal cost; indeed, as the organizers came to recognize, the more activity the group generated, the more it expanded its list—and increased its capacity to generate still more activity. Pariser, who became the organization's face as the publicity-shy Boyd and Blades receded, succinctly summarized the dynamic when he concluded, "Win, lose, or draw, we get stronger." The campaign against the Iraq invasion had been a case in point: All of MoveOn's activity hadn't deterred or even slowed Bush's march to war. But by the time war came they had added another 800,000 names to their e-mail list.

As the Iraq experience demonstrated, MoveOn's growth didn't seem to require political victories in the conventional sense. More important was its role as an outlet for those activists who demanded a steelier resistance to the Republican agenda. MoveOn fed on emotions so heated that they sometimes singed even the group itself. When MoveOn invited members to design an anti-Bush television commercial, two of them (out of some fifteen hundred who participated) submitted ads comparing Bush to Hitler, forcing Boyd to apologize and withdraw the ads from consideration. But the group almost always avoided such embarrassments (despite relying heavily on volunteers) and demonstrated an uncanny ability to connect with the deepest concerns of hard-core liberal activists. "We feel like we have moved into some leadership vacuums," Boyd said, a few weeks after Bush declared the end to major combat operations in Iraq.

Maintaining the leadership of such a turbulent constituency required MoveOn to constantly position itself at the forward edge of Democratic opposition to Bush and the GOP. Through the Bush years MoveOn became the most powerful force in what could be called the confrontation caucus of the Democratic Party. Especially on national security, the group tirelessly pressured Democrats to use more militant tactics against Bush. It launched a petition drive urging Democrats to support Bush's 2003 request for $87 billion to fund the Iraq occupation only if he fired Defense Secretary Donald Rumsfeld and transferred authority for the occupation to the United Nations. In 2003 it called for an independent commission to study Bush's prewar statements. By early 2004 it had raised the stakes by floating the possibility of impeachment, and by launching another petition drive that urged Congress to formally censure Bush over his prewar claims about Iraq.

Self-interest and political strategy both pushed MoveOn toward such aggressive tactics. The petition drives above all were designed to collect new e-mail addresses, the lifeblood for an Internet-based organization. But the messages' fervor also reflected the conviction of the group's organizers that the best way for Democrats to regain power was to fight Bush at every turn, with almost any weapon in reach. The MoveOn leaders viewed elections much as Karl Rove did in the White House: They shared his belief that the key to victory in modern politics was not persuading independent or less partisan voters but generating a huge turnout of core supporters. And the best way to produce such a turnout, they reasoned, was to offer a message of unconditional, unyielding opposition to Bush.

In that belief MoveOn was joined by a second major force that reshaped the Democratic Party during the Bush era: the legion of left-leaning bloggers who congregated on the Internet. Compared to MoveOn the bloggers were a much more decentralized and unruly presence, a guerilla force to MoveOn's teeming infantry. The quality of their work varied widely in quality, sophistication, and at times, it seemed, even sanity. But they provided another lens that focused and sharpened the demands among elements of the Democratic base for a more confrontational response to Bush and the conservative coalition. The "netroots," as they often described themselves, became passionate, if volatile, advocates for a more militant Democratic Party.

Political blogs catering to activists in both parties proliferated during Bush's first term. But liberals turned to the Internet with more urgency than conservatives. Talk radio, dominated by conservative hosts, already provided the right a powerful mechanism for delivering messages to their core supporters. By comparison, a succession of big-name liberal hosts uniformly had flopped. Unable to dent the conservative dominance of talk radio, many Democrats embraced the Internet as their best opportunity to challenge—even to "leapfrog," as Wes Boyd put it—the enormous communications machine Republicans had constructed to stoke their base.

In the Babel of left-leaning Web sites that emerged in the Bush years, the Daily Kos rose to become the most popular and influential. Kos was the eponymous product of Markos Moulitsas Zuniga, a slight, almost elfin young man who ran the Web site from his house in a weathered Berkeley neighborhood known as the Flats. Kos was difficult to capture in a single frame. Online he was bombastic, threatening, and imperious. In person he was soft-spoken and often self-deprecating. To meet him in the flesh was something like pulling back the curtain on the Wizard of Oz.

Moulitsas took a circuitous route to his identity as the fierce Kos. He split his youth between Chicago and El Salvador (his mother's native country), where he lived amid the brutal civil war. After returning to the Chicago suburbs for a rocky adolescence, he enlisted in the U.S. Army at seventeen and spent two and a half years with an artillery unit in Germany. College and law school followed, as Moulitsas contemplated careers as diverse as journalism and composing film scores. He was working as a project manager for a Web-designing company in San Francisco when he started his Daily Kos Web site in May 2002, angered by Bush's direction and inspired by the example of the liberal MyDD Web site founded by Jerome Armstrong, another pioneer in Democrats' use of the Internet. By the next year Moulitsas was running his blog full-time.

After years of uncertainty, Moulitsas had discovered his niche. He quickly found an audience by expressing the unmediated anger of the Democratic base toward Bush, and even more so toward Democrats who cooperated with him, especially on Iraq. Kos, if anything, preached a gospel of confrontation with Republicans even more uncompromising than MoveOn's. His tone was edgier, harsher. The e-mails from Pariser to MoveOn members usually had the earnest and friendly tone of a chat at the corner store. The biting exchanges between Kos and the "Kossacks" who posted responses to him and one another sounded more like arguments at the corner bar. Pariser almost always chose his words carefully, as if mentally measuring how each one would look in print. Kos's emotional posts sometimes seemed to erupt directly from the depths of the Democratic id. In 2004, Kerry's campaign removed its link to the Daily Kos after Moulitsas wrote that he felt "nothing" when four American contractors were killed in Fallujah, because "they are there to wage war for profit." But that same unequivocal, even impulsive, tone created the sense of immediacy that drew readers in large numbers to the site.

Kos wasn't as reliably liberal as the MoveOn community. Although he opposed the Iraq War, he supported the invasion of Afghanistan. His favorite Democrats were not Eastern cultural liberals like Kerry but Westerners who combined economic populism with libertarian views on social issues like gun control. He disdained the conventions of identity politics among Democratic interest groups. In a book Moulitsas coauthored with Armstrong, the two suggested that Democrats were too doctrinaire in demanding support for legalized abortion.

But Kos converged with MoveOn, and almost all of the other prominent bloggers, in his belief that too many Democrats had faltered before the challenge of ascendant conservatism. "The conservatives have declared war on liberalism, and we have been treating it like we can appeal to people on the basis of reason," Moulitsas told one early interviewer. "We need to be down and dirty and absolutely tear them apart." Often contemptuous of Republicans, the mainstream media, and the Washington political establishment, Kos reserved his greatest scorn for Democrats he believed gave comfort to the enemy, either by voting for their initiatives or criticizing other Democrats. Moulitsas raised some money from readers for favored candidates, but he saw his Web site's principal role as arming Democrats around the country with "talking points" they could use to persuade friends and neighbors, much the way conservative talk radio equipped millions of Republican listeners with a common set of arguments and outrages for water-cooler conversations. "I look at this as [training] armies," he said at his home one day early in Bush's second term. "It's training our troops how to fight rhetorically."

All of these streams converged in Dean's 2004 presidential campaign. His candidacy became the first unifying cause for the netroots. Moulitsas was one of Dean's first boosters, and the MoveOn members provided Dean a lift when he finished first in the group's Internet primary in June 2003. Money and support from thousands of grassroots activists, many of them organized through the Internet, provided the fuel for Dean's unlikely ascent to the forefront of the Democratic field through that fall.

That enthusiasm was not enough to save Dean when he undermined his campaign with a succession of ill-considered remarks in the final weeks before the first contest in Iowa. Like the response Pariser generated for his petition opposing military action after 9/11, Dean's fall showed that even the most fervid passions among the Internet activists did not guarantee broad public backing. Dean won only his home state of Vermont as John Kerry swept to the nomination.

But Dean and the activists who fueled his rise left an unmistakable mark on the Democrats. They moved the party further away from the Clinton vision and closer to the confrontational approach that MoveOn and Kos favored. Dean succeeded in shifting the burden of proof to Democrats who cooperated with Bush on almost any front. As Dean ascended, the other Democratic presidential candidates competed to equal the ferocity of his rhetorical attacks on Bush (Richard Gephardt probably took the prize when he took to calling Bush a "miserable failure"). Of more lasting importance, the surge of support for Dean also pressured the other contenders to distance themselves from Bush on Iraq. At Dean's zenith in fall 2003 John Kerry voted against Bush's request for $87 billion to fund the war over the next year. This proved another cautionary moment for Democrats struggling to satisfy the Internet activists: Since Kerry had voted to authorize the use of force, and had even voted to provide the money in an earlier vote, his final vote against the funding became the centerpiece of the Bush campaign's successful general election effort to portray him as an unprincipled flip-flopper. Trying to please his base, Kerry handed Bush a powerful weapon with swing voters. (It only compounded matters when Kerry tried to justify his decision by awkwardly explaining, "I actually did vote for the $87 billion before I voted against it.") "There is no question, no question, that had it not been for Howard Dean, John Kerry would have voted for $87 billion . . . so he wouldn't have voted for it before he voted against it, and that would have been that," said one senior adviser in Kerry's presidential campaign.

If Kerry's early vote against the Iraq funding showed Democrats the danger of surrendering entirely to the Internet activists, the rest of the campaign demonstrated the impossibility of ignoring them. No one imagined that Kerry inspired anything like Dean's personal connection with the new generation of grassroots activists. Yet the determination to defeat Bush still inspired them to unprecedented efforts. In the general election Kerry stunned the political world by nearly matching Bush in fund-raising, largely because of his success in attracting small donors on the Internet. Meanwhile, MoveOn dwarfed its previous efforts; through everything from online fund-raising drives to a nationwide bake sale (called "Bake Back the White House"), it collected another $50 million from small donors for anti-Bush television advertising campaigns and grassroots organizing. Matching funds from wealthy liberals led by financier George Soros added another $10 million to the pile. The total was roughly fifteen times as much as the organization had raised for the election just two years earlier. In all, by the calculation of Tom Matzzie, who helped direct Kerry's Internet operation and later joined MoveOn as its Washington director, Democrats may have raised as much as $300 million on the Internet for the 2004 campaign, nearly one in every six dollars the party collected.

The massive sums collected online, the energetic grassroots organizing conducted by MoveOn, the suppressing fire of invective laid down by Moulitsas and his contemporaries on the liberal blogs all sent a message to Democratic leaders that the new generation of Internet activists had become a constituency too large and valuable to ignore. One of the most cherished beliefs among those activists was that they were liberating Democrats from the demands of wealthy donors and business interests by creating an alternative source of grassroots funding for the party. But one of the most profound truths in politics is that no money, or any other form of support, is free; it all comes with some kind of price tag. With the Internet activists the price was the demand for a more confrontational, warlike party committed to unremitting opposition to Bush at home and abroad. In an e-mail to MoveOn members about a month after Kerry's defeat Pariser made clear those activists would not be shy about presenting that bill. "In the last year, grassroots contributors like us gave more than $300 million to the Kerry campaign and the DNC, and proved that the Party doesn't need corporate cash to be competitive," he wrote. "Now it's our Party: we bought it, we own it, and we're going to take it back."

TOUGHENING ON THE HILL

The same challenges that energized the party at the grassroots toughened it at the summit. Change among congressional Democrats did not come nearly fast enough for the Internet activists who condemned any crack in monolithic opposition to Bush. But change did come to Capitol Hill. During Bush's presidency congressional Democrats steadily renounced the idea of operating as a junior partner in governing and recast themselves as an opposition party dedicated to resisting the majority. Democrats weren't equally bold on all fronts: While in the minority they moved only slowly toward sharpened opposition with Bush on the Iraq War, and remained a safe distance behind Republican critics (principally Senators John Warner, John McCain, and Lindsey Graham) in arguments over the president's policies for interrogating and trying detainees in the war on terror. Yet they fought Bush's central domestic priorities and his overall approach to foreign policy with a fervor and focus that surprised not only Republicans but most Democrats. Bush's aggressive tactics and polarizing proposals encouraged Democrats toward a harder line. But so did the lessons Democrats took from the centrally directed, highly disciplined legislative machine that Republicans constructed after 1994. In the struggle against a White House and Republican congressional majority that locked arms for a coordinated drive to impose its agenda and entrench its power, congressional Democrats remade themselves into something much closer to a mirror image of their adversaries. As congressional Republicans recoiled from compromise and bipartisanship, so did Democrats.

In the Senate, where the rules provided more options for the minority, Democrats opposed Bush and the GOP majority with tactics an earlier generation almost surely would have rejected as too inflammatory. Though soft-spoken and silky in manner, Tom Daschle, the Democratic leader during Bush's first four years, infuriated Republicans with his dogged opposition to Bush's priorities. If anything, Democratic resistance stiffened after Daschle was defeated in 2004 and replaced as Democratic leader by Nevada senator Harry Reid, a three-term moderate with a halting public manner but pugnacious instincts honed during a hardscrabble upbringing and a brief career decades earlier as an amateur boxer.

Under both Daschle and Reid Senate Democrats emulated the Republican minority during Clinton's first two years by consistently filibustering Bush proposals they opposed; but Democrats broke new ground by routinely using the filibuster against Bush's most controversial nominations to the federal appeals courts. When the Republican majority moved to ban the filibuster against judicial nominees, Reid threatened to block all but essential Senate business in retaliation. (The standoff ended when an agreement between a bipartisan "Gang of 14" senators in 2005 preserved the right to filibuster but limited its use against judicial nominees to "extraordinary circumstances.") Both Daschle and Reid strained Senate precedent by refusing to appoint conferees to House-Senate conferences until the Republican leader, Bill Frist, committed to name senators who would defend the Senate version of legislation. (At one point, when Frist said there was no precedent in Senate history for such a preemptive commitment, Reid fired back that there was also no precedent for the routine exclusion of some or all Democrats from the discussions in conference, as Republicans had done on issues such as energy and Medicare.) In 2005, Reid stunned Frist by utilizing a rarely applied Senate rule to force the chamber into a closed session to pressure the majority to complete a long-delayed investigation of Bush's use of prewar intelligence on Iraq. It was a telling measure of the inexorable cycle of escalation that Daschle had also considered the maneuver but decided not to act without agreement from Frist. The first time Frist knew of Reid's move was when the Democrat announced it on the Senate floor. The "notion of one party springing the rule on the other party without warning was so alien," the *Washington Post* noted a few days later, "that senators could not cite a previous example."

House rules did not provide the minority as many opportunities for guerilla warfare. As a result, House Democrats focused on sharpening the contrast with the GOP by maximizing their opposition to its agenda. That required Democratic leaders to apply some of the same tools Republicans had used to maintain order in their ranks since winning the majority in 1994.

House Democrats, aiming to instill more party discipline, had taken the first critical steps in the 1970s to end the reliance on seniority in naming committee chairs. But over the next quarter century that impulse had slackened. After the 1970s, House Democrats only rarely bypassed seniority in naming chairs, and allowed the chairs, once named, to exercise enormous independent authority over the party agenda. Over the same years Democrats likewise made only little progress at imposing more discipline on the rank and file. Vic Fazio, a California representative who rose to chair the House Democratic caucus before leaving Congress after 1998 to become a lobbyist, remembered that "Democrats got into a rut over the many, many years we were in the majority of letting people vote their districts," even if that meant opposing the majority party position. "We had a whip operation," Fazio continued, "but there was never a great deal of focus on the sanctions that would be required to implement the strategy. [The leaders] would plead with people, and people figured, I can still do whatever I want and my status here won't change very much."

As the great sorting out in the electorate reduced the number of conservative Democrats elected to Congress, party loyalty among House

Democrats increased over time. But it still lagged the Republican level, and during Bill Clinton's presidency he faced frustrating, and at times crippling, defections from large numbers of House Democrats on issues from trade to welfare reform to education. No one would confuse the contentious, and sometimes chaotic, relationship between Clinton and House Democrats with the virtually military line of command between the Bush White House and House Republicans.

During Bush's first two years the overall Democratic unity ratings continued to run at high levels. But Democrats still suffered enough defections on enough issues to create demands among liberal interest groups, Internet activists, and even some Democratic legislators for more discipline. That sort of stern hand had never been the style of Dick Gephardt, the persistent St. Louis–area representative who served as the House minority leader from the Republican takeover in 1994 through Bush's first two years. Gephardt's approach was always more to cajole than to threaten; he would engage in tireless negotiation to build party consensus, but he almost never sought to punish Democrats who dissented from it. "Gephardt was very much a pleader, not a demander," said Fazio. "He was very much interested in retaining friendship and goodwill among his colleagues."

The opportunity for a different approach emerged when Gephardt stepped down as minority leader after the 2002 election to run for president. To succeed him Democrats elected Nancy Pelosi, a San Francisco representative with a society page style but roots in the rough and tumble of local Maryland politics. (Both her father and brother had served as Baltimore's mayor.) Pelosi was a conventional liberal Democrat in her views on issues, but she had taken notes during the long years of Republican control. And while she invariably opposed the Republican ends, she absorbed lessons from some of their means, particularly the effort to provide their leaders more leverage to set a unified party course. "Gingrich's whole philosophy was, . . . we have to have a centralized [direction]," said Representative Steny Hoyer, a centrist Maryland Democrat who became majority leader when Democrats regained control of the House in 2006. "I think we've learned from that. I frankly think there was a lot of merit in having a greater unity. Nancy Pelosi believes in that; I believe in that."

Pelosi moved down several paths at once to strengthen her grip and sharpen the Democrats into a more confrontational opposition party. She discouraged Democrats from cosponsoring bills with Republicans, who might later use the Democratic support to tout their commitment to bipartisanship during their reelection campaigns. (To make her point, in one private caucus meeting she told the assembled Democrats, "They don't love you for your mind, they love you for your body.") In the same way, she discouraged the ranking Democrats from negotiating with Republicans on legislation moving through their committees. This was an updated version of the Republican debate twenty years earlier between Gingrich and Bob Michel. Pelosi took the same side as Gingrich: She argued that a minority's goal should not be to tweak the other party's legislation but to develop a clear record of contrast that could be used to unseat the majority in the next election. At times Pelosi directly overruled ranking Democratic members in a manner difficult to imagine from Gephardt. She refused to allow Democrats on the Government Reform Committee to formally participate in the committee's investigation of the administration response to Hurricane Katrina (a decision that embarrassed her when Tom Davis, the committee chairman, produced a surprisingly serious inquiry). In spring 2006, with Republicans raising the specter of impeachment proceedings against Bush as a means of motivating their base to vote in the midterm election, Pelosi went over the head of Representative John Conyers, the ranking Democrat on the Judiciary Committee, to publicly renounce the option.

Just as Gingrich had done, Pelosi also moved to gain more leverage over members by increasing her control over committee assignments. Pelosi pushed through rules changes that increased the leadership's authority to name ranking members on all committees and all members on the most exclusive committees. Members who strayed too often from the party consensus faced tougher questions about their assignments. Colin Peterson of Minnesota was only allowed to retain his ranking member status on the Agriculture Committee after a stormy interview in which he was forced to defend his frequent votes against the dominant party position and his failure to pay dues to the party's campaign committee. When Florida representative Allen Boyd, the sole House Democrat to support private investment accounts under Social Security, flirted with endorsing Bush's proposal, leadership aides anonymously raised the prospect that he might be stripped of his coveted seat on the Appropriations Committee.

Pelosi ultimately didn't remove either from their seats. And when Democrats regained a majority in 2006 the caucus allowed the most senior members of all the permanent committees to assume the chairmanships. But if Pelosi could not match the Republicans in imposing centralized control over the House, she still pushed the Democrats much further in that direction. Over the objection of many senior Democrats she maintained the six-year term limits on committee chairs that provided the Republican leadership more leverage over its members. And early in 2007 she spoke volumes about her intention to set a more united course by forming a special committee to highlight climate change issues after Representative John Dingell of Michigan, the venerable defender of the auto industry and prototypical old bull chairing the House Energy and Commerce Committee, signaled his intention to delay action.

The Democratic congressional leaders demonstrated their determination to learn from Republican tactics perhaps most vividly during the struggle with Bush over restructuring Social Security in 2005. Bipartisan agreement on this front always was unlikely, because Bush, as we've seen, centered his proposal on an idea anathema to most Democrats, private investment accounts funded through the Social Security payroll tax. And all of the factors that we explored in Chapter 8—particularly Bush's inability to build broad public support—also diminished his ability to attract Democratic backing.

But the monolithic congressional Democratic opposition to Bush also reflected the solidifying tendency of Democrats to view opposition as their highest priority. When Bush announced his determination to reshape Social Security immediately after the 2004 election Democrats were at a low ebb, still reeling from his reelection and the Republican gains in the House and Senate. "I can't overstate how overwhelmed we felt in November of 2004," said Susan McCue, the hard-nosed chief of staff at the time for Reid, who became the Democratic leader that month when Tom Daschle lost his bid for reelection in the Republican sweep. Battered congressional Democrats initially feared Bush's drive to restructure Social Security would shatter the party. Instead the fight allowed Democrats to regain their balance and begin their recovery from 2004.

Reid and Pelosi, meeting every Tuesday afternoon at 5:00 P.M., quickly reached two interlocked conclusions. The first was that Democrats would oppose Bush's plan to fund private accounts from the Social Security payroll tax. The second was that they would not offer any alternative, or even negotiate with Bush, until he renounced that idea. Both of these positions presented Democrats with risk, but the second generated the most unease in the party. An array of prominent party consultants argued to the congressional leaders that Bush could portray the Democrats as obstructionists if they failed to offer an alternative.

But Pelosi and Reid never wavered in their belief that the key to success was to maintain the focus solely on Bush's plan by denying him Democratic alternatives to compare it against. Once Democrats offered competing plans, they reasoned, the debate would shift from a binary choice—whether or not to accept Bush's solution—to a much more ambiguous debate over which portions of which plan might contribute to a solution; the question would become not whether to restructure Social Security but how. Despite intermittent misgivings, the Democratic rank and file in both chambers accepted those arguments. None endorsed Bush's plan, and only two House members ever introduced their own.

External pressures helped the Democratic leaders impose internal discipline behind their strategy. MoveOn.org sent one message when it ran television ads opposing Bush's plan in the Florida district of Allen Boyd, the sole House Democrat who had endorsed private accounts. Talking Points Memo, a thoughtful blog maintained by liberal journalist Joshua Micah Marshall, maintained another form of pressure by rigorously tracking the comments of congressional Democrats who indicated even a hint of sympathy for private accounts, a group Marshall devastatingly labeled "the Fainthearted Faction." Pariser and other activists raised the prospect of organizing primary challenges against any Democrat who endorsed Bush's proposal, with Connecticut's Joe Lieberman emerging as an early focus of the threats until he signed the 2005 Senate Democratic letter opposing the president's plan.*

---

* "Lieberman was the hardest to get," said one Democrat involved in organizing the letter. "We were literally running to get the letter out the door before Lieberman could change his mind."

Americans United to Protect Social Security, a nationwide coalition formed as a counterweight to the business groups backing Bush's proposal, proved the most important external force in the debate for Democrats. The emergence of Americans United showed Democrats adapting another component of the Republican legislative machine. Much the way Republicans brought business groups into tightened harness, Americans United operated almost as an extension of the Democratic congressional leadership. Funded primarily by organized labor, and founded around the time of Bush's 2005 State of the Union with the encouragement of Reid and Pelosi, the group worked to build grassroots opposition to Bush's plan across the country. Americans United aimed its efforts at discouraging Republicans from endorsing Bush's proposal, and never directly sought to pressure Democratic legislators. But many of its activities sent Democrats a clear warning of the trouble they could expect if they supported Bush. The group, for instance, hired organizers in several states—including Nebraska, Montana, Louisiana, and North Dakota—with Democratic senators at the top of Bush's target list. In each case the ostensible objective for the group's efforts was local Republicans, but by stirring sentiment in the state against Bush's plan the organizers also created an environment in which Democrats felt safer opposing Bush, and saw greater risk in supporting him. "If we needed to pounce on Democrats," said Brad Woodhouse, the group's communications director, "we would have pounced."

Even with all of this activity swirling outside of Congress, the Democrats still might have splintered over Social Security without the tenacious interventions of their leaders. Pelosi in some respects had the easier task. The rough treatment the Republican majority regularly dealt to the minority encouraged Democrats to stick together in defense; the party's internal rules also gave her more leverage to pressure Democrats through committee assignments. Those tools did not appeal to Reid. Senate Democratic rules, of course, also allowed the caucus to bypass seniority in naming ranking committee members (or chairmen when they were in the majority). But Daschle had never used that weapon and Reid was even less inclined to. Reid venerated seniority as a source of "stability" in Congress, and rejected the notion of using chairmanships as a means of compelling loyalty, much less emulating the Republicans in imposing term limits on chairmen as a method of tightening central control.

That left Reid, like most Senate leaders before him, relying much more on persuasion than coercion. His style on Social Security was informal, insinuating. He would approach Democrats one by one during a slow moment on the Senate floor, or invite them to his office for a quiet chat. His message was that only through unity could the party exert influence in the debate. "I'm not a real cheerleader," Reid said later. "I'm not given to flamboyant speeches, 'give one for the Gipper' and all that kind of stuff. But I've tried to create the reality that we are a team, and if we are going to be able to do some of the things we want to do on a policy basis, we have to stick together."

The breakthrough came early on, when Reid met with Montana senator Max Baucus, the ranking Democrat on the Finance Committee. Baucus had angered other Democrats, especially Daschle, by straying from the caucus to negotiate with Republicans during Bush's first term on taxes and other issues. Reid stressed his desire to let Baucus, as the top Democrat on the committee with jurisdiction over Social Security, take the lead in shaping the party response, and in the process, he nudged Baucus toward the only position—opposition to Bush—that would allow him to play that role in a caucus predisposed against the president's plan. With Baucus brought into line, Bush's prospects of encouraging significant Democratic defections virtually evaporated.

The success of Reid and Pelosi at discouraging Democrats from supporting or even negotiating with Bush on Social Security offered more evidence of their progress at developing the mind-set of an opposition. The price was another log on the fire of partisan confrontation in Washington. By blocking Bush's Social Security plan, Democrats had strengthened their political position and weakened the president's. But they had not brought the country any closer to a consensus on how to handle the genuine challenge of meeting the long-term costs of an aging society.

Most Democrats argued that it made no sense even to begin negotiations with Bush over Social Security, since the two sides started with such contrasting visions of the program. But by the same logic Republican legislators never would have incentive to negotiate with a future Democratic president over restructuring the system. And if the fall of Bush's plan had demonstrated anything it was that Social Security was too big to tackle on a party-line basis. If the parties could not reform Social Security alone, and distrusted each other too much to do it together, the problem never would be addressed short of divine intervention. To make progress on Social Security, the party out of the White House eventually needed to accept the risk of negotiating with a president whose motives it did not entirely trust. Yet the Democratic refusal to negotiate with Bush while he promoted private accounts seemed certain to provide precedent for congressional Republicans to reject negotiations with a future Democratic president committed, for instance, to raising taxes as part of a Social Security solution. Like so many of Bush's legislative victories, the Democratic success on Social Security demonstrated how a legislative strategy focused on party unity could benefit a party in the near term, and even produce a defensible policy decision, but still deepen the cycle of polarization that damaged the country over time.

THE NEW DEMOCRATS AND THE NEW NEW DEMOCRATS

As Democrats sharpened their spears, one group of party leaders fell out of step with the new direction. The Democratic Leadership Council, the organization of centrist Democrats formed after Walter Mondale's landslide defeat in 1984, had been the party's dominant faction in the 1990s. It had served as a principal source of Bill Clinton's New Democrat agenda and the tireless promoters, even after Clinton left office, of his third-way strategy of bridging partisan and ideological differences. But under Bush the DLC allowed itself to become isolated in the party.

During the Bush years the New Democrats of the 1990s faced a prolonged and unforgiving siege from what amounted to a younger generation of New New Democrats who argued that Bush's challenge had rendered the Clinton-era strategies obsolete. The DLC endured endless denunciations from Kos and other left-leaning bloggers. But it also generated complaints from more sympathetic (and temperate) sources. Susan McCue, Reid's chief of staff through January 2007, came to view the DLC as irrelevant, if not counterproductive. "I just remember in my meetings with them that there was such a disconnection between them and reality," she said. "I just felt like the DLC was a bunch of inside-the-beltway thinkers that hadn't really been in the trenches for a long time, and had lost their political edge." Even more strikingly, Simon Rosenberg, a young Democratic operative who in 1996 had founded the political action committee associated with the DLC, distanced himself from the group. "The third way has become an antiquated way of looking at the world," Rosenberg said, "because in essence the third way . . . was predicated on an assumption that Democrats were still running the country and the compromises were done from a position of strength rather than a position of being ideologically rolled by the other side." To underscore his conversion, Rosenberg quietly changed his group's name from the New Democrat Network to the opaque NDN, and drafted as consultants DLC critics like Moulitsas and Joe Trippi, Dean's campaign manager.

The DLC never counseled collaboration with Bush and the GOP majority as much as its opponents alleged. In its New Dem Daily, an online publication in which the DLC explained its views, the group questioned Bush's commitment to bipartisan cooperation from the outset. At several points it argued that Bush "has tried to achieve the maximum feasible change in the image of the Republican Party through the minimum necessary change in its ideology and agenda." Within Bush's first eight months in office the DLC opposed his tax cut, criticized his retreat on global warming, condemned his production-first energy policy, and denounced his restrictions on funding for stem cell research.

But especially in the first years of his presidency, the DLC did not completely rule out cooperation with Bush, and at several points explicitly counseled against abandoning it. On domestic policy the DLC found few opportunities to translate that theory into practice, apart from exhorting Democrats to work with Bush on education reform in 2001. Even when the DLC encouraged Democrats to move in the same broad philosophical direction as Bush—for example, relying on tax credits rather than government programs to expand access to health care—the specifics of Bush's proposals usually left it cold.

It was on foreign and defense policy where the DLC diverged more decisively from the Democratic mainstream. Its message, shaped by the Republican success at painting Democrats as weak on national security in the 1970s and 1980s, insisted that Democrats had to demonstrate their toughness and willingness to use military force. Beneath that umbrella the DLC unreservedly endorsed Bush's decision to invade Iraq. Many leading Democrats, of course, supported Bush when he sought the authority for war in October 2002. But the DLC actively promoted an invasion of Iraq months *before* Bush even floated the possibility. In an essay only five weeks after the September 11 terrorist attacks, the group's New Dem Daily endorsed a prowar speech from Joe Lieberman to Rosenberg's group. Lieberman declared that the United States must be "unflinching in our determination to remove Saddam Hussein from power" with or without support from allies. "[I]f it becomes necessary, as we hope it will not," Lieberman said, "we will benefit from a dose of this administration's previous preference for unilateralism."

As war approached, the DLC marched with Bush step for step into battle. It endorsed the congressional resolution authorizing him to use force against Iraq, and directly echoed Bush's catch-22 argument that the United Nations would demonstrate its irrelevance if it did not support an invasion. When the war came the DLC confidently insisted "there can be no real doubt that the world and the Middle East will be safer, more peaceful and stable without Saddam Hussein."

The group grew more critical of Bush in one significant respect: While in 2001 it urged him to act unilaterally against Iraq, over the next several years it joined other Democrats in accusing Bush of "contempt for allies" and isolating America with his "unilateralist diplomacy." But the group never slackened in its support for the Iraq war. It urged congressional Democrats to back the administration's landmark 2003 request for $87 billion to fund the war (while MoveOn insisted Congress should only provide the money if Bush fired Rumsfeld). As antiwar activists and some Democrats pressed Bush to set a timeline for withdrawing American troops, the DLC denounced the idea. It even mimicked Bush in disparaging such proposals as a policy of "cut-and-run."

The use of such provocative language fit in a long-standing DLC strategy. Al From, the DLC's founder and still its chief executive officer, believed Democrats had to show swing voters who they were in large part by demonstrating who they were not. That meant criticizing other, more liberal elements of the Democratic coalition. In the 1980s and early 1990s the DLC provoked repeated confrontations with Jesse Jackson, then the leading figure in the Democratic left. Under Bush the DLC launched offensives against the new generation of activists, particularly on national security and the war in Iraq. The group urged the party to ostracize prominent liberal voices like filmmaker Michael Moore and MoveOn.org. From and Bruce Reed, who had rejoined the DLC as president after serving as Bill Clinton's chief domestic policy adviser, declared that Democrats could regain the country's trust on national security only by "clearly rejecting our anti-war wing."

More than anything else, this tendency to criticize other Democrats generated the hostility to the DLC from the New New Democrats. Dozens of bloggers argued that it made no sense for Democrats to attack each other while Republicans were waging war against the party so forcefully. To the bloggers it was as if the Democrats were in the siege of Stalingrad and Al From wanted to purge the Trotskyites from the barricades.

This simmering conflict exploded when From and Reed targeted Howard Dean's presidential campaign in a May 15, 2003, memo. Dean was hardly an innocent bystander in this confrontation: His insistence that he represented the "Democratic wing of the Democratic Party" was a barely coded attempt to present the DLC and Bill Clinton as the party's "Republican wing" (later Dean became more explicit in his denunciations of Clinton's direction). From and Reed fired back with both barrels: "What activists like Dean call the Democratic wing of the Democratic Party is an aberration: the McGovern-Mondale wing, defined principally by weakness abroad and elitist, interest-group liberalism at home. That's the wing that lost 49 states in two elections, and transformed Democrats from a strong national party into a much weaker regional one."

The From-Reed salvo was nothing different from the missiles the DLC had aimed at prominent liberals for nearly two decades. But amid the ongoing struggle with Bush and the Republican Congress, the attack generated a much more hostile response not only from liberals but from less ideological party leaders like Terry McAuliffe, the Clinton-appointed chairman of the Democratic National Committee, and even from Simon Rosenberg, who underscored his displeasure by inviting Dean to speak before his group.

The backlash against the DLC attack on Dean showed how thoroughly the martial perspective of the Internet resistance had permeated the party. Quarreling, squabbling, and disagreeing, the activists sprouting across the Internet did not speak with anything approaching one voice. But the central figures in the movement—the leaders of MoveOn, Kos, MyDD, and others—largely coalesced around an edgy alternative to the DLC perspective. Shaped primarily by the experience of combat with a rising Republican coalition and the fear of lasting political subjugation, the New New Democrats formulated a political vision that, like Karl Rove's, sought to profit from polarization, not reverse it. The New New Democrats were like orphans reared in a war zone: resourceful, feral, unsentimental. Their worldview carried the mark of Bush's challenge as clearly as the imprint of a fist on a face.

To the DLC, the New New Democrats were nothing more than old Democrats with new technology—"McGovernites with modems," as Marshall Wittmann, a tart-tongued political analyst at the Progressive Policy Institute, labeled them. That certainly described aspects of the Internet resistance, particularly in its views on foreign policy. Even on domestic issues, the course that the most prominent voices in the movement urged—particularly populist attacks on big business and opposition to free trade—often embraced long-standing goals of the left.

But the movement was more than a re-creation of the 1960s left. Leaders like Moulitsas argued passionately that this uprising was more partisan than ideological. And, in fact, many of the movement's favorite Democrats (Harry Reid, who opposed legal abortion, or Brian Schweitzer, the pro-gun governor of Montana) hardly qualified as conventional liberals. Simon Rosenberg, a shrewd and sympathetic observer, captured the delicate balance of the new movement when he said it inverted the priorities of the 1960s left, which prized ideology and disdained partisan politics. "It's not that [the new movement] is not leaning left; but it's not defined by ideology," he said. "They want to win. They want to win first. . . . What they want more than anything else is [for] people to not accept the inevitable decline of the Democratic Party."

The foundation belief of the New New Democrats was that Republicans had changed the rules of political life, and that Democrats could recover only by reconstituting themselves as a more disciplined and ferocious opposition party. While the DLC considered it dangerous for Democrats and bad for the country to flatly reject compromise with Bush, the New New Democrats maintained that the Republican Party had become too radical to work with. They viewed the modern GOP as something like James Cameron's murderous Terminator: a machine that could not be reasoned or negotiated with, only fought to the death. Indeed, they almost always saw compromise as counterproductive, an invitation for more attacks from the GOP. "Every Democrat who has provided the administration with 'political cover' has been targetted [sic] for political assassination, like [Senators] Jean Carnahan and Max Cleland," Kos wrote early in Bush's second term. "Rove sees compromise as weakness—a sign that the compromising Democrat faces domestic pressures to play nice with the president."

The New New Democrats tried to construct a system of rewards and punishments to steer congressional Democrats toward a harder line on Bush. Any move to confront Republicans was instantly rewarded with torrents of praise on liberal blogs. Almost all gestures toward collaboration with Bush provoked corresponding condemnation and outrage. MoveOn applied the same logic, with more tangible consequences than the bloggers. When the venerable West Virginia senator Robert Byrd helped lead the fight against the Republican efforts to ban the filibuster on judicial nominations in early 2005, the group's PAC raised a breathtaking eight hundred thousand dollars for him from its members in just three days. But MoveOn did not shy away from threatening Democrats, as it did with the Social Security ads that targeted Allen Boyd. MoveOn turned even more heads when it aired an ad in Steny Hoyer's district criticizing him for supporting the Bush-backed bankruptcy legislation in 2005.

Bipartisanship might be possible again some day, the New New Democrats argued, but only if Democrats first stopped the Republican drive for one-party rule; peace would come only after heightened war. Repeatedly they insisted that the Republican rightward turn after 1994 had invalidated Bill Clinton's vision of seeking a middle ground between the parties. At MoveOn, Eli Pariser was often blunt in his insistence that Bush's challenge had rendered Clinton's approach obsolete. "It may be in the 1990s, there was a middle; there isn't a middle now," Pariser said. "You have a Republican Party that is willing to break all the rules and accept no compromises to get what they want. In the face of that, saying, 'I'll meet you halfway' is as sure a recipe for disaster as I know. You have to fight fire with fire."

The New New Democrats rejected as well Clinton's electoral strategy, with its focus on converting swing voters. "Clinton's third way failed miserably," Moulitsas wrote. "It killed off the Jesse Jackson wing of the Democratic Party and, despite its undivided control of the party apparatus, delivered nothing. Nothing, that is, except the loss of Congress, the perpetuation of the muddled Democratic 'message,' a demoralized and moribund party base, and electoral defeats in 2000, 2002 and 2004." To the New New Democrats, Kerry's inability to defeat Bush in 2004 even though the Democrat won both independent and moderate voters proved that Clinton's formula no longer worked amid the polarized passions of the Bush years. "We won the center and it wasn't enough," Moulitsas said. "So, clearly, we have to reach out more to our base."

Starting with that conviction, much of the movement maintained that Democrats could learn more from Bush's strategy than Clinton's. Bush succeeded by unapologetically advancing an agenda aimed at his core supporters; Democrats, they reasoned, could do the same. "Competing against a Republican Party of bold reforms, Democrats have been offering a status quo alternative," one writer insisted on the popular liberal Web site The Raw Story. "The truth is that Democrats need their own George Bush." To MoveOn's Eli Pariser the key lesson of the Bush years was that the "passion" of hard-core followers was "the most powerful political asset around . . . more than money, more than message."

To the DLC, replicating Bush's strategy was a formula for Democratic disaster. That belief underpinned their analysis throughout the Bush years. The DLC leaders rejected the argument that Democrats could prosper by

constructing a mirror image of Bush's political strategy focused on spur-
ring turnout on the left. Polarization, they noted, had barely brought Bush
to a majority in 2004; how, they asked, could it work for Democrats when
there were three conservatives in the electorate for every two liberals? The
DLC leaders remained convinced that the party could recover only behind
a Clinton-like strategy focused on attracting swing voters through centrist
positions that often challenged traditional Democratic constituencies.
"Had the party's last two nominees truly followed Clinton's model," From
wrote a few weeks after Kerry's defeat in 2004, ". . . we might now be talking about an emerging Democratic majority."

Mostly the generational dispute between the New Democrats and the
New New Democrats played out in a war of words. But it became a shooting war in a series of major primary challenges to congressional Democrats
that rocked the party in 2006. These primaries presented another example
of Democrats adopting the tactics of Republicans, particularly the conservative Club for Growth, which had used primaries against congressional
moderates as the ultimate weapon to enforce greater party discipline. Liberals, as on so many other fronts under Bush, sought to apply conservative
means to stiffen Democratic opposition to conservative ends.

Each of the major 2006 Democratic primaries unfolded along a common track, with a liberal challenger, buoyed by enthusiastic support from
the Internet activists, accusing a moderate to conservative incumbent of
collaborating too often with Bush. That dynamic played out in aggressive
challenges to three Democratic House members: Henry Cuellar in Texas
(a frequent Bush supporter), Jane Harman of California (whom critics accused of failing to question Bush's case for war aggressively enough from
her position on the Intelligence Committee), and Albert Wynn of Maryland (one of the most centrist members of the Congressional Black
Caucus). All three survived, but only after difficult campaigns that demonstrated the growing grassroots pressure for tougher opposition to Bush.
Much like the Club for Growth in its initial challenges against Republican
moderates, the Democrats promoting challenges believed they had sent an
effective message even without recording a victory.

For both sides in this internal tussle, the main event in 2006 was the
primary challenge to Connecticut senator Joe Lieberman, the Democrats'

vice presidential nominee only six years earlier. Left-leaning Web sites, like the Daily Kos, and liberal activists in Connecticut began to buzz about the possibility of challenging Lieberman in early 2005, when he initially hinted he might cooperate with Bush on restructuring Social Security. Lieberman dampened that fire when he signed the Democratic letter opposing Bush's plan, but reignited it that December with a speech in which he insisted, "It is time for Democrats who distrust President Bush to acknowledge . . . that in matters of war we undermine Presidential credibility at our nation's peril."

Lieberman's comments amounted to a stick in his own party's eye, and they outraged many Democrats. Among them was Ned Lamont, a wealthy cable television entrepreneur and great-grandson of Thomas W. Lamont, one of J. P. Morgan's most prominent partners. Ned Lamont initially encouraged Lowell P. Weicker, the moderate Republican senator whom Lieberman defeated in 1988, to run against him; when Weicker demurred, Lamont entered the race himself. Lamont joined the contest with no political experience other than some time as a selectman in Greenwich and an unsuccessful bid for a state Senate seat. But he proved a genial and ingratiating campaigner, with a vaguely Kennedy-esque upper-crust flair.

Lamont's campaign struck a chord with Internet activists across the country. Web sites like Kos and MyDD promoted it tirelessly, and Moulitsas even appeared in one of Lamont's ads. MoveOn endorsed Lamont in the primary (as it did the challengers to Cuellar and Wynn). The national Internet activists generated some valuable fund-raising help for Lamont (though with his personal fortune he didn't need much), and the incessant chatter about his campaign on the liberal blogs provided him some credibility, especially with the local media, at a time when virtually no prominent local or national Democrats had endorsed him. But Lamont's candidacy came to prove not so much the direct reach of the New New Democrats as the extent to which their assumptions had penetrated the party at the grassroots.

Many Connecticut Democrats that summer spoke about Lieberman in tones it's easy to imagine French villagers after D-Day using to describe the neighbors who consorted with the Germans. The full flavor of those emotions was on display when Lamont appeared for a late-afternoon rally at a beautiful clock museum in Bristol about a week before the primary. A succession of local Democrats, as they waited for Lamont in the elegant rooms, denounced Lieberman with language that might have been lifted verbatim from Daily Kos or MyDD. "It's not just that he voted for the war, it's that he supported the whole mind-set, and continues to support the mind-set, that justified that unjustifiable war," one woman said. "He enables Republicans to have this veneer of bipartisanship because he is their token Democrat," said another. "I want a senator who is out there challenging them, getting other senators to challenge them, rather than working with them on their crazy policies," insisted a third.

Lieberman, a former chairman of the DLC, and his allies at the organization watched Lamont's rising challenge with mounting horror. It was difficult to dispute the DLC on one point: The New New Democrats had long preached the importance of unity, but it was that wing of the party, not the centrists, widening the Democrats' internal fissures with the primary challenges (albeit in the name of punishing, and thus discouraging, disunity). Yet as the Connecticut campaign proceeded it became evident that Lieberman, like the DLC itself, vastly underestimated the desire among party activists for more forceful opposition to Bush, especially on the war. Lieberman's reputation for independence, once his greatest political asset, became a liability with many Connecticut Democrats, because they saw him as using it primarily to defend Bush against other Democrats. Even a late July endorsement visit from Bill Clinton, who wrapped his arms around Lieberman and testified to his Democratic credentials, could not reverse the tide. On August 8, Connecticut Democrats chose Lamont over Lieberman as their Senate nominee by a comfortable 52 percent to 48 percent.

Lieberman immediately declared his intention to seek reelection in November as an independent. But the leaders among the New New Democrats seemed to view that as little more than a doomed formality. Many of them confidently described Lieberman's defeat as repudiation not only of Bush's politics but also of Clinton's. Pariser, writing in the *Washington Post* two days after the primary, contended that Lamont's victory sounded the death knell for Clinton's policy of triangulation and seeking third-way compromises between the parties. "[T]he policy of seizing the political middle ground no longer makes sense in an era when any attempt at bipartisanship is understood as a sign of Democratic weakness and exploited accordingly," Pariser wrote. "With triangulation passing, a new era of bolder, principle-driven politics can begin."

THE PRECARIOUS BALANCE

Exactly three months after Lamont's victory, on the morning after the November 7 general election, it was the DLC's turn to gloat. Lieberman, capturing a majority of Connecticut independents, over two thirds of Republicans, and even one third of Democrats crushed Lamont to win reelection to a fourth Senate term as an "independent Democrat." The Progressive Policy Institute's Marshall Wittmann, in his Bull Moose blog, exuberantly dug a grave for the netroots activists, or what he called "the nutroots." "There is great joy in Mooseland," Wittmann wrote in a post entitled "KOSenfreude." "The nutroots have struck out. Joe Lieberman has prevailed. The vital center is victorious!"*

That verdict was as premature as the exultations of the Lamont supporters the previous summer. Neither end of the Lieberman saga lent itself to transcendent conclusions. In the primary he was unusually vulnerable because his interpretation of bipartisanship had led him to embrace Bush on the war (and criticize his own party) more effusively than any other Democrat. And in the general election Lieberman was unusually sheltered because the Connecticut Republican Party could not field a viable challenger in the three-way race; if the GOP had found a candidate who won more Republican votes than Alan Schlesinger, the party's hapless nominee, Lamont might have squeezed through to victory. Lieberman's recovery in the general election did not entirely blunt the sting of his defeat in the primary as a cautionary signal to other Democratic senators.

The mixed message of Lieberman's experience captured a larger truth about the Democrats as the Bush presidency wound down. In the GOP

---

* Wittmann was so enthused by the result that he joined Lieberman as his communications director after the election.

under Bush the forces that preached polarization clearly held the upper hand over those who counseled consensus. In the Democratic Party the two sides were more precariously balanced. Those who preferred a more confrontational Democratic Party had gained in strength since Clinton's presidency. But they were not nearly as powerful in the Democratic Party as the voices promoting the comparable strategy inside the GOP.

For the New New Democrats the Bush years were filled with signs of advance. MoveOn expanded its membership (which crossed three million by spring 2005) and the scale of its political operation. In 2006, it not only raised large sums but generated an extraordinary level of grassroots activity, building local organizations aimed at turning out intermittent Democratic voters in dozens of House and Senate races; in many races, the number of its contacts with voters exceeded the Democratic candidate's margin of victory. The readership of Kos and other leading liberal blogs reached impressive heights. Party centrists could point to no comparable inroads on the Internet. The flurry of institution-building that Democrats engaged in during the Bush years (much of it supported by a secretive group of millionaires known as the Democracy Alliance) also fortified the position of the New New Democrats. Almost without exception the new institutions—among them the press watchdog Media Matters for America, the Center for American Progress think tank, Rosenberg's New Politics Institute—came closer to the martial perspective of the new generation than the more nuanced analysis of the DLC.

The influence of the new activists, and the partisan forces that shaped them, was also evident in the Democratic challengers in the 2006 congressional election. Almost all of the 2006 Democrats ran as economic populists, fiercely critical of oil and drug companies and dubious of free trade. Lamont supporters could plausibly argue that although he fell short in November, his primary victory encouraged other Democratic candidates to toughen their opposition to Bush on the war.

But from other angles the 2006 campaign testified to the continuing strength of the original Clinton-era New Democrat vision. Most Democratic candidates stressed fiscal discipline, and almost all praised Bill Clinton's economic record; indeed Clinton himself was rivaled only by Illinois senator Barack Obama as a sought-after speaker for Democratic candidates. Most Democratic candidates, especially in red states and districts, followed Clinton's model in positioning themselves as cultural centrists. And dozens of Democrats (and for that matter many Republicans) ran directly against the partisan polarization in Washington, stressed their independence, and promised to serve as a bridge between the parties if elected.

Above all, the voting results illuminated electoral realities that supported the Clinton analysis and constrained Democrats from moving as far as the GOP toward a consciously polarizing political strategy. Although each side had grown more homogenous in the great sorting out, Democrats remained much more of a coalition party than Republicans. Liberals, as we saw in Chapter 6, constitute a smaller share of the Democratic base than conservatives do of the Republican base. That means Democrats rely more than Republicans on support from moderate voters, a relationship underscored in the 2006 election. As exit polls showed, it was overwhelming support from moderates and independents rather than increased turnout among liberals or Democrats that powered the 2006 Democratic victories. From their first days in power congressional Democrats operated with the awareness that the swing voters who had created their majority could revoke it if they veered too far out of the mainstream. With a more diverse political coalition than Republicans, Democrats could not pursue as narrow and concentrated a vision.

The geographic diversity of the Democratic coalition sent the same message. The Democratic success at widening the battlefield in 2006 left them operating with many more cross-pressured legislators than the GOP. After 2006, more than one in three Democratic senators (eighteen of fifty-one) came from red states that Bush had carried twice. Just five of the forty-nine Senate Republicans, only about one in ten, came from blue states that twice voted against Bush. In the House, Democrats operated with an even greater imbalance in the number of legislators from districts that had supported the other party in the previous presidential election (over one in four Democrats compared to about one in twenty-five Republicans). Like Jacob Javits or John Breaux in earlier generations, these were the legislators with the greatest inherent incentive to find compromise. And the vast majority of them were Democrats.

Other factors also discouraged Democrats from governing with as single-minded a focus on their base as the GOP. Business support for Democrats diminished after 1994, but the party still raised much more money from corporate interests than Republicans did from environmentalists, labor unions, or other groups that collided with industry. Congressional Democrats singled out a few politically unpopular industries—energy companies, pharmaceutical manufacturers—as targets in 2007, and remained cool toward free trade, but did not move nearly as far toward an encompassing anticorporate populism as many of the New New Democrats preferred. As a source of both campaign contributions and economic opportunity, business exerted inescapable influence on both parties, and limited the Democrats' willingness to bang the populist gong. So did the nature of the Democratic political coalition after the cultural re-sorting of the electorate. Democrats, as the 2006 election demonstrated again, now rely heavily on the votes of affluent, socially moderate suburbanites in places like Bergen County, New Jersey, Fairfax, Virginia, and Oakland County, Michigan, who do not feel particularly oppressed by the class system. These were voters likely to be unmoved, and potentially even repelled, by politicians trying to channel the spirit of William Jennings Bryan.

Buffeted by all of these contending forces, Democrats moved into the final Bush years with the advocates of consensus and confrontation still jostling for the steering wheel. Each side in the internal schism, through the first months of 2007, could point to encouraging trends. Key figures in the New New Democrat camp, such as Moulitsas and MoveOn, joined with labor unions in January 2007 to form a Democratic equivalent to the Club for Growth, a political action committee called Working for Us, dedicated to waging primary campaigns against moderate Democrats "who vote to undermine the progressive economic agenda." The New New Democrats also took heart when House Democrats displayed unity reminiscent of the GOP in 1995 to swiftly pass the leadership's "six in '06" agenda. But the centrists' continuing influence was evident in the substance of that agenda—a mostly bread-and-butter program designed to appeal broadly across the party—and was also reflected in the party's emphasis on fiscal discipline. The first stages of the 2008 presidential race displayed the same duality. Hostility toward Bush and the GOP majority among the Democrats' rank-and-file pressured all of the 2008 Democratic presidential contenders to promise bold changes and an aggressive attack on the Republican legacy (with former senator John Edwards, Kerry's 2004 vice presidential nominee, auditioning for the Howard Dean role as the most unforgiving critic). Yet the two leading candidates as the race began, Senators Hillary Rodham Clinton of New York and Barack Obama of Illinois, each promised to pursue national reconciliation and bipartisan compromise, Obama most emphatically. Only on one major dispute did the internal conflict produce an unambiguous winner. On Iraq the tug-of-war inside the party broke decisively toward the advocates of confrontation. Immediately after Democrats gained control of Congress, the New New Democrats mounted a campaign of pressure for aggressive action that quickly overwhelmed centrists, who initially sought to avoid (or at least delay) a direct confrontation with the commander in chief. Bush, as he did so often, strengthened the hands of the most confrontational Democrats by pursuing the policy (his "surge" in American forces) seemingly designed to most provoke the party. Operating with a surprising degree of both speed and unanimity, congressional Democrats moved quickly in 2007 to approve legislation pressuring Bush to begin ending the American role in the war. Bush vetoed their plan, and congressional Democrats, fearful of appearing to undercut the troops still in the field, blinked at using their ultimate weapon to deny funding for the war. But Democratic leaders, confident that the public had turned against both the war and the president, promised to maintain the pressure on Bush by advancing a succession of proposals to wind down America's involvement. As the confrontation persisted, more Democrats than seemed possible even in 2006 displayed no hesitation about a strategy of unrelenting (if not unconditional) warfare with the president over the war.

The overall standoff between the Democrats' two camps through early 2007 reflected not only their contrasting political strengths but the fact that each could claim validation on major issues facing the party. The New New Democrats had understood more quickly than the DLC that Bush's trajectory reduced the opportunity for bipartisan compromise and increased the importance of party unity. The new generation of Democratic activists, in their opposition to war, had also predicted the consequences of invading Iraq more accurately than the centrists—a record that even Al From acknowledged could weaken the hawkish wing of the party for years. But the DLC and its allies had been correct that the path to renewed power for Democrats ran directly through the center of the electorate. And the disintegration of Bush's partisan governing model in his second term suggested that the Democratic centrists were correct on an even larger point in their belief that Democrats could not drive significant progress on the country's major problems without building a legislative and public consensus that extended across party lines.

After the searing partisanship of the Bush years it seemed implausible for Democrats to simply resurrect the Clinton political formula, but the party's reliance on independent voters in 2006 showed it was equally implausible to accept the calls from so many of the New New Democrats for a liberal version of Bush's base-oriented strategy. The 2006 campaign and the early months of the party's congressional control suggested that some broad themes did unite Democrats as they emerged from the crucible of the Bush presidency. On domestic policy Democrats could expect near unanimity on policies (such as raising the minimum wage or increasing access to health care) organized around the principle of expanding opportunity for all Americans who accepted the responsibility of trying to better their lives—an idea captured in the Clintonite shorthand of rewarding people "who work hard and play by the rules." On foreign policy almost all Democrats wanted to restore greater international consent for American leadership by working harder to find common cause with traditional allies alienated during the Bush years. Yet the differences in the party—on policy, message, and political strategy—remained stubborn too. The political challenge for Democrats was to harness the energy and commitment of the new activists without abandoning the impulses toward inclusion, innovation, and consensus that were the most valuable contributions of the Clinton era. Neither side in the Democrats' internecine argument seemed capable of looking far enough beyond their disagreements to forge such a synthesis; if Democrats could develop one at all, it would probably come only through the efforts of the next Democratic president. Polls through mid-2008 consistently demonstrated that the collapse of Bush's polarizing approach provided Democrats their best opportunity since the missteps of Bill Clinton's first two years to strengthen their connection to independent and swing voters, and to rebuild a majority electoral coalition over the Republicans in 2008 and beyond. But if Democrats could not find an agenda and a tone that not only excited their base but also addressed the concerns of those beyond it, they were no more likely to build a lasting political majority than Bush.

Even with new technologies, new ways of communicating, and new alignments in the electorate, the secret of political success did not look much different in the early twenty-first century than it has at any point since at least the age of partisan armies: The party that seeks to encompass and harmonize the widest range of interests and perspectives is the one most likely to thrive. The overriding lesson for both parties from the Bush attempt to profit from polarization is that there remains no way to achieve lasting political power in a nation as diverse as America without assembling a broad coalition that locks arms to produce meaningful progress against the country's problems. The reforms and strategies that might allow a future president from either party to build such a coalition and achieve such progress are the final subjects we explore.

CHAPTER 10

★

BEYOND DIVISION

Nearly sixty years after it issued its exhaustive final report, the American Political Science Association's Committee on Political Parties has been forgotten almost entirely, even among political scientists. Yet in many respects, we live in the political world the committee imagined.

The committee joined students of politics (from such big-name universities as Harvard and Stanford) with practitioners (from institutions such as the State Department, the Council of Economic Advisers, and the Brookings Institution, then one of the nation's first think tanks). It deliberated for nearly four years. And then as we saw in Chapter 3, it published a lengthy report on the state of American politics in September 1950.

The report portrayed an American political system disabled by drift. To the committee the greatest flaw in American politics was too much dissension within the parties and too little distance between them. Because the parties were each so divided between liberal, moderate, and conservative branches, the committee concluded, they could not unify their members behind an effective program for governing the nation. Nor could presidents consistently pass the proposals they promised to the country. The committee wanted unified, mobilized parties that presented unambiguous agendas to the public, and then forcefully pressured their members, from the statehouse to the White House, to support them. "In an era beset with problems of unprecedented magnitude at home and abroad," the committee insisted, "it is dangerous to drift without a party system that helps the nation to set a general course of policy for the government as a whole."

The committee offered a long list of proposals to impose more direction on the parties. It proposed to overthrow the tradition of seniority on Capitol Hill, instead providing party leaders greater authority to deny chairmanships and seats on coveted committees to legislators who consistently voted against the dominant party position on key issues. It urged a one-person, one-vote rule for drawing congressional districts (more than a decade before the Supreme Court finally established the standard). And to increase the national parties' leverage to demand a common course, it proposed to shift to them more control over financing federal campaigns. In the words of the report's title, the committee maintained that all of these changes would lead America "Toward a More Responsible Two-Party System."

The committee's direct impact was modest. All of the proposals listed above proved prescient. But the committee could hardly claim credit when the parties, the courts, and Congress finally implemented those ideas long after it filed its report. Most of the group's signature recommendations, such as establishing elaborate advisory councils to define each party's agenda, were flatly ignored.

And yet, American politics evolved precisely along the lines the Committee on Political Parties promoted and championed. The committee was wrong about the mechanism of change: The parties didn't establish vast new central bureaucracies to coordinate and control their agendas. But it was right about the direction of change. Compared to the committee's day the political parties now are more unified and disciplined. On almost every major issue, the distance between the two parties has widened, even as dissent within the parties has diminished. With the two sides colliding so forcefully on so many issues, few Americans any longer share the committee's fear that "alternatives between the parties are defined so badly" that voters could not recognize meaningful differences between them. Likewise, hardly anyone still worries about too much overlap between the parties in Washington. In all these ways, and more, the practice of American politics has followed the direction that the committee urged.

To which the most appropriate response might be: Beware of what you wish for.

In some ways, as we've seen, the sharpening of the differences between the parties over the past half century has invigorated the political system, exactly as the committee had hoped. The parties now offer the country clearly contrasting directions and bright-line choices. The clash of those contending visions has increased public participation in politics and generated higher turnout on Election Day, good things in any democracy. A much broader diversity of voices and organized constituencies influence national policy today than when the committee filed its report, which is also, on balance, a good thing.

But the emergence of a more adversarial and sharply delineated political system has come with consequences the APSA committee never anticipated. Our modern system of hyperpartisanship has unnecessarily inflamed our differences and impeded progress against our most pressing challenges. We are divided over every major decision we face at home and abroad. In Washington the political debate too often careens between dysfunctional poles: either polarization, when one party imposes its will over the bitter resistance of the other, or immobilization, when the parties fight to stalemate. Either result is a recipe for alienation in large parts of the public. Our political system has virtually lost its capacity to formulate the principled compromises indispensable for progress in any diverse society. By any measure, the costs of hyperpartisanship vastly exceed the benefits.

Why did the Committee on Political Parties' map lead to a destination so different from the one it envisioned? The committee was a creature of its time, the age of bargaining. That era was defined, above all, by panoramic ideological diversity within both parties—the jumble that collected Richard Russell and Hubert Humphrey on one side of the aisle and Robert Taft and George Aiken on the other. The committee's greatest concern was that the parties would be paralyzed by such divergent views, and it aimed its recommendations at creating mechanisms of central control strong enough to force internal agreement.

But the committee did not envision a world in which almost all liberals would congregate in one party and almost all conservatives in the other. It could not, in other words, imagine the great sorting out of the electorate and the changes it triggered in the office-holders each side sent to Washington. By aligning partisanship and ideology, the great sorting out solved the problem that concerned the APSA committee: excessive division within the parties. But the re-sorting of the parties—and all the other forces we have explored in this book—replaced that problem with a different and greater one: excessive division between the parties. In fact, once the parties re-sorted ideologically, many of the changes sought by the committee and other midcentury reformers (like the elimination of seniority on Capitol Hill) actually widened their divisions by allowing the dominant ideological faction on each side to more effectively suppress dissenting views.

We can still find inspiration in the APSA committee's goal of a "responsible party system" that provides focused and purposeful direction to government. But we need a different compass to reach it. Our problem isn't too little partisan discipline but too much partisan rigidity. The committee sought ways to coax any forward motion from two fractured but fundamentally middle-of-the road parties. Now the challenge is to slow the race away from common ground by two parties drawn to the extremes. That will require a new generation of responses tailored to the age of hyperpartisanship.

THE MEDIA MOVES BACK TO THE FUTURE

Before we consider those possible remedies for hyperpartisanship, we need to assess one other powerful pressure for division that the political scientists' committee did not anticipate. Over the past two decades significant elements in the mass media have reverted to the partisan models that defined the American press from the nation's founding through the nineteenth century and into the early years of the twentieth, when newspapers and magazines unambiguously sought to mobilize their readers behind one party and against the other. Just as Joe Cannon would feel comfortable at the side of Tom DeLay or Karl Rove, William Randolph Hearst would understand Rupert Murdoch, Rush Limbaugh, or the Daily Kos. This new media, like paper in fire, fuels the flames of hyperpartisanship.

Even the traditional mainstream media, the major newspapers, magazines, and television stations that seek to operate within the conventional definitions of objectivity and balance, often discourage compromise between the parties. Conflict invariably draws more attention from the traditional press than consensus. In a sense this is understandable: Cars that collide head-on make more noise than those that merge onto a highway uneventfully. But by constantly emphasizing the points of disagreement between the political parties the mainstream press often obscures their opportunities for agreement.

Even with this excessive attraction to conflict, though, the mainstream press promotes national unity in one indispensable manner: It attempts to provide a common set of facts, presented within the traditional boundaries of objectivity, that all sides in the political debate can rely upon to shape their opinions. Loud voices on left and right daily question whether the press meets that ideal of objectivity, and they often make a persuasive case that in individual cases it does not. But the conventions of coverage in the mainstream press, shaped by the standards of balance and fairness, mean that the major media outlets expose readers and viewers to opinions and ideas from across the political spectrum. Every day in the mainstream media, liberals encounter conservative ideas and vice versa, as well as ideas that don't fit easily into either camp (though that group is probably the most underrepresented). This provides an opportunity, however fleeting, for politicians and activists in one faction to persuade Americans in another, and exposes readers and viewers from all points along the political spectrum to ideas contradictory to their own. Needless to say the media doesn't perform this function perfectly. But with all its flaws and limitations, all its blind spots and obsessions, the mainstream mass media still provides the closest thing to a public square where Americans of all viewpoints can meet to obtain a shared foundation of information and assess the challenges and choices facing society.

But the mainstream press's ability to fulfill that role is diminishing. Long gone are the days when any single media institution, much less any single media figure, like CBS's Walter Cronkite, could shape opinion across the entire political spectrum. The principal problem is *not* that the big mainstream media institutions—the national and local television stations, newspapers, and magazines—no longer attract viewers from a wide range of political and ideological perspectives. The best data on where Americans obtain their information comes from an annual survey conducted by the nonpartisan Pew Research Center for the People and the Press. The most recent Pew figures (released in July 2006) show only small differences between the percentage of Republicans (43 percent) and Democrats (41 percent) who read newspapers regularly. Likewise, roughly equal shares of Republicans and Democrats regularly watch local television news. National Public Radio, CNN, and the national network evening news broadcasts* do draw more Democrats than Republicans. But generally the big institutions of the traditional mainstream media still speak to a broad diversity of Americans.

Yet even while retaining diverse audiences the mainstream press's ability to unify is eroding. One reason is declining credibility. Almost every major media institution has seen its overall credibility decline in the Pew surveys since the late 1990s. And on this front, wide partisan differences have emerged. Fox News Channel, which actually fits less in the traditional mainstream media than in the more overtly partisan alternative to it that is emerging, was the media outlet trusted most by Republicans in 2006. But it was trusted by fewer Democrats than any outlet except one (*Newsweek* magazine). Republicans in turn were less likely, sometimes considerably less likely, than Democrats to trust virtually every other mainstream media outlet Pew tested. With the mainstream media's overall credibility not only declining, but splintering, the net effect is that no single media institution possesses broad credibility across both sides of the red and blue divide.

---

* The numbers on the evening network news are subject to varying interpretations. The partisan imbalance on any individual show is relatively small: In the most lopsided case 18 percent of Democrats and 12 percent of Republicans regularly watch ABC's evening news, for instance. But the cumulative gap is wider: Thirty-eight percent of Democrats, but only 24 percent of Republicans, regularly watch *any* of the network news programs, Pew found.

Mostly, though, the mainstream media's ability to function as a bridge is shrinking because its audience is shrinking. Greater choices for readers and viewers, and more time pressures on daily life, have narrowed audiences for the traditional titans of the mainstream media. In 1993, Pew found that six in ten Americans regularly watched one of the nightly network news programs; by 2006 that number had fallen to less than three in ten. The share of Americans who regularly watched local television news dropped over the same period, from more than three fourths to just over one half. The percentage who said they had read a newspaper the day before had dropped from six in ten in 1994 to just four in ten now. Even adding in those who read newspapers online increases the figure only to 43 percent.

As the mainstream media's audience recedes, overtly partisan sources of information are filling more of the space they yield. The mainstream sources of news remain by far the most popular. But compared to forty or even twenty years ago, more Americans now receive information from sources that follow the nineteenth-century model of sharp partisanship. Many of these outlets in the new partisan media are increasing their audiences, even as the traditional media institutions lose ground.

It is hazardous to generalize too precisely about institutions that range from Rush Limbaugh's bombastic but often amusing radio show to the Fox News Channel's hybrid of conventional journalism and embedded advocacy to the gleeful ferocity of thousands of partisan blogs. But there are common threads in the way the new media institutions interact with the political system. The first is that they tend to draw their audiences mostly from one side of the political spectrum. In the Pew survey, for instance, 34 percent of Republicans but only 20 percent of Democrats said they regularly watched Fox. In Rush Limbaugh's radio audience, the survey found, conservatives outnumbered liberals and moderates combined by more than four to one, and on Bill O'Reilly's highly rated Fox show, the ratio was almost two to one. At the other end of the dial, liberals outnumbered conservatives by more than two to one in the audience for the *Daily Show*, Comedy Central's irreverent but left-leaning nightly take on the news. Comparable figures were not available for individual blogs, but reading the comments posted at Daily Kos on the left or Michelle Malkin on the right, it's not hard to see that the vast majority of people visiting these sites are those who share the beliefs expressed there.

The second key is that the central figures in the new partisan media almost universally align with the most combative elements in each party. They typically disparage compromise and applaud confrontation. ("First let's disabuse ourselves of the bipartisanship idea," one leading liberal blogger wrote the morning after the Democrats recaptured the House and Senate in 2006.) Virtually without exception the new partisan media sources reject the standards of objectivity and balance that the mainstream press has long venerated in principle. (Needless to say, the new media voices argue that the mainstream press has failed to uphold those standards in practice.) The new institutions have repeatedly demonstrated their willingness to inject intensely partisan stories into the public debate that may not pass the credibility tests still applied by the mainstream press. The most consequential recent example came in 2004 when the Swift Boat Veterans for Truth group launched an advertising and public relations campaign alleging that John Kerry had exaggerated his combat experiences in Vietnam and did not deserve the medals he had received. Initially the mainstream press devoted little attention to the accusations, and when the big newspapers and networks did turn to it, they mostly debunked the charges. Yet even without attention from the traditional gatekeepers, the accusations still became common knowledge through intensive coverage on Fox, talk radio, and Web sites like the Drudge Report. Mark Mellman, the pollster for Kerry, remembers senior campaign advisers arguing that the senator should not address the allegations because that would only increase their visibility. "There were people in our campaign who would not believe, could not believe, that if it wasn't on the . . . networks or in the *New York Times* and *Washington Post*, that anybody could have heard about it," he recalled. In fact, Mellman said, even before virtually any major mainstream media outlet grappled with the issue, his polls showed that awareness of the charges was "total" across the electorate. "By the time the mainstream media got to it," he continued, "it was too late. By the time they started banging it down, it was already a fact that people had integrated into their thinking."

The institutions in the new partisan media are both a product and a cause of today's polarized political culture. They are growing because they satisfy the desire for unconditional partisan combat in each party's base. But they also feed that emotion by exposing their audiences predominantly or even solely to information that reinforces their preexisting beliefs. Tom Rosenstiel, the director of Pew's Project for Excellence in Journalism, notes that the new partisan media doesn't even accept the *Crossfire* model of promoting argument between antithetical views; it has, he says, created more of a culture of assertion, in which a strongly opinionated host (Limbaugh or Sean Hannity on radio, Lou Dobbs or Keith Olbermann on cable news, Markos Moulitsas on the Internet) points his or her audience toward unambiguous conclusions about the news. To the extent that the new partisan media outlets present opposing views, it is usually to perforate them as misguided or misleading. Like its nineteenth-century ancestor, this is not a culture that prizes nuance, temperance, or balance. When Democratic senator Patrick Leahy early in 2006 raised questions about Bush's authorization of warrantless surveillance by the National Security Agency, Limbaugh accused him of promoting an "Al Qaeda bill of rights." Readers posting comments on liberal Web sites regularly describe Bush or Cheney as fascists. These institutions share a common view of politics as unending combat against a pernicious and malevolent enemy.

Like many developments shaped by hyperpartisanship, these new media institutions can be a source of vitality in political life. They generate passionate debates and inspire activism on left and right. The problem is, they are rigidifying politics even as they help to revitalize it. To the extent that these outlets enlarge their audiences, as they seem likely to do in this climate, they reduce the number of Americans willing to give both sides in the political competition a fair hearing. The political goal of the new partisan media isn't to broaden perspectives—it's to harden allegiances. When the mainstream media does its job well, its effect is precisely the opposite.

Political institutions—the parties, interest groups, candidates—share the goal of hardening allegiances, and they are likewise exploiting new communications tools to do so. Indeed, the growing sophistication of direct communication between political institutions and voters may shape American political life in the coming years even more than the resurgence of partisan media. The major political institutions are developing the capacity for mass communication without the mass media. The Republican National Committee, after the energetic organization-building of the Bush years, amassed some fifteen million names on its mailing list by 2006. MoveOn.org ended the 2006 campaign with more than three million names on its e-mail list. And many other political groups have now accumulated mailing lists that number in the millions.

All of these groups acknowledge that many of those on their lists don't regularly respond to their e-mails. But even if only half or two thirds on these lists routinely open their e-mails, that means the groups are still communicating directly with audiences beginning to approach those generated by the mainstream media. To an even greater extent than in the new partisan media, the groups can speak to this audience in an unfiltered and unchallenged manner, bombarding them with information meant to solidify their allegiance to the cause. The rise of YouTube and social networking sites like MySpace on the Internet is providing candidates, causes, and their opponents mushrooming opportunities to directly broadcast their messages to huge audiences.

Like the rise of the new partisan media, the growing capacity of political causes to communicate directly with massive numbers of Americans invigorates democracy in some respects. It has surely contributed to the rise in activism and voting participation over the past several years. But the growth in direct communication carries the same cost as the new partisan media institutions. It hardens attitudes and encourages conflict.

The direct communication links and the new partisan media have created what amounts to an alternative transmission belt that allows each party to reach its core supporters with a focused message regardless of the story line that is dominating the mainstream press. That is likely to make it easier for each side to mobilize its base against even a president sincerely attempting to build broad consensus. Even the most conciliatory president always does something that antagonizes the other side; the new transmission belt will ensure that those likely to be offended by such decisions are reminded about them constantly. Imagine for a moment that Democratic Illinois senator Barack Obama wins the presidency in 2008 and reaches out by appointing, say, Nebraska Republican senator Chuck Hagel as his secretary of state. Would Rush Limbaugh or Bill O'Reilly focus on that choice—or spotlight the abortion rights advocate with a record of promoting gay-friendly sex education in middle school that he names to a second-tier position in the Department of Health and Human Services? If John McCain wins the presidency and courts the other side by appointing a muscular Democrat such as Richard Holbrooke or Senator Joe Biden as his secretary of state, would the lead item on the Daily Kos or the action alert from MoveOn focus on that decision or on the full-blooded neoconservative McCain names as his national security adviser? To the extent either side even acknowledged this sort of conciliatory appointment it would probably be to label the appointee as a turncoat.

White House veterans from both parties see this clamor as a major new hurdle for any president trying to broaden his or her coalition and narrow the country's divisions. It is tough enough for any president to reach voters in the opposite party when so few elected officials cross party lines to support and validate his ideas. Adding to that a robust and relentless communications infrastructure determined to spotlight the smudge on every canvas, and to do so in the most inflammatory and partisan terms, makes the job that much tougher. "Communication is often very difficult to do, and with all that we know about the fractionation of communication it becomes increasingly difficult to rise above the din," said Harold Ickes, the pugnacious former deputy chief of staff for Bill Clinton and a senior adviser to Hillary Clinton. "The din can be pretty focused and pretty vicious and pretty effective. There is no one medium that one looks to at this point . . . that bestrides the country. So the communications aspect of any national leader has become much more formidable, certainly than in the 1950s and the 1960s, and I think even more so than in the 1990s. . . . Even if you have a set of policies that people generally agree with, to get them to have the center of attention, as opposed to other factors that are being waged in the media, is very, very difficult to do. And I don't know if it can be done."

UNIFYING REFORMS

The rise of the new partisan media is just one reason why no one should expect America to completely reverse all of the forces driving our age of hyperpartisanship. After the great sorting out of the electorate, the partitioning of the country into partisan spheres of influence, the rise of interest groups of left and right, the evolution of the media, and the centralization of leadership authority in Congress it is difficult to imagine us ever returning to a system as consensual as the age of bargaining in its heyday. Given all of that system's flaws, we would not want to precisely re-create it, in any case. But it is possible to construct a political system less confrontational and more productive than today's. It would require action on three broad fronts: unifying reforms, unifying policies, and unifying leadership. Let's examine them in ascending order of importance.

REFORMS OF THE POLITICAL PROCESS

Political reforms that might restrain or even undo polarization come in two categories: those that can be pursued in the near term, and long-term projects that will require years of further discussion before they are seriously considered. On both fronts political scientists and reformers have produced thoughtful proposals. The problem has been building a consensus for reforms that encourage centrism in a political system now driven mostly by its extremes. That remains a conundrum, but the growing evidence of public dissatisfaction with Washington's unrelenting conflict—and the palpable failure of polarized politics to deliver progress against our most serious problems—is creating the opportunity to reconsider these ideas.

An agenda of unity reforms would begin with changes in the process parties use to pick their nominees for president and other offices at every level of government. In most states (twenty-six as of 2006), only registered members of each party can participate in primaries to select that party's nominees for elected office. These so-called closed primaries magnify the influence of hard-core partisans, which means, after the great sorting out, that they also magnify the influence of the most ideological voters on each side. That doesn't guarantee victory for the most ideological candidates, especially in presidential nomination races. In fact, in the modern primary era, a period that traces back to roughly 1952, only three candidates who positioned themselves at their party's ideological vanguard have won a party's presidential nomination: Barry Goldwater in 1964, George McGovern in 1972, and Ronald Reagan in 1980. Far more often the candidate offering the purest ideological appeal has lost to a rival presenting at least a somewhat more balanced approach. Think of Dwight Eisenhower defeating conservative hero Robert Taft for the 1952 Republican nomination; John F. Kennedy topping Hubert Humphrey for the Democratic nomination in 1960; conservatives Jack F. Kemp and Marion G. "Pat" Robertson failing to become much more than nuisances to George H. W. Bush in 1988; and liberals Tom Harkin and Jerry Brown never generating a serious threat to Bill Clinton for the Democratic nod in 1992. Even more recently, as the cycle of polarization has accelerated, the most ideological candidates have not succeeded. In the 2000 Republican race Steve Forbes, the most conservative major contender, never seriously threatened George W. Bush. Four years later the left looked at John Kerry as near beer compared to Howard Dean, but it was Kerry who took home the prize.

So, at least at the presidential level, it's not true that the ideological edge of each party usually can impose its nominee. It's more accurate to say that the ideological vanguard in each party possesses a veto in the presidential nomination process: A candidate completely unacceptable to that base is unlikely to win the nomination. This veto intensifies polarization by narrowing the range of potential nominees. In normal circumstances, under the current dominance of closed primaries, candidates who systematically challenge the priorities of their party's core supporters face a steep climb.* That makes presidential candidates reluctant to pick too many fights with their party's base, or to press their party for too many of the

---

* Bill Clinton, the candidate in recent times who most closely fit that description, won in 1992 largely because many Democrats were unusually open to new approaches after three straight landslide defeats during the 1980s; he also faced a weak field of opponents in which the great champion of traditional liberalism, New York governor Mario M. Cuomo, was conspicuously absent.

policy concessions required to build bipartisan coalitions. Compounding the problem, the base veto over the nomination also compels the nominees into commitments that limit their reach once elected. The best recent example came in the 2000 Republican race when Bush, to preempt Forbes, endorsed the sweeping tax cuts that precluded the possibility of a grand fiscal bargain with Democrats after he took office. It's easy to imagine the next Democratic nominee making commitments on trade or energy that will lace a similar straitjacket.

The best way to dilute the influence of the base is to abandon closed primaries. In varying ways twenty-four states now open their primaries to voters beyond a party's registered partisans. (In almost all of those states closed primaries are impossible because the state does not register voters by party.) Parties should not be required to allow voters from the other party into their primaries. But allowing independent voters into primaries in more states would enable presidential candidates to take more risks to both broaden their coalition and break the political impasse that has blocked progress on our most pressing problems. More independents in the primary electorate could translate directly into more independence for the next president.

Allowing independents to participate in primaries could be equally important in House and Senate elections. Primary challenges have become the nuclear weapon activists on each side use to punish and intimidate legislators who veer too much from party orthodoxy or resist leadership control. Party members in each state and district have the right to determine whether their elected officials have strayed too far from their party's core beliefs, as Connecticut Democrats reasonably concluded about Joe Lieberman in 2006. But allowing independents to contribute to that judgment would provide a fairer gauge of overall opinion in a state, and even within a party's actual electoral coalition. In almost all states, and even in most congressional districts, party nominees need support from independents as well as their hard-core partisans to win election. Why then should only the hard-core partisans be given a vote in determining which candidates voters can choose from in November?

Allowing more independents to vote in party primaries is a straightforward destination, but it's not easy to map out a route to reach it. Lawyers in both parties agree that Supreme Court rulings have left state parties with the last word on who participates in their primaries. And state parties, dominated by partisans, are the last institutions that will see the value of opening decisions to less partisan voices. The only way to change that perspective would be for prominent, centrist elected officials in the states (optimally, governors) to adopt the cause of primary reform, and to press the case that opening primaries to independents would produce stronger general election nominees. Reform of the primary process would not offset all of the current system's incentives for partisanship and polarization, but more open primaries gradually could strengthen consensus-oriented voices in both parties.

The same could be said for another priority of political reformers: changing the rules for drawing districts in the House of Representatives. Redistricting reform isn't the panacea some of its supporters claim, but it also could contribute to a reconstruction of the center in Congress. Advocates of redistricting reform are correct that requiring more legislators to run in competitive districts closely balanced between the parties would encourage more compromise in the House. The difficulty is that redistricting abuse does not appear the principal reason so few House seats are competitive. The larger problem is that after the great ideological and cultural sorting out more communities tilt solidly to one party or the other as the nation politically self-segregates. Still, redistricting abuse makes a bad situation worse, and redistricting reform could produce at least some additional competitive seats in many states.

So far redistricting reform has proceeded on a state by state basis. Precisely for that reason it hasn't proceeded very far. Only six states use independent commissions to draw congressional districts. In addition, Iowa delegates authority for congressional and state legislative redistricting to its Legislative Services Agency, a nonpartisan professional support bureau. The problem with handling redistricting reform in the states is that the dominant party in each state typically opposes changes that might erode its dominance. In 2005, that line of thinking led to the defeat of redistricting reform ballot initiatives promoted by Republicans in California and Democrats in Ohio. In the states, redistricting reform becomes another front in the partisan wars it is meant to pacify.

The Supreme Court has benched itself on the issue by repeatedly refusing to overturn even the most egregious partisan gerrymanders. That leaves Congress as the most viable option for change. Representative John Tanner, a moderate Tennessee Democrat, has proposed legislation that would require every state to establish independent five-member commissions with authority over congressional redistricting. Such a federal mandate for independent redistricting commissions would almost certainly face a legal challenge, though many scholars agree with Tanner that the Constitution's electoral clause (Article I, Section 4) vests Congress with the authority to set the rules governing its election. Even if upheld by the courts, Tanner's solution might not yield results as dramatic as its sponsors hope: The independent redistricting processes in Iowa and Arizona generally have failed to produce many close House races (although two seats switched from Republican to Democrat in each state in 2006). But paired with steps to open the party primaries to independent voters, redistricting reform could send to the House more legislators committed to compromise—and help them maintain an independent course once they arrive.

Many reformers dream of more ambitious long-term changes in the electoral system: more restrictive campaign finance reforms that would further limit the influence of big donors; the replacement of the Electoral College with a direct national popular vote for president; changes in registration laws intended to massively increase voter turnout; and a shift away from single-member districts in the House of Representatives toward an approach closer to the proportional representation systems widely used abroad. None of these ideas is likely to be implemented any time soon, but all would significantly change the dynamics of American politics. Each of these reforms could contribute to a lessening of partisan tensions, or the opposite, depending on how parties and voters react. The possibilities are explored at greater length in an endnote on page 458.

The next step in a near-term reform agenda would be to reassess the way Congress operates. Here the prospects for meaningful change are thinner. It is nice to fantasize about the House majority permitting more open rules for the consideration of legislation. That would allow more bipartisan coalitions to form, but power in the House has always rested on control of the options that reach the floor, and no majority would surrender much of that authority. Similarly, if both parties restored the seniority system as the sole basis for naming committee chairs in the House and Senate, that would also promote more independence. But that won't happen either and probably shouldn't: Absolute deference to seniority provided legislators too much freedom to block their party's proposals with impunity, and made it too difficult for presidents to advance the agendas they promised to the country. Linking committee assignments to loyalty is one of the few effective levers legislative leaders possess, even if Republicans, as on so many things, applied the principle to excess during their years in the majority.

Congressional reform might focus more fruitfully on some of the day-to-day irritants that fray tempers on Capitol Hill. Political scientists Norman Ornstein of the American Enterprise Institute and Thomas Mann of the Brookings Institution, two shrewd longtime congressional observers, joined with a group of Democratic legislators to offer such a package in 2005. The plan's commonsense elements included ensuring representation for both parties on conference committees; limiting floor voting to twenty minutes unless both parties agree to an extension; ensuring at least twenty-four hours for members to review bills before they receive a final floor vote; and reducing the number of earmarked appropriations, which have become a tool both for leadership to strong-arm the rank and file, and for the rank and file to strong-arm lobbyists.

Another corner of Congress that could benefit from new rules is Senate consideration of judicial nominations, one of the most explosive sources of conflict between the parties today. Here the guiding principle ought to be that each of a president's judicial nominees deserves his or her day in court. All nominees should be guaranteed a hearing and a public vote from the Senate Judiciary Committee within a fixed period of time, barring some rare controversy that requires extensive investigation. That would prevent the abusive tactics Senate Republicans used against so many of Bill Clinton's nominees. (The Republican majority blocked twenty-four of Clinton's nominees to the powerful Circuit Courts of Appeals and never held a public vote on any of them; the nominations simply were allowed to expire without action. Of the twenty-four, only two even received hearings from the Judiciary Committee.) The Senate Judiciary Committee should not be allowed to kill a president's judicial nominations without accepting the responsibility of casting a recorded vote.

The same rule, except in rare cases, should apply on the Senate floor. That commitment is necessary to prevent another Senate minority from replicating the excessive use of the filibuster that Democrats directed against so many of George W. Bush's nominees. Future senators would be wise to accept the standard that the bipartisan Gang of 14 formulated to break the dangerous collision over judicial nominations in 2005. Their compromise, as we saw earlier, preserved the right to filibuster judicial nominations, but insisted that that right should be exercised only in "extraordinary circumstances." It would not be practical to codify such a standard in Senate rules (unlike the requirement for timely Judiciary Committee hearings and votes, which could be added). But as an informal guidepost, the "extraordinary circumstances" standard, by guaranteeing all but the most provocative presidential nominees an open vote on the Senate floor, could help lower the tension over judicial nominations.

It might be possible to drain even more of the venom from the war over the courts by ending lifetime tenure for Supreme Court justices, a change that would probably require a constitutional amendment. Proponents of the idea surprisingly include not only liberals but also some conservatives like Northwestern University Law School professor Steven G. Calabresi, a founder of the conservative Federalist Society. The case for change rests on changing behavior among the justices themselves. Since 1970, Supreme Court justices have been serving much longer than their predecessors in earlier generations (more than twenty-six years on average now, compared to about fifteen years through 1970) and retiring at a much older age (seventy-nine, compared to about sixty-eight through 1970). It is as if the Court has added to its oath of office the phrase "until death do us part."

These trends heighten the tension over Supreme Court nominations both by raising the stakes for each appointment (seven presidents could come and go before John Roberts, Bush's choice as chief justice, vacates his position) and reducing the opportunities for each president to nominate justices. A fixed eighteen-year term, the most common term-limit proposal, might help address both problems, but especially the second one. Restricting tenure on the Court to eighteen years would limit the influence of any single justice; more important, once an eighteen-year term limit was fully phased in, each president would be assured one court appointment every two years. That would increase the chances for each party to place its stamp regularly on the High Court. And that could lessen the opposition party's inclination to dig in against each nominee. Term limits carry the risk that the Court would change direction more frequently, generating a kind of constitutional whiplash. But as Calabresi and a coauthor noted, "[E]very other major democratic nation," all of which drafted their constitutions after ours, has rejected unconstrained lifetime tenure for its highest court. More rapid turnover could be a central element of any equation for less conflict over the courts.

Over the long term, a comprehensive agenda of unity reforms also might need to address the fractionation and polarization of the media. It's easier to diagnose the problem—the electorate's growing reliance on overtly partisan media that tends to harden political loyalties rather than test them with competing views—than to devise a solution. These outlets would not be growing on television, radio, and the Internet if there were not a market for them, and the government always must tread carefully when involving itself in political speech. Moreover, these outlets reflect the vitality and energy that represents hyperpartisanship's best contribution to the political system. But democracy is healthier when voters are exposed to diverse views and, with a philosophy centered on adding rather than subtracting voices, it makes sense to explore options to promote that diversity.

The most straightforward possibility would be to restore some version of the Fairness Doctrine. That Federal Communications Commission rule, formally adopted in 1949 but with roots that stretched back to the first days of radio, required radio and television broadcasters to cover important issues and provide reasonable exposure to contrasting points of view. The FCC killed the rule under Ronald Reagan, and when Congress (with support from among others Newt Gingrich, Strom Thurmond, and Jesse Helms) passed legislation restoring it, Reagan vetoed it. The rise of intensely partisan media, especially on radio, followed.

The Fairness Doctrine did not require balance within individual shows; if it was revived, Rush Limbaugh would not have to squeeze Al Franken into his studio. But it would require stations, over periods of weeks or months, to provide a reasonable balance of views in their overall programming. One danger is that a restored doctrine might prompt stations to abandon controversial political subjects rather than meet the fairness requirements, but that seems unlikely on a broad scale at a time when the news/talk format has proven so profitable. A greater hurdle would be updating the rule for the modern media landscape. The Fairness Doctrine only applied to conventional radio and television broadcasters, who were considered "public trustees" because they received valuable government licenses to operate over the public airwaves, a limited resource. Any effort to resurrect the fairness concept would need to determine whether it should apply as well to the other forms of political communication that have emerged since 1987—cable television, satellite radio, Internet Web sites, including those operated by the mainstream media—and if so, how. A new Fairness Doctrine limited to the public airwaves might have too little impact, but one extended beyond the public airwaves might catch too much communication in its net. The legal and conceptual difficulties in solving that riddle would be formidable, if not insurmountable. Still, as Pew's Tom Rosenstiel notes, it may be more difficult to flatly dismiss Washington intervention to encourage a diversity of expression now that the government has resumed regulating media content through the FCC offensive against obscenity, such as the Janet Jackson "wardrobe malfunction" at the Super Bowl. If the federal government can intervene so forcefully to protect America from a fleetingly bared breast, can it really claim no stake in a political debate on the airwaves too often stripped of contrasting views?

One final mechanism for promoting greater consensus also intrigues many political reformers: the possibility that a new competitor could emerge to the two major parties. A viable third party could help reverse the cycle of polarization in American politics by providing an alternative for moderate and less partisan voters, and pressuring the existing parties to compete harder for their support. But creating such a new option is a tall order. No lasting alternative to the major parties has taken root since the Republican Party displaced the Whigs as the principal competitor to the Democrats in the mid–1850s. The fire-breathing Populist Party enjoyed brief success as an alternative to the two major parties in the late nineteenth century but dissolved after William Jennings Bryan absorbed some of its ideas into the Democratic Party in 1896. In the twentieth century independent presidential candidates attracted double-digit support four times: Theodore Roosevelt in 1912; Robert M. La Follette in 1924; George Wallace in 1968; and Ross Perot in 1992. But of those four, only Perot's party appeared again on the presidential general election ballot four years later, and he attracted less than half as much support in 1996 as he did in 1992.

New parties have usually developed when the major parties left substantial constituencies unrepresented, or put another way, when the two major parties failed to serve an identifiable segment of the political market. The Republicans were born in the years before the Civil War in response to the Northern demands for a party unambiguously opposed to the spread of slavery. The nineteenth-century Populists, with a message about constraining corporate power, developed an audience among farmers and small-business owners because neither the Democrats nor Republicans of the day recognized the need for government to counter the new economic behemoths. Perot found a niche because millions of Americans considered both major parties unwilling to balance the federal budget or reform a capital roiling in scandal.

The political system may be experiencing such a market failure again today. By focusing so heavily on their base supporters, the major parties could be opening the space for a third party directed at centrist and independent voters. If both parties continue to slight the center, they are virtually inviting some other force to compete for it.

In 2006, an eclectic group of veteran political consultants and business executives took one step to fill that void. The group launched an effort called Unity08 to nominate a bipartisan, centrist, third-party presidential ticket in 2008 through an Internet-based campaign. The principal organizers represented a kind of over-the-hill gang who had made their deepest imprints on the political system years ago, among them Hamilton Jordan and Gerald Rafshoon, the chief of staff and media adviser respectively for Jimmy Carter; Doug Bailey, a pioneering Republican political consultant; and Angus King, the former two-term independent governor of Maine. But the group operated on the very modern belief that the two parties, through years of unremitting political conflict, had abandoned a substantial centrist constituency disaffected from absolutism on both sides. On the steamy afternoon in May 2006 when the group first unveiled its plans, David Maney, a Denver investment banker who helped to organize the effort, pulled out an index card and drew a curve to show how each party had directed its message at the ideological poles of the electorate. He then swirled a circle around the midpoint of the curve to show where Unity08 wanted to pitch its tent. "The American middle is the biggest single unserved consumer market in America today," he said earnestly. "I'm a business guy. I don't understand: Why isn't somebody going after this part of the market?"

To pursue those voters Unity08 established a Web site where any registered voter could join its party. Its plan is to recruit volunteers from that list to collect the signatures required to place the party on the fifty state ballots. Then, in the first half of 2008, it intends to hold an online convention of its members to pick its nominees for president and vice president. The organizers have said that only presidential and vice presidential tickets that include one Democrat and one Republican, or an independent who selects a running mate from one of the major parties (and a senior cabinet officer from the other), will be allowed to compete.

But in early 2008, the effort collapsed. At least over the past century, the most effective third parties have coalesced around vivid personalities, such as Theodore Roosevelt or Perot. The Unity08 organizers tried to reverse the sequence: They want to build the party and then find a candidate to lead it. And while identifying some issues as "crucial" (such as energy independence, health care, and terrorism) and others as merely "important" (mostly social issues like gun control and gay marriage), the group did not articulate actual policy positions, leaving it to the eventual nominee to define its agenda. Their hope was to avoid alienating voters who dislike the two major parties but don't agree on much else. Yet the effort's failure demonstrated that it requires more tangible goals than just combating partisanship to attract a mass following to a third party.

The problems facing a third party in the contemporary era extend beyond the limitations of this effort. When the country is so evenly divided between the two major parties, many voters sympathetic to a third party will hesitate about "wasting" a vote that might tilt a close election to the candidate they like least—especially after votes for Ralph Nader in 2000 helped tip New Hampshire and Florida, and thus the presidency, from Al Gore to George W. Bush. Today's polarized political climate also makes it difficult for a third-party presidential candidate to win many Electoral College votes: Even a third party that attracts a substantial popular vote faces the risk of finishing second to a Democrat in all the blue states and second to a Republican in all the red ones. And as the Unity08 reluctance to endorse an agenda suggests, uniting the voters dissatisfied with the two parties may not be easy either.

Still, none of these hurdles are disqualifying. Nearly two decades of hyperpartisanship has depleted both parties' public standing to the point where millions of Americans probably are willing to consider a viable alternative. Even as eccentric an option as Perot, after all, won nearly twenty million votes in 1992. It seems implausible that Americans will be satisfied indefinitely with just two political options when they can choose from hundreds of television stations and surf millions of Web sites. Already, a poll commissioned by the Unity08 organizers found that nearly three fourths of Americans agreed that "it would be a good idea for this country to have more choices" in the 2008 presidential race than just the two major parties. The Internet also changes the equation for a third party by making it easier, and less expensive, to find support. As we saw in Chapter 9, the Internet lowers the cost of political organizing by reversing the traditional relationship between causes and supporters: Rather than causes spending heavily to find supporters (through direct mail or advertising), the Internet allows supporters to find the causes and candidates they like at little cost. So far, interests at the ideological edge of each party have succeeded on the Internet more than centrist or moderate movements. But an independent presidential candidate with an edgy political reform message and an outsider image probably could strike a spark too, and use the Internet to build a national political and fund-raising organization far more easily than other third-party rebels like Perot or George Wallace.

In the end, the opportunity for a new competitor is rooted less in technological advances than in political failures. If the major parties continue on their recent trajectories, the backdrop for national politics in the coming years will be continued budget deficits, gridlock on problems like expanding access to health care and reducing reliance on fossil fuels, and poisonous fights over national security, social issues, and Supreme Court appointments. In that environment, someone will respond to the demand for a more consensual and pragmatic leadership. One of the two parties could do it by offering a more expansive agenda and inclusive style. But if they don't, all of the structural barriers discouraging a new political alternative may not prevent one from emerging.

A Unifying Agenda

Political reform could be the first step toward reconstructing a more pragmatic and consensual politics. But reform is a means toward an end: its principal value is to create an environment that encourages more politicians to offer comprehensive and unifying responses to our most pressing problems.

In the parties' current configuration Democrats probably would find it easier than Republicans to offer a policy agenda aimed at national reconciliation. The reason is twofold. Republicans have succeeded more than Democrats with a policy agenda targeted primarily at their base supporters, and thus feel less incentive to change—although the party's sharp losses in 2006 might alter that equation at least somewhat. By contrast Bill Clinton's presidency, the most recent model of success for Democrats, came much closer to a consensus approach. More important, liberals constitute a smaller share of both Democratic voters and office-holders than conservatives do among Republicans. That means Democrats possess a greater incentive than Republicans to reach out beyond their ideological vanguard and usually face somewhat less resistance when they do.

Still, these differences are relative. Any agenda aimed at both narrowing our differences and comprehensively attacking our problems requires the blending of ideas that one party favors and the other resists. Each party would need to accept ideas it has opposed as the price of convincing the other party to do the same. That means constructing such an agenda would be painful for leaders in either party but impossible for neither. The path to a new American consensus could begin on the right or the left, so long as it points toward the center, not the extreme.

It is beyond the capacity of this author—and perhaps any single author—to identify acceptable compromises on all the challenges we face. But the history we have explored points toward three principles that should guide the search for a new policy consensus:

- involve all segments of society in seeking solutions;
- ask all segments of society for concessions and sacrifice in devising solutions;
- use all the tools available to us in formulating solutions.

These principles could help lead us out of the current impasse in two respects. They offer the opportunity for a *political* breakthrough. Policies organized around these ideas provide the ingredients to build coalitions between diverse social and economic interests with roots in each of the two major parties. That would increase the odds of overcoming reflexive partisanship among elected officials and activists in Washington. Second, policies forged through these principles offer the opportunity for *substantive* breakthroughs. Today, with too many in each party only willing to embrace ideas acceptable to their core supporters, we cannot pursue comprehensive solutions. Instead we are reduced to addressing problems from only one direction—more production *or* more conservation as the answer on energy; more enforcement *or* legalization as the answer on immigration; more government control *or* personal responsibility as the key on health care. It is as if we are trying to cut a piece of paper by using only one blade of a scissors.

Let's consider a few examples of how we might attack problems more productively by using the three principles listed above. Nowhere is a new approach more necessary than on the interlocked challenges of reducing America's dependence on foreign oil and limiting the emissions of the gases associated with global warming. Progress on either front has been stalemated by a politics of subtraction, in which each party has directed its greatest effort toward blocking the priorities of the other—more production on one side, more conservation and promotion of renewable energy sources on the other. When Congress and President Bush agreed on energy legislation in 2005, after four years of bruising legislative combat, Democrats and their allies in the environmental movement prevented Republicans from including their principal proposals to increase supply (particularly greater access to drilling in the Arctic National Wildlife Refuge prized by environmentalists) while Republicans, the White House, and their allies in the energy, auto, and utility industries blocked the most ambitious Democratic efforts to reduce demand (such as mandating higher fuel economy for cars and trucks). The result was that when one nonpartisan group analyzed the final product, they discovered that after four years of debate and maneuver through a deeply divided capital, President Bush and the two parties in Congress had produced a program that reduced America's dependence on foreign oil by . . . absolutely nothing.

An approach built on shared sacrifice, and using all the tools available to American society, would marshal carrots and sticks to address supply and demand simultaneously. It would begin by acknowledging that this challenge cannot be met from only one direction. It is implausible to center any long-term energy plan on more production of domestic oil not only because of the imperative to reduce greenhouse gas emissions, but because our oil needs dwarf our capacities: The United States uses one quarter of the world's oil but holds less than 3 percent of its proven reserves. Equally, though, the massive fixed investments in cars, homes, factories, and offices makes it impractical over the near term to count on vast reductions in energy use or a radical shift toward renewable fuels like wind and solar (which now contribute only a meager 6 percent of our total energy needs, much of that from hydropower).

A grand compromise on energy would start by allowing oil companies greater access to domestic oil and gas supplies from environmentally sensitive areas, particularly through greater offshore drilling, coupled with tougher penalties for spills or environmental damage. Then it would use all the tools available to Washington to promote more conservation and a transition toward renewable energy sources that produce fewer greenhouse emissions.

The first step in that mission would be more federal research spending on technologies that hold the long-term promise of reducing reliance on fossil fuels—a list that ranges from solar and wind energy for electricity, to cars powered by cellulosic ethanol produced from agricultural waste, or even more distantly, vehicles run on hydrogen fuel cells. The next step requires government actions to accelerate the movement of those ideas from the lab to the marketplace. Those interventions are central to a comprehensive approach, because the availability of a technologically appealing alternative isn't always, or even usually, enough to spur change in auto, utility, and energy companies, all operating with enormous investments in the status quo.*

In a comprehensive energy agenda the federal government would use a wide array of levers to accelerate the transition to new technologies. It would apply its massive purchasing power to help catalyze the market for solar energy or vehicles run on alternative fuels, the way its purchases for the space program helped create the first market for semiconductors. It would expand tax incentives for new alternatives, like the purchase of energy-efficient homes and hybrid cars. And it would impose mandates that require change. Washington could require utilities to produce a fixed percentage of their electricity from renewable energy sources, a mandate that nearly half the states have already adopted but Bush and House Republicans have blocked at the federal level. An even more valuable step would mandate further improvement in fuel economy for the cars and trucks sold in America. Until Congress mandated increases in 2007, Washington has not raised fuel economy standards for passenger cars since 1989, and only slightly improved them for trucks and SUVs; the result is that the fuel economy of passenger vehicles sold in the United States now lags the average not only in Europe and Japan but even China.

The most sweeping incentive for energy change would be for the nation to follow California's landmark decision in 2006 to mandate reductions in greenhouse gas emissions through a so-called cap-and-trade plan. California's plan requires a 25 percent reduction in greenhouse gas emissions

---

* The absence of such steps was the key flaw in the energy agenda Bush developed during his second term. Although he moderated his initial bias toward fossil fuel production to support more federal research spending on alternative sources of energy, his ideological opposition to government mandates led him to oppose federal requirements (discussed following) that would push companies to bring that research to market rapidly. Only after Democrats won control of the House and Senate in 2006 did Bush bend by accepting higher fuel economy standards for cars and trucks, although he continued to oppose mandatory reductions in carbon emissions.

by 2020 but will allow companies to buy and sell credits for meeting their targets. By imposing a cost for greenhouse emissions the plan increases the economic incentive to develop and commercialize low-emission alternatives to fossil fuels—which also contribute to lessening America's reliance on imported oil. (A direct tax on the carbon emissions in fossil fuels could achieve much the same effect.) In fact, all of these approaches—more government procurement, new standards for the utility and auto industries, limits on greenhouse emissions—would use public-sector tools to encourage private-sector innovation.

Taken together, the central elements of a grand bargain would tie a short-term increase in domestic oil and gas production to government steps aimed at speeding a long-term shift toward cleaner energy sources that simultaneously reduce our dependence on foreign oil. One final piece might be necessary to build a congressional majority for such an approach: As Democratic senator Barack Obama of Illinois has proposed, the auto companies might be induced to accept higher fuel economy standards and requirements to build more hybrid vehicles if Washington agreed to absorb some of the heavy burdens they face in providing pensions and health care for retirees.

There is something for everyone to dislike in this grand bargain. Democrats content to beat up on oil companies or provide subsidies to alternative fuels would need to stare down the United Auto Workers, which has myopically joined with the auto industry in opposing tougher fuel economy standards. Republicans committed to greater domestic oil production would need to confront both their ideological resistance to new government mandates and the entrenched opposition of some business interests. Environmentalists would accept more offshore drilling. Oil companies would accept carbon caps that encourage a long-term shift away from fossil fuels. Consumers would face higher energy prices until technological advances improved efficiency and lowered the cost of new alternatives. Every interest in the debate would sacrifice. But all also would gain, and more important, after decades of polarized stalemate, the nation could use all the tools available to move toward a more secure and environmentally sustainable energy future.

The same principles offer a way forward on health care. The values of shared risk and shared responsibility provide the best hope of expanding coverage to the uninsured and controlling costs for those with insurance. On this front, innovative states are carving the path Washington can follow. The most important recent breakthrough came in Massachusetts in 2006 while Republican Mitt Romney held the governorship and Democrats controlled both chambers of the state legislature. The two sides agreed on the most ambitious effort to expand access to health care since the collapse of Bill Clinton's proposal in 1994.

The Massachusetts plan requires all state residents to buy health insurance, the way states now require all drivers to purchase car insurance. But the state agreed to cover the full cost for families with incomes below the federal poverty level and to subsidize premiums, on a sliding scale, for those earning up to three times that amount. All employers that did not insure their workers were required to contribute to a state fund providing the subsidies. The plan linked the expansion of coverage with reforms in the health insurance market by creating an innovative insurance exchange intended to allow individuals and small businesses to choose among an assortment of policies. And it provided health insurers more freedom to offer stripped-down, less-expensive policies, especially for young people. Finally, the state expanded eligibility for public health insurance to more children from working-poor families.

The plan represented an exquisite balancing of interests and the creative coupling of policy tools usually considered incompatible. It divided responsibility for funding expanded coverage between government, individuals, and business. It used both public programs and private insurance to reach the uninsured. It advanced some of the top conservative priorities in the health care debate by demanding personal responsibility (through the mandate on individuals) and providing more flexibility for insurers. But it also embraced key priorities of the left by expanding coverage and demanding contributions from employers. Most important, by requiring everyone to purchase insurance, including the young and healthy, and then pooling the uninsured to buy coverage together through the new state exchange, the plan protected the foundation of social insurance—the idea that insurance should share risk between the young and old, the healthy and sick.

The Massachusetts plan didn't strike the perfect balance on all these issues. It required, for instance, much too small a contribution from employers who do not insure their workers. Nor did it match the plan in neighboring Vermont, also devised by a Republican governor and a Democratic legislature to control costs (and thus reduce premiums) by mandating more comprehensive management of chronically ill patients, who consume most health care spending. A national health care plan would add new elements, like a limit on the tax preference for employer-provided health care (an idea favored both by President Bush and some leading Democratic health care thinkers) to help fund the subsidies for uninsured working-poor families. (The lack of a sufficient dedicated funding source is the principal weakness of the plan approved in Massachusetts.)

In each party there are many activists who consider the Massachusetts model too incremental, a Band-Aid for a terminally flawed health care system that requires massive surgery. On the left, many still believe the only long-term solution for health care is to radically centralize control under government through a single-payer system that eliminates private insurance; on the right an equal number believe the only answer is to radically decentralize the system by shifting more responsibility and risk away from government and employers toward individuals. Eventually one side in this argument may assemble a coalition of public and institutional support sufficient to impose such a fundamental change on the other. But that day, if it ever comes, is far away. To wait for it before acting would be like telling a cancer patient to forgo chemotherapy while waiting for a miracle cure that science might someday develop. A national Massachusetts-style health care reform might be only the first step toward more fundamental change. But like a grand bargain on energy, it offers the potential for practical progress and reconciliation around the themes of shared sacrifice and the application of all the tools available to society.

The same principles of inclusion and mutual concession offer the best compass on many of the other challenges now dividing us. To calm the virulent argument over immigration and advance both security and economic needs, a guest worker program could be joined with tougher enforcement at the border and in the workplace, and a pathway to legalization for the estimated twelve million illegal immigrants already in the United States. To confront the unsustainable growth in spending on federal entitlement programs for the elderly (Social Security, Medicare, and Medicaid), tax increases could be linked to benefit cuts such as reducing payments to more affluent seniors and indexing the retirement age to increases in life expectancy. To maximize the benefits of free trade (lower prices for American consumers; new markets for the best American producers) while minimizing the cost, we could shift our focus from the stalemated debate over dictating tougher labor and environmental standards on developing countries toward measures that provide more economic security to the Americans most directly hurt by global competition—ideas such as guaranteed health care, improved pension security, and publicly funded wage insurance that would temporarily offset up to half of the lost income if a displaced worker is forced to take a new job at lower wages. On all of these issues, as well as with energy and health care, progress requires not so much an intellectual breakthrough as a political accommodation.

The cultural issues that provide so much of the octane for today's polarized politics present a more complex challenge. In a society so powerfully shaped by cultural and religious differences, we cannot eliminate disagreement over controversies such as abortion, gay rights, and gun control. But even if a complete truce is an unreasonable goal, it could be possible to lessen hostilities on cultural issues through an approach centered on the principle of federalism.

Under a federalism approach states, rather than the federal government, would take the lead whenever feasible in shaping answers to culturally divisive questions. The most culturally conservative states—primarily in the South, the Plains, and portions of the Mountain West—could adopt policies that reflect the prevailing values in their borders; the cosmopolitan states along the East and West coasts and in portions of the upper Midwest could do the same. David Gelernter, a contributing editor at the conservative *Weekly Standard*, summarized the case for this strategy when he wrote, "True federalism accommodates profound national disagreement by allowing each state to tailor the local climate to suit itself. Federalism is an escape valve that lets polarizing bitterness blow off into the stratosphere."

In practice, this approach would force each side in the cultural argument to acknowledge that it cannot impose its vision on the entire society. Liberals would concede that Montana and Texas will allow greater access to guns than New York or California. Conservatives would abandon the effort to pass a federal constitutional amendment banning gay marriage and acknowledge that states, which have traditionally regulated marriage, should set the rules for same-sex unions. Some of the tension on these issues might then drain away as states settled into a new equilibrium.

Following that logic, some analysts on both sides of the issue believe that the federalism principle could help defuse the unending clash over abortion, the most intractable of the social disputes. If a constitutional amendment or future Supreme Court decision overturned *Roe v. Wade*, the Court's 1973 decision establishing a nationwide right to abortion, the procedure would not be banned. Rather, the decision on whether to prohibit or permit abortions would return to the states. Many of the red culturally conservative states where antiabortion sentiment is high would bar it (in some cases simply by allowing pre-*Roe* abortion bans to spring back into effect), while blue states would likely continue to provide a right to abortion.

In theory, coastal cosmopolitans who support abortion rights might be more willing to accept a ban in Texas or Tennessee so long as it remains available in their communities. Bible-belt evangelicals might be more willing to accept legal abortion in Brentwood and Soho so long as it is prohibited where they live. Each side in the argument could control their immediate experience at the price of allowing the other side to do the same. Eventually, proponents of this strategy believe, the issue could lose much of its sting.

That scenario isn't outside the realm of possibility, but it does not seem the most likely outcome. The activists on each side see abortion as a moral absolute. For many supporters abortion rights represent a statement of equality for women no more negotiable, or acceptably subject to state-by-state infringement, than the claim of African Americans to civil rights. For abortion opponents the practice amounts to the taking of an innocent life, an evil no more negotiable, or acceptably subject to state-by-state authorization, than murder. Moving the struggle over abortion from

Washington to the states amid such emotions is less likely to end the war than to widen it.

Before the states reached a new equilibrium every one of them, even those with preexisting laws, would be compelled to reconsider and debate its rules on abortion. In dozens of states the issue would eclipse all others. Even states with a clear preponderance of opinion (Mississippi or Texas on one side; New York or California on the other) would experience passionate and heated argument. In states where opinion is more evenly divided, like Pennsylvania or Ohio, the struggles over abortion laws could ignite full-scale political conflagrations fanned by national money and media attention. In both sets of states, but especially the latter, abortion could dominate state campaigns for years, as candidates promise to protect or overturn the outcome of the initial decisions. Even supporters of the federalism approach for abortion, like Jeffrey Rosen, a thoughtful George Washington University law professor, admit, "[T]he overturning of *Roe* would probably ignite one of the most explosive political battles since the civil-rights movement, if not the Civil War."

Though the federalism option might in some respects bring us closer to an armistice on abortion, all of these considerations suggest the issue is more likely to mark the limits of such a strategy. On balance, the least contentious approach would maintain a national right to abortion while protecting state flexibility at the margins (on issues such as parental notification for minors) and pursuing whatever common ground is available on related questions, such as reducing unwanted pregnancies. No single solution can extinguish the dispute over abortion; the best the country can hope for is to deny fuel to the fire by building consensus to combat unwanted pregnancies and using a federalism strategy to resolve as many other combustible cultural arguments as possible.

On foreign policy, which has divided America more than any other issue under Bush, the opportunities may be greater to set a united course. This front could also benefit from the central element of a consensus strategy on domestic issues such as health care or energy: using all of the tools available to us. To advance America's interests around the world and enhance its security at home, a unifying foreign policy would deploy all of the nation's assets, not just its military strength, but its economic and cultural influence and its relationships with traditional allies. Such a foreign policy agenda could accept Bush's goal of promoting democracy as a worthwhile and even noble ambition, but it would recognize that the United States is more likely to advance this goal if it enlists other democracies to the cause rather than presenting it to the world as a uniquely American mission (a sure recipe for backlash). With Iraq tragically demonstrating the limits of using military force to build democratic societies, more balanced models for promoting liberty might inspire greater consensus at home and abroad. The European Union, for instance, helped spread freedom throughout Eastern Europe and to the doorstep of the Muslim world in Turkey by requiring countries seeking the benefits of membership to provide free elections and to protect individual rights. A foreign policy aimed at promoting greater consensus would ask whether the EU model could be applied to some new international system (perhaps a club of democracies, as some in each party have proposed) that rewards countries moving toward democracy with economic and diplomatic benefits.

Once America resolves its military commitment in Iraq—a job certain to top the agenda for the next president if Bush does not complete it first—the opportunity to reconstruct consensus on foreign policy may be much greater than it now appears. To an extent probably unmatched since the height of the cold war, Americans agree on the principal threat facing the nation: Virtually all segments of U.S. society consider Islamic radicalism a hostile and dangerous force. At the same time the limitations—and in Iraq outright failure—of Bush's inordinately militaristic, unilateral, and partisan national security strategy have created a broad constituency for a more comprehensive and inclusive approach (that would include the elements of Bush's vision with the broadest support, such as the focus on democracy and efforts to link foreign aid to democratic and social reform in poor countries). One exhaustive national poll completed early in 2007 found majority support in both parties for a foreign policy that stressed bipartisanship at home, cooperation with allies, and increased emphasis on economic and diplomatic means, rather than military force, to promote American interests. Such broad guidance from the public doesn't answer the most difficult question for a president: when to use to military force to respond to threats like Iran's movement toward nuclear weapons. But it does provide a framework for the steps a president must take—exhausting other options, establishing international consensus, working if possible with allies, and involving both parties at home—to build domestic consent for such a momentous decision.

A commitment to pursuing such consent could contribute more than any of these specific guidelines to restoring greater consensus in foreign policy. No analyst (especially not this one) can divine a list of predetermined rules that guarantees broad acceptance of a president's foreign policy. The world constantly presents a president with new challenges and dilemmas; the key to ensuring that most Americans support the response is to include a broad range of opinion in devising it. Richard Lugar, the Republican senator who chaired the Senate Foreign Relations Committee during much of Bush's presidency, offered the best guidance when he wrote: "The bolder the president's foreign policy, the more essential is his understanding of constitutional power sharing and the more sophisticated must be his arrangements for obtaining congressional advice and consent."

The same could be said about domestic issues. The bolder a president's agenda, the greater its potential to polarize the country—unless it is shaped by the desire to harmonize diverse views. The policy principles explored in the last several pages—broad consultation, shared sacrifice, using all the tools available—and the political reforms discussed before that offer one potential formula for reducing political conflict and increasing productive agreements. Others could surely devise alternative, and even more promising, paths; the specifics of these ideas matter less than the spirit behind them. The one thing certain is that no alternative will significantly narrow our divisions without a president determined to breathe life into it. A president cannot tame hyperpartisanship alone, but without a president dedicated to that cause, the nation will never surmount the divisions now debilitating it. That brings us to the final and most significant change necessary for constructing a more productive and less confrontational political system: presidential leadership committed to unifying the country.

Unifying Leadership

No serious practitioner or student of politics today imagines, as many of America's founders did, that one class of leaders can synthesize the interests of all, or that broad, undivided consensus is the natural state of society. More than two centuries of experience have demonstrated that conflict is a constant in American politics precisely because conflict is a constant in American life. Conflict, in fact, is the element in any society that makes politics necessary. In a democracy the central role of politics should be to resolve conflict. Containing disagreements, building consensus, negotiating compromise between opposing interests, establishing a national direction that most people can support: This is what political leaders, at their best, have done throughout American history. This is the essence of their jobs. Without conflict, politics would be administration.

Mediating conflict and bounding contention does not mean eliminating disagreement. Politics is now, as it has always been, a clash of interests. But throughout American history the most far-sighted politicians, at every level of government, have refused to simply bear arms for one interest group against another. Instead they have tried to construct agreements that harmonize those opposing groups in a manner that produces progress for the nation as a whole. Constructing such agreements, in fact, is the principal way politicians contribute to the health of American society.

Great legislators throughout American history have displayed that harmonizing impulse. But in our system it is the president who has the greatest opportunity to fashion agreements that move America forward. The president is the sole political leader elected by the entire country (except for the vice president, the caboose the president drags up the hill). In our system no other figure is as suited to look beyond partisan, factional, or regional interests to the national interest. If a president does not bring the nation together, no one else can do so around him.

Presidents have employed very different styles to advance their goals. Yet the best of them have recognized that building consensus is a central part of their job. Harriet Beecher Stowe once wrote that Abraham Lincoln demonstrated his great might less by standing firm than by bending in ways that brought others to his cause. Lincoln's strength, she wrote, "is like the strength not so much of a stone buttress as of a wire cable . . . swaying to every influence, yielding on this side and on that to popular needs, yet tenaciously and inflexibly bound to carry its great end." In their finest hours Lincoln's successors have all recognized that. Looking back through American history, it is clear that there is no single path to success for a president. But as we've seen, the surest path to failure is to lose the ability to hear and respond to all the voices in our diverse society. Presidents who divide rarely conquer.

No single president (not even George Washington or Abraham Lincoln) ever devised a perfect strategy for minimizing social conflict in America, and none probably ever will. But many have contributed insights and approaches that stand as valuable guideposts to those aspiring to heal our current divisions.

Perhaps the most explicit articulation of consensus as a value came from Theodore Roosevelt. Roosevelt certainly did not produce the golden mean—an agenda that balanced precisely the claims of business and labor to advance the national interest. But his instinct was to seek such a mean. The search was influenced by ambition, the lust for attention, and ego. But it also reflected a belief that at a moment of great social division, one purpose of leadership was to bridge divides. Roosevelt feared a society with widening class divisions and a political system that reinforced rather than narrowed them. Roosevelt saw reform as the sole opportunity to reverse a drift toward intensifying conflict that might culminate in revolution.

Roosevelt's response, articulated more precisely after he left the White House, was twofold. At the broad level he urged Americans to pursue choices that reflected the national interest, rather than factional, regional, or class interests. As part of a series of 1910 campaign speeches for insurgent Republicans, Roosevelt in Osawatomie, Kansas, on August 31 declared: "The New Nationalism puts the national need before sectional or personal advantage." At the specific level Roosevelt's response was to embrace an extended reform agenda that responded to the material concerns of the discontented. During his presidency, as we saw in Chapter 2, he moved only modestly in that direction out of reluctance to break completely with his party's old guard congressional leadership. Freed from those limitations Roosevelt, after his presidency, embraced a bold panorama of reform. During his campaigning in 1910 he delivered speeches and wrote articles praising the progressive income tax, a steep inheritance tax, and tougher regulation of railroads. In his independent 1912 bid for the White House Roosevelt also endorsed "stricter regulation of manufacturing, minimum wage and maximum hour laws, abolition of child labor, employers' liability provisions, and government-backed pensions and insurance." This agenda did not match the promises of security for average Americans that Franklin Roosevelt formulated a generation later, and it conspicuously excluded African Americans, but it was for the time an astonishing platform that showed how far Roosevelt would break from the small-government ideological assumptions that had shaped him to establish a new consensus capable of responding to popular discontent.

And yet Roosevelt also argued constantly for restraint, and for a balancing of interests. "If I could ask but one thing of my fellow countrymen, my request would be that, whenever they go in for reform, they remember the two sides, and that they always exact justice from one side as much as from the other," he warned in his Osawatomie speech. Even as Roosevelt moved toward the progressives on a broad range of issues, he admonished them to moderate their demands and to subject their expectations to the discipline of political reality. In the final speech of his independent 1912 campaign, to a mass rally in New York, Roosevelt urged his party "to be just to all, to feel sympathy for all, and to strive for an understanding of the needs of all."

Roosevelt's pleas to minimize self-interest in politics carried more than a whiff of political self-interest. A politics built solely around class division may have terrified Roosevelt so much in part because he understood that the struggling classes outnumbered the thriving. Yet in these arguments he advanced a theory of political change that valued both constructive reform and social cohesion. Roosevelt's great fear was a country separated across class lines. But his analysis applies just as well to a nation divided along cultural lines or by contending visions of how America should pursue its role in the world. Roosevelt recognized the importance of maintaining public consent while pursuing a personal vision. And he understood that encouraging national unity should be a priority for the nation's leadership—a priority important enough to shape the pace and scope of a president's agenda. "I . . . ask that we work in a spirit of broad and far-reaching nationalism," he insisted in Osawatomie. "We are all Americans. Our common interests are as broad as the continent."

Through the decades other presidents offered similar counsel, if rarely as eloquently or expansively. Franklin Roosevelt's description, early in the New Deal, of the unique responsibility of the president remains resonant today: "to find among many discordant elements that unity of purpose that is best for the Nation as a whole." Dwight Eisenhower, in a letter he wrote near the end of his two terms as president to New York governor Nelson Rockefeller, underscored the critical insight that crafting compromise lies at the heart of a politician's responsibility. While as a matter of "moral truth or basic principle" issues often inspire absolutist beliefs cast in "black or white," Eisenhower wrote, "the task of the political leader is to devise plans among which humans can make constructive progress. This means that the plan or program itself tends to fall in the 'gray' category. This is not because there is any challenge to the principle or the moral truth, but because human nature itself is far from perfect." Ronald Reagan, lionized today by conservatives for his resolve, actually demonstrated in his dealings with Mikhail Gorbachev the strength a political leader can derive from adjusting his course to new events and seizing unexpected opportunities for agreement. Bill Clinton, through his New Democratic agenda, showed that ideas previously considered antagonistic—opportunity and personal responsibility, fiscal discipline and government activism—could be joined together with productive results, both substantively and politically.

All of these insights can provide direction for a president committed to restoring the nation's common purpose. But they are more a destination than a map for reaching it. Even a president who accepts national reconciliation as a goal still faces the practical challenge of navigating toward it in a political current that now flows toward conflict.

How can a president convert an impulse for unity into action? The most important step, by far, would be to campaign on, and in office propose, a policy and political reform agenda of the sort described above—a plan that attempts to use all the tools available against our most difficult problems. But even that answer begs another question: How can a president create an environment conducive to agreement on such a boundary-shattering agenda?

The answer should begin in the formation of an administration. Shrewd presidents, as we've seen, sometimes extend their reach by appointing members of the opposite party to central positions in their cabinet or White House staff. Franklin Roosevelt did it by naming Republicans Henry Stimson and Frank Knox as secretaries of war and the Navy before World War II. John F. Kennedy installed Republican Douglas Dillon, Eisenhower's undersecretary of state, as his treasury secretary. Richard Nixon brought iconoclastic Democrat Daniel Patrick Moynihan into the White House as a senior domestic policy adviser. Bill Clinton picked Republican senator William Cohen as secretary of defense in his second term. Not all cross-party appointments worked so well. Presidents benefited little from symbolic appointments to second-tier positions. And sometimes the culture clash is so great that an administration rejects an appointment from the other party the way a body rejects a transplanted organ. But more often, cross-party appointments can provide a president with credibility and contacts that multiply his power. A president can achieve the same effect by filling a Supreme Court vacancy with a nominee from the opposition party—something presidents, perhaps surprisingly, have done a dozen times in American history.

The next step could be to create a culture of experimentation. Franklin Roosevelt's promise of "bold, persistent experimentation" ought to be a watchword for every president. To help break the impasse between the parties on domestic issues a president could challenge the two sides to take their competition from the level of theory to practice by allowing each other to field test some of their ideas on the most difficult domestic problems. A Democratic president could accept a test of private school vouchers for children in some underperforming urban school systems if Republicans agreed to a test of universally funded preschool in others. A Republican president could agree to fund state experiments guaranteeing universal health care coverage if Democrats agree to test conservative proposals to exempt small businesses from more state health insurance mandates.

This approach would not apply to all issues, but a strategy of experimentation could build broader consensus for ideas that demonstrate results and inspire more creativity as well. The fear of political backlash against an unsuccessful program too often prevents Washington from fresh thinking; a culture of experimentation could encourage greater boldness by increasing the tolerance in the public and political system for failure. It was precisely such benefits that Lyndon Johnson had in mind when he told Doris Kearns Goodwin that he wished the public had allowed him to structure his Great Society more in this manner. "I wish the public had seen the task of ending poverty the same way as they saw the task of getting to the moon, where they accepted mistakes and failures as a part of the scientific process," Johnson said. "I wish they had let us experiment with different programs, admitting that some were working better than others. It would have made everything easier. But I knew that the moment we said out loud that this or that program was a failure, then the wolves who never wanted us to be successful in the first place would be down upon us at once, tearing away at every joint, killing our effort before we even had a chance."

Next, to build credibility across the partisan divides, a president can search for opportunities to demonstrate independence from his party's most powerful organized constituencies. One of the most revealing measures of a president's leadership is his willingness to confront his party's vested interests to advance the national interest when the two conflict. The liberal New York Republican senator Jacob Javits, in his penetrating 1964 book *Order of Battle*, argued that the Republican Party, as the historic party of business, incurred the obligation to demand that business operate in the public interest. That same insight remains valid today, and equally applicable to Democrats with organized labor and environmentalists, or Republicans and Christian conservatives. A president who pursues policy concessions from his own side can increase his leverage to ask it of the other. (Such a balanced approach would be the political underpinning of a policy agenda built on using all the tools available against our problems.) And, paradoxically, by demonstrating independence a president will likely help his party grow, and thus enhance its capacity to defend the interests it must sometimes discipline. When a party is eclipsed by its constituency groups, both lose.

The next key would be to organize a president's time to allow more regular opportunities for legislators from both parties to hear his thinking and share their own. Most decisions in Washington are driven by impersonal calculations of interest, but personal trust and goodwill are the grease in the engine of government, most noticeable when they are absent. The more time a member of Congress has spent exchanging ideas with a president, the more likely he is to give him the benefit of the doubt, and to temper his words even when he disagrees. The iconoclastic Republican senator Chuck Hagel speaks for many on Capitol Hill when he says legislators, especially from the opposition party, are more likely to decide "a line call" in the president's favor if they trust him and believe they have been given a fair opportunity to make their case. When a member "has been with the president a couple of times, the president has called him in, [he is more likely to say], 'I don't know about this, Mr. President, but there's a connection [so] I'll give you this one,' " Hagel said. "That happens in life many, many times on big things."

Members of Congress always have an insatiable desire for a president's time, so it's not surprising that legislators from both parties like Hagel, Richard Lugar, and Tom Daschle all point to more interaction between Capitol Hill and the chief executive as a key to reducing conflict in the capital. But Bill Clinton reached a similar conclusion after his eight years in the White House. Clinton said that as president he often found his thinking prodded most by regular contact with senators and House members, especially those who approached issues from different angles than he did. "Sometimes, someone like Richard Lugar would come in and say something, and I knew he was really smart, and he just had a whole different take on it than I did," Clinton recalled. "When he talked to me I didn't think he was a Republican trying to trip up a Democratic president; I thought he was a guy with a different point of view. So I found it valuable." Even North Carolina Republican senator Jesse Helms, an implacable opponent on almost all issues, changed Clinton's thinking about reorganizing the State Department, a prime Helms cause. "I was totally against what he wanted to do in the beginning," Clinton remembered. "In the end, we wound up with a compromise."

In the White House Clinton spent hours talking with politicians from both parties. Dozens of legislators can tell stories of receiving calls at home from Clinton to chew over a speech they had delivered on the House or Senate floor. Hagel said that even as a Republican senator he enjoyed easier access to offer dissenting views on foreign policy issues to Clinton than to George W. Bush. "Clinton used to do that all the time," Hagel said. "Clinton would have you down, and he'd sit there with two or three of you. And he would go around and say, 'What do you think, Chuck? NATO enlargement? You think NATO enlargement is a good idea? How many? Where is this going?' It was a president actually thinking through that." Lugar remembered being summoned to sit with Clinton in small groups debating how to respond to the Mexican currency crisis or India's test of a nuclear weapon. But, looking back, Clinton said he would have been better served by devoting even more time to open-ended discussions with members from both parties about each side's concerns. "If I had to do it over again, I would block out significantly greater time . . . to just bring these guys in and let them say whatever the hell they want to say to me," he said. "You know, most of these people are pretty smart. Most of them didn't get there by accident. Most of them love our country, and most of them have something to say. And I found that people that I ordinarily, superficially, would not have that much in common with would be quite helpful."

That was one of several practical guidelines Clinton, in a lengthy conversation for this book, offered for a future president committed to reconciliation. This isn't the place to recapitulate all the strengths and weaknesses of Clinton's governing style (which were explored at greater length in Chapter 5). Clinton didn't always succeed in constructing consensus—in fact, he failed spectacularly in his first two years, and later divided the country through his personal behavior in the Monica Lewinsky scandal. But he also displayed more creativity than any president in modern times at reframing issues like crime, welfare, and the federal budget to create new coalitions and resolve old disputes. From his setbacks as much as his successes Clinton has developed keen insights into the ways a president can reach out to those beyond his traditional coalition.

His guidelines start with the approaches we have just discussed: formulating ideas that blend priorities of each party; encouraging experiments; making appointments across party lines, and maintaining an open door to legislators from both sides. Beyond that, Clinton portrayed the construction of consensus as something very much like the construction of a house: a complex job that requires precision, tenacity, and patience. His ideas included:

- *Stay aware of opposing views.* Clinton said he tried "all the time" to keep up with conservative criticisms of liberalism. He believed the opposition could sometimes pinpoint weaknesses in an idea that supporters were unlikely to air. As president, Clinton instructed his White House staff to flag for him articles criticizing his policy proposals. "I told people, I'm not interested, too much, in people's political attacks, or a political puff piece, a supportive piece," he said. "But if there is an op-ed where somebody says, 'I think the president is wrong on this policy and here's why,' I want to see that." No matter which party wins the White House in 2008, Clinton says, "the president's time should be organized differently, so that there are consistent opportunities for him to meet with leaders" from the key constituencies in the other party—"not to give up everything you believe, but to try to bring the country together."

- *Build bipartisan trust and momentum.* Another lesson Clinton drew from his experience is that the parties are more likely to reach agreements when it becomes a habit. In retrospect, he said, he agreed with those who say that after the bruising, partisan battle over his first budget, he would have been wiser to move next to reforming welfare, an issue on which he shared substantial common ground with Republicans, rather than health care, where the parties began much further apart, and ultimately failed to agree.

  "By far the better choice," he said, "would have been to go to the American people and say, 'Look, look at this budget fight; we are simply too divided to take on something as big as health care. I am going to offer these things that will make the situation better, one, two, three, now, and I am going to undertake a yearlong effort to develop a bipartisan consensus. We're going to do it after the next election however you vote, and let's take up welfare reform [first].' "

• *Be tough, not extreme.* Presidents cannot completely avoid conflicts, and should not try to, Clinton said; they must be willing to fight for things they believe in even if they "think the country is fifty-fifty, or our position is unpopular." Even when a president makes a decision that leaves voters uncertain (as Clinton did by intervening in Bosnia and Kosovo), he said, they will likely defer to him if he has convinced them he reaches reasonable judgments. (That's a conclusion similar to Hagel's observation about the relationship between a president and Congress.) Clinton also said presidents need not hesitate about responding forcefully to those who forcefully oppose them. "People don't think you're polarizing or too left wing or crazy or anything if somebody hits you between the eyes with a two-by-four and you deck them back—you give an answer," he said.

But, Clinton continued, presidents must always resist the hardening of disagreement into permanent hostility. "I just think you have to use encompassing language, and you always have to be reaching out and act like you're not tone deaf, that you respect people who disagree with you, and you're trying to find common ground," he said. "Sometimes people just got a position that you disagree with, and sometimes they have to take a position that doesn't permit any principled compromise. But even then there is some value in letting them know their government doesn't consider them pariahs because they disagree. I mean, the National Rifle Association, those members pay taxes just like everybody else." That observation led to his next point.

• *Hug your opponents close.* Few instincts will help a president more, Clinton concluded, than constantly searching for issues on which he can work with interests that usually oppose him. Clinton, for instance, did that by recruiting evangelical Christians to his campaign for Third

World debt relief in 2000, pursuing alliances with Republican governors on welfare reform, and encouraging Hillary Clinton to partner
with Tom DeLay on foster care. Once Clinton directed Bruce Reed,
his domestic policy adviser, to scour an early manifesto on compassionate conservatism written by Republican senator Dan Coats and
his aide Michael Gerson (later Bush's eloquent speechwriter) to find
areas where they could agree. "That's what you do," Clinton said. "You
look for things where you do have common ground, and you don't ask
people to give up what they believe. Either on the left or the right;
don't ask them. And let them litigate the next election on whatever
the issues are. But to pretend that because you disagree on these things,
you've got to demonize the other guy and paralyze the country, that is
the error."

• *Cast a broad net.* Like many political strategists, Clinton believes that
with the electorate so sharply divided, no president is likely to win
support from more than 55 percent of voters in the foreseeable future.
Bush's political team and many liberal activists argue that the only
rational response to that environment is to focus a party's agenda primarily on its own base. But Clinton said that that choice can lead a
president toward a narrowing and polarizing perspective. A president's
goal, he said, should be to craft an agenda and direction that might
potentially appeal not only to his own party, but to independents
and moderates in the other. "You want your issues, your package—
something in there—to have appeal to two thirds of the people, even
though you know as a practical matter, unless the other guy commits
armed robbery, you can't get more than 55 percent," he said. Even if a
president only wins 51 percent of the vote, Clinton argued, aiming to
speak to 65 percent of the electorate will provide a better compass for
his administration than accepting the premise that nearly half the
country is forever beyond his reach.

Other presidents operated with at least some of these insights, and
even Clinton's closest advisers would concede he didn't always meet the
standards for inclusion and outreach that he identified. No political rival

who ever collided with Clinton would confuse him with Gandhi. Yet these approaches offer practical tools that could help a unity-minded president encourage more consensus between the parties and reduce, though not eliminate, their conflicts. Nor do Clinton's suggestions, and the other ideas discussed here, exhaust the list of options available to a creative leader. A president who viewed leadership as more of an interactive than a solitary process, for instance, could proactively summon the leading inter-ests in our most difficult debates to search for common ground. On health care, a president could ask the heads of General Motors and Wal-Mart to sit with the leaders of the major health care unions and consumer groups to explore areas of agreement, and to pinpoint their remaining disagree-ments. On energy issues, oil and utility executives could be brought together with environmentalists and climate scientists.

Such a convening style of leadership would tap the energy of voters and interest groups alike exhausted by the warfare in Washington. Indeed, one of the most striking expressions of frustration with hyperpartisanship dur-ing the second half of Bush's presidency was the proliferation of odd-couple coalitions that formed in the hope of breaking the deadlock between the parties. During a single extraordinary week in January 2007, Washing-ton saw the announcement of a coalition of business, labor, religious, and immigrant groups to promote comprehensive immigration reform; a part-nership between ten major companies and four leading environmental groups to support a new offensive against global warming; and two sepa-rate business-labor-consumer alliances calling for universal health care, including one mammoth alliance that brought together the Business Roundtable, the AARP (the giant lobby for seniors), and the Service Em-ployees International Union, one of the most innovative unions in orga-nized labor. It was as if the political system had outsourced its historic responsibility for forging social consensus to the private sector. "I don't think we have that culture anymore in Washington where a president brings labor and business together, or environmentalists, and says, 'I really want to work this out,' " Andy Stern, the SEIU president, said a few weeks after his coalition with the Business Roundtable and AARP was an-nounced. "There is a lot more willingness to find common ground outside the political process right now than inside."

Shrewd politicians would recognize the emergence of these coalitions as a signal of the political opening for a more conciliatory and convening style of leadership after all the partisan acrimony we have explored in this book. Imagine a new president who sought the counsel of not only his allies but his opponents, and who told the country he (or she) would seek to break our most difficult deadlocks by blending the ideas of both sides. Imagine further that such a president told the country that he would accept some ideas counter to his own preferences to encourage others to do the same. Surely such a president would face howls of complaint about ideological betrayal from the most ardent voices in his own coalition. But that president also might touch a deep chord with voters waiting to be summoned to a common crusade of shared sacrifice and mutual concession. It has always been true that a president can score points by shaking a fist at his enemies. But a president who extends a hand to his enemies could transform American politics.

If one party begins a genuine effort to repair our divides, the other will face a momentous choice: to dynamite the bridges or to join in their construction. The saboteur's instinct is now deeply bred into American politics; yet if the country responds to a politics of reconciliation, a party seeking to derail it would risk ceding the center of the electorate, and a lasting electoral majority, to its rival. Hyperpartisanship's most positive contribution has been the fervor, creativity, and passion that it has inspired in millions of Americans. If the parties conclude they must compete over the means of uniting America, rather than in finding new ways to divide it, the same invigorating energies that have fed the rise of hyperpartisanship could fuel its demise.

BEYOND DIVISION

Sometimes the nation has faced conflicts that are truly "irrepressible" as William Seward, Abraham Lincoln's rival for the 1860 Republican presidential nomination and then his secretary of state, described the collision over slavery. Although Lincoln dreamed of a gradual response that would set slavery on the road to extinction, and great nineteenth-century legislators like Henry Clay and Daniel Webster searched for compromises that would postpone the reckoning, Seward was probably right that no political accommodation could prevent the eventual explosion. The same was almost certainly true of Southern segregation a century later. In these instances political confrontation (and worse in the bloodshed during the Civil War and the civil rights movement) was the inescapable price of progress.

Yet these examples are much less common than the ideologues on each side would insist. And even when the direction of American policy is made unmistakable by history, the best path for reaching that destination is almost always subject to debate, dispute, and compromise. A political leader always can choose whether to raise a new wall between Americans or to raze the walls that already divide us. The Depression demanded that Franklin Roosevelt pursue federal intervention in the economy that exceeded anything America had previously experienced, an inherently polarizing mission. Yet, as we saw in Chapter 2, especially in his first years FDR pursued that mission in a manner that harmonized as many interests as possible. The measure of his success is that he constructed a consensus over government's role in the economy—a pathway between the laissez-faire of American tradition and the more intrusive level of government control common in Europe—that in most respects still endures today. Likewise, the aftermath of World War II presented national leaders with the inherently polarizing mission of devising for the United States a more engaged role in world affairs than it had ever before accepted. Yet Harry Truman, working with Arthur Vandenberg, designed a consensus for contesting the cold war that also lasted for decades.

In any case, very few (if any) of the problems we face today are as inherently divisive as those challenges. We have not failed to provide universal health care, reduce our reliance on foreign oil, or balance our long-term obligations and assets because they present irrepressible conflicts. Even on foreign policy we face a dispute over means, not ends. We are so polarized today not because we face problems immune to agreement but because so many political incentives now discourage compromise.

Critics often point out that bipartisan accommodation has its drawbacks, too, and they are right. The most indefensible example was the

bipartisan gentleman's agreement to turn away from segregation for decades, but the age of bargaining's comity also came at the cost of neglect to
problems, from inner-city poverty to the environment and the suppression
of the most impassioned voices on each side. Politics is a human institution (perhaps the most human), and every institution shaped by human
hands is flawed. Every alternative carries a price. Government that is
divided between the parties can promote more bipartisan cooperation,
but it can also induce paralysis and stalemate. A commitment to consensus
can lead a president to important agreements, but it can also totter into
timidity.

That risk would be present in any presidency committed to national
reconciliation. But it is far from insurmountable. The pursuit of unity need
not translate into split-the-difference minimalism. The best remedy for
timidity is boldness. A president committed to consensus is not doomed to
modest measures located exactly halfway between the existing preferences
of the two parties, or to tepid solutions that avoid offense by only tinkering
at the edges of genuine challenges. Instead, a unifying president can create
national consensus by pursuing inspiring goals and boldly demanding sacrifice from all segments of society to achieve them: universal health care
that requires Democrats to accept a mandate on individuals and Republicans to accept a mandate on employers; a plan to reduce reliance on foreign oil that requires environmentalists to accept more domestic production
and industry to accept tougher mandates for conservation and the use of
alternative energy; entitlement reforms that raise more revenues but also
reduce benefits to sustainable levels, especially for the affluent. Division is
not a necessary ingredient of ambition, and balance, not caution, is the key
to restoring national consensus.

Seeking consensus, in fact, is not a cautious act. A true strategy of consensus is a risky enterprise. It requires a president to chart a new path and
then hold new ground inherently vulnerable to attacks from both parties.
It demands leadership at least as forceful as polarization, but leadership
applied to a more constructive end. It requires not just the small-minded
conflation of resolve with stubbornness, but the empathy to understand
the priorities of others (at home and abroad) outside of a president's usual
coalition of supporters, and the creativity to address their needs while still

advancing his own. It means mustering the national interest to surmount the parochial interests that reinforce the current impasse. It means betting and believing that for all the differences Americans now express, a solid and sustainable majority of them can be persuaded to act not upon what divides them, but on what unites them.

If a president offered this kind of leadership, the responsibility would shift to where it ultimately belongs in a democracy: the American people themselves. If most Americans want a more cooperative politics, they need to reward it on Election Day. Politics is a business of contagions; ideas that work in one campaign are almost instantly adopted in others. Lindsey Graham, the South Carolina senator, is surely correct when he says that when more national candidates win elections by promising "leadership, not partisanship" and a commitment "for the common good over a special-interest need," then politicians will fall over each other "to meet you in the middle."

One of the most venerable theories about presidential elections is that the nation almost always elects a president who responds to the flaws it has found in his predecessor. John F. Kennedy was more vibrant and energetic than Eisenhower; Carter more honest than Nixon; Reagan tougher than Carter; George H. W. Bush "kinder and gentler" than Reagan; Clinton more engaged and energetic than Bush; the second Bush more morally upright in his personal life than Clinton. If that pattern holds, Americans in 2008 will be searching for two things above all in the successor to George W. Bush: competence in the management of government's day-to-day challenges, and the creativity and flexibility to construct more consensus at home and around the world. There are signs the political system is already responding to those yearnings. Many of the 2008 presidential candidates in both parties touted their own commitment to unity as they announced their campaigns early in 2007. Precisely because Bush proved so polarizing he has, ironically, virtually guaranteed that the next president will reprise the sentiment, if not the words, of his pledge to govern as a "uniter, not a divider."

All of the men and women auditioning to succeed Bush may sincerely intend to promote reconciliation, yet constructing a more pragmatic, productive, and unifying politics will require not only sincerity but fortitude.

No one should underestimate the difficulty of taming the powerful forces in each party, and in the underlying workings of the modern political system and the mass media, that now feed on division. A president committed to political peace will earn the scars to prove it.

But he or she also can find inspiration in the president who repaired the worst rupture American society has ever known. Toward the end of the real Civil War, Abraham Lincoln challenged both sides in the struggle with perhaps the greatest speech in American history. On March 4, 1865, as the North marched toward victory through the shattered South, Lincoln used his second inaugural address not to revel in triumph but to remind all Americans of their complicity in the carnage. In Lincoln's demanding and prophetic vision, the "mighty scourge of war" represented God's punishment "to both North and South" for the sin of slavery, the divine judgment that "every drop of blood drawn with the lash, shall be paid by another drawn with the sword." Even while Americans bled against each other in battle, Lincoln spoke not as the champion of one faction in the fight but as the guardian of the united country he held in his heart. His words were stern but healing, for he recognized that even at the moment of greatest division in American history, when the nation expressed its differences with iron and fire rather than ballots and speeches, the fate of all Americans remained inextricably linked in a common destiny. To bind up the nation's wounds after our modern, metaphoric, second Civil War does not require Lincoln's soaring moral vision and transcendent empathy. But it does require our contemporary leaders to absorb and act upon Lincoln's conviction that what unites America is always greater than what divides it.

Amid the clamor and contention of our unending political conflict, it is easy to lose sight of that powerful truth. Yet Americans today, no less than every generation that preceded them, are bound by their common aspirations for opportunity, community, security, and a better life for their children. These shared purposes loom over our disagreements like mountains over a valley. The work awaiting America is big enough to demand all of our energies. We will either enlist all of our talents to finding answers to our great challenges, or the answers will remain beyond our reach.

The leaders who reunite America after our long and destructive cycle of extreme partisanship will not extinguish all our conflicts. But they will summon us to lift our eyes to our shared national interests, which remain today, as Theodore Roosevelt described them nearly a century ago, "as broad as the continent." The partisan, ideological, cultural, and geographic fault lines in American life are jagged and deep. But from the towering heights of our common dreams, those differences all look very small.

ACKNOWLEDGMENTS

TO PRODUCE this book on a tight deadline, I incurred many debts.

Robert Barnett, my agent, believed in this idea and encouraged me to pursue it from its first stirrings. His calm confidence and unflappable efficiency provides a wonderful safety net for the authors lucky enough to work with him.

Among Bob's many virtues is that he steered me toward Penguin, which provided me the opportunity to work with a great group of professionals. I approached this book on a sturdy foundation because of the confidence that Ann Godoff demonstrated in me and the project from our first meeting forward. Scott Moyers led me through the process with friendship and keen advice. If he wasn't such an outstanding editor, Scott could have been a great jockey: I've never met an editor with as intuitive an understanding of when to stroke and when to push an author. No writer could have asked for a more insightful, involved, and encouraging collaborator. Laura Stickney, at a critical moment, answered an array of questions on style and procedure, and then steered the manuscript through to completion. Joseph Perez produced an arresting cover.

I enjoyed tremendous help from two outstanding research assistants from Stanford University. Emma Vaughn brought tenacity, creativity, and infectious enthusiasm to a challenging array of research assignments, and her thorough work helped me hone the themes and sharpen the organization of the work. When Emma moved on, she recommended Megan Stacy, who ferreted out even the most obscure facts with her own trademark blend of determination and inventiveness. Without the long hours both devoted to the project, I could not have met my schedule. Later, Heather Gehlert and Shira Toeplitz stepped in to conduct timely research on specific projects.

I also received invaluable assistance from friends and colleagues who provided data critical to the project. Alan Abramowitz of Emory University took hours away from his own book on political polarization to run the historical polling data from the University of Michigan on ideological, partisan, and voting behavior that provided the spine for Chapter 6; his assistance was a model for scholarly collaboration. Likewise John C. Green of the University of Akron, perhaps our premier student of religion and politics, also produced tables of historical data that greatly enriched my understanding of the changing relationship between cultural affinity and political allegiance.

Susan Pinkus, the polling director of the *Los Angeles Times*, and her colleagues Claudia Vaughn and Jill Richardson, have provided me with mounds of polling data and replied with good humor no matter how complicated or rushed my requests. I owe as much to Maura Strausberg, the librarian at the Gallup Organization, who has cheerfully tolerated and swiftly met my unending and sometimes mystifyingly obscure data requests not only for this book but for years of newspaper reporting. The same is true about Gary Langer of the ABC Polling unit, as well as Andy Kohut, the director of the Pew Research Center for the People and the Press, and his associates Scott Keeter and Michael Dimock. Gary C. Jacobson of the University of California (San Diego), the author himself of an insightful book on how the country has divided over President Bush, graciously provided a different set of historical polling figures.

Robin Cochran, the endlessly resourceful research librarian in the *Los Angeles Times*'s Washington bureau, helped me track down answers and unearth obscure citations with speed, goodwill, and an apparently bottomless supply of outstanding alt-country music recommendations.

Clark Bensen of Polidata once again proved himself the Bill James of political statisticians. Massie Ritsch and Doug Weber of the Center for Responsive Politics provided valuable analysis of fund-raising trends.

Portions of Chapter 9 originally appeared in *National Journal*, which I thank for permission to reprint the material.

This book in many respects represents the culmination of the more than two decades I have spent writing about American politics, so I also want to thank some of those who have provided me the opportunity to study the modern electoral system. Richard Frank, the old-school editor of the *National Journal*, gave me my first chance to cover politics; Shelby Coffey allowed me to continue my education at the *Los Angeles Times;* during a brief detour into weekly magazine journalism, James Fallows offered me insights about politics and prose that still color my thinking; Michael Parks welcomed me back to the *Los Angeles Times;* John Carroll and Dean Baquet, two of the finest editors any reporter could ever ask for, provided me unparalleled freedom to explore the trends in political life and agreed to the leave I needed to finish this book; Doyle McManus and Tom McCarthy in the *Times's* Washington bureau not only supported my work and enriched it with their insights over the years, but suppressed the urge to summon me back into the fray while I finished this manuscript during periods of political tumult in Washington (as did Scott Kraft and Doug Frantz back in Los Angeles). Don Frederick of the *Times* has sharpened my sentences and protected me from mistakes for many years. I also owe much to Tom Hannon, the former political director of CNN, who allowed me to share my work on television, and also shared with me his encyclopedic knowledge of American politics.

I've also been blessed with colleagues, friends, and sources who have offered me their ideas and insights about politics, policy, and Washington over the years, and listened patiently as I worked through my own. I cannot name them all, but I would especially like to thank Richard Cohen of the *National Journal*, who also took the time to review the manuscript and provided keen critiques, and Dan Balz of the *Washington Post*, my coauthor on another political book, who provided a patient sounding board for the inevitable authorial frustrations on this work, and also shared transcripts of interviews with Newt Gingrich that helped answer key questions for Chapter 5. Over the years my understanding of politics has also benefited from the conversation and friendship of Michael Duffy of *Time* magazine; Janet Hook, Peter Wallsten, Tom Hamburger, Greg Miller, Joel Havemann, David Savage, Paul Richter, Josh Meyer, Ricardo Alonso-Zaldivar, and Aaron Zitner of the *Los Angeles Times;* Adam Nagourney of *The New York Times;* Mark Halperin of *Time* magazine; Chuck Todd of NBC News; Harold Meyerson of the *American Prospect;* Bill Kristol of the *Weekly Standard;* Tim Russert and Betsy Fischer of NBC; Patrick Reap and Paul Steinhauser of CNN; Roger Simon of the Politico; and the many talented men and women who populate the traveling carnival of the national political press corps.

The list of political practitioners who have spent time with me sharing their insights for this book, and my work at the *Los Angeles Times*, could fill another book. I would like to thank a few who have been especially generous with their time and influential on my thinking. I have been interviewing, questioning, and learning from Stanley B. Greenberg and Bill McInturff for twenty years, and each gave graciously of his time for this book; I consider both to be friends, tutors, and models of rigorous and insightful analysis. Bill and his colleague Alex Bellone went beyond the call in providing me unpublished data from their surveys and the surveys of others. Matthew Dowd's partisan loyalties have evolved over time, but his friendship, candor, honesty, and the sophistication of his insights have remained rock solid wherever he hangs his hat. The same is true of Mark McKinnon (who also doubles as another excellent source of music recommendations). Karl Rove and Ken Mehlman demonstrated an admirable commitment to public debate by answering detailed questions and explaining their thinking, even after I had written columns in the *Los Angeles Times* that made clear my concerns about aspects of their design. Mark Mellman shared critical insights from his own long experience in the trenches, especially about the 2004 Democratic campaign.

Many others were generous in making themselves available for lengthy interviews for this book despite busy schedules. In that group I would especially like to thank Representatives Tom Davis (who surely knows as much about American politics as anyone else on Capitol Hill), Jeff Flake, Steny Hoyer, Allen Boyd, Ellen Tauscher, and Jim Moran; Senators Chuck Hagel, Lindsey Graham, Richard Lugar, Harry Reid, Pat Leahy, and Edward M. Kennedy; former Senate majority leader Tom Daschle; former speaker Newt Gingrich; former Democratic leader Richard Gephardt; John Breaux; John Feehery; Nick Calio; and former representatives Tony Coelho, Vin Weber, and Vic Fazio. Paul Weyrich and Ed Feulner were invaluable in helping to understand the rise of the conservative movement in Washington. In conversations over the past few years Simon Rosenberg, Al From, Bruce Reed, Will Marshall, Eli Pariser, Tom

Matzzie, Markos Moulitsas Zuniga, and Ruy Teixeira, from very different perspectives, all illuminated the contemporary struggles among Democrats. Finally, former president Bill Clinton was giving with his time and candid with his observations.

Almost every one of these interviews occurred only because of the cooperation of efficient and responsive press assistants, but I would especially like to thank Jim Manley, Jay Carson, Laura Capps, Mike Buttry, Wes Hickman, Andy Fisher, and Trevor Fitzgibbon (who also tracked down some elusive citations) for their interventions.

My family sustained me through this book. My brother, Harold, and sister, Lenore, endured the daily status reports and helped keep me on an even keel. My sons, Taylor and Danny, provided inspiration, patience while I closeted myself in the office, and partners for baseball, *Buffy*, and the occasional stadium tour whenever I stole away from the computer. Danny also proved himself an able proofreader.

My wife, Eileen, brought tea, the intermittent Twizzler, and unflagging encouragement; the nation's energy problems wouldn't look nearly so daunting if we could somehow tap the enthusiasm, joy, and effortless grace she brings to everything she does. She is truly spring in bloom.

My only regret is that my mother, Shirley, didn't live to see this book completed, but her encouragement, humor, and quiet determination are present in every word I write.

NOTES

PREFACE: A DAY IN JUNE

3. "one step ahead of an angry mob": Maura Reynolds, "DeLay, 'the Hammer,' Goes Out With a Bang," *Los Angeles Times,* June 9, 2006.
4. "In preparing for today": Tom DeLay, *Congressional Record,* June 8, 2006, pp. H-3548–3549.
5. "Zuniga, a former Army Officer": Ronald Brownstein, "The Internet And Democrats," *National Journal,* July 2, 2005.

CHAPTER 1: AMERICA DIVIDED

11. "In our politics": Richard Hofstadter, *The Idea of a Party System: The Rise of Legitimate Opposition in the United States, 1780–1840* (Berkeley: University of California Press, 1969), p. 72.
12. "People want you to": Lindsey Graham, interview by author, Washington, D.C., July 18, 2006.
12. "There is no dialogue": Richard Gephardt, interview by author, Washington, D.C., August 4, 2006.
17. "Men who have been intimate": Thomas Jefferson to Edward Rutledge, 1797, at etext.virginia.edu/jefferson/quotations/jeff0750.htm.
18. "The two political parties are": Ken Mehlman, interview by author, Washington, D.C., April 19, 2006.
20. changes in residential patterns: Bill Bishop, "The Schism in U.S. Politics Begins at Home," *Austin American Statesman,* April 4, 2004.
20. Today, three fourths: CBS/*New York Times* polls, November 1980 and June 2006, collected by Public Opinion Strategies.
20. One study found: Institute for Politics, Democracy, and the Internet in collaboration with the Campaign Finance Institute, "Small Donors and Online Giving: A Study of Donors to the 2004 Presidential Campaigns," March 2006, p. 5.
21. "neglected grievances": Hofstadter, *The Idea of a Party System,* p. 15.
21. "call it off": James N. Giglio, *The Presidency of John F. Kennedy* (Lawrence, KS: University Press of Kansas, 2006), p. 180.
21. forced him to move: Ibid., p. 181.
23. half the voters: Morris P. Fiorina, with Samuel J. Abrams and Jeremy C. Pope, *Culture War? The Myth of a Polarized America* (New York: Pearson Longman, 2006), p. 55.

24. An even greater number: "Evans Witt, Election Landscape 2008: Summary of Poll Findings," Princeton Survey Research Associates, May 22, 2006.
24. "The country doesn't like": Stanley B. Greenberg, interview by author, Washington, D.C., April 6, 2006.
24. "there is a big opportunity": Matthew Dowd, interview by author, Washington, D.C., July 10, 2006.

CHAPTER 2: THE AGE OF PARTISAN ARMIES

27. even hired: Michael Kazin, *A Godly Hero: The Life of William Jennings Bryan* (New York: Alfred A. Knopf, 2006), p. 66.
28. as many as 5 million people: Ibid., pp. 67–68.
28. "the struggling masses": Jules Witcover, *Party of the People: A History of the Democrats* (New York: Random House, 2003), p. 283.
29. For only four: Dan Balz and Ronald Brownstein, *Storming the Gates: Protest Politics and the Republican Revival* (Boston and New York: Little Brown & Co., 1996), p. 363.
29. often split both parties: David J. Rothman, *Politics and Power: The United States Senate, 1869–1901* (Cambridge, MA: Harvard University Press, 1966), p. 87.
29. "No one exercises": Ibid., p. 41.
30. "industrial nation-building": Everett Carll Ladd, Jr., *American Political Parties: Social Change and Political Response* (New York: W. W. Norton & Co., 1970), p. 288.
30. "Government is force": Matthew Josephson, *The Politicos, 1865–1896* (New York: Harcourt, Brace & Co., 1938), p. 443.
31. "Never before": William E. Leuchtenburg, *The Perils of Prosperity, 1914–1932*, 2nd ed. (Chicago: University of Chicago Press, 1993), p. 103.
32. Cannon removed: Horace Samuel Merrill and Marion Galbraith Merrill, *The Republican Command, 1897–1913* (Lexington, KY: University Press of Kentucky, 1971), p. 298.
32. Taft replied: Ibid., p. 282.
32. "[T]he unity of the party": Rothman, *Politics and Power*, p. 107.
33. "What you say goes": Merrill and Merrill, *The Republican Command*, pp. 18–19.
33. the acid judgment of Taft: Ibid., p. 160.
33. after the dynamic: John Milton Cooper, Jr., *The Warrior and the Priest: Woodrow Wilson and Theodore Roosevelt* (Cambridge, MA, and London: Belknap Press, 1983), p. 80.
33. continued to battle: Leuchtenburg, *The Perils of Prosperity*, pp. 97–98, 128.
33. even Herbert Hoover: Ibid., p. 253.
34. work within the GOP: James Holt, *Congressional Insurgents and the Party System, 1909–1916* (Cambridge, MA: Harvard University Press, 1967), pp. 81–94, 106–20.
34. to lower tariffs: Merrill and Merrill, *The Republican Command*, pp. 292, 319.
34. as much as 90 percent: Keith T. Poole et al., "Party Polarization: 1879–2006," November 20, 2006, at voteview.com/Polarized_America.htm#POLITICALPOLARIZATION.
34. returning to such heights again: David Brady et al., "The Decline of Party in the U.S. House of Representatives, 1887–1968," *Legislative Studies Quarterly*, August 1979, pp. 381–407, and Poole et al., "Party Polarization: 1879–2006."
36. Reed instructed the clerk: L. White Busbey, *Uncle Joe Cannon: The Story of a Pioneer American* (New York: Henry Holt and Co., 1970), pp. 175–77.

37. Cannon seized authority: Elizabeth Sanders, "Economic Regulation in the Progressive Era," in Julian Zelizer, ed., *The American Congress: The Building of Democracy* (Boston and New York: Houghton Mifflin Co., 2004), p. 340.
37. Beveridge . . . once described: Merrill and Merrill, *The Republican Command*, p. 18.
37. The Four's power rested: Ibid., p. 18.
37. investments with wealthy men: Ibid., p. 21.
38. Initially they resisted: Ibid., p. 49.
38. "promoted their friends": Rothman, *Politics and Power*, p. 60.
38. Cannon wrote: Merrill and Merrill, *The Republican Command*, p. 194.
38. "It would be": Cooper, *The Warrior and the Priest*, p. 85.
38. Roosevelt considered modest: Ibid., p. 82.
38. "he has seen": "Nelson Aldrich" in Zelizer, *The American Congress*, p. 336.
38. Roosevelt did try to soothe: Cooper, *The Warrior and the Priest*, p. 79.
39. discouraged him from pursuing: Ibid., pp. 81–83.
39. Roosevelt never felt: Ibid.
39. Senate Democrats could not: Matthew Josephson, *The President Makers: The Culture of Politics and Leadership in an Age of Enlightenment, 1896–1919* (New York: Frederick Ungar, 1969), pp. 228–236.
39. progressive Republicans joined with Democrats: Sanders, "Economic Regulation in the Progressive Era," in Zelizer, *The American Congress*, p. 342.
39. to purge dissident: Merrill and Merrill, *The Republican Command*, p. 303, and Arthur S. Link, *Woodrow Wilson and the Progressive Era: 1910–1917* (New York: Harper Torchbook, 1963), p. 5.
40. In his final two years: Merrill and Merrill, *The Republican Command*, pp. 315–20.
40. by unifying his party: Link, *Woodrow Wilson and the Progressive Era*, pp. 34–35.
40. "Like a British Prime Minister": Leuchtenburg, *The Perils of Prosperity*, p. 49.
41. "Nearly every leading Republican": John Milton Cooper, Jr., *Breaking the Heart of the World: Woodrow Wilson and the Fight for the League of Nations* (Cambridge: Cambridge University Press, 2001), p. 7.
41. Even the Republican Progressives: Holt, *Congressional Insurgents and the Party System*, pp. 81–95, 106–20.
41. the one first-term priority: Ibid., p. 112.
41. Even the *New Republic: New Republic*, November 7, 1914, quoted in Holt, *Congressional Insurgents and the Party System*, p. 86.
42. Several prominent independents: Ibid., p. 161.
42. did not receive support: Ibid.
42. "The dominant spirit": Ibid.
43. resistant to . . . ideas: Link, *Woodrow Wilson and the Progressive Era*, p. 32.
43. Roosevelt may have: Cooper, *Breaking the Heart of the World*, p. 11.
43. Wilson followed: Ibid., p. 17.
43. La Follette described Wilson: Holt, *Congressional Insurgents and the Party System*, p. 148.
44. "in every European quarrel": Cooper, *The Warrior and the Priest*, p. 310.
44. a genuine difference: Cooper, *Breaking the Heart of the World*, p. 8.
44. only eight senators: Ibid., p. 112.
44. just 12 percent wanted: Ibid., p. 58.
44. "made almost no effort": Cooper, *The Warrior and the Priest*, p. 263.
44. "wish me to continue": Cooper, *Breaking the Heart of the World*, p. 31.
44. it backfired, badly: Ibid.
44. named him as both: Ibid.

45. once published an article: James MacGregor Burns, *The Deadlock of Democracy: Four-Party Politics in America* (Englewood Cliffs, NJ: Prentice-Hall, 1963), p. 119.
45. He did not take: Lewis L. Gould, *The Most Exclusive Club: A History of the Modern United States Senate* (New York: Basic Books, 2005), p. 83.
45. Though friendly with: Cooper, *Breaking the Heart of the World*, p. 37.
45. sent letters to British negotiators: Ibid., pp. 38–39.
45. Lodge announced: Ibid., p. 56.
45. No one missed: Ibid.
45. Wilson denounced: Ibid., p. 70.
45. negotiated some changes: Ibid., pp. 86–87.
46. following a Root suggestion: Ibid., p. 106.
46. tried to position: Ibid., pp. 129–30.
46. First they blocked: Ibid., p. 147.
46. tried to leverage Democrats: Ibid., p. 148.
46. renouncing any compromise: Ibid., p. 149.
46. pressured Senate Democrats: Ibid., p. 262.
46. Each failed: Ibid., pp. 266–68.
47. "not heroism, but healing": Leuchtenburg, *The Perils of Prosperity*, p. 89.
48. "The law that builds up": Arthur M. Schlesinger, Jr., *The Crisis of the Old Order, 1919–1933* (Boston: Houghton Mifflin Co., 1957), p. 57.
48. "The sole function of government": Ibid., p. 238.
49. government's principal role: David Kennedy, *Freedom from Fear: The American People in Depression and War, 1929–1945* (New York and Oxford: Oxford University Press, 1999), p. 47.
49. Eventually he proposed: Ibid., p. 84.
49. Hoover also resisted: Schlesinger, *The Crisis of the Old Order*, pp. 225, 240–41.
50. limited his attacks: Ibid., p. 421.
50. He named to his initial cabinet: Ibid., p. 472.
51. "bold, persistent experimentation": Ibid., p. 290.
51. took an emotional journey: Ibid., p. 454.
51. who had supported him: Gould, *The Most Exclusive Club*, p. 126.
51. direct federal relief grants: Patrick Maney, "The Forgotten New Deal Congress," in Zelizer, *The American Congress*, p. 452.
51. He even enlisted: Kennedy, *Freedom from Fear*, p. 135.
51. Roosevelt accepted the arguments: Maney, "The Forgotten New Deal Congress," in Zelizer, *The American Congress*, p. 453.
52. "to find among": James MacGregor Burns, *Roosevelt: The Lion and the Fox, 1882–1940* (New York and London: Harvest/HBJ, 1956), p. 183.
52. drew broad support: Gould, *The Most Exclusive Club*, p. 130.
52. "ever used the word 'Democrat' ": Arthur M. Schlesinger, Jr., *The Coming of the New Deal* (Boston: Houghton Mifflin Co., 1959), p. 504.
52. "cement our society": Burns, *Roosevelt: The Lion and the Fox*, p. 183.
53. Burns memorably called: Ibid.
53. Increasing resistance: Kennedy, *Freedom from Fear*, pp. 328–29.
53. he could still declare: Ibid., p. 319.
53. "the royalists of the economic": Burns, *Roosevelt: The Lion and the Fox*, p. 274.
55. only after laborious resistance: Ibid., pp. 343–44.
55. "The Roosevelt of 1938": William E. Leuchtenburg, *The White House Looks South: Franklin D. Roosevelt, Harry S. Truman, Lyndon B. Johnson* (Baton Rouge, LA: Louisiana State University Press, 2005), p. 127.

55. Kentucky, Alabama, and Florida: Michael Barone, *Our Country: The Shaping of America from Roosevelt to Reagan* (New York: The Free Press, 1990), p. 120.

55. George reportedly replied: Leuchtenburg, *The White House Looks South*, p. 129.

55. the last . . . to become law: Burns, *Roosevelt: The Lion and the Fox*, p. 344.

Chapter 3: The Age of Bargaining

57. he sniped at: Harold L. Ickes, *The Secret Diary of Harold L. Ickes, The Inside Struggle: 1936–1939, Vol. II* (New York: Simon & Schuster, 1954), p. 179.

57. laughed out loud: "Tired Mule," *Time*, August 9, 1937.

57. similar tongue-lashings: Robert S. Allen, "Roosevelt Fights Back," *The Nation*, August 21, 1937.

57. wrote one Washington journalist: Ibid.

58. Burns correctly concluded: Burns, *Roosevelt: The Lion and the Fox*, p. 315.

58. "It is the politician's task": Doris Kearns, *Lyndon Johnson and the American Dream* (New York: Harper & Row, 1976), p. 141.

58. took the bus: Edward L. Schapsmeier and Frederick H. Schapsmeier, *Dirksen of Illinois: Senatorial Statesman* (Urbana and Chicago, IL: University of Illinois Press, 1985), p. 69.

58. an afternoon walk: D. B. Hardeman and Donald C. Bacon, *Rayburn: A Biography* (Austin, TX: Texas Monthly Press, 1987), p. 409.

59. when he learned of: Ibid., p. 308.

59. Eisenhower sometimes invited: Ibid., p. 392.

59. ate breakfast every day: Gould, *The Most Exclusive Club*, p. 193.

59. "I'd vote for him": James J. Kenneally, *A Compassionate Conservative: A Political Biography of Joseph W. Martin Jr., Speaker of the U.S. House of Representatives* (Lanham, MD: Lexington Books, 2003), p. 48.

60. "If senators didn't join": Howard E. Shuman, Legislative and Administrative Assistant to Senators Paul Douglas and William Proxmire, 1955–1982, Oral History Interviews, Senate Historical Office, Washington, D.C., July 29, 1987.

60. "That's vanity": Richard Reeves, *President Kennedy: Profile of Power* (New York: Simon & Schuster, 1993), p. 319.

61. "The biggest danger": Kearns, *Lyndon Johnson and the American Dream*, p. 154.

62. political scientists spoke of: Burns, *The Deadlock of Democracy*.

62. Shelley found that the largest group: Mack C. Shelley II, *The Permanent Majority: The Conservative Coalition in the United States Congress* (University, AL: University of Alabama Press, 1983), p. 151.

63. The Senate divided: Ibid.

63. "with a wink and a nod": Robert Mann, *The Walls of Jericho: Lyndon Johnson, Hubert Humphrey, Richard Russell, and the Struggle for Civil Rights* (New York: Harcourt Brace & Co., 1996), p. 75.

63. it won most of the fights: Shelley, *The Permanent Majority*, pp. 34, 38.

64. Shelley found the conservative: Ibid., p. 103.

64. the numbers were similar: Ibid.

65. enough Republicans joined: *Congressional Quarterly Almanac 1956* (Washington, DC: Congressional Quarterly, 1956), pp. 411–17.

65. kill the legislation decisively: Ibid., pp. 411–17.

65. "The consequence": Burns, *The Deadlock of Democracy*, p. 260.

66. "consarned S.O.B. so-called": Witcover, *Party of the People*, p. 444.

66. "My greatest troubles": Stephen E. Ambrose, *Eisenhower: Volume Two, The President* (New York: Touchstone, 1985), p. 152.

66. "unalterably opposed": Robert J. Donovan, *Eisenhower: The Inside Story* (New York: Harper & Brothers, 1956), p. 239.

66. Senate Democrats provided: *Congressional Quarterly Almanac 1954* (Washington, DC: Congressional Quarterly, 1954), p. 294.

67. demand they be diluted: Tom Wicker, "Again That Roadblock in Congress," *New York Times*, August 7, 1960.

67. only two petitions: Ibid.

67. still lived in: Julian E. Zelizer, *On Capitol Hill: The Struggle to Reform Congress and Its Consequences, 1948–2000* (Cambridge, England: Cambridge University Press, 2004), p. 56.

67. inspecting a barn: Wicker, "Again That Roadblock in Congress."

67. blocking all of them: *Congressional Quarterly Almanac 1960* (Washington, DC: Congressional Quarterly, 1960), pp. 232, 277, 319, 320.

67. One journalist described him: Hardeman and Bacon, *Rayburn*, p. 461. The journalist was Robert Donovan, then of the New York *Herald Tribune*.

68. "radical, wild-eyed": Zelizer, *On Capitol Hill*, p. 57.

68. But only six: Wicker, "Again That Roadblock in Congress."

68. the speaker floated the purge: Hardeman and Bacon, *Rayburn*, p. 455.

68. threatened to vote: Ibid., p. 453.

69. a *Time* magazine correspondent: Ibid., p. 458.

69. "We can't lose this one": Zelizer, *On Capitol Hill*, p. 57.

69. by a mere five votes: Ibid., p. 59.

69. "We repudiate": Ibid.

69. "the worst fight": Hardeman and Bacon, *Rayburn*, p. 448.

70. never fell below 49 percent: These and subsequent figures on presidential approval by party from Gallup surveys, provided by Gary Jacobson, University of California at San Diego, June 2006.

70. "an era when": American Political Science Association, Committee on Political Parties, "Toward a More Responsible Two-Party System," September 1950, p. v.

70. "when both parties are weakened": Ibid., p. 17.

70. "Alternatives between the parties": Ibid., pp. 3–4

71. "dangerous cycle of drift": Burns, *The Deadlock of Democracy*, p. 340.

71. "While the demands": Ibid., p. 7.

71. "The difference between": Albert Clark, "Leaders Favor Rallying Behind Nixon, Trying Democrats' Hard Sell," *Wall Street Journal*, April 16, 1958.

71. "It should be evident": Barry M. Goldwater, "A Conservative Sets Out His Credo," *New York Times*, July 31, 1960.

72. "its lowest point": Clifton Brock, *Americans for Democratic Action: Its Role in National Politics* (Washington, DC: Public Affairs Press, 1962), p. 155.

73. consistently held the chairmanships: Shelley, *The Permanent Majority*, p. 66.

73. from outside the South surged: Ibid., pp. 140, 142.

73. significantly outnumbered the Southerners: Ibid.

73. Southerners held more: Ibid., p. 66.

73. at least as often: Ibid., pp. 69, 71.

73. Five of the eleven: Author calculations from *Congressional Quarterly Almanac 1961* (Washington, DC: Congressional Quarterly, 1961).

73. When the session opened: *Congressional Quarterly Almanac 1961*, p. 25.

74. each supporting Kennedy: Ibid., p. 628.

74. "conservative power": Zelizer, *On Capitol Hill*, p. 34.
74. first laid siege: Ibid., p. 33.
75. "If there is to be": Howard E. Shuman, "What's the Matter with Congress?" *New Republic*, April 1, 1957.
75. block Wagner's antilynching legislation: Gould, *The Most Exclusive Club*, p. 149.
75. to eliminate the poll tax: Ibid., p. 165.
75. (the level set in 1917): Ibid., pp. 70–71.
75. actually raised the hurdle: Ibid., pp. 201–2.
75. in Georgia, one: Zelizer, *On Capitol Hill*, p. 67.
75. through the 1950s: Ibid., p. 65.
76. rural districts plummeted: Ibid., p. 74.
76. defeated the aging Smith: Ibid., p. 72.
76. then lost the seat: Ibid., p. 73.
77. "The consequences of this system": Shuman, "What's the Matter with Congress?"
77. Clark . . . wrote Lyndon Johnson: Zelizer, *On Capitol Hill*, p. 55.
77. When Senator Stephen Douglas: Rothman, *Politics and Power*, p. 14.
77. In 1925, Republicans removed: Nelson W. Polsby, *How Congress Evolves: Social Bases of Institutional Change* (Oxford and New York: Oxford University Press, 2004), p. 33.
77. Democrats did not punish: Ibid.
77. calls from liberals to strip: Brock, *Americans for Democratic Action*, p. 111.
77. Nor did Democrats: Polsby, *How Congress Evolves*, p. 58.
80. deficits faced resistance: Arthur M. Schlesinger, Jr., *A Thousand Days: John F. Kennedy in the White House* (New York: Greenwich House, 1983), p. 650.
80. Kennedy's personal preferences: Ibid., pp. 649–50.
80. To satisfy Wilbur Mills: Ibid., p. 1003.
82. Congress finally loosened: Robert Dallek, *Franklin D. Roosevelt and American Foreign Policy, 1932–1945* (New York: Oxford University Press, 1979), p. 204.
82. the Senate . . . blocked Roosevelt: Ibid., p. 227.
83. his first instinct: James MacGregor Burns, *Roosevelt, The Soldier of Freedom, 1940–1945* (New York and London: Harvest/HBJ, 1970), p. 38.
83. When Landon balked: Ibid.
83. Roosevelt unveiled a master stroke: Ibid.
83. Senators in both parties complained: C. David Tompkins, *Senator Arthur H. Vandenberg: The Evolution of a Modern Republican, 1884–1945* (Lansing, MI: Michigan State University Press, 1970), p. 194.
83. encouraged him in the . . . journey: Burns, *The Soldier of Freedom*, p. 274.
83. Roosevelt repudiated him: Ibid., p. 276.
83. an idea first planted: Tompkins, *Senator Arthur H. Vandenberg*, p. 199.
83. appointed Democratic senator Tom Connally: Arthur H. Vandenberg, Jr., with the collaboration of Joe Alex Morris, *The Private Papers of Senator Vandenberg* (Boston: Houghton Mifflin Co., 1952), p. 147.
83. "were recognized": Francis O. Wilcox Oral History, Truman Presidential Library, February 1, 1984.
84. His grandfather had attended: Tompkins, *Senator Arthur H. Vandenberg*, p. 1.
84. even as a teenager: Ibid., p. 3.
84. As a young editor: Ibid., p. 8.
84. Vandenberg continued to occupy: Ibid., pp. 103, 115.
85. in a private tirade: Dallek, *Franklin D. Roosevelt and American Foreign Policy*, p. 191.
85. he wrote that year: Tompkins, *Senator Arthur H. Vandenberg*, p. 177.

85. he mused in his diary: Vandenberg Jr., *The Private Papers of Senator Vandenberg*, p. 41.

85. with suggestions from: Tompkins, *Senator Arthur H. Vandenberg*, p. 238.

85. "I do not believe": Ibid., p. 239.

86. over phrases such as: Richard H. Rovere, *The American Establishment and Other Reports, Opinions, and Speculations* (New York: Harcourt, Brace & World, 1962), p. 187.

86. "I tried manfully": James T. Patterson, *Mr. Republican: A Biography of Robert A. Taft* (Boston: Houghton Mifflin Co., 1972), p. 341.

86. He did not agree: Melvyn P. Leffler, *A Preponderance of Power: National Security, the Truman Administration, and the Cold War* (Stanford, CA: Stanford University Press, 1992), pp. 95, 292–95.

87. Truman instructed Lovett: Robert A. Lovett Oral History, Truman Presidential Library, July 7, 1971.

87. "with a sheaf of telegrams": Ibid.

87. drafted a resolution: Vandenberg Jr., *The Private Papers of Senator Vandenberg*, p. 404.

87. One month after: Ibid., p. 411.

87. Truman accepted: Dean Acheson, *Present at the Creation: My Years in the State Department* (New York and London: W. W. Norton, 1987), p. 224.

87. pass the Senate: *Congressional Quarterly Almanac 1947* (Washington, DC: Congressional Quarterly, 1948), p. 270.

87. credited the senator: Acheson, *Present at the Creation*, p. 235.

87. the administration accepted: Charles L. Mee, Jr., *The Marshall Plan: The Launching of the Pax Americana* (New York: Simon & Schuster, 1984), p. 240.

87. cleared the Senate: *Congressional Quarterly Almanac 1948* (Washington, DC: Congressional Quarterly, 1948), p. 216.

87. Acheson told him to check: Acheson, *Present at the Creation*, p. 242; James Chace, *Acheson: The Secretary of State Who Created the American World* (New York: Simon & Schuster, 1998), p. 186.

88. Truman, in his diary: Alonzo L. Hamby, *Man of the People: A Life of Harry S. Truman* (New York and Oxford: Oxford University Press, 1995), p. 403.

88. an excellent choice: Ibid.

88. Acheson concluded it would be: Acheson, *Present at the Creation*, p. 277.

88. Truman and Acheson accepted: Ibid., p. 285.

88. the Senate approved: *Congressional Quarterly Almanac 1949* (Washington, DC: Congressional Quarterly, 1949), p. 349.

88. "in my hand a list": Hamby, *Man of the People*, p. 529.

89. Truman's initial reaction: Chace, *Acheson*, p. 261.

89. negotiate . . . with Japan: Ibid., p. 262.

89. gave Dulles the assignment: Ibid.

89. an extremely effective negotiator: Leffler, *A Preponderance of Power*, p. 429.

89. undertook a speaking tour: Acheson, *Present at the Creation*, p. 633.

89. easily cleared the Senate: *Congressional Quarterly Almanac 1952* (Washington, DC: Congressional Quarterly, 1952), Vote 7, p. 177.

CHAPTER 4: THE AGE OF TRANSITION

93. "I want—and I intend": Robert Dallek, *Flawed Giant: Lyndon Johnson and His Times, 1961–1973* (New York and Oxford: Oxford University Press, 1998), p. 198.

94. On April 11, 1965: *Congressional Quarterly Almanac 1965* (Washington, DC: Congressional Quarterly, 1966), p. 68.

94. the source of bitter frustration: Giglio, *The Presidency of John F. Kennedy*, p. 103.

94. impulsively shifting: Kearns, *Lyndon Johnson and the American Dream*, p. 250.

94. without changing a word: *Congressional Quarterly Almanac 1965*, p. 67.

96. an elaborate chart: Kearns, *Lyndon Johnson and the American Dream*, p. 233.

96. "For God's sakes": Michael Beschloss, ed., *Reaching for Glory: Lyndon Johnson's Secret White House Tapes, 1964–1965* (New York: Simon & Schuster, 2001), p. 240.

96. "What the hell": Ibid., p. 197.

96. Johnson saw himself: Kearns, *Lyndon Johnson and the American Dream*, p. 221.

96. Before Johnson would finalize: Ibid., pp. 222–23.

96. Johnson invited the legislators: Ibid., p. 223.

96. "I did not, I do not": Rowland Evans and Robert Novak, *Lyndon B. Johnson: The Exercise of Power* (New York: New American Library, 1966), p. 470.

97. Johnson's original conception: Dallek, *Flawed Giant: Lyndon Johnson and His Times*, p. 207.

97. Johnson quickly embraced it: Ibid., p. 208.

97. Among Johnson's major bills: Author calculations from *Congressional Quarterly Almanac 1965*.

98. He drove away: Kearns, *Lyndon Johnson and the American Dream*, p. 320.

98. "Under siege, however": Ibid., p. 319.

98. "taken in": Dallek, *Flawed Giant*, p. 367.

98. "Most of the protests": Ibid., p. 467.

100. agreements between the two parties produced: Melvin Small, *The Presidency of Richard Nixon* (Lawrence, KS: University Press of Kansas, 1999), p. 153.

100. Nixon and a bipartisan congressional coalition produced: Ibid., pp. 198–99.

101. Republicans to the left: Ibid., p. 39.

101. more than one third: *Congressional Quarterly Almanac 1970* (Washington, DC: Congressional Quarterly, 1971), Vote S–180, p. 33–S.

101. John Sherman Cooper joined with: Stephen E. Ambrose, *Nixon: The Triumph of a Politician, 1962–1972* (New York: Simon & Schuster, 1989), p. 358.

101. Seventeen Senate Republicans: *Congressional Quarterly Almanac 1969* (Washington, DC: Congressional Quarterly, 1970), Vote 135, p. 29–S.

101. a little girl in Deshler, Ohio: Barone, *Our Country*, p. 454.

102. "The one great objective": Small, *The Presidency of Richard Nixon*, p. 30.

102. "open to new ideas": Ibid.

102. He offered to appoint: Ibid., p. 36.

102. Nixon also proposed: Ibid., pp. 175, 188, 192, 212.

102. decisions that angered liberals: Ibid., pp. 173, 179.

102. "The president is no longer": Ibid., p. 154.

103. "Emphasize—anti-Crime": Ambrose, *Nixon*, p. 374.

103. In his speeches he contrasted: Ibid., p. 348.

103. as much as one fifth: Small, *The Presidency of Richard Nixon*, p. 200.

103. Nixon told Harry Dent: Ibid., p. 168.

103. The nomination failed: *Congressional Quarterly Almanac 1970*, Vote 112, p. 21–S.

104. he escalated . . . into Laos: Small, *The Presidency of Richard Nixon*, p. 71.

104. in Cambodia: Ibid., pp. 71–72, 75.

104. He mined the North Vietnamese: Ibid., p. 89.

107. when James Roche: Justin Martin, *Nader: Crusader, Spoiler, Icon* (Cambridge, MA: Perseus Publishing, 2002), p. 55.

107. a coruscating, exhaustively researched: Ibid., p. 45.

107. did Nader explode into the public: Ibid., p. 59.

107. much tougher federal regulation: *Congressional Quarterly Almanac 1966* (Washington, DC: Congressional Quarterly, 1967), pp. 269, 272.

108. "indrawn and ingrown": William S. White, *Citadel: The Story of the U.S. Senate* (New York: Harper and Brothers, 1956), p. 8.

108. "walks apart, very often": Ibid.

108. "Few issues appeared": David Vogel, *Fluctuating Fortunes: The Political Power of Business in America* (New York: Basic Books, 1989), p. 7.

109. signed into law half a dozen: Ibid., p. 26.

109. do not even mention: Jeffrey M. Berry, *The New Liberalism: The Rising Power of Citizen Groups* (Washington, DC: Brookings Institution Press, 1999), p. 4.

109. five major new environmental organizations: Ibid., p. 65.

109. John Gardner . . . took out: Berry, *The New Liberalism*, p. 29.

110. "public interest conglomerate": Vogel, *Fluctuating Fortunes*, p. 101.

110. all doubled roughly: Kirkpatrick Sale, *The Green Revolution: The American Environmental Movement, 1962–1992* (New York: Hill and Wang, 1993), p. 23.

110. Membership in the Sierra Club: Ibid., p. 23.

110. twenty-nine significant pieces: Berry, *The New Liberalism*, p. 72.

111. a *Harvard Business Review* survey: Vogel, *Fluctuating Fortunes*, p. 35.

111. a more proactive agenda: Jerome L. Himmelstein, *To the Right: The Transformation of American Conservatism* (Berkeley: University of California Press, 1990), pp. 129–51.

112. "Business must learn the lesson": Lewis F. Powell, Jr., memo to Eugene B. Sydnor, Jr., "Attack on American Free Enterprise System," August 23, 1971.

112. offices or lobbyists in the capital exploded: Vogel, *Fluctuating Fortunes*, pp. 197–198.

112. the number of political action committees: Ibid., p. 207.

112. the 1972 opening of: Ibid., p. 198.

112. doubled its membership: Ibid., p. 199.

112. probably did less to expand: Godfrey Hodgson, *The World Turned Right Side Up: A History of the Conservative Ascendancy in America* (Boston and New York: Houghton Mifflin Co., 1996), pp. 62–63.

113. formed the Eagle Forum: Ibid., p. 175.

113. in an unused soda-bottling plant: Ibid., p. 170.

113. AEI had been a voice: James Allen Smith, *The Idea Brokers: Think Tanks and the Rise of the New Policy Elite* (New York: The Free Press, 1991), p. 175.

113. The idea . . . came from: Ibid., p. 200.

114. "Here before my eyes": Paul Weyrich, interview by author, Washington, D.C., August 2006.

114. with seed money from . . . Coors: Lee Edwards, *The Power of Ideas: The Heritage Foundation at 25 Years* (Ottawa, IL: Jameson Books, 1997), p. 9.

115. a 1,093-page volume: Ibid., p. 48.

115. A group initially called: "The Human Rights Campaign: A Historical Snapshot," at hrc.org/Content/NavigationMenu/About_HRC/HistoricalSnapshot.htm.

115. closed its doors in 1989: Balz and Brownstein, *Storming the Gates*, p. 311.

116. a higher priority than liberals: Sidney Blumenthal, *The Rise of the Counter-Establishment, From Conservative Ideology to Political Power* (New York: Harper & Row, 1988), p. 66.

117. "change the agenda": Paul Weyrich, interview by author, August 2006.

117. a rebellion among the New Right: Hodgson, *The World Turned Right Side Up*, pp. 227–30.

118. a small-time inventor . . . named Howard Jarvis: Robert Kuttner, *Revolt of the Haves: Tax Rebellions and Hard Times* (New York: Simon & Schuster, 1980), pp. 39–41.

119. almost five times that: Data provided by Michael J. Malbin, Campaign Finance Institute, June 2006.

119. Senators likewise: Ibid.

120. "I don't socialize at all": Alan Ehrenhalt, "In the Senate of the '80s, Team Spirit Has Given Way to the Rule of Individuals," *Congressional Quarterly*, September 4, 1982.

120. "Bob Michel was": John Breaux, interview by author, Washington, D.C., April 11, 2006.

120. "[I]n so many of its critical moments": White, *Citadel*, p. 197.

120. "They didn't report the drunks": Howard E. Shuman, Legislative and Administrative Assistant to Senators Paul Douglas and William Proxmire, 1955–1982, Oral History Interviews, Senate Historical Office, Washington, D.C., September 17, 1987.

121. "nobody paid any attention": Alan Ehrenhalt, "Media, Power Shifts Dominate O'Neill's House," *Congressional Quarterly*, September 13, 1986.

121. More investigative reporting: Michael Schudson, "Congress and the Media," in Zelizer, *The American Congress*, p. 651.

121. Television first aimed: Donald A. Ritchie, *Reporting from Washington: The History of the Washington Press Corps* (New York: Oxford University Press, 2005), pp. 188–89.

121. starting with Walter Cronkite's CBS broadcast: Ibid., p. 195.

121. Mudd marked television's arrival: Ibid., p. 200.

121. Cable News Network inaugurated: Ibid., p. 210.

121. "the House of Representatives was a backwater": Richard Gephardt, interview by author, August 4, 2006.

122. inaugurated a series of folksy: "The 1960s: A Multi-Media View from Capitol Hill," Dirksen Congressional Center, at: dirksencenter.org/emd_audio/aboutproject.htm.

123. "big, fat, and out of control": Gil Troy, *Morning in America: How Ronald Reagan Invented the 1980s* (Princeton, NJ, and Oxford: Princeton University Press, 2005), pp. 99–100.

123. "There was dissent or unrest": Richard Gephardt, interview by author, August 4, 2006.

123. Wright . . . advanced the transformation: David W. Rohde, *Parties and Leaders in the Postreform House* (Chicago: University of Chicago Press, 1991), pp. 105–6.

123. "What has happened over those years": John Breaux, interview with author, April 11, 2006.

124. the Senate slightly curbed: Zelizer, *On Capitol Hill*, p. 175.

124. "an ineluctable and irresistible force": White, *Citadel*, p. 183.

124. stripped two Southern Democrats: Polsby, *How Congress Evolves*, p. 58.

124. another Southerner suffered: Ibid., p. 60.

125. support from the proliferating: Zelizer, *On Capitol Hill*, p. 133.

125. immediately used the power: Polsby, *How Congress Evolves*, pp. 65–68.

125. Reuss . . . captured the sense of upheaval: Zelizer, *On Capitol Hill*, p. 168.

125. "A party support record": Ann Cooper, "Committee Assignments Finished, Chairmen Picked, Congress Is Ready to Work," *Congressional Quarterly*, January 27, 1979.

125. House Democrats didn't oust: Polsby, *How Congress Evolves*, p. 122.

125. Coelho . . . had difficulty: Tony Coelho, interview by author, Washington, D.C., July 7, 2006.

125. Aspin, was nearly removed: Polsby, *How Congress Evolves*, pp. 123–24.

126. even Whitten moved much closer: Barbara Sinclair, *Party Wars: Polarization and the Politics of National Policy Making* (Norman, OK: University of Oklahoma Press, 2006), p. 91.
126. on a blackboard: Ibid., p. 87.
126. "There's nothing that can be done": Schlesinger, *A Thousand Days*, p. 723.
126. "replaced with a merit system": John Feehery, interview by author, Washington, D.C., April 12, 2006.
128. Carter's vote actually declined more: Marjorie Connelly, "Who Voted: A Portrait of American Politics, 1976–2000," *New York Times*, November 12, 2000.
130. In one early 1982 survey: Gallup poll, April 25, 1982. Breakdowns by party provided by Gary Jacobson, University of California (San Diego).
131. A coalition of 150 groups: Blumenthal, *The Rise of the Counter-Establishment*, p. 232.
131. Some 700,000 people crowded: Troy, *Morning in America*, p. 138.
131. "war, pestilence, famine and death": Ibid., p. 93.
131. from about 40 percent of Democrats: Author calculations from Gallup surveys provided by Gary Jacobson.
132. Opposition from moderate Republican senators: *Congressional Quarterly Almanac 1982* (Washington, DC: Congressional Quarterly, 1983), pp. 403–5.
132. opposition from Specter and . . . Mathias: *Congressional Quarterly Almanac 1985* (Washington, DC: Congressional Quarterly, 1986), p. 237.
133. Reagan . . . offered him the ambassadorship: Lou Cannon, *President Reagan: The Role of a Lifetime* (New York: Public Affairs, 2000), p. 440.
133. he understood the value of compromise: Ibid., pp. 153–54.
134. Reagan replaced her with . . . Ruckelshaus: Ibid., pp. 469–70.
134. the treaty drew support: Ibid., pp. 700–1.
134. "Reagan . . . kept a relatively open": Ronald Brownstein, "Resolute in Rhetoric, Reagan and Bush Part Ways in Deed," *Los Angeles Times*, June 14, 2004.
136. "Reaganism completely defeated": Grover Norquist, interview by author, Washington, D.C., July 18, 2006.

CHAPTER 5: THE AGE OF TRANSITION II: THE RISE OF HYPERPARTISANSHIP

137. "There is a model I work off": Susan F. Rasky, "From Political Guerilla to Republican Folk Hero," *New York Times*, June 15, 1988.
137. "It is my tactic": David Rogers, "Assault from the Right: Rep. Gingrich Fights Democrats," *Wall Street Journal*, May 23, 1984.
137. "My interest is in creating": William Johnson, "New-wave right Congressman preaches a pop conservative vision," *Toronto Globe and Mail*, July 25, 1985.
137. "I'm tough in the House": Dave Montgomery, "Gingrich Persists in Angering Foes," *St. Louis Post-Dispatch*, January 2, 1988.
138. "I have an enormous": Lois Romano, "Newt Gingrich, Maverick on the Hill . . .," *Washington Post*, January 3, 1985.
139. "Ed . . . we don't talk about changing": Edwin Feulner, interview by author, Washington, D.C., June 27, 2006.
139. Michel would sometimes drive home: Polsby, *How Congress Evolves*, p. 125.
139. "If you think you are the subordinate": Newt Gingrich, interview by author, Washington, D.C., July 10, 2006.

139. younger Republican members . . . voted: Rohde, *Parties and Leaders in the Postreform House*, p. 122.

139. to seek advice from Richard Nixon: Balz and Brownstein, *Storming the Gates*, p. 118.

139. with a small group that included: Ibid., pp. 118–19.

140. "a confrontational activism": Romano, "Newt Gingrich, Maverick on the Hill . . ."

140. Gingrich visited the fledgling Heritage: Edwin Feulner interview, June 27, 2006.

140. He encouraged Paul Weyrich: Paul Weyrich, interview by author, Washington, D.C., August 2006.

140. "I called the head of the NFIB": Newt Gingrich interview, July 10, 2006.

141. the COS championed a marriage: Dan Balz and Charles R. Babcock, "Gingrich, Allies Made Waves and Impression," *Washington Post*, December 20, 1994.

141. Among the regular viewers was . . . Limbaugh: Rush Limbaugh, interview, *Evans & Novak* (CNN), November 15, 1997.

141. "sick institution" and "Tammany Hall . . .": Richard E. Cohen, Kirk Victor, and David Baumann, "The State of Congress," *National Journal*, January 10, 2004.

141. O'Neill's words violated: Balz and Brownstein, *Storming the Gates*, pp. 120–21.

141. rose to applaud Gingrich: Rogers, "Assault from the Right: Rep. Gingrich Fights Democrats."

141. "Tip made a critical error": Tony Coelho, interview by author, Washington, D.C., July 7, 2006.

142. Gingrich sought to expel: Balz and Brownstein, *Storming the Gates*, p. 123.

142. A long, tangled confrontation: Ibid., pp. 123–25.

142. Gingrich encouraged younger Republicans: Newt Gingrich, interview by Dan Balz and Ronald Brownstein, Washington, D.C., July 12, 1995.

142. "I'd say, . . . 'Be bold. Have courage . . .' ": Ibid.

142. extended beyond words to fists: Mark Nelson, "Hostility in House Becoming Physical," *Dallas Morning News*, July 15, 1985.

142. "I always thought that": Newt Gingrich interview, July 12, 1995.

143. "It totally blurred all the issues": Steven V. Roberts, "One Conservative Faults Two Parties," *New York Times*, August 11, 1983.

143. "forcing a polarization of the country": Nina Easton, *Gang of Five: Leaders at the Center of the Conservative Crusade* (New York: Simon & Schuster, 2000), p. 159.

143. "The minority party doesn't win elections": Eric Pianin, "House GOP's Frustrations Intensify," *Washington Post*, December 21, 1987.

143. Michel walked out . . . without clapping: Steven V. Roberts, "Congress, New Conflict a Threat to Old Ways," *New York Times*, May 19, 1984.

143. "he didn't want to hurt the establishment": Tony Coelho interview, July 7, 2006.

144. "Our caucus started to get more and more aggressive": Ibid.

144. to award an Indiana seat: Balz and Brownstein, *Storming the Gates*, p. 122.

144. "who were Gingrich-ites": Newt Gingrich interview, July 10, 2006.

144. Wright threatened Democrats: Rohde, *Parties and Leaders in the Postreform House*, p. 114.

145. Republicans complained that Democrats: Sara Fritz, "Minority in Each House Frustrated," *Los Angeles Times*, May 21, 1985.

145. Wright infuriated Republicans: Janet Hook, "GOP Snipes at How Democrats Run House," *Congressional Quarterly*, May 28, 1988.

145. Wright kept the vote open: Sinclair, *Party Wars*, p. 118.

145. Gingrich ran more on a platform of injecting: Balz and Brownstein, *Storming the Gates*, p. 133.

146. Congress could simply go home: Michael Duffy and Dan Goodgame, *Marching in Place: The Status Quo Presidency of George Bush* (New York: Simon & Schuster, 1992), p. 82.

147. he infuriated them: Balz and Brownstein, *Storming the Gates*, p. 178.

148. "we could make it so unbelievably expensive": Ibid., p. 140.

148. "it was contrary to what we were doing": Ibid., p. 135.

149. Clinton promised voters during his march: Clinton acceptance speech to Democratic convention, July 16, 1992, at: presidency.ucsb.edu/shownomination.php?convid=7.

150. "He was omnivorous": Bruce Reed, interview by author, July 5, 2006.

150. even as two thirds of voters said they disliked: *Los Angeles Times* exit poll, November 7, 2000. Fifty-eight percent said they liked Clinton's policies, while 65 percent said they disliked him personally.

152. voted with their party more often: "Party Unity History," *Congressional Quarterly*, January 9, 2006.

153. For every dollar in tax increases: Balz and Brownstein, *Storming the Gates*, p. 95.

153. by the most tenuous of margins: Ibid., p. 97.

153. Domenici . . . told Clinton's budget director: John F. Harris, *The Survivor: Bill Clinton in the White House* (New York: Random House, 2005), p. 86.

154. Business groups . . . spent sums estimated: Haynes Johnson and David S. Broder, *The System: The American Way of Politics at the Breaking Point* (Boston and New York: Little Brown & Co., 1996), pp. 194–95.

154. weighed in at 1,342 pages: Ibid., p. 10.

155. even Bob Dole . . . and . . . Haley Barbour: Balz and Brownstein, *Storming the Gates*, p. 98.

155. "health reform is faster, smaller": Paul Starr, "What Happened to Health Care Reform," *American Prospect*, Winter 1995.

158. Gingrich engineered a change in House rules: *Congressional Quarterly Almanac 1994* (Washington, D.C.: Congressional Quarterly, 1995), pp. 1–10; Sinclair, *Party Wars*, pp. 122–30.

158. "you ascend by loyalty": Tom Davis, interview by author, Washington, D.C., June 22, 2006.

158. Gingrich said his principal motivation: Newt Gingrich interview, July 10, 2006.

159. Gingrich further tightened his control: Sinclair, *Party Wars*, p. 126.

159. only if they committed to work for every element: Don Fierce, interview by author, Washington, D.C., June 30, 2006.

159. the Republican House approved nine of the ten: Sinclair, *Party Wars*, p. 127.

159. On average, 98 percent of House Republicans voted: Balz and Brownstein, *Storming the Gates*, p. 294.

160. only a single Republican House member voted against: *Congressional Quarterly Almanac 1995* (Washington, D.C.: Congressional Quarterly, 1996), Vote H–345, p. H–98.

160. Senate Democrats and Republicans had adopted rules: Sinclair, *Party Wars*, p. 194.

160. neither party had used them: Donald Ritchie (Senate historian), interview by author, Washington, D.C., June 28, 2006.

160. "Ownership of a seat . . . is pretty well established": Tom Daschle, interview by author, Washington, D.C., April 13, 2006.

161. The average senator voted with his or her party: Calculations from "Party Unity History," *Congressional Quarterly*, January 9, 2006.

161. The number soared past forty: Cohen, Victor, and Baumann, "The State of Congress."

161. filibuster against fully half of Clinton's: Sinclair, *Party Wars*, p. 213.
161. Not a single Republican senator voted against: *Congressional Quarterly Almanac 1995*, Vote S–232, p. S–39.
162. once again, every Senate Republican . . . voted for it: *Congressional Quarterly Almanac 1995*, Votes S–296, p. S–49, and H–458, p. H–130.
162. broke the momentum of the new Republican majority: To this day Gingrich insists the government shutdowns did not hurt the GOP. "There's no evidence in any polling data that it cost us anything," he said. "We thought you had to be that serious to get to a balanced budget, and we thought being that serious communicated biologically in a way that caving and being acceptable to the Georgetown cocktail party crowd would not have done. Totally different models of how you run the country" (Newt Gingrich interview, July 10, 2006). To support his claim Gingrich correctly notes that Republicans held their congressional majority in 1996. But Gingrich's argument fails to acknowledge that Clinton's recovery, which began with the budget fight, changed the nature of that majority. It forced congressional Republicans to defer their hopes of sweeping, even revolutionary, cutbacks in government and instead accept compromises with Clinton that often expanded government's reach. By ending any chance Republicans might consolidate their control over Washington in 1996, the government shutdown set back the conservative agenda for years.
163. "I do not want a pile of vetoes": Harris, *The Survivor*, p. 175.
164. "it was liberating for him": Harold Ickes, interview by author, Washington, D.C., May 8, 2006.
165. Clinton and Lott narrowed many: Trent Lott, *Herding Cats: A Life in Politics* (New York: Regan Books, 2005), pp. 129–44.
166. So did much of his cabinet: Harris, *The Survivor*, p. 237.
166. the share of single women in poverty: Ronald Brownstein, "State of the Debate: Recent books on the Clinton legacy," *American Prospect*, February 25, 2002.
166. the number of children in poverty: Ibid.
166. "They had been humbled": Bruce Reed interview, July 5, 2006.
167. the tax burden . . . declined: "Historical Effective Federal Tax Rates: 1979 to 2004," Congressional Budget Office, December 2006. The federal income tax rate for families in the middle fifth of the income distribution dropped from 17.3 percent in 1993 to 16.6 percent in 2000.
168. "We were like two graduate students": Newt Gingrich interview, July 10, 2006.
168. Reed imagined future agreements: Bruce Reed interview, July 5, 2006.
168. "a capitulation . . . to fear": "No Deal," editorial, *Weekly Standard*, May 12, 1997.
168. The Heritage Foundation issued: Matt Rees, "Cutting the Tax-Cut Pie," *Weekly Standard*, May 25, 1997.
168. Dan Quayle . . . complained: Ceci Connolly and Terry M. Neal, "Quayle Questions Leaders Loyalty," *Washington Post*, August 23, 1997.
168. a coup against Gingrich: Janet Hook, "Gingrich Survives New Try to Unseat Him as Speaker," *Los Angeles Times*, July 17, 1997.
168. both Armey and DeLay had participated: Ibid.
168. Lott . . . faced similar grumbling: John King, "GOP Conservatives Grumble over Lott's Deal-making Compromises," Associated Press, May 4, 1997.
169. Gingrich . . . defended the budget deal: Jeanne Cummings, "Gingrich Rips Republicans Critical of Budget Accord," *Wall Street Journal*, August 26, 1997.
169. "I used to tell my members": Newt Gingrich interview, July 10, 2006.
169. "We're fudging the differences . . ." said Tom Pauken: Donald Lambro, "GOP Conservatives Slap Budget Plan as Bad Deal for Party," *Washington Times*, May 25, 1997.

169. "people with bigger dreams": "Rosty's Tax Cut," editorial, *Wall Street Journal,* July 30, 1997.

170. "we'd run out of things to agree on": Bruce Reed interview, July 5, 2006.

170. "slowed to a trickle": *Congressional Quarterly Almanac 1997* (Washington, D.C.: Congressional Quarterly, 1998), p. 5–19.

170. legislation blocking Clinton's top education reform: Janet Hook and Ronald Brownstein, "Logjam Augurs Partisan Strife for Congress," *Los Angeles Times,* November 12, 1997. See this for a summary of the legislative breakdowns that fall.

170. Democrats . . . compounded the sense of confusion: Ibid.

170. spent over $2 million on thirty-two hearings: *Congressional Quarterly Almanac 1997,* p. 1–9.

170. seventeen impatient Republicans . . . filed a resolution: Times Staff and Wire Reports, "17 in GOP Seek Impeachment Study," *Los Angeles Times,* November 6, 1997.

171. surveys all found that at least: See surveys by Gallup, December 12–December 13, 1998; ABC/*Washington Post,* December 15, 1998; and CBS/*New York Times,* December 16, 1998.

172. in the House all but four Republicans voted: *Congressional Quarterly Almanac 1998* (Washington, D.C.: Congressional Quarterly, 1999), Votes H–543–546, pp. H–154–156.

172. in the Senate . . . fifty of the fifty-five Republicans voted to convict: *Congressional Quarterly Almanac 1999* (Washington, D.C.: Congressional Quarterly, 2000), Votes S–17–18, p. S–7.

172. "We were impeaching each other": John Breaux, interview by author, Washington, D.C., April 11, 2006.

172. the welfare reform agreement drew support: Gallup survey August 5–August 7, 1996, question 15. Results by party provided by Gallup.

172. supported the budget agreement: Gallup survey August 22–August 25, 1997, question 13. Results by party provided by Gallup.

Chapter 6: The Great Sorting Out

175. packed his wife Tricia: Lott, *Herding Cats,* p. 49.

175. Lott was born: Ibid., pp. 7–13.

176. ever disagreeing about politics until: Ibid., p. 16.

177. "He certainly evolved": Ralph Neas, interview by author, Washington, D.C., June 21, 2006. All subsequent Neas quotes in this section are taken from the same interview.

178. "the ranks of the clueless": Lott, *Herding Cats,* p. 37.

178. shared the support for segregation: David M. Halbfinger and Jeffrey Gettleman, "In Lott's Life, Long Shadows of Segregation," *New York Times,* December 15, 2002.

178. "time had come": Lott, *Herding Cats,* p. 41.

179. "I'm not a Democrat": Ibid., p. 52.

179. "crossed the Rubicon": Ibid.

179. he stunned Colmer: Ibid., p. 53.

179. fewer than one in every ten: Ibid.

180. even remove his own wastes: Steven A. Holmes, "Lobbyist on Civil Rights Wins Despite Hostility," *New York Times,* December 2, 1991.

180. nearly went to work for the Reagan: Ralph Neas interview, June 21, 2006.

182. "an embarrassment to the nation": "Lott's Latest Apology Misses the Point," People for the American Way, press release, December 13, 2002.

183. the most comprehensive study ever made of attitudes: Herbert McClosky, Paul J. Hoffmann, Rosemary O'Hara, "Issue Conflict and Consensus Among Party Leaders and Followers," *American Political Science Review,* June 1960, pp. 406–27.

183. significantly different views on twenty-three: Ibid., p. 411.

184. The two groups expressed similar views: Ibid., p. 410.

184. "their followers differ only moderately": Ibid., p. 426.

185. significant shares on both sides: V. O. Key, Jr., *Public Opinion and American Democracy* (New York: Alfred A. Knopf, 1961), p. 444.

185. On noneconomic issues . . . the NES surveys: Angus Campbell, Philip E. Converse, Warren E. Miller, and Donald E. Stokes, *The American Voter: Unabridged Edition* (Chicago and London: University of Chicago Press, 1976), p. 198. Also, Gerald M. Pomper, "Toward a More Responsible Two-Party System? What, Again?" *Journal of Politics,* November 1971, p. 926.

185. "Extremism in the defense of liberty": Goldwater acceptance speech to 1964 GOP convention at: washingtonpost.com/wp-srv/politics/daily/may98/goldwaterspeech.htm.

187. accepts interracial dating: "The 2004 Political Landscape: Evenly Divided and Increasingly Polarized," Pew Research Center for the People and the Press, p. 45, November 5, 2003. See question t-52 for woman's place. In Gallup surveys the percentage of Americans saying homosexuals should have equal rights in job opportunities has increased from 56 percent in June 1977 to 89 percent in May 2006.

193. In all, liberals outside the South: The Democratic vote in House races among liberals outside the South has increased from 73 percent in the 1970s to 85 percent in this decade. In Senate races the increase has been from 71 percent to 90 percent; in the presidential race from 71 percent to 89 percent. Calculated from National Election Studies in 2006 by Alan Abramowitz, Emory University.

195. those "differential images . . . have prevailed": Key, *Public Opinion and American Democracy,* p. 434.

195. Both skilled and unskilled workers: Ibid.

195. Bill Clinton, Al Gore, and John Kerry all won handily: Marjorie Connelly, "How Americans Voted: A Political Portrait," *New York Times,* November 7, 2004.

196. The difference between the two closest: The ANES Guide to Public Opinion and Electoral Behavior, at: electionstudies.org/nesguide/2ndtable/t9a_1_2.htm and electionstudies.org/nesguide/2ndtable/t9a_1_1.htm.

197. Greenberg . . . speaks for many political strategists: Stanley B. Greenberg, interview by author, Washington, D.C., April 6, 2006.

198. Republicans run better with those who attend: John Green and Mark Silk, "The New Religion Gap," *Religion in the News,* Fall 2003, at: trincoll.edu/depts/csrpl/RINVol6No3/2004%20Election/religion%20gap.htm.

198. Even Jewish voters: See John C. Green, *The Faith Factor: How Religion Influences the Vote* (Westport, CT: Praeger Press, 2007).

200. on a beautiful late October day: Author notes on Clinton appearance, October 24, 1996.

201. "from places like Hoboken and Jersey City": Tom Turcol and Thomas Fitzgerald, "Race Intensifies Here Over War," *Philadelphia Inquirer,* October 19, 2004.

202. roughly $700 million between them: "2004 Presidential Election," Center for Responsive Politics, at: opensecrets.org/presidential/index_2004./asp.

203. most revealing to compare highly competitive elections: Calculations on margins of victory in the 1960, 1976, 2000, and 2004 elections provided by Clark Bensen, Polidata, Inc.

206. the midpoint of the two parties has become: Gary C. Jacobson, "Party Polarization
      in National Politics: The Electoral Connection," in Jon R. Bond and Richard Fleisher
      (eds.), *Polarized Politics: Congress and the President in a Partisan Era* (Washington,
      DC: Congressional Quarterly Press, 2000), p. 12.

206. the centrist Senate Republicans were squeezed: These forces first felled Ed Brooke
      and Clifford Case in 1978. Both faced primary contests from more conservative
      challengers. Brooke fended off his challenge from radio talk show host Avi Nelson.
      But he was weakened further by an achingly public divorce dispute, and lost the
      general election to neoliberal Democrat Paul Tsongas; John Kerry won the seat when
      Tsongas retired for health reasons in 1984, and Republicans have never held it again.
      In New Jersey Case lost his primary to Jeffrey Bell, an engaging young aide in Ronald
      Reagan's 1976 presidential campaign, who accused the incumbent of voting too often
      with Jimmy Carter; but Bell lost the seat to another neoliberal Democrat, Bill
      Bradley, that fall. Democrats held the seat after Bradley's retirement, and Republicans
      have never recaptured it, either.
        New York two years later saw a variation on the theme. Alfonse M. D'Amato, a
      genially overbearing local Republican official from Long Island, challenged Javits on
      the grounds that he was too old and voted too often with Carter. D'Amato won the
      primary, and he narrowly won the general election too, when Javits remained in the
      race on the Liberal Party line and split the state's Democratic-leaning vote. D'Amato
      then tenaciously held the seat until 1998, when the ambitious, equally tenacious
      Democrat Charles E. Schumer beat him in an atmosphere shaped by the high
      emotions surrounding the Republican drive to impeach Clinton. Schumer won
      reelection in 2004 and seems in no danger of surrendering the seat to the GOP any
      time soon.
        Others of the Republican moderates, such as Charles Percy in 1984, simply lost to
      Democratic challengers in states evolving away from the GOP. In other cases
      Democrats captured seats when the centrist Republicans retired, as Patrick Leahy did
      when Aiken finally stepped down in Vermont in 1974 or Barbara Mikulski did when
      Mathias stepped aside in Maryland in 1986. Both Democrats have held those seats
      ever since as well.

208. the number of close House general election races has fallen dramatically: In 2002 and
      2004, the first two elections in the new districts drawn after the 2000 census, the
      number of close House elections tumbled to the lowest level in the past half century.
      Redistricting isn't the only cause of that trend: Incumbents enjoy many other
      advantages, especially in fund-raising. But the table following leaves little doubt that
      the 2000 redistricting marked a sharp break from earlier experience. The table tracks
      the number of close, and one-sided, House races in each of the past six decades. It
      shows a decline in competition beginning in the 1960s, punctuated by a severe
      reduction in the average number of close races after 2000. In 2006 gale-force
      discontent among voters created a larger circle of competitive races, with Republicans
      losing districts from Ohio to Texas that were designed to provide their candidates
      with lopsided advantages. Yet even in that storm, the defenses constructed for
      incumbents after 2000 limited the damage: Although the number of close races
      increased amid the voter backlash in 2006, the total remained well below the peaks
      reached during other elections marked by voter upheaval, like 1958, 1966, 1974, and
      1982. (In 1958, 106 House races were decided by ten percentage points or less; the
      numbers were seventy-six in 1966, ninety in 1974, and seventy-two in 1982.)

209. "Your only threat is a primary": Richard Gephardt, interview by author, Washington,
      D.C., August 4, 2006.

COMPETITIVENESS IN HOUSE RACES

Elections	Average number of House races won by 10% or less	Average number of House races won by 30% or more	Ratio
1952–60	92	182	1–2.0
1962–70	77	202	1–2.6
1972–80	71	238	1–3.4
1982–90	51	263	1–5.1
1992–2000	67	225	1–3.4
2002–2004	29	280	1–9.6
2006	60	230	1–3.8

Source: Clark Bensen, Polidata, Inc.

212. who report splitting their tickets: Figures from NES surveys provided by Alan Abramowitz, Emory University. The percentage of voters who supported one party for president and another party in House elections rose from 16 percent in the 1960s to 27 percent in the 1970s, fell to 25 percent in the 1980s, before declining to 20 percent in the 1990s and 17 percent in this decade. The percentage of voters who supported one party for president and another party in Senate elections rose from 18 percent in the 1960s to 26 percent in the 1970s, before declining to 23 percent in the 1980s, 16 percent in the 1990s, and 14 percent in this decade.

214. and 70 percent of their Senate seats: The three states that split their votes between 2000 and 2004—Iowa, New Hampshire, and New Mexico—provided the final House and Senate members for each party after 2006. In the House the figures were four for the Republicans and six for the Democrats; in the Senate, the numbers were four for the Republicans and two for the Democrats.

215. "Parts of the electorate are locked in": Matthew Dowd, interview by author, Washington, D.C., July 10, 2006.

215. "Public esteem . . . is declining": Stanley B. Greenberg interview, April 6, 2006.

216. The last time Pew performed this exercise: "The 2005 Political Typology: Beyond Red vs. Blue," Pew Research Center for the People and the Press, May 10, 2005.

217. "umbrella party" . . . "programmatic coherence": Ladd, *American Political Parties*, pp. 43, 53.

CHAPTER 7: THE PRESIDENT OF HALF OF AMERICA

222. "I'm a uniter": Author notes from Bush appearance, June 14, 1999.

222. "Bob doesn't pass out compliments easily": Ronald Brownstein, "The Candidates and How They Govern," *Los Angeles Times*, July 16, 2000.

223. instantly put him at ease: Ibid.

223. he routinely popped in unannounced: Ibid.

223. Each time he accepted compromises: Ibid.

224. "To the extent people want to work": Ibid.

224. Most Texas legislators . . . reached similar verdicts: Ibid. Bill Ratliff, a Republican who chaired the powerful State Senate Finance Committee, thought Bush often tried to position himself as the bridge between the contending factions in the legislature. "Most of the time, he calls in two or three [legislators] from each side and gets them to talk to each other, with him inserting comments or expressing opinions in some cases," Ratliff said. "It's almost a moderator or mediator role, but a mediator with strong opinions where the limits are." Robert Junell, a Democrat who chaired the House Appropriations Committee, agreed. "The governor is a big picture guy," he said. "Does he know the details? Yes. But is he willing to negotiate on the details? Absolutely. What he wants to see is us not get hung up on that." Brownstein, "The Candidates and How They Govern."

224. The National Review suggested: Ramesh Ponnuru, "The Front-Runner," National Review, December 22, 1997.

225. "he seems to have a fairness": Paul Sadler, telephone interview by author, June 1, 1999.

225. "balance their budget on the backs": Tim Weiner, "Criticism Appears to Doom Republican Budget Tactic," New York Times, October 1, 1999.

226. "I will bring Americans together": Bush to RNC gala, author notes on prepared text, April 26, 2000.

226. "Some people thought they were apologizing": Grover Norquist, interview by author, Washington, D.C., July 18, 2006.

227. "Tonight I chose to speak": CNN Transcript of Bush remarks, December 14, 2000.

228. offered to appoint him as energy secretary: John Breaux, interview by author, Washington, D.C., April 11, 2006.

228. "his message was, I want to work": Tom Daschle, interview by author, Washington, D.C., April 13, 2006.

228. "an ability to communicate": Edward M. Kennedy, telephone interview by author, April 6, 2006.

228. "When we had issues": Ibid.

228. an education reform bill that won majority support: Congressional Quarterly Almanac 2001 (Washington, D.C.: Congressional Quarterly, 2002), Vote H–497, p. H–170, and Vote S–371, p. S–76.

229. the president's team largely believed: Matthew Dowd, interview by author, Washington, D.C., July 10, 2006.

230. "[T]he suggestion that somehow": Dick Cheney interview, Face the Nation (CBS), December 17, 2000.

230. Rove told a private gathering: Tom Hamburger and Peter Wallsten, One Party Country: The Republican Plan for Dominance in the 21st Century (Hoboken, NJ: John Wiley & Sons, 2006), p. 87.

230. "He didn't see it that way": Nick Calio, telephone interview with author, undated, 2003.

231. three Republican defectors joined with Senate Democrats: Daniel J. Parks, "It's the Day of the Centrist As Bush Tax Cut Takes a Hit," Congressional Quarterly, April 7, 2001.

231. "The president could have gotten": Ronald Brownstein, "Good Bush, Bad Bush . . ." Los Angeles Times, April 8, 2001.

232. Democrats . . . began formulating sharply contrasting: Tom Daschle, with Michael D'Orso, *Like No Other Time: The Two Years That Changed America* (New York: Three Rivers Press, 2003), pp. 91–95.

232. instead had committed to a strategy: Tom Daschle interview, April 13, 2006.

232. charged that Bush would divide the country: Robert A. Rosenblatt, "Despite Attacks, Bush Remains Firm on Tax Cut," *Los Angeles Times*, December 18, 2000.

232. while the president was leaving for a foreign: Daschle, *Like No Other Time*, p. 101.

233. "The mind-set of too many people": Karl Rove, interview by author, Washington, D.C., July 17, 2006.

234. Cohesion within the parties reached levels: Keith T. Poole et al., "Party Polarization: 1879–2006," November 20, 2006, at voteview.com/Polarized_America.htm# POLITICALPOLARIZATION.

234. Republicans voted together at a rate: Author calculations from "Party Unity History," *Congressional Quarterly*, January 9, 2006.

234. On average, Republican House members: Ibid.

235. supported the resolution authorizing the use of force in Iraq: *Congressional Quarterly Almanac 2000* (Washington, D.C.: Congressional Quarterly, 2001), vote S–237, p. S–48, and vote H–455, p. H–142.

235. No more than four Senate Democrats: Don Stewart (office of Senator John Cornyn), e-mail to author, February 16, 2005.

235. Overall . . . Democrats voted together: Author calculations from "Party Unity History," *Congressional Quarterly*, January 9, 2006.

235. "operating in two political worlds": Matthew Dowd, "The Politics of Polarization," *Washington Post*, December 16, 2002.

236. I saw the effect: Ronald Brownstein and Faye Fiore, "Sunday Division Has a New Equation," *Los Angeles Times*, June 13, 2004. All quotes from Edina are taken from this article.

237. asked Americans for one-word descriptions: "Iraq Prison Scandal Hits Home, But Most Reject Troop Pullout," Pew Research Center for the People and the Press, May 12, 2004.

238. he is not the centrist as president: Ronald Brownstein, "Bush Moves by Refusing to Budge," *Los Angeles Times*, March 2, 2003.

239. "I can't tell you how many Democrats": Karl Rove interview, July 17, 2006.

240. "If we have chemistry": Tom Daschle interview, April 13, 2006.

240. Bush did invite Daschle and his wife: Ibid.

240. Reid . . . said that he had had only one personal: Harry Reid, interview by author, Washington, D.C., August 4, 2006.

240. "Never had a call": Ibid.

240. "The breakfasts are like this": Ibid.

241. " 'Why don't we have him over' ": Ibid.

242. "That was constantly our conversation": Brownstein, "Bush Moves by Refusing to Budge."

242. "It was his very dictatorial expressions": Tom Daschle interview, April 13, 2006.

243. "there was never a dialogue": Richard Gephardt, interview by author, Washington, D.C., August 4, 2006.

243. Breaux . . . expressed just as much frustration: John Breaux interview, April 11, 2006.

243. "That was part of the plan": Nick Calio, interview by author, Washington, D.C., September 2006.

244. "There was no good cop": Tom Daschle, telephone interview by author, December 19, 2006.

244. "I don't think the president has been as good": Tom Davis, interview by author, Washington, D.C., June 22, 2006.

244. "It was just a waste of time": Chuck Hagel, interview by author, Washington, D.C., September 12, 2006.

244. Lugar . . . said he had participated: Richard Lugar, interview by author, Washington, D.C., December 15, 2006.

245. "they simply wanted congressional *support*": Ibid. Lugar attributed much of the administration's disregard for Congress to Vice President Cheney's views on the primacy of executive power, especially in wartime. "I don't blame it all on the vice president's pronouncements, but he frequently would indicate that we're at war, and the president has inherent powers to deal with this, so whether it was Abu Ghraib, or human rights situations, or interrogations, or torture, always there was the thought that you've got to understand this is a new ball game, this is a new enemy, the president has a responsibility here. You folks may feel you have a little bit of responsibility too, but nevertheless there is one place where this situation finally resides, the responsibility for this. So help out if you can; if you can't, why nevertheless, the president is the president, this is the arbiter of what is going to happen here." But Lugar also believed that Bush's lack of experience in foreign affairs before taking office, and his determination to demonstrate resolve, contributed to his reluctance to move much beyond talking points in his discussions with senators. "It's not, I think, that the president doesn't really want to have these conversations," Lugar said. "In part, I think he feels he cannot show weakness, that he cannot show lack of resolve. So even while he'd like to get an idea in the situation, he doesn't want to drop, I think, that guard." (Richard Lugar interview, December 15, 2006.)

245. "a lot of missed opportunities": Edward Kennedy interview, April 6, 2006.

247. "I remember coming to work thinking": Ellen Tauscher, interview by author, Washington, D.C., December 12, 2006.

248. the vote among Democrats flipped: *Congressional Quarterly Almanac 2003*, vote S–262, p. S–49, and vote S–459, p. S–82.

248. "they wanted an all-Republican bill": Edward Kennedy interview, April 6, 2006.

248. "the olive pit in the jelly donut": Ellen Tauscher interview, December 12, 2006.

248. "we have chosen the latter every time": Jeff Flake, interview by author, Washington, D.C., May 13, 2006.

249. the campaign targeted about three fourths: Matthew Dowd interview, July 10, 2006.

249. "everything was about persuading": Ken Mehlman, interview by author, Washington, D.C., April 19, 2006.

249. "look at the numbers": Ibid.

250. "We thought there was very little pliability": Karl Rove interview, July 17, 2006.

250. "People . . . have made a decision": Ibid.

250. "That was a landslide": Matthew Dowd interview, July 10, 2006.

250. it identified three top priorities: Ken Mehlman interview, April 19, 2006.

251. "You are kidding yourself": Karl Rove interview, July 17, 2006.

251. courted not only white evangelical ministers: Hamburger and Wallsten, *One Party Country*, pp. 129–35.

252. "They knew him, and it wasn't good": Matthew Dowd interview, July 10, 2006.

252. "accountability moment": Jim VandeHei and Michael A. Fletcher, "Bush Says Election Ratified Iraq Policy," *Washington Post*, January 16, 2005.

253. "[T]he people are gonna say": Brian Williams, "President Bush talks to Brian Williams," MSNBC.com, August 29, 2006.
254. "[W]e've got to be careful about the language": President Bush, "Remarks to Freedom House and a Question and Answer Session," March 29, 2006, at: Weekly Compilation of Presidential Documents, March 31, 2006.
254. "when you do hard things": ABC News, "Bush Not Worried About Low Approval Ratings," February 28, 2006. This is a transcript of a Bush interview with Elizabeth Vargas of ABC.
255. The rough-and-tumble . . . didn't bother him: Karl Rove, "Lessons from a Larger-than-Life President," *Time*, July 3, 2006.
255. The policy process . . . always pivoted more: One insight into this mind-set came from the celebrated Downing Street memo written by a young British diplomat in July 2002 after meetings between the head of the British Foreign Intelligence Service and American officials. "Bush wanted to remove Saddam, through military action, justified by the conjunction of terrorism and WMD [weapons of mass destruction]," the diplomat, Matthew Rycroft, wrote to senior officials in London. "But the intelligence and facts were being fixed around the policy." The memo, first published by the *Sunday Times* of London in May 2005, is available at: downingstreetmemo.com/memos.html. See also, Michael Isikoff and David Corn, *Hubris: The Inside Story of Spin, Scandal, and the Selling of the Iraq War* (New York: Crown, 2006), pp. 15–20.
256. survey, completed just three days before: "March 2003 News Interest Index," Pew Research Center for the People and the Press, March 18, 2003, question 5.
256. the president told Rove at their first: Karl Rove interview, July 17, 2006.
257. he ignored suggestions . . . from Lieberman: Lieberman supported the war more steadfastly, and at greater political cost, than any prominent Democrat. But even Lieberman through 2006 did not believe he had much input into Bush's thinking about the war. In a December 2005 speech Lieberman urged Bush to form a bipartisan group of legislators that would meet regularly with senior administration officials to assess strategy for Iraq. Lieberman cited as inspiration Henry Stimson's service across party lines for Franklin Roosevelt in World War II, Arthur Vandenberg's bipartisan collaboration with Harry Truman at the dawn of the cold war, and the experience of other countries like Great Britain in uniting competing parties into coalition governments during major conflicts.

The White House could not have missed the suggestion; Lieberman offered it in the same speech when he took the enormous political risk of urging Democrats to temper their criticisms of Bush on the war. Just in case he didn't hear about Lieberman's remarks, the senator sent him the proposal in a letter the next day. Yet Lieberman saw no evidence that Bush or his aides ever seriously considered his idea of a bipartisan war cabinet until after the 2006 election. "I think they appreciate when I am supportive, and they don't appreciate when I am critical," Lieberman said on his campaign bus a few days before his primary defeat in August 2006. "Occasionally I will call up someone like [Bush's national security adviser Stephen] Hadley, throw out an idea, and he responds to it, but obviously there was no real reaction to that proposal I made for a bipartisan working group on Iraq, except for the pro forma meetings that were held [with former officials], which were not bad, but never really amounted [to much]." Joe Lieberman, interview by author, on his campaign bus in Connecticut, July 28, 2006. For Lieberman's original suggestion see, Remarks of Senator Joe Lieberman (D-CT), Center for Strategic and Budgetary Assessment Forum on Next Steps for Successful Strategy in Iraq, December 6, 2005.

257. "I'm the decider": President Bush, "Remarks on Nomination of Rob Portman," April 21, 2006, at: Weekly Compilation of Presidential Documents, April 21, 2006.
257. "I'm the decision maker": Michael Abramowitz and Jonathan Weisman, "Bush Defies Lawmakers to Solve Iraq," *Washington Post*, January 27, 2007.
259. cut taxes another $726 billion: *Congressional Quarterly Almanac 2003* (Washington, D.C.: Congressional Quarterly, 2004), pp. 1–5.

Chapter 8: The 51 Percent Solution: Republican Strategy in the Bush Years

265. "They were clearly right": Bill McInturff, interview by author, Alexandria, VA, June 2006.
266. "We had no one to talk to": Don Fierce, interview by author, Washington, D.C., August 2006.
267. their "majority maker": Balz and Brownstein, *Storming the Gates*, p. 198.
267. initially launched . . . in 1989: Grover Norquist, telephone interview by author, November 29, 2006.
268. "If you want to play in our revolution": Nicholas Confessore, "Welcome to the Machine," *Washington Monthly*, July–August 2003.
268. In the most egregious cases: Thomas E. Mann and Norman J. Ornstein, *The Broken Branch: How Congress Is Failing America and How to Get It Back on Track* (Oxford and New York: Oxford University Press, 2006), pp. 183–84. Also, Confessore, "Welcome to the Machine."
268. "it worked brilliantly": Steve Elmendorf, interview by author, Washington, D.C., December 14, 2006.
269. DeLay famously displayed a book: Confessore, "Welcome to the Machine."
269. the Democratic share . . . plummeted: Doug Weber (Center for Responsive Politics), e-mail to author, June 30, 2006.
269. never again exceeded 42 percent: Ibid.
270. "where we are putting our shoulders": Bill Miller, interview by author, Washington, D.C., November 22, 2006.
270. "a process where elected officials": Don Fierce interview, August 2006.
272. "he's our leader": Tom Davis, interview by author, Washington, D.C., June 22, 2006.
272. "his success would be their success": Nick Calio, interview by author, Washington, D.C., September 2006.
273. "assumed a parliamentary system": Tom Davis interview, June 22, 2006.
273. "probably beyond the normal tension": Vin Weber, interview by author, Washington, D.C., November 20, 2006.
273. "They are always dictating": Tom Davis interview, June 22, 2006.
274. One panel alone: "Congressional Oversight of the Clinton Administration," Minority staff, Committee on Government Reform, January 17, 2006.
274. 140 hours of sworn testimony: Susan Milligan, "Congress Reduces Its Oversight Role," *Boston Globe*, November 20, 2005.
274. "no congressional committee ever subpoenaed: Senior administration official, telephone interview by author, November 14, 2006. The official requested anonymity.
274. The sole congressional subpoena: Ibid.
274. Committee . . . in February 2004 agreed: Jonathan Weisman, "Panel Set to Release Just Part of Report on Run-Up to War," *Washington Post*, September 7, 2006.

274. to testify under oath: Senate Democratic aide, telephone interview by author, November 9, 2006. The aide requested anonymity.

275. He did not convene another public hearing: The hearings were dated May 7, and September 9, 2004.

275. both publicly called on Warner to stop: Helen Dewar and Spencer S. Hsu, "Warner Bucks GOP Right On Probe of Prison Abuse," *Washington Post*, May 28, 2004.

275. " 'mesmerized by cameras' ": Dewar and Hsu, "Warner Bucks GOP Right."

275. "We're not in a position": Eric Schmitt, "Congress's Inquiry Into Abuse of Iraqi Prisoners Bogs Down," *New York Times*, July 16, 2004.

276. "I've been accused of being disloyal": Chuck Hagel, interview by author, Washington, D.C., September 12, 2006.

276. "If we were able to get somebody": Richard Lugar, interview by author, Washington, D.C., December 15, 2006.

277. he viewed with some regret: In conversation, Lugar questioned whether he should have followed the precedent of another Foreign Relations Committee chairman, Democratic senator William Fulbright, who convened televised hearings in 1966 to challenge the Vietnam policies of Lyndon Johnson, a president from his own party. "It is a legitimate question, why don't you launch a situation like Senator Fulbright, going full bore trying to bring [the policy] down," Lugar said. "And I don't deny there is some effect in all that." But Lugar said he concluded that he could best exert influence through quieter means. "I always felt that probably my greater strength was personal chemistry with the person himself, whoever the president is, even if the contact is infrequent, or if it's letters or memos," he said. Yet in the end, as we saw in Chapter 7, Lugar acknowledged that Bush had shown little interest in recommendations from him, or any other senator, on Iraq. By renouncing public pressure in the hope of private influence, Lugar, somewhat tragically, achieved neither. Richard Lugar interview, December, 15, 2006.

277. "functioning like a parliament": Chris Shays, telephone interview by author, November 15, 2006.

277. each side informally agreed to a moratorium: Fred Wertheimer (Democracy 21), telephone interview by author, November 4, 2006.

278. House Republicans rescinded the rules: *Congressional Quarterly Almanac 2005* (Washington, D.C.: Congressional Quarterly, 2006), pp. 5-6, 5-7.

278. Hastert sent an unmistakable signal: Mann and Ornstein, *The Broken Branch*, pp. 189–90.

278. favorable treatment in . . . earmarks: Jeff Flake, interview by author, Washington, D.C., May 13, 2006, and Tom Davis interview, June 22, 2006.

279. passed over . . . on six of those thirteen: Sinclair, *Party Wars*, p. 137.

280. said that the Senate was unlikely: Sheryl Gay Stolberg, "Despite G.O.P. Gain, Fight Over Judges Remains," *New York Times*, November 5, 2004.

280. "The problem is that he's a liberal": G. Gordon Liddy interview, *Hannity and Colmes* (Fox News Channel), November 16, 2004.

280. at back-to-back ninety-minute meetings: Helen Dewar, "Specter Seeks, Gets Support," *Washington Post*, November 17, 2004.

281. "quick committee hearings": Sheryl Gay Stolberg, "G.O.P. Colleagues Backing Specter in Judiciary Post," *New York Times*, November 19, 2004.

281. not to use his position: Steve Goldstein, "Specter Wins Panel's Backing," *Philadelphia Inquirer*, November 19, 2004.

281. "We feel like a message was sent": Mary Curtius, "GOP Colleagues Rule for Specter," *Los Angeles Times*, November 19, 2004.

282. all but nine Republicans in the Senate: "The National Taxpayer Protection Pledge," Americans for Tax Reform, at: atr.org/pledge/national/incumbents.html.
282. "I see it more as corralling": Grover Norquist, interview by author, Washington, D.C., July 18, 2006.
282. "RINO Senators . . . believe": "McCain & Co Undermine War on Terror," Center for Individual Freedom, e-mail, September 21, 2006.
282. ran a full-page cover photo: "Wrong," *National Review*, November 9, 2006.
282. "at this point are almost dangerous": John Mercurio, "LindseyMentum?" National Journal.com, September 28, 2006.
283. "If you do step out": Lindsey Graham, interview by author, July 18, 2006.
283. "What's happened in politics": Ibid.
283. one South Carolina GOP official launched: Mercurio, "LindseyMentum?"
284. an organization founded in the early 1980s: Paul Starobin, "Welcome to the Club," *National Journal*, January 28, 1995.
284. surprisingly lost momentum: Stephen Moore, interview by author, Washington, D.C., February 10, 2005.
284. Moore's critical insight: Ibid. All subsequent descriptions of club activities are from interviews with Moore, February 10, February 21, and March 25, 2005.
285. House moderates regularly pressed: John Feehery, interview by author, Washington, D.C., April 12, 2006.
285. saw the group as a useful means: Ibid.
285. "The moderates tended to be much more careful": Ibid.
286. "things they were for": Karl Rove, interview by author, Washington, D.C., July 17, 2006.
287. "it was not a grudging marriage": Vin Weber interview, November 20, 2006.
288. "we knew we couldn't go get": Matthew Dowd, interview by author, Washington, D.C., July 10, 2006.
288. Rove recognized: For studies on the similarities between voters and nonvoters, see for example Ruy A. Teixeira, *The Disappearing American Voter* (Washington, D.C.: Brookings Institution Press, 1992).
288. Rove explained the answer he reached: Karl Rove interview, July 17, 2006.
288. "Make a perfect list of all the voters": John G. Nicolay and John Hay, *Complete Works of Abraham Lincoln* (New York: Lamb Publishing Co., 1905), pp. 142–45.
288. "the critical phrase": Karl Rove interview, July 17, 2006.
289. in 2002 . . . independents split evenly: Stanley Greenberg, "Re: 2002 Congressional Vote by Demographic Groups," Greenberg, Quinlan, Rosner Research, November 8, 2002.
289. Nor did Republicans attract more defections: Greenberg, "Re: 2002 Congressional Vote." Also, "A Look at Voting Patterns of 115 Demographic Groups in House Races," *New York Times*, November 9, 1998.
289. Republicans slightly outnumbered Democrats: Greenberg, "Re: 2002 Congressional Vote."
289. "When I went down to Crawford": Karl Rove interview, July 17, 2006.
290. It spent three fourths of its money in 2004: Matthew Dowd interview, Washington, D.C., July 10, 2006.
290. "All tactical decisions . . . from that": Ibid.
290. Dowd set a straightforward: Matthew Dowd, telephone interview by author, August 19, 2004.
291. Those matches revealed clear patterns: Ken Mehlman and Brian Jones, interview by author, Washington, D.C., April 19, 2006.

291. "I am going to find the needle": Ken Mehlman, interview by author, April 19, 2006.

292. it tilted its buying away: Matthew Dowd interview, July 10, 2006.

292. other element became evident: Ronald Brownstein, "Bush Aims to Solidify His Base," *Los Angeles Times*, August 22, 2004.

292. led to some surprising decisions: Matthew Dowd interview, July 10, 2006.

293. "The technology matched with the evolution": Mark McKinnon, interview by author, Washington, D.C., April 2006.

293. Bush raised . . . while Kerry collected: "2004 Presidential Election," Center for Responsive Politics, at: opensecrets.org/presidential/index.asp.

294. "we were clearly under 50 percent": Mark McKinnon, interview by author, Alexandria, Va., September 7, 2006.

294. Over 122 million Americans voted: "Statistics of the Presidential and Congressional Election of November 2, 2004," Clerk of the House of Representatives, June 7, 2005.

294. Kerry won nearly 59 million: Ibid.

294. Bush won nearly 62 million: Ibid.

294. "We had plenty of energy": Stanley B. Greenberg, interview by author, Washington, D.C., April 6, 2006.

295. also increased his margins: Marjorie Connelly, "How Americans Voted: A Political Portrait," *New York Times*, November 7, 2004. Also see *Los Angeles Times* 2004 exit poll at: latimes.com/news/nationworld/timespoll/.

295. Bush actually *lost* ground: Ibid.

295. Bush increased his share . . . among Republicans: Connelly, "How Americans Voted: A Political Portrait."

295. Dowd met his goal: Ibid.

295. he held Kerry to 43 percent . . . or less: Author calculations from 2004 election results.

296. He reduced the Democratic margin in eleven: Ronald Brownstein, "GOP's Future Sits Precariously on Small Cushion of Victory," *Los Angeles Times*, November 15, 2004.

296. was actually 30 percent larger in 2004: The calculation is based on exit poll findings. In 2000, the Edison/Mitofsky exit poll found that blacks constituted 10 percent of the electorate. That means they provided about 10.6 million of the 105,594,000 votes cast. Gore carried 90 percent of the black vote, which would translate into roughly 9,503,460 votes; Bush carried 8 percent, which would equal about 844,752 votes. That left Bush with a net deficit of approximately 8,658,708 among black voters. In 2004, the exit poll found that blacks constituted 12 percent of an electorate that had swelled to 122,349,000. That meant the 88 percent of the black vote Kerry carried translated into roughly 12,920,054 votes; Bush's 11 percent equaled about 1,615,007. In 2004, then, Bush's deficit among black voters reached 11,305,047, about 30 percent larger than his shortfall in 2000.

296. the smallest margin . . . for a reelected president: Brownstein, "GOP's Future Sits Precariously on Small Cushion of Victory."

296. only Woodrow Wilson . . . won a smaller share: Ibid.

298. "I earned capital in the campaign": President Bush, news conference November 4, 2004, at: Weekly Compilation of Presidential Documents, November 5, 2004.

298. "we have waited our entire lives": Janet Hook, "Bush, GOP Downsize Ambitions for 2006," *Los Angeles Times*, December 25, 2005.

299. "This is an exhausted administration": Ibid.

301. In some surveys even decisive majorities: Ronald Brownstein, " 'Culture of Life' Issues Split GOP," *Los Angeles Times*, March 28, 2005.

302. largely confined to Republicans: Gallup survey, January 7–9, 2005, question 19. Results by party supplied by Gallup.

302. measured opinion . . . again in April 2005: Gallup survey, April 1–2, 2005, question 12. Results by party supplied by Gallup.

303. Bush's advisers and allies believed: Mark McKinnon interview, September 7, 2006, and Terry Nelson, interview by author, Washington, D.C., September 22, 2006.

303. "if you lived in a red state": Terry Nelson interview, September 22, 2006.

303. Reid . . . remembers being: Harry Reid, interview by author, Washington, D.C., August 4, 2006.

304. signed a letter declaring: Letter to President Bush from Senate Democrats, March 3, 2005.

304. Nelson denounced his Republican: David DiMartino (press secretary for Ben Nelson), telephone interview by author, September 11, 2006.

304. "It was a casualty": Allen Boyd, interview by author, Washington, D.C., January 9, 2007.

305. the Senate passed . . . with sixty-two votes: Nicole Gaouette, "Senate Passes Sweeping Bill on Immigration," *Los Angeles Times*, May 26, 2006.

305. "The job of the speaker": Dennis Hastert, "Reflections on the Role of the Speaker," Cannon Centenary Conference, House Document No. 108–204, November 12, 2003.

305. allowing a vote on raising the minimum wage: Newt Gingrich, interview by author, Washington, D.C., July 10, 2006.

306. to force the renegotiation: Ronald Brownstein, "House GOP Resistance Presents Bush a Clear Test of Leadership," *Los Angeles Times*, November 29, 2004.

306. passed the Senate 96–2: *Congressional Quarterly Almanac 2004* (Washington, D.C.: Congressional Quarterly, 2005), p. 11–3.

306. surrounded by the congressional Republicans: Nicole Gaouette, "Bush Signs Fence Bill, Pushes Back," *Los Angeles Times*, October 27, 2006.

307. to just 29 percent in 2006: Edison/Mitofsky exit poll for 2006, at: cnn.com/ ELECTION/2006/pages/results/states/US/H00/epolls.0.html.

307. Nearly 45 million in 2005: "Census Bureau Revises 2004 and 2005 Health Insurance Coverage Estimates," press release, March 23, 2007.

307. the number of Americans in poverty: Ibid.

307. the total without health insurance: Ibid.

307. the nation's dependence on foreign oil: "Overview of U.S. Petroleum Trade," Energy Information Administration, at: eia.doe.gov/emeu/mer/pdf/pages/sec1_15.pdf.

308. every other . . . reached at least 62 percent: Author calculations from Gallup surveys.

308. just 4 percent of Democrats: Gallup survey, May 5–7, 2006.

309. They were, in fact, the lowest: This is based on Gallup surveys on presidential approval. Data on results by party provided by Gary C. Jacobson, University of California (San Diego).

309. "It's a downward spiral": Nick Calio interview, September 2006.

310. "The terrorists win and America loses": "Remarks by the President at a Georgia Victory 2006 Rally, Statesboro Georgia," Office of the (White House) Press Secretary, October 30, 2006.

310. "validate" Al-Qaeda's belief: Michael Abramowitz, "Cheney Remark Rankles Pelosi," *Washington Post*, February 24, 2007.

311. "If we had done better": Chris Shays interview, November 15, 2006.

312. "there is no sheriff in town": Fred Wertheimer interview, October 4, 2006.

313. "that is the potential": Karl Rove interview, July 17, 2006.

313. "the young Hispanic": Ibid.
313. "All of these things": Ibid.
314. "the side that is winning": Ibid.
314. "alive and well and likely to reemerge": Peter Baker, "Rove Remains Steadfast in the Face of Criticism," *Washington Post*, November 12, 2006.
314. "There must be a counterculture": "Blunt Speech on GOP Future," Roy Blunt press release, November 9, 2006.
315. Hewitt went further yet: Hugh Hewitt, "The Road Not Taken: Forfeiting a Majority," Townhall.com, November 8, 2006.
315. Hewitt helped establish a new conservative group: "Our Mission," Victory Caucus, at: victorycaucus.com/index.php?option=com_content&task=view&id=17&Itemid=34.
315. "I believe they rejected us": "McCain Calls for Common Sense Conservatism at GOPAC Dinner," John McCain press release, November 16, 2006.
316. When political analyst Rhodes Cook: Rhodes Cook, "1994 and 2006: A Comparison," *Rhodes Cook Letter*, December 2006, p.4.
317. the nature of the coalition that had assembled: All figures are from Edison/Mitofsky exit polls posted by CNN.com for 2004 at: cnn.com/ELECTION/2004/pages/results/states/US/H/00/epolls.0.html and 2006 at: cnn.com/ELECTION/2006/pages/results/states/US/H/00/epolls.0.html.
318. advantages . . . reached staggering proportions: 2006 Senate exit polls at: cnn.com/ELECTION/2006/.
318. 63 percent of independent voters said: Kellyanne Conway (the polling company), e-mail to author, December 6, 2006.
318. "It's one of the first votes": "Sheldon Whitehouse for Senate: 'Think About It,' " nationaljournal.com, September 14, 2006.
319. a regional and "minority party": Ken Mehlman, "RNC Chairman Ken Mehlman Addresses the Republican Governors Association": speech, November 30, 2006.
319. "the American people made it clear": "Far Right Solely Responsible for Democratic Gains," Republican Main Street Partnership, press release, November 7, 2006.
319. "should cause Republicans to rethink": "Degringolade," *National Review*, December 4, 2006.
320. Dowd nearly sputtered with outrage: Matthew Dowd interview, July 10, 2006.
321. "I don't think a series": Ibid.
321. "where do people go": Ibid.
322. winning a majority of independents: "The gubernatorial contest," *Los Angeles Times* Exit Poll, November 9, 2006, at: latimes.com/news/custom/timespoll/.
323. the party of "doubt and defeat": Ronald Brownstein, "Partisan Rhetoric Even in Wartime Sets Bush Apart," *Los Angeles Times*, October 29, 2006.
323. "This whole politics of division": Matthew Dowd, telephone interview by author, October 25, 2006.
323. "That should be the takeaway": Ibid.
323. "What they need to take out of it": Ibid.

CHAPTER 9: THE OPPOSITION IN AN AGE OF POLARIZATION

326. "really are a minority party": Markos Moulitsas Zuniga, interview by author, Berkeley, Calif., April 22, 2005.
328. "stand up to Bush more strongly": Mark Mellman, interview by author, April 2, 2006.

329. A year earlier they had: Louis Jacobson, "Digital Democrats 'Move On,' " *National Journal*, October 18, 2003.

329. "We were hearing people": Joan Blades, interview by author, Berkeley, Calif., December 4, 2003.

329. "people must have gone wild": Joan Blades, interview by author, Berkeley, Calif., December 4, 2003.

329. hundreds of thousands: Wes Boyd interview, December 4, 2003.

329. half a million names: Wes Boyd, telephone interview by author, June 18, 2003.

329. "We were . . . fully prepared": Wes Boyd interview, December 4, 2003.

330. raised more than 3 million: Wes Boyd interview, June 18, 2003.

330. as a permanent institution: Wes Boyd interview, December 4, 2003.

330. Pickering agreed to place: George Packer, "Smart-Mobbing the War," *New York Times Magazine*, March 9, 2003.

330. The combined petition urged: "Justice Not War, U.S. Statements of Opposition to War and Support for Just, Effective Solutions," undated document from 9–11peace.org.

330. "The next Monday I checked": "Democracy in Action," FC Now, The Fast Company Weblog, March 14, 2004.

330. more than 500,000 names: "Worldwide Call for Justice, Stability, Cooperation," 9–11 peace.org press release, October 9, 2001.

330. "to counsel patience": Eli Pariser, e-mail to author, April 18, 2005, with undated message from MoveOn to members.

331. he contacted the group: Eli Pariser, interview by author, New York City, November 20, 2003.

331. nearly doubling the group's e-mail list: Wes Boyd interview, June 18, 2003. According to Boyd, the group's membership was five hundred thousand after Clinton's impeachment.

331. raised nearly $2 million: Eli Pariser interview, November 20, 2003.

332. the famous Lyndon Johnson "daisy": Meg Kinnard, "Anti-War Group Revives Daisy Ad," NationalJournal.com, January 17, 2003.

332. "virtual march on Washington": Packer, "Smart-Mobbing the War."

332. it collected instead four hundred thousand dollars: Joan Blades interview, December 4, 2003.

332. just four paid staff members: Wes Boyd interview, June 18, 2003.

332. succinctly summarized the dynamic: Eli Pariser interview, November 20, 2003.

332. another eight hundred thousand names: Wes Boyd interview, June 18, 2003.

333. ads comparing Bush to Hitler: Howard Kurtz, "Anti-Bush Ad Contest Includes Hitler Images," *Washington Post*, January 6, 2004.

333. "moved into some leadership vacuums": Wes Boyd interview, June 18, 2003.

333. only if he fired . . . Rumsfeld: Eli Pariser, "$87 Billion: What Do You Think?" MoveOn.org e-mail, September 15, 2003.

333. it called for an independent commission: "Misleader," ad in *New York Times*, June 19, 2003.

333. floating the possibility of impeachment: "Censure the President!" MoveOn.org and Win Without War press release, February 5, 2004.

334. contemplated careers as diverse: Ronald Brownstein, "The Internet and Democrats," *National Journal*, July 2, 2005.

335. running his blog full-time: Markos Moulitsas Zuniga, telephone interview by author, May 10, 2005.

335. Kerry's campaign removed its link: Brownstein, "The Internet and Democrats."

335. Democrats were too doctrinaire: Jerome Armstrong and Markos Moulitsas Zuniga, *Crashing the Gate: Netroots, Grassroots, and the Rise of People-Powered Politics* (White River Junction, VT: Chelsea Green Publishing, 2005), pp. 58–62.

335. "The conservatives have declared war": Kara Platoni, "Party Central," *East Bay Express*, December 15, 2004.

336. "I look at this": Markos Moulitsas Zuniga interview, April 22, 2005.

337. it collected another $50 million: Tom Matzzie (MoveOn.org), e-mail to author, April 5, 2005.

337. as much as $300 million on the Internet: Brownstein, "The Internet and Democrats."

338. "we bought it, we own it": Eli Pariser, Justin Ruben, and the whole MoveOn PAC team, "Who will lead the Democratic Party?" MoveOn.org Political Action e-mail, December 9, 2004.

340. "notion of one party springing": Charles Babington, "Senate's Closed-Session Move Borne Out of Daschle's Strategy," *Washington Post*, November 3, 2005.

340. "there was never a great deal of focus": Vic Fazio, interview by author, Washington, D.C., December 18, 2006.

341. "Gephardt was very much": Ibid.

341. "Gingrich's whole philosophy": Steny Hoyer, interview by author, Washington, D.C., May 19, 2006.

342. She refused to allow: Ronald Brownstein, "Partisan Snub of Republican Katrina Inquiry Now Looks Petty," *Los Angeles Times*, February 19, 2006.

342. with Republicans raising the specter of impeachment: Charles Babington, "Democrats Won't Try to Impeach President," *Washington Post*, May 12, 2006.

342. Peterson . . . was only allowed: Erin P. Billings, "Democrats on 'Exclusives' Face Review," *Roll Call*, January 24, 2005.

343. "I can't overstate": Susan McCue, interview by author, Bethesda, Md., December 26, 2006.

344. quickly reached two interlocking conclusions: Ibid.

344. in the Florida district of Allen Boyd: "MoveOn Launches Ad Campaign," MoveOn.org press release, January 31, 2005.

344. Pariser . . . raised the prospect of organizing: Eli Pariser, interview by author, Brooklyn, N.Y., April 2005.

345. with the encouragement of Reid and Pelosi: Brad Woodhouse, interview by author, Washington, D.C., December 14, 2006. All descriptions of Americans United activities are taken from this interview.

346. "I'm not a real cheerleader": Harry Reid, interview by author, Washington, D.C., August 4, 2006.

348. "there was such a disconnection": Susan McCue interview, December 26, 2006.

348. "an antiquated way of looking": Simon Rosenberg, interview by author, Washington, D.C., May 30, 2006.

348. the group questioned Bush's commitment: "Ten Kinds of Bipartisanship," New Dem Daily, January 9, 2001.

348. "has tried to achieve the maximum": Ibid.

348. opposed his tax cut: "The President's Speech to Congress: Too Good to Be True," New Dem Daily, February 28, 2001.

348. criticized his retreat on global warming: "Some Like It Hot: Bush Looks on the Sunny Side of Global Warming," New Dem Daily, March 15, 2001.

348. condemned his . . . energy policy: "Bush: The First 100 Days," New Dem Daily, April 30, 2001.

348. denounced his restrictions ... for stem cell: "Stem Cell Cop Out," New Dem Daily, August 10, 2001.

348. explicitly counseled against abandoning it: "Idea of the Week: How to Define Partisan Differences," New Dem Daily, November 8, 2002.

348. usually left it cold: "Bush's Health Care Agenda: You're On Your Own," New Dem Dispatch, March 2, 2006.

349. "[I]f it becomes necessary": "Lieberman Speaks Out on War Goals," New Dem Daily, October 17, 2001.

349. It endorsed the congressional resolution: "A Time for Resolve," New Dem Daily, October 3, 2002.

349. and directly echoed Bush's catch–22 argument: "Multilateralism On Trial," New Dem Daily, January 23, 2003.

349. the world ... will be safer ... without Saddam Hussein: "A Time for Unity and Resolve," New Dem Daily, March 18, 2003.

349. "contempt for allies": "Idea of the Week: Succeed in Iraq," New Dem Daily, May 28, 2004.

349. "unilateralist diplomacy": "Idea of the Week: Being Bigger Than Bush on Iraq," New Dem Daily, October 17, 2003.

349. It urged congressional Democrats to back: Ibid.

349. "cut-and-run": "Democrats Draw Lessons from Iraq," New Dem Daily, June 22, 2004.

350. "clearly rejecting our anti-war wing": Al From and Bruce Reed, "The Road Back," Blueprint magazine, Volume 2004, Number 5.

350. "What activists like Dean call the Democratic wing": Al From and Bruce Reed, "The Real Soul of the Democratic Party," DLC Memo, May 15, 2003.

351. McAuliffe ... and even from Simon Rosenberg: Ronald Brownstein, "Centrists Losing Ground in Democratic Tug of War," Los Angeles Times, June 21, 2003.

351. "McGovernites with modems": Marshall Wittmann, "McGovernites with Modems," The Bull Moose, May 9, 2006.

351. "it's not defined by ideology": Simon Rosenberg interview, May 30, 2006.

352. "Rove sees compromise as weakness": Kos, "No Compromise!" Daily Kos, February 24, 2005.

352. raised a breathtaking eight hundred thousand dollars: Brownstein, "The Internet and Democrats."

352. it aired an ad in Steny Hoyer's: "Steny Hoyer and GOP Reps Targeted," MoveOn press release, April 15, 2005.

353. "You have to fight fire with fire": Eli Pariser interview, April 2005.

353. "Clinton's third way failed miserably": Markos Moulitsas Zuniga, "Problems on the Left," Washington Post, May 7, 2006.

353. "We won the center and it wasn't enough": Interview with Markos Moulitsas Zuniga, April 22, 2005.

353. "Democrats need their own George Bush": Chris Burke, "Where's my Bush?" rawstory.com, undated post.

353. "the most powerful political asset around": Eli Pariser interview, April 2005.

354. "truly followed Clinton's model": Al From, "Building on Clintonism," Blueprint, vol. 2005, no. 1.

355. "we undermine Presidential credibility": "Remarks of Senator Joe Lieberman, Center for Strategic and Budgetary Assessment Forum," Senator Joe Lieberman press release, December 6, 2005.

355. initially encouraged Lowell P. Weicker: Ned Lamont, telephone interview by author, January 18, 2006.

356. denounced Lieberman with language that might: Author interviews with attendees at Lamont rally in Bristol, Conn., July 30, 2006.

356. Even . . . Bill Clinton: David Broder, "Former President Joins Rally for Lieberman," *Washington Post*, July 25, 2006.

356. "[T]he policy of seizing the political middle ground": Eli Pariser, "The Death of Triangulation," *Washington Post*, August 10, 2006.

357. "There is great joy in Mooseland": Marshall Wittmann, "KOSenfreude," Bull Moose, November 8, 2006.

358. an extraordinary level of grassroots activity: "Election 2006: People-Powered Politics," MoveOn.org political action report, November 2006.

360. "who vote to undermine the progressive": "About Us," Working for Us PAC, at: workingforuspac.org/pages/about/.

362. even Al From acknowledged could weaken: Al From, interview by author, Washington, D.C., December 18, 2006.

Chapter 10: Beyond Division

366. "In an era beset": American Political Science Association, Committee on Political Parties, "Toward a More Responsible Two-Party System," September 1950, p. 17.

366. "alternatives between the parties are defined": Ibid., p. 3.

370. who read newspapers regularly: "Pew Research Center Biennial News Consumption Survey," Pew Research Center for the People and the Press, July 30, 2006, p. 57.

370. roughly equal shares . . . watch local television: Ibid., p. 63.

370. do draw more Democrats: Ibid., p. 37.

370. trusted by fewer Democrats: Ibid., p. 48.

370. Republicans . . . were less likely: Ibid., p. 48.

370. the evening network news are subject: Ibid., pp. 36–37.

371. because its audience is shrinking: Ibid., p. 1.

371. 34 percent of Republicans . . . regularly watch Fox: Ibid., p. 37.

371. In Rush Limbaugh's radio audience: Ibid., p. 38.

371. in the audience for the *Daily Show*: Ibid., p. 38.

372. "let's disabuse ourselves": Matt Stoller, "And Now to the Bickering," MyDD, November 8, 2006.

372. "There were people in our campaign": Mark Mellman, interview by author, Washington, D.C., April 2, 2006.

373. "Al Qaeda bill of rights": "Limbaugh Falsehood: 'Leahy Opposes NSA Intercepts of the Enemy,'" Media Matters for America press release, February 10, 2006. This release includes a transcript of Limbaugh on February 6, 2006, when he made the remarks.

374. audiences beginning to approach: Network evening news programs now attract audiences of eight to ten million; cable news programs generate a combined prime-time audience of less than three million; only about twenty major newspapers now measure their circulation above five hundred thousand.

375. "it becomes increasingly difficult": Harold Ickes, interview by author, Washington, D.C., May 8, 2006.

376. In most states . . . only registered members: "Primaries Open and Closed," FairVote, at: fairvote.org/index.php?page=1801.

379. left state parties with the last word: Ben Ginsberg, telephone interview by author, January 11, 2007; Joe Sandler, telephone interview by author, January 11, 2007.

379. Only six states use independent: Thomas Mann, "Redistricting Reform: What is Desirable? Possible?" in Thomas E. Mann and Bruce E. Cain, eds., *Party Lines: Competition, Partisanship, and Congressional Redistricting* (Washington, DC: Brookings Institution Press, 2005), p. 101.

379. the defeat of redistricting reform: Juliet Eilperin, "You Can't Have a Great Election Without Any Races," *Washington Post,* November 13, 2005.

380. Tanner . . . has proposed: "It's Up to Congress to Fix Redistricting, Say Lawmakers and Reform Advocates," John Tanner press release, July 18, 2006.

380. The possibilities are explored: The highest priority for many political reformers is to reduce the influence of big donors in politics through tighter limits on campaign contributions and greater reliance on public funding. That might be advisable for other reasons, but its impact on polarization likely would be mixed. Further limiting contributions from labor and business could create more flexibility for both parties to pursue legislative compromises that bite the hand of their biggest contributors. But even if business could not contribute a cent, it would always wield influence because of its role in driving the economy and providing jobs. Labor's influence already rests more in its ability to mobilize its members on Election Day than in its money. Reducing contribution limits to promote greater reliance on small donors might even fuel more political confrontation. In both parties small donors, drawn from the activist core, tend to be more ideological and partisan than big donors, many of whom are willing to work with both parties to advance their (often self-interested) goals. Tom Matzzie, who helped direct John Kerry's Internet operation in 2004, said small donations usually poured in at the highest rate when the campaign sent out messages promising to fight Bush more fiercely; Republicans report similar results when they wave the bloody shirt at Democrats. Small donors now provide big incentives for intense partisanship, and increasing their role would only intensify that pressure.

How about another top priority for many reformers: replacing the Electoral College with a direct popular vote for president? This idea, which would require a constitutional amendment, has many virtues and drawbacks not directly related to our topic of excessive partisan conflict. From the perspective of restraining partisanship, scrapping the Electoral College might also produce a mixed result. On the ledger's positive side, a direct popular vote could encourage presidential candidates to offer a broader appeal by pressuring them to compete for every vote in every state; neither side could entirely write off states in the other side's camp, as the winner-take-all Electoral College system encourages them to do today. That would combat the dangerous tendency now evident in each party to retreat into regional enclaves and abandon the goal of speaking to, and for, the entire country.

But an election decided by a national popular vote could also push candidates to conclude, as the Bush campaign did in 2004, that their money is more efficiently spent turning out another one of their base voters than converting a swing voter wavering between the parties. Because a national popular vote would place such a premium on turnout, it is easy to imagine the Republican candidate camping out outside Dallas or Atlanta mobilizing their core supporters with a highly partisan message, and Democrats doing the same in downtown Los Angeles or Detroit. For all its flaws the Electoral College in one respect pushes candidates away from the extremes: In years when the country is closely divided, the system provides the decisive role to states where neither party dominates. And that ensures an indispensable role for the swing voters who typically tip those battleground states. The direct popular election of the president might give those swing voters a louder say, but it could just as easily amplify the voices of hard-core partisans. Ultimately, the effect of such a basic change would pivot on the choices the parties make in response to it.

Those who support a nationwide popular vote for president often pair it with another set of long-term reforms: measures to massively increase voter participation. In their impact on excessive partisanship, these ideas could also cut both ways. The best proposals to increase participation range from moving Election Day to a weekend (or making it a holiday) to automatically registering all Americans to vote once they turn eighteen. (See Steven Hill, *10 Steps to Repair American Democracy* [Sausalito, CA: PoliPointPress, 2006], pp. 35–47.)

Contrary to common assumptions, most studies have concluded that significantly enlarging the electorate probably would not change the balance of power between the parties. Studies of nonvoters usually find that they don't differ much in their partisan allegiance or views on issues from those who do vote; nonvoters are united more by their lack of information about, or connection to, the political process. But, precisely because of those characteristics, nonvoters as a group would not approach campaigns from a deeply ideological perspective. Bringing more of them into the electorate could enlarge the constituency for a more pragmatic problem-solving politics. On the other hand, importing so many voters with few firm beliefs and even less information also could create a more receptive audience for divisive and demagogic appeals. Adding more voters always strengthens democracy, but no one can say with much confidence how much, if at all, it would weaken the forces sustaining today's political warfare.

Other proposals aim to rethink House elections. These ideas focus on reducing the winner-take-all aspect of House races to increase the influence of a district's minority views—a dynamic that could push House members toward less absolutism and more compromise. The most intriguing of these proposals would abandon the current system of electing representatives solely through single-member districts. Instead, the House would be chosen through larger "multimember" districts in which voters would elect two, three, four, or more representatives at once. Many variants on this system exist, but the best scramble the electoral dynamics in ways that could combat hyperpartisanship. One approach, known as "cumulative voting," provides residents a number of votes equal to the number of seats in the district and allows them to split the ballots in any way they want; so in a three-member seat a voter could cast three votes for one candidate or one vote for three candidates or any combination in between. Another approach, called "choice" or "ranked" voting, allows voters to rank their choices for a district's seats and distributes those preferences through a complex formula to produce the winners.

These systems, also known as "proportional representation," are more common abroad but are not completely alien to the American experience. Some states used multimember districts to elect their House members early in the nineteenth century until Congress banned the practice in 1842 (Mann, in Mann and Cain, *Party Lines,* p. 96). Illinois used a multimember system with cumulative voting to elect its state legislature until 1980 (for 110 years in all) (Hill, *10 Steps to Repair American Democracy,* p. 63). A few city and county governments use variations on the multimember system to elect local officers as well. In 2006, voters in Minneapolis and Oakland approved referenda establishing systems with similar principles for all of their local elections.

Steven Hill, a political analyst and political reformer at the centrist New America Foundation, energetically made the case for the idea in his provocative book *10 Steps to Repair American Democracy.* The great virtue of a multimember election system with cumulative or choice voting is to allow more views from any region to be represented in the House. Today Democrats might win all the House seats in a big state's urban centers while Republicans win all the rural seats. But, as Hill notes, under a multimember system with those voting schemes, each party would almost certainly win some seats in what is now the other party's sphere of influence. The reason is that multimember districts lower the threshold needed to win. In a three-member district, for instance, any candidate who received at least 25 percent of the vote would capture a seat. That would allow the parties to win House seats in all the places where they attract support from a solid minority but rarely reach 50 percent of the vote. These systems also allow voters to support candidates from both parties for the same offices at the same time, which increases the value of politicians who can appeal across partisan lines.

By electing more legislators from communities that generally lean toward the other party (inner-city Republicans, rural Democrats), the multimember system could produce a more diverse legislature more receptive to compromise. That was exactly the experience in Illinois, as Hill found in his interviews with veterans of the statehouse there. One Republican legislator, who later went on to election in Congress, told Hill, "By its nature the system encouraged moderate viewpoints to be brought to bear. There's a great deal more independence for each member than there is under the present system" (Hill, *10 Steps to Repair American Democracy*, p. 67). With that effect, multimember districts could help combat the rigidity that has afflicted the House as each party's membership has grown more ideologically homogenous. But the great strength of multimember districts—encouraging diversity—is also its principal weakness. By lowering the threshold for victory the system makes it easier for fringe and extremist candidates to win seats in the House. If adopted widely enough, multimember districts would even increase the risk that no party wins a House majority, forcing one of the major parties to bargain with a minor party (or parties) to reach 218 votes. Electing more fringe candidates, and possibly requiring the major parties to bargain with them to organize the House, probably are deeply unappealing prospects for most Americans, and they would need to be balanced against the advantage of promoting more diverse representation in any future discussion of multimember districts and cumulative or choice voting.

381. The plan's commonsense elements: Mann and Ornstein, *The Broken Branch*, p. 233.

381. The Republican majority blocked twenty-four: Ronald Brownstein, "Senate Should Act So Judges Get Their Day in Court," *Los Angeles Times*, May 6, 2002.

382. justices have been serving much longer: Steven G. Calabresi and James Lindgren, "Term Limits for the Supreme Court: Life Tenure Reconsidered," *Harvard Journal of Law and Public Policy*, Summer 2006.

383. each president would be assured: Ibid.

383. "[E]very other major democratic nation": Ibid.

383. The FCC killed the rule: "Fairness Doctrine," Museum of Broadcast Communications, at: tv/archives/etv/F/htmlF/fairnessdoct/fairnessdoct.htm.

384. it may be more difficult: Tom Rosenstiel, interview by author, Washington, D.C., January 11, 2007.

386. "the biggest single unserved consumer market": David Maney, interview by author, Washington, D.C., May 31, 2006.

387. nearly three fourths of Americans agreed: Evans Witt, "Election Landscape 2008: Summary of Poll Findings," Princeton Survey Research Associates International, May 22, 2006.

390. absolutely nothing: Alliance to Save Energy, "Comprehensive Energy Bill Moves Toward Efficiency . . . ," July 27, 2005; and Ronald Brownstein, "U.S. Energy Policy Ought to Send Iran a Lasting Message," *Los Angeles Times*, January 22, 2006.

390. uses one quarter . . . but holds less than 3 percent: "Recommendations to the Nation on Reducing U.S. Oil Dependence," Energy Security Leadership Council, December 2006, p. 14.

390. a meager 6 percent: "Annual Energy Review, 2005," Energy Information Administration, July 2006, p. 46.

391. now lags the average not only in Europe: "Recommendations to the Nation on Reducing U.S. Oil Dependence," Energy Security Leadership Council, p. 35.

391. California's plan requires a 25 percent: Marc Lifsher and Jordan Rau, "State on Verge of Greenhouse Gas Restrictions," *Los Angeles Times,* August 31, 2006.

392. As . . . Obama . . . has proposed: Barack Obama, "Securing Our Energy Future," Speech to Resources for the Future, Washington, D.C., September 15, 2005.

393. The Massachusetts plan requires: "Health Care Reform: Conference Committee Bill," Massachusetts Joint Caucus for House Members, April 3, 2006, and Ronald Brownstein, "Healthcare Bill Is a Vital Sign of Bipartisan Progress," *Los Angeles Times,* April 9, 2006.

395. "True federalism accommodates profound": David Gelernter, "Back to Federalism," *Weekly Standard,* April 10, 2006.

397. "[T]he overturning of *Roe* would . . . ignite": Jeffrey Rosen, "The Day After *Roe,*" *Atlantic Monthly,* June 2006.

398. whether the EU model could be applied: Ronald Brownstein, "For Democracy to Take Root, It Must Be the Work of Many Hands," *Los Angeles Times,* January 24, 2005.

398. found majority support in both parties: Steven Kull, et al., "Opportunities for Bipartisan Consensus—2007," Program on International Policy Attitudes, University of Maryland, January 2007, pp. 5–7.

399. "The bolder the president's foreign policy": Richard G. Lugar, *Letters to the Next President* (Bloomington, IN: Author House, 2004), p. 267.

401. "not so much of a stone buttress": Burns, *The Deadlock of Democracy,* p. 73.

401. Roosevelt saw reform as the sole . . . opportunity: Ibid., p. 113.

401. "puts the national need before": Theodore Roosevelt, "The New Nationalism." Speech at dedication of the John Brown Battlefield, Osawatomie, Kansas, August 31, 1910, at: presidentialrhetoric.com/historicspeeches/roosevelt_theodore/newnationalism.html.

402. he delivered speeches and wrote articles: Theodore Roosevelt, "The Progressives, Past and Present," *Outlook,* September 3, 1910, and Theodore Roosevelt, "The Pioneer Spirit and American Problems," *Outlook,* September 10, 1910.

402. Roosevelt also endorsed "stricter . . .": Cooper, *The Warrior and the Priest,* p. 190.

402. conspicuously excluded African Americans: Ibid., p. 210.

402. "If I could ask but one thing": Roosevelt, "The New Nationalism."

402. "to be just to all": Cooper, *The Warrior and the Priest,* p. 202.

403. "we work in a spirit": Roosevelt, "The New Nationalism."

403. "to find among many discordant": Burns, *Roosevelt: The Lion and the Fox,* p. 183.

403. "the task of the political leader": Fred Greenstein, *The Hidden-Hand President: Eisenhower as Leader* (New York: Basic Books, 1982), p. 52.

404. a dozen times in American history: Ronald Brownstein, "To Fill O'Connor's Shoes, Bush Might Want to Cross the Aisle," *Los Angeles Times,* September 12, 2005.

405. "I wish the public": Kearns, *Lyndon Johnson and the American Dream,* p. 291.

405. Javits, in his penetrating 1964 book: Jacob K. Javits, *Order of Battle: A Republican's Call to Reason* (New York: Atheneum, 1964), pp. 129–37.

406. are more likely to decide a "line call": Chuck Hagel, interview by author, Washington, D.C., September 12, 2006.

462

NOTES

406. "someone like Richard Lugar would come in": Bill Clinton, interview by author, Washington, D.C., October 4, 2006. All subsequent quotes from Clinton in this section are taken from the same interview.
407. "What do you think, Chuck": Chuck Hagel interview, September 12, 2006.
407. Lugar remembered being summoned: Richard Lugar, interview by author, December 15, 2006.
410. Once Clinton directed Bruce Reed: Bruce Reed, telephone interview by author, January 26, 2007.
411. "There is a lot more willingness": Andy Stern, telephone interview by author, January 31, 2007.
415. when more national candidates win: Lindsey Graham, interview by author, Washington, D.C., July 18, 2006.
416. In Lincoln's demanding and prophetic vision: Abraham Lincoln, "Second Inaugural Address," in Andrew Delbanco, ed., *The Portable Abraham Lincoln* (New York: Viking, 1992), pp. 320–21.

BIBLIOGRAPHY

Acheson, Dean. *Present at the Creation: My Years in the State Department.* New York and London: W. W. Norton, 1987. (Paperback edition.)

Ambrose, Stephen E. *Eisenhower: Volume II. The President.* New York: Touchstone, 1985.

———. *Nixon: The Triumph of a Politician, 1962–1972.* New York: Simon & Schuster, 1989.

Armstrong, Jerome, and Markos Moulitsas Zuniga. *Crashing the Gate: Netroots, Grassroots, and the Rise of People-Powered Politics.* White River Junction, VT: Chelsea Green Publishing, 2005.

Baker, Peter. *The Breach: Inside the Impeachment and Trial of William Jefferson Clinton.* New York: Scribner, 2000.

Balz, Dan, and Ronald Brownstein. *Storming the Gates: Protest Politics and the Republican Revival.* Boston and New York: Little Brown & Co., 1996.

Barnes, Fred. *Rebel-in-Chief: Inside the Bold and Controversial Presidency of George W. Bush.* New York: Crown Forum, 2006.

Barone, Michael. *Our Country: The Shaping of America from Roosevelt to Reagan.* New York: The Free Press, 1990.

Berry, Jeffrey M. *The New Liberalism: The Rising Power of Citizen Groups.* Washington, DC: Brookings Institution Press, 1999.

Beschloss, Michael (ed.). *Reaching for Glory: Lyndon Johnson's Secret White House Tapes, 1964–1965.* New York: Simon & Schuster, 2001.

Blum, John M. *Joe Tumulty and the Wilson Era.* Boston: Houghton Mifflin, 1951.

Blumenthal, Sidney. *The Rise of the Counter-Establishment: From Conservative Ideology to Political Power.* New York: Harper & Row, 1988.

Bond, Jon R., and Richard Fleisher. *Polarized Politics: Congress and the President in a Partisan Era.* Washington, DC: CQ Press, 2000.

Brock, Clifton. *Americans for Democratic Action: Its Role in National Politics.* Washington, DC: Public Affairs Press, 1962.

Burns, James MacGregor. *Roosevelt, The Soldier of Freedom, 1940–1945.* New York and London: Harvest/HBJ, 1970.

———. *Roosevelt: The Lion and the Fox, 1882–1940.* New York and London: Harvest/HBJ, 1956.

———. *The Deadlock of Democracy: Four-Party Politics in America.* Englewood Cliffs, NJ: Prentice-Hall, 1963.

Busbey, L. White. *Uncle Joe Cannon: The Story of a Pioneer American.* New York: Henry Holt and Co., 1970.

Campbell, Angus, and Philip E. Converse, Warren E. Miller, and Donald E. Stokes. *The American Voter: Unabridged Edition.* Chicago and London: University of Chicago Press, 1976 (reprint); John Wiley & Sons, 1960.

Cannon, Lou. *President Reagan: The Role of a Lifetime*. New York: Public Affairs, 2000.

Caro, Robert. *The Years of Lyndon Johnson: Master of the Senate*. New York: Alfred A. Knopf, 2002.

Chace, James. *Acheson: The Secretary of State Who Created the American World*. New York: Simon & Schuster, 1998.

Clinton, Bill. *My Life*. New York: Alfred A. Knopf, 2004.

Clinton, Hillary Rodham. *Living History*. New York: Simon & Schuster, 2003.

Continetti, Matthew. *The K Street Gang: The Rise and Fall of the Republican Machine*. New York: Doubleday, 2006.

Cooper, John Milton, Jr. *Breaking the Heart of the World: Woodrow Wilson and the Fight for the League of Nations*. Cambridge: Cambridge University Press, 2001.

———. *The Warrior and the Priest: Woodrow Wilson and Theodore Roosevelt*. Cambridge, MA, and London: Belknap Press, 1983.

Cox, Gary W., and Jonathan N. Katz. *Elbridge Gerry's Salamander: The Electoral Consequences of the Reapportionment Revolution*. Cambridge: Cambridge University Press, 2002.

Dallek, Robert. *Flawed Giant: Lyndon Johnson and His Times, 1961–1973*. New York and Oxford: Oxford University Press, 1998.

———. *Franklin D. Roosevelt and American Foreign Policy, 1932–1945*. New York: Oxford University Press, 1979.

Daschle, Tom, with Michael D'Orso. *Like No Other Time: The Two Years That Changed America*. New York: Three Rivers Press, 2003.

Davidson, Osha Gray. *Under Fire: The NRA and the Battle for Gun Control*. New York: Henry Holt, 1993.

Donovan, Robert J. *Eisenhower: The Inside Story*. New York: Harper & Brothers, 1956.

Duffy, Michael, and Dan Goodgame. *Marching in Place: The Status Quo Presidency of George Bush*. New York: Simon & Schuster, 1992.

Easton, Nina. *Gang of Five: Leaders at the Center of the Conservative Crusade*. New York: Simon & Schuster, 2000.

Edwards, Lee. *The Power of Ideas, The Heritage Foundation at 25 Years*. Ottawa, IL: Jameson Books, 1997.

Eilperin, Juliet. *Fight Club Politics: How Partisanship Is Poisoning the House of Representatives*. Lanham, MD: Rowman & Littlefield Publishers, 2006.

Evans, Rowland, and Robert Novak. *Lyndon B. Johnson: The Exercise of Power*. New York: New American Library, 1966.

Farrell, John Aloysius. *Tip O'Neill and the Democratic Century*. Boston, New York, and London: Little Brown & Co., 2001.

Fiorina, Morris P., with Samuel J. Abrams and Jeremy C. Pope. *Culture War? The Myth of a Polarized America*. New York: Pearson Longman, 2006.

Fleischer, Ari. *Taking Heat: The President, the Press, and My Years in the White House*. New York: William Morrow, 2005.

Garrett, Major. *The Enduring Revolution: How the Contract with America Continues to Shape the Nation*. New York: Crown Forum, 2005.

Giglio, James N. *The Presidency of John F. Kennedy*. Lawrence, KS: University Press of Kansas, 2006.

Gould, Lewis L. *The Most Exclusive Club: A History of the Modern United States Senate*. New York: Basic Books, 2005.

Greenstein, Fred. *The Hidden-Hand President: Eisenhower as Leader*. New York: Basic Books, 1982.

Hamburger, Tom, and Peter Wallsten. *One-Party Country: The Republican Plan for Dominance in the 21st Century*. Hoboken, NJ: John Wiley & Sons, 2006.

Hamby, Alonzo L. *Man of the People: A Life of Harry S. Truman.* New York and Oxford: Oxford University Press, 1995.

Hardeman, D. B., and Donald C. Bacon. *Rayburn: A Biography.* Austin, TX: Texas Monthly Press, 1987.

Harris, John F. *The Survivor: Bill Clinton in the White House.* New York: Random House, 2005.

Hill, Steven. *10 Steps to Repair American Democracy.* Sausalito, CA: PoliPointPress, 2006.

Himmelstein, Jerome L. *To the Right: The Transformation of American Conservatism.* Berkeley: University of California Press, 1990.

Hodgson, Godfrey. *The World Turned Right Side Up: A History of the Conservative Ascendancy in America.* Boston and New York: Houghton Mifflin, 1996.

Hofstadter, Richard. *The Age of Reform.* New York: Vintage Books, 1955.

———. *The Idea of a Party System: The Rise of Legitimate Opposition in the United States, 1780–1840.* Berkeley: University of California Press, 1969.

Holt, James. *Congressional Insurgents and the Party System, 1909–1916.* Cambridge, MA: Harvard University Press, 1967.

Ickes, Harold L. *The Secret Diary of Harold L. Ickes: Volume II, The Inside Struggle: 1936–1939.* New York: Simon & Schuster, 1954.

Javits, Jacob K. *Order of Battle: A Republican's Call to Reason.* New York: Atheneum, 1964.

Johnson, Haynes, and David S. Broder. *The System: The American Way of Politics at the Breaking Point.* Boston and New York: Little Brown & Co., 1996.

Josephson, Matthew. *The Politicos, 1865–1896.* New York: Harcourt, Brace & Co., 1938.

———. *The President Makers: The Culture of Politics and Leadership in an Age of Enlightenment, 1896–1919.* New York: Frederick Ungar, 1969.

Kaplan, Richard L. *Politics and the American Press: The Rise of Objectivity, 1865–1920.* Cambridge: Cambridge University Press, 2002.

Kazin, Michael. *A Godly Hero: The Life of William Jennings Bryan.* New York: Alfred A. Knopf, 2006.

Kearns, Doris. *Lyndon Johnson and the American Dream.* New York: Harper & Row, 1976.

Kenneally, James J. *A Compassionate Conservative: A Political Biography of Joseph W. Martin, Jr., Speaker of the U.S. House of Representatives.* Lanham, MD: Lexington Books, 2003.

Kennedy, David M. *Freedom from Fear: The American People in Depression and War, 1929–1945.* New York and Oxford: Oxford University Press, 1999.

Key, V. O., Jr. *Public Opinion and American Democracy.* New York: Alfred A. Knopf, 1961.

Kuttner, Robert. *Revolt of the Haves: Tax Rebellions and Hard Times.* New York: Simon & Schuster, 1980.

Ladd, Everett Carll, Jr. *American Political Parties: Social Change and Political Response.* New York: W. W. Norton & Co., 1970.

Leffler, Melvyn P. *A Preponderance of Power: National Security, the Truman Administration, and the Cold War.* Stanford, CA: Stanford University Press, 1992.

Leuchtenburg, William E. *The White House Looks South: Franklin D. Roosevelt, Harry S. Truman, Lyndon B. Johnson.* Baton Rouge, LA: Louisiana State University Press, 2005.

———. *The Perils of Prosperity, 1914–1932,* 2nd ed. Chicago: University of Chicago Press, 1993.

Link, Arthur S. *Woodrow Wilson and the Progressive Era: 1910–1917.* New York: Harper Torchbook, 1963.

Lott, Trent. *Herding Cats: A Life in Politics.* New York: Regan Books, 2005.

Lugar, Richard G. *Letters to the Next President.* Bloomington, IN: Author House, 2004.

Mann, Robert. *The Walls of Jericho: Lyndon Johnson, Hubert Humphrey, Richard Russell, and the Struggle for Civil Rights.* New York: Harcourt, Brace & Co., 1996.

Mann, Thomas E., and Bruce E. Cain (eds.). *Party Lines: Competition, Partisanship, and Congressional Redistricting.* Washington, DC: Brookings Institution Press, 2005.

Mann, Thomas E., and Norman J. Ornstein. *The Broken Branch: How Congress Is Failing America and How to Get It Back on Track.* Oxford and New York: Oxford University Press, 2006.

Martin, Justin. *Nader: Crusader, Spoiler, Icon.* Cambridge, MA: Perseus Publishing, 2002.

Mee, Charles L., Jr. *The Marshall Plan: The Launching of the Pax Americana.* New York: Simon & Schuster, 1984.

Merrill, Horace Samuel, and Marion Galbraith Merrill. *The Republican Command, 1897–1913.* Lexington, KY: University Press of Kentucky, 1971.

Mickelthwait, John, and Adrian Wooldridge. *The Right Nation: Conservative Power in America.* New York: Penguin Press, 2004.

Nicolay, John G., and John Hay. *Complete Works of Abraham Lincoln, Volume I.* New York: Lamb Publishing Co., 1905.

Patterson, James T. *Mr. Republican: A Biography of Robert A. Taft.* Boston: Houghton Mifflin Co., 1972.

Podhoretz, John. *Bush Country: How George W. Bush Became the First Great Leader of the 21st Century—While Driving Liberals Insane.* New York: St. Martin's Griffin, 2005.

Polsby, Nelson W. *How Congress Evolves: Social Bases of Institutional Change.* Oxford and New York: Oxford University Press, 2004.

Poole, Keith T., and Howard Rosenthal. *Congress: A Political-Economic History of Roll Call Voting.* New York and Oxford: Oxford University Press, 1997.

Rae, Nicol C. *The Decline and Fall of the Liberal Republicans: From 1952 to the Present.* New York and Oxford: Oxford University Press, 1989.

Reeves, Richard. *President Kennedy: Profile of Power.* New York: Simon & Schuster, 1993.

Ritchie, Donald A. *Reporting from Washington: The History of the Washington Press Corps.* New York: Oxford University Press, 2005.

Rohde, David W. *Parties and Leaders in the Postreform House.* Chicago: University of Chicago Press, 1991.

Rothman, David J. *Politics and Power: The United States Senate, 1869–1901.* Cambridge, MA: Harvard University Press, 1966.

Rovere, Richard H. *The American Establishment and Other Reports, Opinions, and Speculations.* New York: Harcourt, Brace & World, 1962.

Sale, Kirkpatrick. *The Green Revolution: The American Environmental Movement, 1962–1992.* New York: Hill and Wang, 1993.

Schaller, Thomas F. *Whistling Past Dixie: How Democrats Can Win Without the South.* New York: Simon & Schuster, 2006.

Schapsmeier, Edward L., and Frederick H. Schapsmeier. *Dirksen of Illinois: Senatorial Statesman.* Urbana and Chicago, IL: University of Illinois Press, 1985.

Schlesinger, Arthur M., Jr. *The Crisis of the Old Order, 1919–1933.* Boston: Houghton Mifflin Co., 1957.

———. *The Coming of the New Deal.* Boston: Houghton Mifflin Co., 1959.

———. *A Thousand Days: John F. Kennedy in the White House.* New York: Greenwich House, 1983.

Sinclair, Barbara. *Party Wars: Polarization and the Politics of National Policy Making.* Norman, OK: University of Oklahoma Press, 2006.

Small, Melvin. *The Presidency of Richard Nixon.* Lawrence, KS: University Press of Kansas, 1999.

Smith, James Allen. *The Idea Brokers: Think Tanks and the Rise of the New Policy Elite.* New York: The Free Press, 1991.

Tompkins, C. David. *Senator Arthur H. Vandenberg: The Evolution of a Modern Republican, 1884–1945.* Lansing, MI: Michigan State University Press, 1970.

Troy, Gil. *Morning in America: How Ronald Reagan Invented the 1980s.* Princeton, NJ, and Oxford: Princeton University Press, 2005.

Vandenberg, Arthur H., Jr., with the collaboration of Joe Alex Morris. *The Private Papers of Senator Vandenberg.* Boston: Houghton Mifflin Co., 1952.

Vogel, David. *Fluctuating Fortunes: The Political Power of Business in America.* New York: Basic Books, 1989.

White, William S. *Citadel: The Story of the U.S. Senate.* New York: Harper and Brothers, 1956.

Witcover, Jules. *Party of the People: A History of the Democrats.* New York: Random House, 2003.

Wood, Gordon S. *The Radicalism of the American Revolution.* New York: Vintage Books, 1991.

York, Byron. *The Vast Left-Wing Conspiracy.* New York: Crown Forum, 2005.

Zelizer, Julian E. (ed.). *The American Congress: The Building of Democracy.* Boston and New York: Houghton Mifflin Co., 2004.

Zelizer, Julian E. *On Capitol Hill: The Struggle to Reform Congress and Its Consequences, 1948–2000.* Cambridge: Cambridge University Press, 2004.

INDEX

hyperpartisanship (*cont.*)
  need for leadership reform, 400–412
  need for reform of policy agenda, 388–400
  need for reform of political process, 376–388
  need for unity reforms, 376–412
  positive consequences, 20–22
  reasons for existence, 25–26
  role of 1994 midterm election, 156
  role of ideologues, 21–22

Ickes, Harold, 50, 164, 375
ideologues
  insufficient challenge from conciliators, 25
  relative number, 23
  and rise of hyperpartisanship, 21–22
  role in American politics, 21–22
ideology vs. partisanship, 61–62, 72, 188–192, 368
Imhofe, James, 275
immigration reform
  Bush's plan, 251, 254, 260, 304–305, 306
  coalition of interest groups, 411
  under Johnson, 94–95, 97
  as part of unifying agenda, 394–395
  under Reagan, 134
impeachment
  and Bush, 342
  and Clinton, 18, 171–172, 173, 174, 283, 309, 329
  and Nixon, 105
independent voters, adding to primary process, 378–379
Ingalls, John J., 30
interest groups
  become force in political structure, 106, 107–108
  conservative vs. liberal, 116, 130, 263–266
  DeLay's ties to, 281
  New Right groups, 113–116
  role in sharpening of ideological differences between political parties, 186, 281–282
  role of business, 108–109, 112
  social movement representation, 109–112
Internet
  activists as constituency, 338
  bloggers on, 334–336, 338, 358
  and Dean campaign, 328, 336–337
  and Fairness Doctrine, 384
  first convention of Daily Kos readers, 5–7
  and Kerry campaign, 337, 338
  and Lamont campaign, 355, 356
  and MoveOn.org, 329, 330–331, 332, 338
  role in connecting citizens to politics, 20–21
  and third-party issue, 387
Investment Company Institute, 268
Iran-Contra scandal, 131
Iraq Study Group, 257, 310
Iraq War
  Abu Ghraib prison scandal, 236, 275
  in aftermath of 2006 midterm election, 361–362

Bush's policy, 236, 256–258, 260, 298–299, 309–310
conflict over policy, 274–275, 338
Downing Street memo, 447n
and Hagel, 244
shortage of congressional oversight, 274–275
isolationism, 82, 85

Jackson, Andrew, 28
Jackson, Henry, 102
Jackson, Janet, 384
Jackson, Jesse, 350, 353
Jarvis, Howard, 118
Javits, Jacob, 62, 101, 206, 207, 405
Jefferson, Thomas, 17, 28, 172
Jeffords, James, 232, 272
John Birch Society, 112
Johnson, Hugh S., 52
Johnson, Lyndon
  approval ratings, 15–16, 70, 97, 99, 308
  and automobile safety standards, 107–108
  comparison with George W. Bush, 258
  comparison with Hoover, 98
  comparison with Nixon, 105
  comparison with Wilson, 96, 98
  as conciliator, 185
  desire for experimentation, 405
  and election of 1964, 97, 187–188
  and federal aid to education, 93–94
  party divisions during administration, 19, 97, 99–100
  problem-solving orientation, 60, 61
  relationship with Congress, 58, 60, 78–79, 93–100
  as senator, 58, 60
Jones, Paula, 171
Jordan, Hamilton, 385
judicial appointments, 259, 280–281, 298, 381–382

K street project, 267–271
Katrina (hurricane), 298, 299, 342
Kefauver, Estes, 121
Kelly, Ed, 50
Kemp, Jack F., 117, 377
Kennedy, Edward M., 128, 228–229, 245, 247–248
Kennedy, John F.
  appointment of Republicans to central positions, 230, 404
  approval ratings, 70
  bipartisan agreement on tax plan, 219
  and civil rights movement, 21
  comparison with Eisenhower, 415
  comparison with Reagan, 132
  and election of 1960, 203, 377
  and federal health insurance for elderly, 94
  liberal frustration with, 72